D0087525

# Enduring Legacies

## Native American Treaties and Contemporary Controversies

EDITED BY
**BRUCE E. JOHANSEN**

FOREWORD BY
**VINE DELORIA, JR.**

PRAEGER

Westport, Connecticut
London

**Library of Congress Cataloging-in-Publication Data**

Enduring legacies: Native American treaties and contemporary
  controversies / edited by Bruce E. Johansen; foreword by
  Vine Deloria, Jr.
     p.   cm.
  Includes bibliographical references and index.
  ISBN 0–313–32104–3 (alk. paper)
     1. Indians of North America—Legal status, laws, etc. 2. Indians of
  North America—Treaties. I. Johansen, Bruce E. (Bruce Elliott), 1950–
  KF8205.E53   2004
  346.7301'3—dc22        2003064908

British Library Cataloguing in Publication Data is available.

Library of Congress Catalog Card Number: 2003064908
ISBN: 0–313–32104–3

First published in 2004

Praeger Publishers, 88 Post Road West, Westport, CT 06881
An imprint of Greenwood Publishing Group, Inc.
www.praeger.com

Printed in the United States of America

The paper used in this book complies with the
Permanent Paper Standard issued by the National
Information Standards Organization (Z39.48-1984).

10 9 8 7 6 5 4 3 2 1

# Contents

# Foreword

*Vine Deloria, Jr.*

Like no other group of indigenous peoples, now submerged in a society of immigrants, treaties define our relationship with the United States politically and with the body politic emotionally. Most people have never seen the text of a treaty, and far fewer have seen the text of a treaty written on large sheets of paper and parchment with fading black ink at the end of each line where the pen of the secretary was running out of ink. Yet there is an attachment to the idea of a treaty that stirs great emotions and calls us to maintain a high ethical standard in our dealings with each other.

England and France began the treaty-making process in the earliest days of colonization. The negotiations were conducted in traditional Indian fashion and lasted nearly two weeks with first a ceremony of condolence to "wipe away the tears" caused by the infractions committed by both sides since the previous treaty. This ceremony was followed by a ceremony called "polishing the covenant chain." This chain was initially an imaginary silver belt of alliance that had become tarnished when both sides failed to fulfill the spirit of the previous treaties. Once forgiveness was given, each day was devoted to a speaker from one of the parties, the initial speaker announcing his understanding of the previous conditions that had been agreed upon and the responding speaker, the following day, giving the perspective from the other side.

American colonists adopted this format; until 1778, in the middle of the American Revolution, treaties involved considerable discussion and a general agreement on the future conduct of both parties. The first treaty with the western tribes, and these people would be frontier Indian nations living just beyond the Demarcation Line of the Proclamation of 1763, was actually with the Cherokees and was conducted in traditional fashion. Treaties by the respective colonies, now regarding themselves as states, continued in the old format until the treaty with the Delawares in 1778. At that time, the United States sought to use a format that had formal articles and a legal format, unique, actually, to the United States and not duplicated by Great Britain in its treaties with the Hindu states in India that were being negotiated at the same time. Since the 1778 treaty was held for the purpose of getting the permission of the Delawares for the United States to cross their lands to attack Vincennes and the settlements in the Indiana Territory, the United States obviously wanted a written document to prove the legality of its actions.

Using the instrument of formal articles and provisions was continued until around 1914 when the last of the allotment agreements was concluded. By that time, many western tribes had lost their leadership or been so disrupted that they lacked spokesmen to plead their cases. The old chiefs who had influence, such as Red Cloud and Washakie, were dead or very old men; the policy had been to seek to negate their influence by insisting on a majority vote of the adult males of a tribe, hoping that they would favor short-term benefits such as per capita payments rather than long-term planning. Eventually, a voice vote was taken after a lengthy summary of the agreement's provisions. Diplomatic negotiations thus degenerated into simply seeking Indian consent for a proposed course of action. In legislative proposals, this format dominated the relationship between the United States and Indians until the Indian Reorganization Act (1934).

Tribes filing claims with the Indian Claims Commission had to give their permission first to hire lawyers, second to approve the claim, and third to agree to any stipulations the lawyers might make in the course of pursuing the claim. Gradually, tribal governments were able to assert their rights so that Taos Pueblo, for example, was able to convince the Indian Claims Commission to exclude the Blue Lake area from its claim so that the Pueblo could attempt to get this site returned to them. This action brought to the forefront the negotiating process and within a decade the idea of negotiating the terms of "settlement acts" meant a restoration of bargaining power on behalf of the Indian nations.

While formal negotiations were submerged in the rush to allot the reservations beginning in the 1890s, tribes did seek relief in the state and federal courts for actions they saw as violations of treaty promises. Such famous cases as *Lone Wolf v. Hitchcock* (1903) and *United States v. Winans* (1905), along with a multitude of litigation over the provisions of the agreements made by the Five Civilized Tribes in the dissolution of their tribal lands meant that specific phrases contained in treaties became the subject of intense activity in the courtrooms. This activity has not ceased, reaching its high point in a series of cases in the 1960s and 1970s. Foremost of this surge in successful litigation was *United States v. Washington* (1975), in which the Indians of Washington State were awarded up to half the fish returning to waters covered by treaties negotiated during the 1850s. Following this case (which was upheld by the U.S. Supreme Court), fishing rights became a legal issue in Oregon, Michigan, and Wisconsin. Today, as much litigation is conducted dealing with treaty rights as we have in any other area of federal Indian law. Combined with the movement to negotiate the difficult questions once the issue has been joined, Indians are now giving the treaties the status they deserve.

The essays in this book give the scope and flavor of contemporary treaty-rights activities. The most difficult cases have not yet been joined, however, and the prospect ahead is to soon enter a time when whole sets of treaties may be partially litigated and partially determined in court. Since use of settlement acts has been a process favored by Congress and the recent administrations, we can look forward to considerable activity in this area. There is a great need for more Indian scholars to devote an increasing amount of time to researching and articulating the conditions under which treaties were made and upgrading the understanding of the public as to the importance of these documents. This book certainly will need a sequel in the future, and historians may well regard this development as marking the high point of the Indian renaissance.

# Acknowledgments

First, we acknowledge Mother Earth for her sustenance. In addition, the editor wishes to express an appreciation to all the contributors, as well as the people who have made his work as author and editor possible for many years: wife Pat Keiffer, department chair Deb Smith-Howell, editor Heather Staines, and the staff of the University of Nebraska at Omaha Criss Library.

# Introduction

*Bruce E. Johansen*

Treaties are so fundamental to the lives of Native Americans and their nations in the United States that life without them would be difficult to imagine. Most contemporary issues are rooted in laws that derive a large amount of their sustenance from the treaties. Treaties are, therefore, vibrant documents that define important issues in our time, providing this book's subject matter and reason for being.

This book examines only a small fraction of the 371 treaties (and many other agreements resembling treaties) that the United States negotiated with Native American tribes and nations beginning with the Delawares in 1778 even before national independence was legally confirmed. This book is an attempt to maintain a "national conversation" on the treaty basis of important contemporary laws and issues that will require elaboration (as Vine Deloria, Jr., writes in the Foreword) by future work. While the texts of the treaties are available, discussion and other annotation of them in a context that gives them contemporary meaning has been scarce.

## QUESTIONING DEFINITIONS OF SOVEREIGNTY

I am indebted to Barbara Gray-Kanatiiosh for providing a description of a talk given by Deloria at the Arizona State University Law School March 6, 2001, during which he questioned popular contemporary assertions utilizing simplistic notions of Native American sovereignty. Native sovereignty, said Deloria, is not based on the fictions created by the parameters of federal Indian law, but rather on the "fact that we were nations of people occupying Turtle Island long before the Europeans came to our lands" (Gray 2001, 14). According to Gray's account, Deloria said that the legal definition of *sovereignty* is Eurocentric. In addition, the term is anthropocentric in that it is based on a perspective where everything revolves around humans. It perpetuates a worldview where power is centralized at the top.

Custodianship may be a far better term than *sovereignty,* especially in describing Native American attitudes toward the Earth. "Perhaps," wrote Gray, "If Deloria is correct, it would be harder for the federal Government to deny our right to be custodians of our lands, peoples, and cultures" (Gray 2001, 14).

While it is true that the treaties evidence a measure of collective identity and independence to native peoples in the United States, we should be careful not to claim for them more than they can legally or conceptually deliver. The sovereignty of treaties is defined in U.S. law by limits defined in the decisions written by U.S. Supreme Court Chief Justice John Marshall during the 1820s and 1830s that define Native polities as "domestic dependent nations." Having said that, it also is useful to keep in mind the Onondaga leader Oren Lyons's assertion that sovereignty is often self-defined, that sovereignty is as sovereignty does. Deloria and Lyons's points of view are mutually complementary. In fact, during his talk, Deloria quoted Lyons: "Sovereignty is practiced. You don't ask for the colonizer to recognize it" (Gray 2001, 14). Readers will find the tensions between established legal precedent and ad hoc assertion of rights evident throughout this book.

## LINGUISTIC AND CULTURAL MISUNDERSTANDINGS

Treaties, at least until early in the nineteenth century, were state-to-state negotiations regarding rights and property. From the distance of decades and centuries, treaties may seem overly clear-cut. Viewed from the scene of their execution, they were anything but that; negotiations were fraught with many linguistic and cultural misunderstandings. Many treaty negotiations were conducted not only in a language (English) that many native participants did not completely understand, but according to assumptions of European property rights that were foreign to them.

In *Brave Are My People,* for example, Frank Waters describes a "purchase" by Miles Standish and two companions of a tract of land fourteen miles square near Bridgewater, for seven coats, eight hoes, nine hatchets, ten yards of cotton cloth, twenty knives, and four moose skins. When native people continued to hunt on the land after it was "purchased" and were arrested by the Pilgrims, the Wampanoag sachem Massasoit protested

> What is this you call property? It cannot be the earth. For the land is our mother, nourishing all her children, beasts, birds, fish, and all men. The woods, the streams, everything on it belongs to everybody and is for the use of all. How can one man say it belongs to him only? (Waters 1993, 28)

While Standish and his companions thought they had carried away an English-style deed, Massasoit argued that their goods had paid only for use of the land in common with everyone.

Differences in attitudes toward the land vis à vis European cultures recur time and again in the statements of Native American leaders recorded by Euro-American observers, in many areas of North America. Tecumseh, rallying Native allies with an appeal for alliance about 1805, said "Let us unite as brothers, as sons of one Mother Earth. . . . Sell our land? Why not sell the air. . . . Land cannot be sold" (Grinde and Johansen 1995, 31).

Because attitudes toward land tenure varied, negotiations which Europeans took to involve acquisition of land from Native people often involved a high degree of intercultural misunderstanding. When the English colonists of New England thought they were *buying* land, Native Americans often took the same agreements to mean that they were agreeing to *share* it.

The very concepts of land ownership and centralized government regulation often were foreign to Indian leaders who negotiated treaties. Native Americans very often did not completely understand what they were signing, and even when they did, the Senate sometimes unilaterally changed treaty provisions before ratification. Treaties often were signed with Native "leaders" who had been recruited by treaty commissioners who failed to realize that the treaties had little or no support among the people of the nation being represented as the contracting party.

During negotiations for the 1851 Fort Laramie Treaty (sometimes called the Horse Creek Treaty), the United States representatives insisted that the Sioux designate one leader to speak for all of them. The Sioux refused, after which the United States negotiators designed Conquering Bear as the Sioux's leader without the consent of the people he was supposed to be leading. The problem was compounded three years later when Conquering Bear was killed by U.S. Army troops during the Grattan fight near Ft. Laramie. The Sioux had a great deal of trouble comprehending why the Army had killed the chief who had earlier been handpicked as the Sioux's supposed "leader."

Judge George Boldt, in *United States v. Washington* (1974), pointed out that treaty negotiations in the Pacific Northwest often were carried out in three languages—English, Chinook (a trade jargon with limited vocabulary), and a Native language. The use of Chinook severely limited both parties' ability to communicate complex concepts. Because of the disadvantages at which treatymaking often placed Indians, the Supreme Court has held that treaties should be construed as the Indians would have understood them [*Tulee v. Washington,* 315 U.S. 681, 684–85 (1942)]. Treaties, according to Supreme Court rules of construction, are also to be interpreted to accomplish their protective purposes, according to legal scholar William S. Canby, Jr., "with ambiguities to be resolved in favor of the Indians" [*Carpenter v. Shaw,* 280 U.S. 363 (1930)].

## OUTLINE OF THE BOOK

The legal context of treaty law in Canada is evolving as this book is being written; a window on this evolution (which somewhat resembles the process undergone in the United States almost two centuries ago with the opinions of Justice Marshall) is provided in an essay on Canada's own Marshall Decision (no legal relation to its southerly namesake). As in the United States, control of and access to land and resources are basic to the definition of Native treaty rights in Canada. In this case, the testing ground has become the lobster-trapping areas adjacent to the village of Burnt Church, New Brunswick, and (by legal extension) forests and mines across the country. The legal process of defining Native rights to these resources much resembles the struggle over salmon and other fish and shellfish in the United States.

Granville Ganter, an assistant professor of English at St. John's University in Queens, New York, takes a detailed, historically nuanced look the two decades following the settlement of lawsuits brought principally by the Penobscots and Passamaquoddies. First, these lawsuits were nationally significant for their scope: the plaintiffs established a serious treaty-supported claim to roughly two-thirds of Maine's land area. Second, the settlement was (and remains) important for its basis: the several "non-intercourse" acts passed by the U.S. Congress during the late eighteenth and early nineteenth centuries. These laws were passed to prevent state governments and private interests from taking native land fraudulently by requiring federal oversight. The laws were regularly ignored throughout the Northeast and so, in our time, have become a basis for several lawsuits.

The 1980 Maine Indian Claims Settlement Act, according to Ganter, "was a landmark moment in twentieth-century U.S.-Native relations." The Penobscots and Passamaquoddies received a settlement of $81 million, federal recognition, the right to purchase at least 300,000 acres of land at fair market value, and limited immunity from state laws. In addition to being the largest compensation package awarded to a Native American group prior to 1980, the successful prosecution of the Maine land claim and settlement was part of a family of several other eastern tribal land claims in the late 1970s and early 1980s, which included those of the Pequots and the Narragansetts. Several Haudenosaunee (Iroquois) settlement negotiations in Upstate New York are still pending, with the federal and state governments having tentatively consented to settle with the Oneidas for a figure in the vicinity $500 million.

Robert W. Venables provides a fresh view of the Treaty of Canandaigua, signed in 1794, in which the United States recognized the independent status of the Six Nations of the Iroquois Confederacy. From 1794 to the present day, this treaty has been the legal keystone of relations between the United States and the Six Nations of the Iroquois Confederacy. The treaty is at the center of the Six Nations' land claims and their rights to govern their own reservations. The matter of native governance in Upstate New York resonates through several contemporary debates in addition to active pursuit of land claims. The Iroquois have been involved in economic development, including casinos and sales of gasoline and cigarettes, among other commodities, without state taxes. Border-crossing rights to and from Canada (for people as well as goods) also have been a point of conflict in our time. As Professor Venables points out, this was not a treaty of conquest, and it contains strong guarantees of sovereignty, points of reference for the contemporary national debate over that subject.

John C. Mohawk, in "The Iroquois Land Claims: A Legacy of Fraud, Politics, and Dispossession," makes a case that "The current wealth that is enjoyed in New York and the United States as a whole was built on a foundation of illegally taken land and stolen natural resources." The stakes of the land claims amount to hundreds of thousand of acres, including some notable real estate, such as a large part of metropolitan Syracuse. Present-day land claims, writes Mohawk, "test whether this theft will be acknowledged and at least partially paid for." According to Professor Mohawk's analysis, "the Empire State was created when the state government violated federal law and illegally obtained 98 percent of the native lands and forced 95 percent of the Haudenosaunee people to flee from their aboriginal land. They were subsequently subjected to coercion and sometimes outright fraud and the result was that the nations lost all but a tiny fraction of their original homelands. The Cayuga and Oneida lost practically all their lands." Present-day claims comprise redress for a small fraction of that loss.

The rise of the Turning Stone Casino in Oneida Country, New York, has been accompanied by a debate among the Oneidas as to whether its founder, Ray Halbritter, is asserting the legal support of Native nationhood for what is, essentially, solely a business venture. The controversy in Oneida is important not only for its economic aspects, but also because the U.S. Supreme Court in 1974 issued the Oneidas what is, in effect, an I.O.U. for 250,000 acres of illegally taken land that has yet to be made good. Ray Halbritter's government is also sitting at that negotiating table, no matter how solid its legal support may be.

Barbara Alice Mann provides a detailed look at the circumstances leading to the negotiation of the Greenville Treaty (in 1795), by which most of the present-day state of Ohio was legally defined. This treaty grew out of a historical context that many people who are not experts on it may find surprising. This record includes the most substantial defeat of the United States Army in its nineteenth-century battles with American Indians. Mann finds existing analysis of the Greenville Treaty to be often inaccurate and incomplete, as well as historically misleading.

In some cases, errors of large magnitude were made during treaty negotiations. In 1868, for example, the Treaty of Fort Laramie granted the Sioux land in northern present-day Nebraska that had long been occupied by the Poncas. The Sioux, traditional enemies of the Poncas, fully approved of the U.S. Army's intervention to force the Poncas off their land and into exile in Indian Territory, later called Oklahoma. This mistake in treaty negotiation gave rise to a long march homeward by Standing Bear and other Poncas, which in turn created the conditions that caused a landmark case to be brought in Omaha during 1879 under which Standing Bear and his party were held to be human beings under United States law, able to legally return to their homeland. After several decades of bureaucratic battling, the Poncas finally reacquired some of the land taken from them by the error in the Treaty of Fort Laramie. In this volume, Jerry Stubben, who is of Ponca heritage, begins with the origins of the Poncas and brings the story to the present with the most complete narrative to date of the Poncas' revival.

Also in the context of the U.S. Army's Indian wars, Hugh J. Reilly takes a fresh look at the treaty context of incidents at Wounded Knee in 1890. Readers may be surprised to learn that the U.S. Army still officially regards what happened at Wounded Knee as a "battle" and not a "massacre," much as it was reported by Army public-information officers to the non-Indian press in 1890. The reason for this awesomely out-of-date interpretation has a great deal to do with the large number of Medals of Honor awarded after the "battle," twenty of them, as many as were given in some of the nation's major wars. If the Army were to admit that Wounded Knee actually was a massacre, the medals probably would have to be revoked.

As in the case of Washington State fish, treaties have been used by the Osage in Oklahoma to protect their rights to oil, an instructive story in a history that features so many other instances in which Native peoples have been defrauded of their resources. This account is provided to us by Teresa Trumbly Lamsam who is herself Osage, a member of a family that has long been prominent in tribal government.

The Osages arrived in Indian Territory (soon to become Oklahoma) in 1871, having purchased 1.5 million acres from the Cherokees, their last stop on a long string of treaty-impelled migrations through Missouri and Kansas. They didn't know it at the time, but nature had a surprise for them. In 1896, at the dawn of the automotive age, their land was found to be underlain by copious stores of oil and gas. How did they keep the oil? What emerged was an historical irony: in the case of the Osages, allotment legislation, originally meant to break up collective tribal identity and rights in favor of individual landholding and Anglo-Saxon-style property rights, was used at a key juncture to uphold collective Osage control of oil and other mineral rights. The key was the insertion of a clause to that effect into the legislation, passed in 1906, which initiated allotment for the Osages. At every turn, the Osage tribal government has protected its rights to manage oil production for the common good of the nation, even as private interests have tried to assail it. Through several decades, the Osages have used legal resources to lobby Congress to use its plenary power vis à vis Native nations to maintain its right to manage the nation's natural resources.

We conclude this collection with two journeys into racial fantasies, appreciating, as always, a candle in the darkness from Vine Deloria, Jr., who observes that while race has lost most of its force as an intellectual concept, racism is alive and well. Kennewick Man, a 9,300-year-old skeleton, has been turned into a vehicle for racial wish-fulfillment by a number of people who would like to believe that the first Americans came from Europe. This line of reasoning suits anti-treaty activists, the subject of the final chapter, just fine. If Europeans were first, they reason, then American Indians owe them the rent. Like inventors of most fantasies, lack of evidence doesn't seem to pose a problem.

We hope that these accounts will provide support for a systematic, national inquiry into the value of treaties and the legal context in which they reside for Native peoples (and many non-Natives as well) in our time.

## REFERENCES

Canby, W. C., Jr. 1981. *American Indian law.* St. Paul: West Publishing.

Deloria, V., Jr. 1974/1985. *Behind the trail of broken treaties: An Indian declaration of independence.* Austin: University of Texas Press.

Gray, B. (Kanatiiosh) 2001. Vine Deloria spoke: I listened, will you? *Indian Time (Akwesasne)* 19(48):14.

Grinde, D. A., Jr., and B. E. Johansen. 1995. *Ecocide of Native America: Environmental destruction of Indian lands and peoples.* Santa Fe, NM: Clear Light.

*United States v. Washington,* 384 F. Supp. 312 (1974).

Waters, F. 1993. *Brave are my people: Indian heroes not forgotten.* Santa Fe: Clear Light Publishers.

Wilkinson, C. F. 1987. *American Indians, time, and the law: Native societies in a modern constitutional democracy.* New Haven, CT: Yale University Press.

# 1

# The "Lobster War," the Marshall Decision, and Emerging Canadian First Nations' Treaty Rights

*Bruce E. Johansen*

A Canadian Supreme Court ruling supporting aboriginal subsistence rights has electrified debate over Native American economic potential and sparked non-Indian backlash. The immediate flashpoint has been the Burnt Church Mi'kmaq Reserve in New Brunswick, where non-Indian lobstermen have destroyed several thousand Native lobster traps. Nonnatives also desecrated a sacred site, and at least three people were injured in scuffles associated with the "lobster war."

The Canadian Supreme Court's Marshall Decision, announced September 17, 1999, guarantees Canada's First Nations access to the natural resources of their aboriginal territories for subsistence purposes, the basis of economic infrastructure. The ruling is similar to some in the United States, notably the "Boldt Decision" on fishing rights in the Pacific Northwest, handed down in 1974, and later affirmed by the U.S. Supreme Court. If anything, the Marshall Decision is broader than the U.S. rulings because it is not restricted to a single resource, such as fish.

As in the Boldt Decision, the Canadian Supreme Court in the Marshall case attempted to determine what the original treaties meant to their signers. Both decisions also invoked an aboriginal right to a reasonable standard of living from fishing. In the United States, this standard has been interpreted to include livelihood by commercial sale of fish, which also figures into the Canadian case. As in the United States, the meaning of these terms has been left to judicial interpretation. Boldt's ruling was strictly limited initially to certain types of fish (and later expanded to shellfish), leaving little legal wiggle room. In the Canadian case, the scope of the Marshall case was left wide open in the initial ruling and then tempered.

## THE SUPREME COURT'S "CLARIFICATION"

Two months after its initial decision, the Canadian Supreme Court issued a "clarification" of the Marshall Decision which denied that the ruling granted indigenous communities aboriginal access to forest, mineral, and oil resources on government-owned lands. The second decision generally restricted the court's action in Marshall to fishing rights. The court also said that native fishermen on the east coast of Canada are subject to federal regulations, which could include a closed fishery, as they exercise their treaty rights to hunt, fish, and gather resources for a "moderate livelihood." The court said that the Canadian federal government may step in to ensure there is "fairness" and recognition of the "historical reliance upon, and participation in, the fishery by non-aboriginal groups" (Bourrie 1997).

The Canadian Supreme Court, in a 6 to 0 ruling, said that its original decision had been misinterpreted both by indigenous groups and nonnatives who asserted that it gave the Mi'kmaq free access to all fish and game in eastern Canada and made them immune from government regulations.

The Canadian Supreme Court issued its clarification as First Nations in Nova Scotia claimed rights to large tracts of land throughout the province in a case that could transform the logging industry in the same fashion that the 1999 Marshall Decision reshaped the Atlantic fishery. Lawyers for thirty-five Natives convicted of illegally harvesting lumber told the Nova Scotia Supreme Court in Halifax February 4, 2002, according to a Canadian newspaper account, "that they have aboriginal title spelled out in eighteenth-century treaties to cut and sell trees on Crown property" ("Natives Lay Claim" 2002).

According to one observer, "The Supreme Court said that the Marshall Decision granted the Mi'kmaq year-round fishing rights for eels because Ottawa did not provide a justification for closing that fishery. Eels are not an endangered species and there is no significant nonnative commercial fishery, it notes. The courts add, however, that the government could justify restrictions for native fishermen, such as a closed season, to conserve other species such as lobster, scallops, cod and crabs" (Bourrie 1997). Because of this, the same observer reasoned that "Conservation always has been recognized to be a justification of paramount importance to limit the exercise of a treaty and aboriginal rights." The court says, "It is up to the Crown to initiate enforcement action in the lobster and other fisheries if and when it chooses to do so" (Bourrie 1997).

As the legal limits of the Marshall Decision were being defined by the court, its street-level implications were being played out in Burnt Church, where Indian and non-Indian fishing people jostled over the resources that Canada's legal system sought to allocate. The incidents on the Burnt Church Reserve brought back memories for anyone who observed fishing-rights disputes in the states of Washington and Wisconsin between the 1960s and 1980s. "Substitute 'walleye' for 'lobsters,' and it seems about the same," remarked two activists from Wisconsin (McNutt and Grossman 2000). Similarly, one could substitute "salmon" for "lobsters," as well as "Boldt" for "Marshall," and find a very similar, but earlier, history along Puget Sound. Images of Canadian officials swamping Native boats off Burnt Church recalled similar memories three decades earlier at Frank's Landing, Washington.

## A HISTORY OF THE MARSHALL RULING

A decade after the confrontation at Kanesatake (Oka) energized Canadian debates related to First Nations' treaty rights, land claims, and economic infrastructure across Canada, the Marshall Decision is only the tip of a proverbial legal iceberg. Across Canada, by the turn of the millennium on the Christian calendar, the courts were being used as never before to seek rulings to establish Canadian First Nations' access to the resources that comprise, in the words of the Marshall ruling, a "moderate livelihood." From Vancouver Island to the urbanized islands along Toronto's waterfront and the Atlantic shores of Nova Scotia, several treaty-based struggles have become subjects of controversy.

The Marshall ruling was based on agreements between the British and Native leaders during 1760 and 1761, after the British defeated the French at Montreal. The most notable of these agreements is the Treaty of Swegatchy, negotiated in 1760. While the first conflict has been over lobster in the Maritime provinces, the Supreme Court ruling's impact may encompass other forms of subsistence. Legal debate is already underway regarding whether the ruling will allow increased Native harvests of lumber. The ruling also may shape hunting, trapping, and even mining, as well as fishing rights.

The Mi'kmaqs, who have some of the highest unemployment rates in Canada (up to 85 percent in some communities), have been testing the Marshall Decision in several ways. The most notable assay into Mi'kmaq economic development has been lobster, but some Mi'kmaq also have been catching salmon and cutting timber on Crown (publicly owned) lands as well. Their attorneys have hinted that they believe that even mining activities could be covered under the Marshall ruling. They also assert that the Mi'kmaqs' proper geographic scope for assertion of resource rights is the entire province of Nova Scotia, because the Mi'kmaqs used all of the present-day Canadian province (as well as other adjacent lands) as aboriginal territory.

The landmark case was initiated after a Mi'kmaq, Donald Marshall, Jr., of Cape Breton, Nova Scotia, was arrested for taking and selling 210 kilograms of eel out of season. The Canadian Supreme Court overturned a lower-court conviction of Marshall, finding that peoples have a right to fish regardless of season, with or without a license.

Donald Marshall, Jr., knew the Canadian legal system quite well before the Supreme Court ruled on the fishing-rights case that now bears his name, Marshall served more than eleven years in prison for the murder of Sandy Seal; later evidence traced the murder to Roy Ebsary. The long view of legal history clearly indicated that Marshall had been framed by the police of Sydney. The case became the subject of a prize-winning Canadian documentary film.

On September 17, 1999, the Supreme Court of Canada ruled that Donald Marshall, a Nova Scotia Mi'kmaq, should not have been convicted of illegally catching eels because a treaty signed in 1760 gave the peoples a right to hunt and fish freely. That fall, Native lobster fishermen at Burnt Church set traps after the province's official season had ended. (The official season lasts six months and ends on June 30.)

Marshall's fishing case initially did not fare well in Nova Scotia's provincial courts. During March of 1997, the Nova Scotia Court of Appeal upheld a provincial court ruling that Donald Marshall, Jr., had illegally caught and sold 210 kilograms of eels.

All three appeals-court judges ruled in favor of the federal government's position, against Marshall. Judges in both courts concluded that Marshall couldn't maintain a defense based on the 1760 treaty for having caught eels out of a season defined by the Canadian government. In the Supreme Court, however, by a vote of 5 to 2, justices upheld Marshall's reasoning under the terms of the Treaty of Swegatchy, signed in 1760, as Montreal was being surrendered to the British. While references to the treaty exist in archival documents, all copies of the document's actual text have been lost.

"It's a great shot in the arm and a major milestone in the history of the Mi'kmaq people," said Bruce Wildsmith, one of Marshall's attorneys, regarding the Marshall Decision. "Mind you, it's only as good as what governments and courts make of it" (Marshall Decision 1999).

## THE "LOBSTER WAR"

The Supreme Court's ruling in Marshall's case caused an immediate impact in Mi'kmaq country. Lobster traps came out of storage after the government-mandated season had ended. In the meantime, the New Brunswick government appealed for calm as many non-Indians worried that unlicensed hunting, fishing, and harvesting by the Mi'kmaqs and other aboriginal people could threaten their own livelihoods.

During late September of 1999, roughly 600 nonnative lobster fishermen demanded that the Canadian federal government force the Mi'kmaqs to pull their traps, or "They'll yank them from the sea themselves" (Toughill 1999, n.p.). The nonnatives said that their livelihoods were at stake. The tip of Nova Scotia that juts toward Maine contains some of the richest lobster harvests in the world. A fisherman with the standard 375 traps can easily clear $60,000 (before taxes) for six months of cold, hard work. A license to get into the trade sells for $200,000 (Toughill 1999, n.p.). The possibility of such income is tempting to the 20,000 Mi'kmaqs and Maliseet in the area, in whose committees unemployment runs as high as 85 percent.

Soon after the Marshall ruling, about 4,000 Mi'kmaq traps had been set, drawing the ire of nonnative fishermen who demanded that the federal government halt Mi'kmaq fishing out of season. On October 1, Department of Fisheries and Oceans Minister Herb Dhaliwal refused, saying that the Mi'kmaqs had a right to fish that had been denied them for two centuries. Nonnatives who earn their livings taking lobster began destroying Native traps early in October. The nonnatives said they were sabotaging the Native traps to ensure conservation of the species. They contended that lobsters caught out of season are too young, hungry, and easy to catch.

During the initial confrontations following the Marshall ruling, two Mi'kmaq pickup trucks and an empty summer cottage were burned. Soon, Natives organized to protect their traps, using peace-keepers in combat fatigues whom some in the press called "warriors," although they were unarmed and scoffed at comparisons to Mohawk Warriors who had maintained a lengthy confrontation near Oka, Quebec (on land claimed by Kanesatake Mohawks), more than ten years ago.

After a year of increasing pressure from nonnative lobster fisher-men, following futile efforts to arrange a truce by negotiator Bob Rae, the Department of Fisheries and Oceans (DFO) ordered the Mi'kmaq fishery closed. Within a week, gunshots were being fired around Burnt Church, as DFO boats—Royal Canadian Mounted Police (RCMP) Zodiacs and police catamarans—as well as helicopters swooped into the waters off Burnt Church to disengage roughly 1,300 Mi'kmaq lobster traps that the DFO had deemed illegal. (The government's rationale, following the arguments of the nonnative lobster trappers, was that conservation required the closure of the Mi'kmaq fishery. The DFO was defining that term itself because the Supreme Court, in its Marshall ruling, had left the matter vague.)

Canadian federal authorities moved in under cover of darkness Sunday, August 13, 2000, in Burnt Church to seize hundreds of lob-ster traps that they insisted had been laid illegally by Mi'kmaq fisher-men. Enraged Mi'kmaqs, who have been trying to establish their own fishery, said that officers on about a dozen government boats had pointed guns at them. People on shore reported hearing the sounds of boats being rammed, along with screaming. At one point, Native fishermen tried to drive the federal fisheries police away by pelting them with bait. Doug Dedam, a native fisherman, said the federal officials nearly sank his small dory.

The boat-borne battles along the shores of Burnt Church became very rough at times. Tracy Sinclair, 21, a McGill University student from North Bay, Ontario, traveled to Burnt Church to act as an observer on behalf of the Mi'kmaqs.

> Sinclair continued to film all that was going on when one of
> the RCMP Zodiacs rammed into them [the boat on which
> she was filming]. Sinclair was thrown from her seat, almost
> falling out of the boat. The police rammed into them again,
> causing their boat to flip over, sending Sinclair and the
> other three passengers into the water. (Zemel 2000, 10)

Sinclair and three other occupants of the tipped boat were then hauled out of the water, arrested and handcuffed. Sinclair's camera was seized by the RCMP as evidence. The Canadian Broadcasting Corporation reported this incident September 14, after which the RCMP denied any part in tipping the boat in which Sinclair had been traveling.

The federal agents also were forced to restrain nonnative trappers from joining them in removing Mi'kmaq traps. The DFO agents turned back 48 nonnative boatloads of trappers intent on pulling Mi'kmaq traps themselves. The Mi'kmaqs had previously called an end to their own trapping season October 7, so within a few days the situation settled into a tense standoff, as the lobsters began their annual migration to deeper water.

Following their confrontations with police, several Mi'kmaq fishermen took a five-week course in hand-to-hand combat with the express purpose of sharpening their skills for the next time the fisheries police came calling. "We're tired of being victims of their brutality," said Chief Reg Maloney of the Indian Brook Mi'kmaq band (Lambie 2000). A newspaper account described the Mi'kmaq fishermen as preparing to meet DFO agents during the 2001 Mi'kmaq lobster-trapping season, to begin in July, 2001. "They're in good physical shape and they have a few tricks up their sleeves," said Maloney (Lambie 2000). A fisheries official said that Mi'kmaqs who exercise their physical skills on DFO officers will probably be charged with resisting arrest. By the end of October, 2000, the DFO had confiscated about 1,700 Mi'kmaq lobster traps (Lambie 2000).

During the first week of October, 2000, about the same time the last Mi'kmaq trapper pulled his lobster gear out of the water, fisheries officials seized a half-ton truck and thirteen salmon from two Burnt Church men. Federal rules allow the Burnt Church Mi'kmaq to catch as many as 416 salmon using up to thirteen gillnets between July 1 and October 22.

Shocked by the ferocity of the non-Indian backlash to their fishing activities, leaders of thirty-five Native bands along Canada's Atlantic Coast agreed during the first week of October to ask aboriginal fishing people to suspend their activities for a month. What remained to be seen was how many of the Native fishing people would accept the moratorium. Under terms of the proposed moratorium, nonnative lobster interests also would be required to shelve their traps, something many of them were not willing to do, especially during the last few weeks of mild weather before the onset of winter.

Asked his reaction by two reporters from the *Toronto Star,* Donald Marshall called the non-Indian response "racist." He continued: "If . . . Canadians don't accept what's happened, then it's too god-damned bad. I proved my point, and the truth hurts, I guess." The reporters, Valerie Lawton and Kelly Toughill, wrote that Marshall made this statement with "eyes wet, body shaking and . . . voice trembling." "I proved my point," he said, "and I guess it hurts" (Lawton and Toughill 1999, n.p.).

## UNRESOLVED ISSUES

The Supreme Court ruling in the Marshall case left two important issues open to interpretation. First, what is meant by a harvest suitable for a "moderate livelihood?" In the Marshall case, the Canadian Supreme Court said that the treaty limited the Mi'kmaq's fishing-harvest rights to daily needs, including "food, clothing, and housing, supplemented by a few amenities" (Mofina 1999, A-3).

Audrey Marshall commented in *The Eastern Door,* a newspaper published on the Kahnawake Mohawk Reserve near Montreal:

> The Aboriginal people of this country have a treaty right to partake in the commercial fishery, and limits on that right are subject to conservation. The Supreme Court of Canada grants the Mi'kmaq the right to trade their catch for necessities, interpreted to mean a moderate livelihood. However, the Supreme Court failed to clarify the definition of "moderate livelihood," which leaves it wide open to interpretation. . . . The Department of Fisheries and Oceans, an agent of the Crown [federal government], is defining and interpreting "moderate livelihood" on its [own] premise, without consulting the aboriginal people. . . . (Marshall 2000, 3)

A second question is left unanswered in the Marshall Decision: Which resources are defined as subject to the decision? While the Mi'kmaqs asserted that logging is covered, some officials of the Nova Scotia provincial government disagreed. For example, Brad Green, provincial aboriginal affairs minister, asserted that the Marshall Decision refers specifically to hunting and fishing, but not to logging. (The Supreme Court opinion does refer to "gathering,") Green also said that all hunting and fishing rights are subject to reasonable restrictions, such as conservation needs.

"I'm not expecting chaos, I'm not expecting a crisis," Green said. "The aboriginal peoples of New Brunswick are responsible. I think they are obviously pleased with the decision, and they should be. . . . It will facilitate our understanding as a government of the rights of aboriginal people. It should make it easier to sit down and discuss with them how those rights can be exercised with the least number of restrictions" (Marshall Decision 1999).

Supporters of the Marshall Decision's interpretation of treaty relations pointed to support in the Canadian Charter of Rights and Freedoms. Section 25 of the charter states that "The guarantee in this charter of certain Rights and Freedoms shall not be construed so as to abrogate or derogate from any Aboriginal, Treaty, or other Rights or freedoms that pertain to the Aboriginal people of Canada, including (a) any Rights or Freedoms that have been recognized by the Royal Proclamation of October 7, 1763, and (b) any Rights or freedoms that now exist by way of land-claims agreements or may be so acquired" (Marshall 2000, 3).

According to Audrey Marshall, writing in *The Eastern Door,* "The aboriginal people of this country have been left out of the commercial fishing industry for hundreds of years, and it is the nonnative fishermen who monopolize and capitalize on the commercial fishery. Moreover, the nonnative fishermen are the culprits who depleted the fishing industry in the Maritimes and did not consider environmental implications . . ." (Marshall 2000, 3).

Non-Indian hunting and fishing groups generally have come out against liberal interpretation of the Marshall ruling, stressing (as did non-Indian interests in the northwest fishing "wars" more than thirty years ago) that unlicensed Indian exploitation of resources will threaten their conservation and perpetuation. (The non-Indian interests almost never examine their own role in resource depletion.) Steven Chase, president of the New Brunswick Salmon Council, a private conservation organization, said that serious concerns exist regarding the effects of unlimited aboriginal fishing on depleted stocks of Atlantic salmon. Chase described his concerns in a letter to Canadian Prime Minister Jean Chretien. "We didn't know who else to turn to," Chase wrote. "The federal government has a primary responsibility for aboriginals. We're looking for the prime minister to take a leadership role and make sure the conservation principle is observed" (Marshall Decision 1999).

The Canadian federal government announced during the year 2000 that it is willing to spend hundreds of millions of dollars to sign interim fishing agreements that would include fishery licenses, equipment, and training for First Nations fishermen. The federal government during 2000 also launched a first round of negotiations, potentially worth $160 million, in an attempt to implement the Marshall ruling. By March of 2001, the federal government had reached agreements with thirty of the thirty-four First Nations affected by a fishery that was being reorganized along lines now defined as legal by the Canadian Supreme Court. Two of the affected First Nations were too late in agreeing to participate, while lobster trappers at Burnt Church, New Brunswick, and Indian Brook, Nova Scotia, refused to sign. Trappers at the Burnt Church Reserve refused to agree to a forty-trap limit advocated by federal officials. Members of the Burnt Church Reserve also voted to take charge of their own fishery rather than negotiate with Ottawa.

## CONSERVATION OR CONTROL?

Following police expropriation of Mi'kmaq lobster traps, several Canadian lawyers with extensive experience in aboriginal and treaty rights issued a statement saying that they "are of the opinion that the Department of Fisheries and Oceans has made a serious error of law in its interpretation of the Marshall Decision." This error had been compounded, said the lawyers, by governmental overreaction to the situation at Burnt Church. The lawyers' statement continued:

> The Department of Fisheries and Oceans acts as if it has the absolute right to regulate the Treaty Fishery in Atlantic Canada. It does not have that right. In fact, the department has a limited ability to regulate the treaty fishery. In order for it to exercise that function, it must meet specific criteria. . . . In its clarification of the Marshall Decision, the Supreme Court of Canada said that the government must establish that the limitations on the treaty right are imposed for a pressing and substantial public purpose. However, first there must be consultation with the aboriginal people concerned. Limitations must go no further than is required. (Birenbaum, et al. 2000)

In other words, the provincial and federal government may not use "conservation" as a cover to deny aboriginal peoples' rights to sustenance. This debate echoes the use of "conservation" as a state rationale for its control of the Washington salmon fishery during the 1960s and early 1970s, before Judge Boldt's initial ruling and his subsequent assumption of control over the fishery.

The Canadian courts thus found themselves walking a legal highwire between two very distinct, competing groups: Native Americans exercising their economic-subsistence rights as they see them under the Marshall ruling, and non-Indians who believe that aboriginal people are being granted rights to hunt, fish, gather (and, perhaps, mine minerals and cut timber) at times or in places denied to non-Indians.

By April 2001, no new fishing agreements had been signed between Canada's federal government and the lobster-harvesting First Nations. Mi'kmaq chiefs were advised by their lawyers to stand up for their treaty rights by refusing to negotiate. For lawyer Bruce Wildsmith, the equation was clear. Native chiefs who signed agreements were signing away their treaty rights. "They're clearly signing them away for the life of the agreement. But that's not the problem. The problem is what's going to be made of these agreements in the future?" (First Nations 2001).

Wildsmith said that signing agreements with the federal government could set a precedent and limit treaty rights under later interpretations of the Marshall Decision. In the meantime, federal Fisheries Minister Herb Dhaliwal spoke repeatedly of his department's success because thirty-two of thirty-five Atlantic bands had signed one-year agreements with the federal government. Ottawa's lead negotiator said during April 2001 that indigenous fishing people were becoming more reluctant to sign. "I don't think we'll get as many as we got last year," Jim McKenzie said April 7 during a panel discussion with fishermen (Canadian Negotiator 2001).

According to Dhaliwal, fishermen who refused to negotiate would still be allowed to harvest, but without aid from the government. "What they will not be able to have access to is the resources in terms of equipment, training, mentoring," said Dhaliwal (First Nations 2001). During 2000, fishing agreements provided approximately $200 million (Canadian) in licenses, fishing equipment, and training to native fishermen. Much of the money was spent purchasing licenses from non-Indian fishermen.

Nova Scotia Chief Lawrence Paul said that the federal government was trying to deal with the Mi'kmaq in the same way that the British Crown had hundreds of years ago. "They still have the same mentality, 'Give them a couple of beads and a few mirrors and stuff and we'll get what we like.' You know those days are gone and gone forever" (First Nations 2001).

During the summer of 2001, Canada's national fisheries bureaucracy continued to tighten its administrative interpretation of the Marshall Decision, raising the risk of a new confrontation in the lobster-trapping grounds in the waters near the Burnt Church reserve. The federal move came, according to an account in Canada's *National Post,* "after Ottawa's offer of a deal to resolve the Burnt Church fishing dispute met with a wall of silence from Mi'kmaq leaders" (Blackwell 2001, n.p.). According to a bluntly worded statement from Dhaliwal, the government had decided that it would now allow the native community to trap lobster only for food and ceremonial purposes, not for commercial sale, and only until October 20, 2001. Furthermore, the DFO restricted the legal fishing zone, allowing only 900 traps to be placed in a limited area directly in front of the reserve. The Mi'kmaq had proposed to set 5,600 traps. Dhaliwal said his department would vigilantly enforce the new zone and the prohibition on commercial sales, raising the specter of a repeat of conflicts resembling those of the previous fall, when fisheries officers tried to stop lobster trapping and clashed violently with Native fishermen.

Wilbur Dedam, the Burnt Church chief speaking for the reserve's lobster trappers, rejected the government's edict, as he said that the Mi'kmaqs' constitutionally guaranteed rights should allow a larger lobster catch over a broader area. Dedam said the native community in northeastern New Brunswick was not opposed to discussion of such issues with the Fisheries Department. "But I must insist that we are opposed to signing any federal interim agreement which fails to respect our aboriginal and treaty rights" (Blackwell 2001, n.p.). "It remains the position of Burnt Church not to enter into an interim agreement as proposed by the federal government . . . but to fish under our own fisheries management plan," Dedam said (Lawlor 2001).

Nonnative fishermen, drawing support from a report of a consultant hired by the government, warned that a large Mi'kmaq fall fishery would seriously cut into their catch and undermine the lobster population as a whole. They demanded that the Burnt Church fishery be completely shut down as of the end of August. On August 26, a flotilla of about twenty nonnative fishing boats motored into the waters off Burnt Church. Burnt Church Mi'kmaq accused the nonnative fishermen of cutting their trap lines, but the nonnatives denied that allegation.

Federal Fisheries Department officers seized native lobster traps in waters near the Burnt Church reserve on August 30, 2001 in what one band member described as an "act of aggression" (Native Lobster 2001). "We're still assessing the damage and exactly what happened," said James Ward, a Mi'kmaq warrior and co-author of the Mi'kmaq band's fisheries management plan. "But there definitely were traps taken. I'd describe it as a hit-and-run operation and certainly, it can only be considered an act of aggression" (Native Lobster 2001). Jim Jones, a spokesman for the federal Fisheries Department in Moncton, New Brunswick, said eighty-six traps were seized during the midmorning raid on waters, which Ottawa considers outside the legal fishing zone for the Burnt Church Reserve (Native Lobster 2001). Fisheries boats patrolled Miramichi Bay on Thursday, making sure there were no more traps outside the allowable zone.

During early July 2002, the three-year struggle by native fishermen on the Burnt Church Reserve to set their own trapping regulations suffered a major setback as Provincial Court Judge William McCarroll ruled that aboriginal fishermen must abide by federally set fishing rules. McCarroll convicted Mark Simon and John Duplessis of Burnt Church on four counts of violating Department of Fisheries and Oceans regulations. Each was fined $2,000 for fishing lobster during a closed season (Cox 2002, A-5). This ruling was the first direct interpretation of the Marshall ruling. Simon and Mr. Duplessis acknowledged that they set traps during October 2000, months after the federally defined season had closed. But they said they had the right to fish according to band regulations. Burnt Church chief Wilbur Dedam said yesterday's court decision was a slap in the face and the band is looking to appeal it. "It's a very sad day for the Native community of Burnt Church," he told reporters outside the Miramichi courthouse (Cox 2002, A-5). This case was one of several pending against Native fishermen before Canadian courts.

## THE MARSHALL RULING AND LOGGING

Wildsmith argued from the Marshall Decision during the trial of Joshua Bernard, a New Brunswick Mi'kmaq charged with illegal possession of Crown (public) timber. "The Marshall case is extremely significant," Wildsmith said. "We're going to have to put the point to [Judge Dennis Lordin] and he is going to have to decide whether logs are in the same position as eels" (Marshall Decision 1999).

Natives in New Brunswick have been fighting for years for the right to harvest lumber from Crown land. One lower court found that they had such a right, but that ruling was later overturned by a higher court. The Canadian Supreme Court later refused to hear the case.

As resource-based conflicts surfaced among Mi'kmaqs and their neighbors, their attorneys were preparing to argue in court that the Mi'kmaqs own the entire province of Nova Scotia because none of the province had been ceded by treaty. This is a crucial question in Canada, where the transfer of only a small part of the land was accompanied by treaty negotiations, a much lower proportion than in the United States. By various estimates, roughly 85 percent of Quebec, for example (most of the country outside major urban areas) was never ceded by treaties. The logging case centered around thirty-five Mi'kmaq loggers who cut timber from Crown land, saying they have a treaty right to do so. Lawyer Wildsmith said this is the "next phase" of the Marshall Decision. "Nova Scotia and the Maritime provinces are prime candidates for having unceded aboriginal title," said Wildsmith. ". . . They [the Mi'kmaq] were using and occupying all of Nova Scotia and they never did anything in their treaties or otherwise to give up their interest in that land" (Toughill 2000, n.p.).

During early March 2001, a provincial court judge ruled that Native peoples do not have historic rights to vast stretches of land throughout Nova Scotia. In a decision read to about 100 people crowding his courtroom, Judge Patrick Curran ruled that the Mi'kmaqs were guilty of illegally harvesting lumber in the province and do not possess aboriginal title to those areas of land.

Curran's ruling was not a complete repudiation of the Marshall ruling, nor of the treaty on which it was based. This decision meant that Natives cannot harvest trees on Crown land without the government's authorization. The case was being watched closely by other provinces, including New Brunswick, where a similar case was making its way through the courts. "The eighteenth-century Mi'kmaq might have had some claim to coastal lands . . . but those lands did not include any of the cutting sites," Judge Curran said in his ruling (Court Rules 2001).

Curran said that the Mi'kmaqs' Treaty of Swegatchy did not set out any right "of which harvesting timber for sale is the modern equivalent" (Court Rules 2001). Stephen Marshall, Jr., one of the men charged with illegal logging, said he was disappointed with the decision. "I was hoping he would go in our favor," said Marshall, who lives on the Millbrook Reserve near Truro, Nova Scotia (Court Rules 2001).

The stakes in this case are larger than the harvest of a few trees. Some non-Indians had speculated that a decision by Judge Curran in favor of the Mi'kmaq loggers would have allowed Nova Scotia's Mi'kmaq bands to claim unextinguished aboriginal title to all of Nova Scotia (Court Rules 2001). A valid claim by the Mi'kmaqs under the Marshall Decision also could cast a legal cloud across leases held by lumber companies operating on property that the Mi'kmaqs say they never ceded.

The logging case began in July 1999 and produced 9,000 pages of transcripts, twenty volumes of historical evidence, reviewed treaties from 1760, and included testimony from several Native elders and anthropologists. Crown lawyers argued there was no basis to Native claims that they have title to all Crown land in the province because they were sharing it with settlers. They also disputed whether the Natives used the trees for commercial purposes and whether commercial sale is covered under the Marshall ruling's guarantee of a "moderate livelihood."

A year later, a small number of Mi'kmaq still faced charges from the summer 2000 "lobster wars" at Burnt Church. Given the wayward path of the Marshall case through the Canadian Supreme Court, no one is really sure, absolutely, whether Canadian aboriginal people may legally trap lobsters under the Treaty of 1760. The Mi'kmaq have surmised that they have that right, and many non-Indian lobster fishermen have assumed the opposite.

## LAND CLAIMS ACROSS CANADA

Canada's attempts to come to terms with the fact that most of its land was never ceded by treaty extend well beyond its Atlantic shores. The shock waves of the Oka occupation spread across Canada during the summer and early fall of 1990, from Nova Scotia to British Columbia. Canada's attempt to explain Native unrest provoked the multivolume, multimillion-dollar report of the Royal Commission on Aboriginal Peoples during the middle 1990s. One of the commission's most prominent proposals advocated a speedier land-claims process across Canada.

The Canadian federal policy developed to settle historic land claims that was established after the Oka standoff is an "abject failure,"

The Mohawk "Warriors" helped kick-start native land claims in Canada. (*Louis Hall*)

according to its director (Laghi 2001, n.p.). Jim Prentice, a Calgary-based lawyer, said the system is "in gridlock," with native claimants growing restless. After eight years of work, the Indian Claims Commission has resolved only a handful of cases, while at least 450 are still in process (Laghi 2001, n.p.). The backlog is growing by fifty to sixty cases a year. The "unacceptably slow" rate of claim resolution is undermining confidence in the process, according to Prentice (Laghi 2001, n.p.).

Even as the general land-claims process languishes, some notable progress has been made in the courts, and sometimes at the provincial level. For example, the Fishing Lake First Nation of Saskatchewan has been offered almost $38 million (Canadian), one of the largest land claims in the history of the province. Chief Allan Paquichan said that the band is planning to put most of the money into a trust (Saskatchewan 2001).

The Nuu-chah-nulth, a group of about 6,500 people that claims the west coast of Vancouver Island (including Pacific Rim National Park), has been negotiating a tentative treaty agreement with British Columbia and the Canadian federal government. The Nuu-chah-nulth are the largest aboriginal group on Vancouver Island; their traditional territory includes the tourist town of Tofino and environmentally sensitive Clayoquot Sound, from Barkley Sound to Kyuquot Sound (Meissner 2001).

The Nuu-chah-nulth treaty settlement is the third such agreement reached with aboriginal groups since 1993 when First Nations, British Columbia (BC), and the Canadian federal government formed a commission "to negotiate modern-day land claims treaties" (Meissner 2001). The Sliamon (in the Powell River area) and the Sechel, on the BC coast northwest of Vancouver, have reached tentative agreements leading to negotiation of final treaties. Outside of the formal treaty process, the Nisgras (in northwestern BC) during August of 1999 reached agreement on compensation of about $500 million and 2,000 square kilometers. The group gave up its right to make future claims as well as its tax-exempt status.

The tentative settlement with the Nuu-chah-nulth, which has been under negotiation since 1993, includes cash and land. Parties to the negotiations have not disclosed how much of each is being considered. The Nuu-chah-nulth originally asked for $950 million (Canadian) and 3,336 square kilometers of land. The government originally offered $204 million and 340 square kilometers. Peter Smith, speaking for the Aboriginal Affairs Ministry, said that the tentative agreement with the Nuu-chah-nulth contains no provisions for whale hunting, a point of contention because the Nuu-chah-nulth have traditionally hunted whales. They have said they will not give up their traditional right to hunt whales.

On March 10, 2001, the Nuu-chah-nulth Tribal Council initialed a $250-million treaty agreement with the provincial and federal governments lacking participation by one of its chairmen and one of its twelve tribes. Richard Watts, the Nuu-chah-nulth Tribal Council's southern regional chairman, and representatives of the Ehahtteshat First Nation, skipped the signing ceremony on the Tseshaht Reserve near Port Alberni. Ehattesaht councillor Sharon Doucette said her nation withdrew from the negotiating table after the band's 240 members met on their Northern Vancouver Island Reserve. Doucette said the agreement in principle did not meet the band's needs. The band was getting lost in the shuffle of negotiations because of its isolated location, Doucette said. "It is, at times, difficult to get our needs met. . . . The agreement in principle doesn't meet probably half of our needs" (Tribe Skips 2001).

The agreement gave the Nuu-chah-nulth $243 million and 550 square kilometers of land. "What we've got here is the best that we could do," said Nelson Keetlah, Nuu-chah-nulth's chairman representing the central region. "The best that we could do with what we have" ("Tribe Skips" 2001). The agreement is a framework for negotiation of a final treaty, which is expected in about two years. Trevor Proverbs, the province's chief negotiator, said Nuu-chah-nulth negotiations received a boost from the signing of a treaty agreement between the governments and the Sliamon Tribal Council of the Sunshine Coast. "I wouldn't describe (the Sliamon agreement) as a blueprint or a template," Mr. Proverbs said. "That did provide us with a foundation on which to build" (Tribe Skips 2001).

The agreement in principle found a rocky road to ratification. By mid-April 2001, two of the largest of the fourteen Nuu-chah-nulth communities, one-third of their population, had rejected the proposed agreement. The people of Ahousaht voted 74 percent against the proposal; Tseshaht voted 92 percent against the proposal. As of April 4, six First Nations had voted in favor of the agreement. Three tribal council members—Hesquiaht, Nuchahtlaht, and Ehahtteshat—had not yet participated in the ratification vote.

Because so much of Canada never was ceded by treaty, a case involving Sarnia, Ontario, has been watched closely. According to an opinion issued by the Ontario Court of Appeal on December 21, 2000, the land on which much of Sarnia has been built was surrendered improperly by the Chippewa nearly a century and a half ago, but it cannot be returned to its original owners because the cost to Canadian society would be too high. The court ruled that the present owners of the land bought it and built homes in good faith, so a land transfer would cause unfair "havoc and hardship" (Makin 2000). "Aboriginal rights are an integral aspect of the Canadian legal landscape," said a consensus statement of the five judges who composed the opinion. "Their shape, definition, and enforcement do not, and cannot, exist in a vacuum," wrote the five justices (Coulter Osbourne, George Finlayson, David Doherty, Louise Charron, and Robert Sharpe) (Makin 2000).

The land in question, 1,030 hectares, is now occupied by 2,000 businesses and other organizations, five schools, five churches, and several hundred private homes. The area claimed by the Chippewa is worth "hundreds of millions of dollars" (Makin 2000). A lawyer representing the Chippewa, Earl Cherniak, said that his clients were extremely disappointed by the ruling, especially by the introduction of equity, in a legal sense, between the interests of present-day owners and legal support for aboriginal title. The land at issue in this case is protected under an 1827 treaty with the Chippewas. The land was sold twelve years later to a speculator, Malcolm Cameron, by three Chippewas. The treaty requires collective agreement of the affected Chippewas to sell land; no such consensus was ever sought, or reached. The land was deeded to Cameron in 1853 when the Canadian government issued letters of patent "in the mistaken belief that the land had been properly surrendered" (Makin 2000).

About 1,500 people comprising the Mississauga band of New Credit, Ontario, say they never surrendered one of Toronto's defining features, the Toronto Islands along Lake Ontario. The native band, whose reserve is 95 kilometers from the islands, assert that it owns some of the land earmarked for Toronto waterfront development related to the 2008 summer Olympic games. The Mississaugas "is awaiting a Justice Department ruling on whether Ottawa considers its land claim legally valid" (Southworth 2001). If the answer is "yes," negotiations will follow regarding compensation.

The Toronto Islands, near downtown, are now occupied by yacht clubs, an airport, a residential village, and several popular parks. Roughly 650 people live on the islands in 250 private houses built on land leased from the city of Toronto. The Mississaugas sold much of the land under present-day Toronto to the British during 1787 and 1805. Lloyd King, a Mississauga elder, said that the 1787 treaty lacked required signatures. King also said that participants in the 1805 treaty, known as the Toronto Purchase, said they did not know what they were signing. The Mississauga band has never accepted the provisions of the 1805 treaty; they contend that the Toronto Islands were not part of the deal.

## METIS' IDENTITY LEGALLY RECOGNIZED

In another extension of Canadian aboriginal treaty rights (and economic infrastructure), the Ontario Court of Appeal ruled February 23, 2001 that the Metis (mixed-race First Nations and French) are a fullfledged aboriginal people with constitutional rights comparable to those of Native Americans. The court said that governments in Canada should stop treating the estimated half-million Canadian Metis as a fictional people and that the "honour of the Crown" requires that they be properly shielded under the Canadian Constitution. "The basic position of the government seems to have been to deny that these rights exist—absent a decision from the courts to the contrary," Justice Robert Sharpe wrote for the 3 to 0 majority, which included Chief Justice Roy McMurtry and Justice Rosalie Abella (Makin 2001). The ruling affirmed two lower-court decisions in the case.

Metis spokesmen were quoted in the press as being overjoyed by the ruling. Gerald Morin, president of the Metis National Council, said the ruling will aid the Metis in realizing their constitutional rights, including self-government. "It sends a message to all governments across Canada and to Ottawa that clearly these rights exist—we are a people; we exist in this country" (Makin 2001).

"This is the first recognition by the courts of our existence as a people," said Jean Teillet, a lawyer for Steve and Rod Powley, who initiated the case by hunting moose out of season. "In effect, this judgement is a confirmation that the Metis people have harvesting rights in this province—and that this right has priority over other users" (Makin 2001). Teillet said that the Metis' harvesting rights will eventually extend to subsistence (noncommercial) harvesting of fish and trees, as well as hunting. Teillet also said that the ruling is a "long-awaited repudiation of a historic policy in Canada which sought to assimilate the Metis through shame and neglect." Teillet continued, "I think politicians felt that when they hanged Louis Riel in 1837, the Metis people would disappear off the face of the planet. The government of Ontario made it its business to wipe [Metis] people out of the province, but they lost one today" (Makin 2001). "We have had swift and sweet justice provided to the Metis nation today by the Ontario Court of Appeal," said Tony Belacourt, president of the Metis Nation of Ontario (Prittie 2001).

The Powleys, father and son, began their legal challenge during 1993 in the Sault Ste. Marie area, as the two men killed a bull moose and took the carcass home. They later were charged under the Fish and Game Act with unlawfully hunting (and possessing) a moose without a license. The charges were dismissed at trial in 1998, and early in 2000, an Ontario Superior Court judge upheld the trial judge's decision.

The provincial government later declined to appeal the Metis ruling to Canada's Supreme Court. Ontario Premier Mike Harris said that the provincial government was most concerned about "proper planning and management of our wildlife here in the province of Ontario" (Prittie 2001). The court also said that Ontario may curtail moose hunting in the interest of conservation, a type of measure that has been used to control the exercise of Native American fishing rights in the United States (as well as lobster trapping in New Brunswick).

Attorneys for the province argued that the Metis are an undefined group and, therefore, their hunting does not comprise a continuous cultural tradition. The judge took a different tack, however. "There was considerable evidence from lay and expert witnesses that the Metis have been victims of discrimination, ostracism, and overt hostility from the nineteenth century forward," wrote Judge Sharpe (Makin 2001). The court directed the provincial government to proceed with "immediate dispatch" to negotiate a new hunting regime that recognizes the Metis' aboriginal rights (Prittie 2001).

## KANESATAKE (OKA) TEN YEARS LATER

The 1990s were a tumultuous decade for treaty-grounded claims to land and resources for Canada's First Nations. The decade began with a months-long armed standoff at the Kanesatake Mohawk Reserve near Oka, Quebec, provoked by the town's plan to extend a municipal golf course onto land for which the Mohawks have a treaty-based claim.

The Mohawks' land base near Oka had been shrinking for almost four centuries by 1990, when armed confrontation made the village famous across Canada. The first European-American incursion into Mohawk territory occurred during 1609 and 1610, when Samuel de Champlain arrived with Algonquian allies. In 1717, France's King Louis XV granted land to which his nation possessed no legal title, granting 2,300 acres for a mission meant to introduce the Mohawks to European-style farming. Great Britain took control of the area, and the ground on which the mission sat, after 1763.

A land and governance agreement that had been ratified by a margin of two votes was signed in late December 2000 for the Kanesatake Territory, adjoining Oka, Quebec, site of a seventy-eight-day armed standoff during 1990 which is often credited with initiating Canada's recent array of First Nations land-claims cases. The agreement "recognizes an interim land base for the native community and its legal status under the Constitution" (Widely Opposed 2000). The agreement also calls for harmonizing of laws between the Kanasatake Reserve and the municipality of Oka.

The agreement was ratified by the community by a vote of 239 to 237, with fewer than half of about 1,000 eligible voters casting ballots. Many Mohawk traditionalists opposed the agreement because it was negotiated with the government-sponsored band council, which is recognized as Kanesatake's legitimate governing body by the agreement. "No band council or individuals have the moral or ethical right to negotiate instruments that will impact on our children, grandchildren, and beyond," said a statement issued by Walter David on behalf of the traditionalists (Widely Opposed 2000). The traditionalists said that by tradition the negotiations should have been held by clan mothers who hold title to the land. The traditionalists want to establish a government at Kanesatake outside of Canadian government sanction.

The Kanesatake Interim Land Base Governance Bill was introduced to the Canada's Senate March 27, 2001 after joint negotiations between the Kanesatake Band Council and the Ministry of Indian Affairs and Northern Development. The act gives the Kanesatake Mohawks governance over the fifty-seven lots of Mohawk-owned lands spread out in the municipality of Oka. "It was a very close vote. There were two votes over that voted in favor of the land governance code and act," said Canatonquin (Gregoire n.d.). "It's final recognition by the government of our self-government," said Grand Chief James Gabriel. "We'll be out of the Indian Act. It's a very major step and it's historic" (Gregoire n.d.). The Kanesatake lands will now be recognized as lands reserved for the Mohawks of Kanesatake under the Constitution Act of 1867.

"I'm very enthusiastic and very confident," said Gabriel. "It was hard to attract investors because no one was sure what laws apply" (Gregoire n.d.). The agreement grants the Kanesatake Band Council the ability to enact laws and describes that provincial and federal laws apply to land use. Gabriel believes the agreement will benefit the Kanesatake community. "We're very confident that this will turn things around for us," said Gabriel (Gregoire n.d.).

## REFERENCES

Atlantic Indian tribes balk at signing new fisheries deals with Ottawa. 2001. Associated Press in *Boston Globe,* March 9. http://www.boston.com/dailynews/068/region/Atlantic_Indian_tribes_balk_at:.shtml.

Birenbaum, J., S. Birks, D. Bruce Clarke, T. Cutcliffe, D. English, O. Fuldauer, N. G. Gilby, S. C. B. Gilby, C. Gillespie, R. S. Maurice, C. S. Metallic, M. Montour, G. Morin, J. O'Reilly, A. Orkin, S. Thibodeau, H. Sioui Trudel, B. Wildsmith, K. J. Winch, and E. Zscheile. 2000. Fisheries and oceans makes legal error at Burnt Church. September 7. portfolio@newswire.ca.

Blackwell, T. 2001. Return of violence feared in Burnt Church Native fishery dispute. *National Post (Canada)*, August 28, n.p. http://www.nationalpost.com.

Bourrie, M. 1997. Supreme Court scales back indigenous rights. Interpress Service, November 22. http://www.tips.org/IPS/human.NSF/86afef403a5ab0ca802565b0004cc6df/4700159811f7c6338025683c004ea873?OpenDocument.

Canadian negotiator expects fewer tribal chiefs to sign fishing deals. Associated Press in *Boston Globe*, April 7, 2001. http://www.boston.com/dailynews/097/region/Canadian_negotiator_expects_fe:.shtml.

Court rules Natives don't have logging rights. Canadian Press in Toronto *Globe and Mail*, March 8. 2001.

Cox, K. 2002. New Brunswick Natives lose court fight over fishing. *Toronto Globe and Mail*, July 10, A-5.

First Nations advised not to sign new fishing agreements with Ottawa. 2001. Canadian Broadcasting Corporation News On-line. April 2. http://cbc.ca/cgi-bin/view?/news/2001/04/02/native010402.

Gregoire, M.-L. Kanesatake land governance recognized by federal government. *The Six Nations and New Credit Ontario News*. N.d. http://www.tekanews.com/page2.html.

Laghi, B. 2001. Policy for land claims abject failure. *Toronto Globe and Mail*, January 2, n.p.

Lambie, C. 2000. N[ova] S[cotia] Natives get combat training for Lobster Wars; "Tired of being the victim." *National Post*, December 22. http://www.nationalpost.com.

Lawlor, A. 2001. Strict enforcement planned at Burnt Church. *Toronto Globe and Mail*, August 28.

Lawton, V., and K. Toughill. 1999. Chiefs call temporary truce in fish war. *Toronto Star*, October 7, n.p.

Makin, K. 2000. Natives fail in bid to regain land. *Toronto Globe and Mail*, December 22. http://www.globeandmail.com/gam/national/20001222/UCHIPN.html.

———. 2001. Court recognizes Metis as a distinct people. *Toronto Globe and Mail*, February 24. http://www.globeandmail.com.

Marshall, A. 2000. Commentary: Charter protects rights of aboriginal people. *Eastern Door (Kahnawake Mohawk Territory)*, September 15, 3.

Marshall Decision used in Native logging case. 1999. Canadian Press. September 21. http://www.lawcanada.com/news/sept99/sept21c99.shtml.

McNutt, D. and Z. Grossman. 2000. Midwest Treaty Network, Madison, Wisconsin. Personal communication, September 5.

Meissner, D. 2001. Treaty nears for Vancouver Island's largest aboriginal group. *Vancouver Sun*, March 4. http://www.canada.com/vancouver/vancouversun.

Mofina, R. 1999. Treaty ruling causing "chaos;" federal cabinet may suspend top court ruling on Native fishing. *Ottawa Citizen*, September 28, A-3.

———. 2001. Native lobster dispute heats up as officers seize traps off Burnt Church. *National Post*, August 30. http://www.nationalpost.com.

Natives lay claim to Nova Scotia forests. 2002. Canadian Press in *Toronto Globe and Mail*, February 5, A-6.

Prittie, J. 2001. Court orders Ontario to recognize Metis and their right to hunt; Province has year to work out deal; Harris may appeal. *National Post*, February 24. http://www.nationalpost.com.

Saskatchewan Indian band ponders $38 million. 2001. Canadian Broadcasting Company News, March 6. http://cbc.ca/cgi-bin/view?/news/2001/03/06/sask_landclaim010306.

Southworth, N. 2001. A Native band has turned to Ottawa in bid to reclaim land it says was never surrendered to the British. *Toronto Globe and Mail*, January 15. http://www.globeandmail.ca/gam/national/200101115/UNATIM.html.

Toughill, K. 2000. Mi'kmaq own entire province, N[ova] S[cotia] court told. *Toronto Star*, December 9. n.p.

———. 1999. Nova Scotia fishermen fear violence as feud brews. *Toronto Star*, September 27, n.p.

Tribe skips agreement ceremony. 2001. Canadian Press in *Toronto Globe and Mail*, March 11. http://www.globeandmail.com/servlet/RTGAMArticle HTMLTemplate/D/20010311/wtribeagree?tf=RT/fullstory.html.

Widely opposed "historic" land deal at site of 1990 Oka conflict is signed. Canadian Press, December 22. http://www.canoe.ca/nationalticker/canoe-wire.Oka-Lands.html.

Zemel, K. D. 2000. Burnt Church human rights observer arrested. *Eastern Door* (*Kahnawake Reservation*), October 20, 10.

# 2

# Sovereign Municipalities? Twenty Years after the Maine Indian Claims Settlement Act of 1980

*Granville Ganter*

The 1980 Maine Indian Claims Settlement Act (MICSA) was a landmark moment in twentieth-century U.S.-Native relations. Based on treaty records from the 1790s onward, members of the Maine Wabanaki (Abenaki) confederacy, whose name means "people of the dawn," successfully argued that they were entitled to compensation for illegal land sales and seizures performed by the states of Massachusetts and Maine. In exchange for vacating their claims to nearly two-thirds of the state of Maine, the Wabanakis, principally the Penobscots and Passamaquoddies, received a settlement of $81 million, federal recognition, the right to purchase at least 300,000 acres of land at fair market value, and limited immunity from state laws. In addition to being the largest compensation package awarded to a Native American group prior to 1980, the successful prosecution of the Maine land claim and settlement was part of a family of several other eastern tribal land claims in the late 1970s and early 1980s, which included those of the Pequots and the Narragansetts (Benedict 2000, 33–53). Beneficiaries of the unprecedented size of the Maine agreement, several Haudenosaunee settlement negotiations in upstate New York are still pending, with the federal and state governments having tentatively consented to settle with the Oneidas for a figure in the vicinity of $500 million (Higgins 2002, 1; Dewan 2002).

As important as it was, the Maine settlement did not equally include all of the Maine Wabanakis, namely, the Maliseets and

Micmacs. Under MICSA, the Houlton Band of Maliseets obtained federal recognition and $900,000 for land trust acquisition, but they remained subject to Maine's regulatory laws in ways that the Passamaquoddies and Penobscots were exempt. The Aroostook Band of Micmacs were not included at all in 1980 because they did not have sufficient documentation at the time. Eleven years later, the Micmacs negotiated a separate settlement with the United States, gaining federal recognition and $900,000 to be spent toward land trust acquisition. Because they were not a party to the 1980 Settlement Act, they do not feel bound by it, a situation that makes them unique among the Maine Wabanakis (MITSC 1995, 1; *Aroostook* 1991; Phillips 2002).

In fact, the Micmacs consider themselves fortunate because the other Maine Wabanakis—the Passamaquoddies, the Penobscots, and the Maliseets—have found the 1980 Settlement posed some serious obstacles to their economic growth and environmental health. Because the courts have steadily upheld the state's claims of regulatory control over many aspects of Wabanaki political life—and blocked the construction of casinos—some Wabanakis have declared that the 1980 Settlement should be scrapped (*At Loggerheads* 1997, i). Others believe that the settlement can be built upon, but its provisions need to be modified and rearticulated so that basic Native sovereignty is better acknowledged in their political relations with the state of Maine.

Since 1983, when the Penobscots' high stakes beano game (a form of bingo) was shut down by the Supreme Court at the request of the state of Maine, the Passamaquoddies and Penobscots have been in dispute with the state over jurisdiction and authority over Indian lands (Benedict 2000, 109, 180). In November 2000, three tribal leaders were threatened with jail because they refused to surrender documents pertaining to paper mill pollution in their ongoing fight to clean up the Penobscot river. The chiefs argued that the state's demand violated their sovereign rights (Murphy 2002). The courts of appeal, however, ruled that the Passamaquoddies and Penobscots had no such sovereignty in that case. These rulings echoed important court decisions in 1995–1996 on the casino issue, which also maintained that the state of Maine held extensive regulatory authority over the nations who agreed to the 1980 Settlement.

Although MICSA was a great financial victory for the Passamaquoddies and Penobscots, it explicitly equated the regulatory rights of those Indian nations with those of state municipalities. Because of differing interpretations over the scope of Native sovereignty, the settlement generated extraordinary conflict between the State of Maine and the Wabanakis. For their part, the Wabanakis argue that Maine has refused to acknowledge their aboriginal claim to national sovereignty, which exists *in addition* to the municipality provisions of the settlement (Chavaree 1998). The state, in turn, argues that the Indians are trying to lay claim to a form of sovereignty that was explicitly extinguished by mutual agreement in 1980. At present, disputes about sovereignty have become so bitter that both the state and Native leaders are in the process of reviewing the 1980 Settlement.

## THE 1980 SETTLEMENT

The Maine Indian Claims Settlement Act of 1980 was based on state purchases of Penobscot and Passamaquoddy land that violated the U.S. Trade and Intercourse Act of 1790, reconfirmed and amended several times in the early nineteenth century (Prucha 1994,

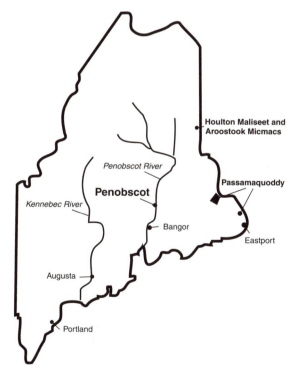

Maine's native territories. (*Map by Granville Ganter*)

99–104). Originally drawn up to protect the U.S. government from land-grabbing by private investors, the Intercourse Act (or as it was later called, the Non-Intercourse Act) stipulated that all sales of Indian lands need to be attended by a U.S. Commissioner and ratified by Congress. In this sense, the act benefited the Indian nations by establishing only one federal avenue for land sales. The law minimized their vulnerability to the corruption of local and state governments. It also acknowledged the sovereign status of Native nations residing within or near U.S. territory.

The law was originally conceived, however, to serve the sovereign interests of the U.S. government. By outlawing the unsupervised purchases of private investors, who were actively buying swaths of Native land large enough to be turned into separate states or even countries, the federal government was simply trying to assert its own control over state and private land acquisition (Taylor 1995; Royster 1999). Nonetheless, the Intercourse Act was sometimes successfully invoked by Native nations to force governmental inquiry into fraudulent land purchases, such as the New York Senecas' petitions against the Ogden Land Company sale of 1826 (Manley 1950, 149–68).

It wasn't until 1957, however, that the leaders of Passamaquoddies and Penobscots discovered proof that land they had sold to the states of Massachusetts and Maine was forfeited in federally unsanctioned purchases. Until that time, they had been under the jurisdiction of Maine's Department of Indian Affairs, not recognized by the federal government, and thus ineligible for federal subsidies. Since the 1800s, the Wabanakis had two nonvoting representatives to the state legislature (which remain today), but they were otherwise very poor and marginalized. The per capita income of the Passamaquoddies in the late 1960s was $400 a year (Benedict 2000, 4). In 1957, Louise Sockabesin produced from a shoebox a copy of a 1794 sale of Passamaquoddy land to the state of Massachusetts that was never ratified by the United States (Brodeur 1985, 69). By the early 1970s, the Wabanakis had put together an impressive legal alliance, organized and headed by Tom Tureen, which included Barry Margolin, Robert Mittel, Robert Pelcyger, and Stuart Ross. They won an important victory in 1975 when the U.S. District Court Judge Edward Gignoux ruled that the Non-Intercourse Act applied to the Passamaquoddy, and they earned federal recognition (84–95). In addition to adding support for several other important Non-Intercourse Act suits brought by eastern Native tribes and nations, the Passamaquoddy's victory guaranteed them federal subsidies long into the future. Today, government-sponsored programs provide much of the employment on Maine's reservations (Young and Graettinger 2002, 1).

By 1977, it became clear that the Passamaquoddies and Penobscots could press their claim to twelve and a half million acres of Maine land, which would displace 350,000 homeowning whites as well as several massive timber and paper companies. Their arguments were compelling enough that Peter Taft, head of the Justice Department's Land and Natural Resources Division, wrote in a memo to Judge Gignoux that the Indian claim was "potentially the most complex litigation ever brought in the federal courts, with social and economic impacts without precedent, and incredible potential litigation costs to all parties" (99).

At the behest of President Jimmy Carter, a task force was appointed to settle the Wabanaki claim out of court in late 1977. As Carter's term of office began to draw to a close, however, and Ronald Reagan's election seemed imminent, negotiations were rushed. Both the Wabanakis and the state of Maine had much to lose. Reagan had vowed to quash the settlement if it were still pending when he was elected, and the Wabanakis were worried that time was running out (Stevens n.d.; Benedict 2000, 111). The U.S. Court of Appeals and the Maine Supreme Court had upheld the sovereign status of the Passamaquoddies and the Penobscots in 1979, and the State of Maine was anxious that it was fighting a losing case (Brodeur 1985, 120–23). By March of 1980, a tentative agreement was reached, and it was at that stage endorsed by a vote of the participating Wabanakis. Shortly afterward, the governor and the legislature of Maine passed the Maine Implementing Act in April. The Maine agreement was then ratified by the U.S. Congress with some significant additions to federal law and was signed by President Carter in early October 1980.

The 1980 settlement concerned state law, finances, and land. First, it revised the laws that are applicable to Natives and Native land in Maine—the Maine Implementing Act. Second, it established a $27 million trust to be shared equally between the Passamaquoddies and Penobscots, tax-free and with interest paid quarterly. Most importantly, it set aside $54.4 million to buy 300,000 acres to add to Passamaquoddy, Penobscot, and Maliseet territory. These new land acquisitions would be held in trust for the Wabanakis by the United States and would be subject to alienation and land management oversight by the U.S. Secretary of the Interior. Although the Houlton

Maliseets got $900,000 of this money for land trust acquisition, they did not get independent municipality status in their relationships with the state of Maine, nor did they get a trust fund (MITSC 1995, 16–17).

The 1980 settlement was a great financial victory for the majority of the Wabanakis, but it also held enormous benefits for the state of Maine. First, the federal government paid the $81 million settlement cost. Maine paid nothing. Second, the state cleared title to all of its lands. The Implementing Act states that all Indian land claims were henceforth extinguished in Maine. (The state presently believes that even Aroostook Micmac claims were extinguished by the Act, but since they were not included in the Implementing Act, the federal government treated with them independently in 1991—a situation whose advantage the Micmacs are presently studying (Phillips 2002). Third, Maine was able to dismantle its Department of Indian Affairs, divesting itself entirely from 150 years of supervision of some of the poorest Native populations in the country. The U.S. government would henceforth provide subsidies and care for the Wabanakis. (Again, until 1991 the Aroostook Micmacs were treated as if they did not exist.) Finally, and most important, even though Maine had rid itself of *responsibility* for the management of Indian affairs in Maine, it retained extensive *regulatory authority* over the territory of the Passamaquoddies, Penobscots, and Maliseets.

The crucial sections of the Maine Implementing Act that define this authority, 30 M.R.S.A. 6204-6, appear to restrict the sovereign powers of the Indian nations in Maine to jurisdiction over "internal tribal matters." In the Implementing Act, the Passamaquoddy and Penobscot nations are defined like state municipalities, not like independent sovereigns. Except as otherwise provided in the act, the Passamoquoddies and Penobscots

> have, exercise, and enjoy the rights, privileges, powers and immunities of a *municipality,* including the power to enact ordinances, and collect taxes; be subject to all the duties, obligations, liabilities, and *limitations of a municipality;* and be subject to the laws of the State, except that "internal tribal matters" are not subject to regulation by the State. Internal tribal matters include membership in the Tribe or Nation, the right to reside within the respective Indian territories, tribal organization, tribal government, tribal

elections, and the use or disposition of Settlement Fund income. (quoted in *At Loggerheads* 2000, 11, emphasis mine)

According to the state's interpretation of this provision, the Native nations are thus at liberty to manage their own internal government, tribal membership, fiscal management, and legal system for minor infractions, but like city governments, they are otherwise regulated by the state on almost any issue of consequence. Particularly when it comes to financial or environmental development, the definition of a *state issue* is a determination initially made by *state* supervisory agencies. In other words, the state argues that the Wabanakis are like teenagers living in their parents' basement: they are free to make their beds or not, feed themselves as they may, but if they want to do anything their parents deem questionable, like have a card game on Friday night or take action on their plumbing needs, they need their parents' approval.

Although this is not a very complimentary characterization of the limitations of Native sovereignty under MICSA, and one which Wabanaki leaders currently dispute, the domestic analogy of parent and child has a long-standing tradition in American law, going back to the Marshall court decisions in the 1820s and 1830s. In a famous ruling in *Cherokee Nation v. Georgia* (1831), Justice John Marshall qualified Indian independence by denominating Native governments as "domestic dependent nations." Because of the paradoxes inherent in this concept, the words *anomalous* or *anomaly* are often used to describe both the type of sovereignty the Native nations have in the eyes of the U.S. courts, as well as the nature of the treaties made with them (Prucha 1994).

Wabanaki leaders argue that an exclusive focus on the municipality provisions of the Maine Implementing Act disregards their simultaneous aboriginal rights as sovereign peoples which existed long prior to European imperialism ("Maine Tribal" 2002, A-5; Cohen 1971, 122–26). In an essay in the Winter 1998 issue of *Wabanaki Legal News*, Penobscot counsel Mark Chavaree quotes from Senate reports made during the MICSA negotiations that explicitly state that MICSA should not be interpreted as reducing Native sovereignty—municipality status is an addition to their powers, not a limitation of it (Chavaree 1998). The courts, however, have not been persuaded by these arguments during the 1990s.

There is a second problem relating to the Maine Implementing Act, however, that occurred at the federal level. The federal government was conscious that Maine's foremost concern during the 1980 Settlement was to maintain authority over trade and government within the bounds of the state. Thus, the federal act which *ratified* the Maine Implementing Act included provisions that reaffirmed the Wabanaki's former status as "state" Indians. Sections of 1980 Maine Settlement Act, 25 U.S.C. 1725 and 1735, state that federal laws and regulations that confer special status to Indians and that also *preempt* the jurisdiction of the State *are inapplicable in Maine.* Also, any federal law enacted after October 10, 1980 for the benefit of Indians which would *effect* or *preempt* the laws of the State of Maine "shall not apply within the State of Maine, unless [it] is specifically made applicable within the State" (quoted in *At Loggerheads* 2000, 13, emphasis mine). Wabanaki leaders point out that these federal provisions were drawn up *after* Wabanaki votes on the Implementing Act and thus did not reflect Native consent (13).

The paradox of the federal 1980 Settlement Act is that the Wabanakis lost elements of their federal recognition. The U.S. government ratified the Maine Implementing Act and henceforth excluded the Wabanakis from some types of federal legislation expressly designed to have national effect. Because few legislators will be likely to incur the ill-will of their Maine colleagues by including specifically "Maine" clauses to national Indian legislation, the Wabanakis are doubly held under the thumb of the state of Maine: first by the *municipality* provisions of the Maine Implementing Act, and second, by federal law that segregates them from national legislation that might otherwise bear on their status. In the two decades since the 1980 Settlement, federal legislation pertaining to casinos and pollution have made the Wabanakis painfully aware of the importance of maintaining regulatory authority over their own lands.

## MAINE INDIAN TRIBAL-STATE COMMISSION (MITSC)

Despite the negative aspects of the 1980 Settlement, its initial appeal was mutual. The Wabanakis wanted land restitution and some money with which to rebuild their traditional way of life. Maine wanted assurances that it could control commerce and law within the state's boundaries (Brodeur 1985, 125). Both sides knew that disagreements were bound to arise and new laws created or modified. To negotiate the evolution of the compromise, which both sides recognized would take years to work out, the Maine Implementing Act provided for the establishment of an advisory body called the Maine Indian Tribal-State Commission (MITSC). The MITSC is composed of nine members: four appointees from the state, two each from the Passamaquoddies and Penobscots, and a chairperson chosen by the appointees. MITSC is charged with reviewing the effectiveness of the Implementing Act; to make recommendations on land acquisition; to promulgate fishing rules; to conduct fish and wildlife studies; and to review petitions by tribes for extensions to the reservations. The MITSC's budget has varied over the years but in 2001 it was just over $40,000 (*At Loggerheads* 2000, 17). From this small budget, MITSC employs a part-time Executive Director, Diana Scully, who has served in that capacity since 1990.

A 1997 state-sponsored review of the relationship between the Indians and the State of Maine, *At Loggerheads,* concluded that, although Native-State relationships were poor, the MITSC had performed a number of tasks well: work on fish and wildlife rules, and review of trust land applications. It also had developed an educational function that the framers of the Implementing Act had not envisioned. In 1995, the MITSC produced an educational video, *Wabanaki: A New Dawn,* and it has often provided testimony to the state legislature on Native issues. The MITSC has also become the central source for information about the Settlement and its legacy, as well as the facilitator of State-Tribe interactions. Director Scully reports that much of the agency's time is simply spent responding to information requests from the public because the state of Maine no longer has a Department of Indian Affairs (MITSC 1995, 17; Scully 2002).

In the *At Loggerheads* report, however, both state and Wabanaki representatives voiced concern that the MITSC had very little power and was not living up to its potential as a mediator for the discussion of tribal-state relations. Both the state and the tribes tend to feel that the MITSC is biased toward the other side. The MITSC itself presently feels frustrated by its small budget, its lack of access to independent legal council, and its generally unrecognized efforts on behalf of the legislature (31–33). As a result of being primarily an advisory body, the MITSC has been unable to defuse the tensions that have developed over the past decade over how to realize the spirit of the Implementing Act.

Despite its lack of enforcement power, the MITSC's role as a mediator has brought some positive results. The MITSC has brokered an annual Assembly of Governors and Chiefs from the late 1990s to the present. In these meetings, representatives from the state, including Governor Angus King, met with the Chiefs and Governors of the Wabanakis to air their concerns. During meetings from 1999 to 2001, all parties expressed a desire for increasing the MITSC's involvement. In the unofficial minutes of the last meeting (yet to be ratified), December 7, 2001, representatives from several of the Wabanaki groups and nations voiced their satisfaction with Governor King's recent attempts to listen and respond to their concerns. Passamaquoddy state legislative representative Donald Soctomah pointed out accomplishments, such as the marine resources bill, offensive place names legislation (to remove the word *squaw* from state discourse), and the education bill to teach Native history in elementary schools, LD 291. Penobscot Chief Barry Dana remarked that a new era of Tribal-State relations seemed to be dawning, but he also insisted that the state needed to view the tribes as a separate and sovereign form of government that does not infringe on the state's sovereignty (Assembly of Governors and Chiefs 2001, 6).

## WATER POLLUTION AND SOVEREIGNTY

Despite the publically optimistic tone of recent Assemblies of Governors and Chiefs, bitter disputes between the Wabanakis and the state have occurred in the past ten years over water quality and pollution controls. Maine's largest rivers have been significantly polluted by mercury and dioxin. The toxic effects of mercury poisoning, such as birth defects, have been known for many years but dioxin is a more recently acknowledged threat. Maine's paper production industry generates many kinds of organochlorides called dioxins, but the most stable is 2,3,7,8 tetrachloridibenzo-p-dioxin, or TCDD. TCDD is the organochloride most commonly referred to as *dioxin*. It is indisputably carcinogenic and one of the most toxic synthetic substances known to man (Ranco 2001, 43, 174–78). It is of interest to researchers because it seems to be potent even in trace amounts, causing cancer in unusual and unpredictable ways. The Lincoln paper mill, thirty-five miles north of the principal Penobscot reservation of Indian Island, produced TCDD until 1999 as a result of the hot chlorine bleaching process it used to create high quality paper (179, 7–9). (Lincoln's parent company, Eastern Pulp and Paper, filed for bankruptcy in 2000 (Young 2000)). Because of the high levels of dioxin in the rivers, the Environmental Protection Agency (EPA) has posted warnings since the 1980s that people shouldn't eat more than

16 ounces of fish per month from stretches of the Penobscot river if they want to protect their health. Pregnant women shouldn't eat *any* fish taken from south of the Lincoln mill (Ranco 2001, 10). These are the same types of warnings presently encountered on the piers of New York City's East River.

Each of Maine's high-quality paper mills produce many tons of dioxin-related organochlorides a day, but the kind of pollution that these plants produce has other consequences as well. Maine's paper mills have stained many of Maine's rivers, like the Androscoggin, dark brown, nearly black. Waterfalls downstream from the plants are coffee colored and smell bad. The rivers have a stiff brown foam that cakes in the eddies. No one knows exactly which pollutants cause the foam. Wabanakis note that frogs and turtles do not seem to behave normally when the mills discharge effluent (Ranco 2001, 14). There are no laws that speak to the psychological effect that this type of pollution produces. For this reason, Wabanaki leaders ask the state to also consider the *cultural* effects of pollution.

The Wabanakis have a long-standing relationship to Maine rivers, not only as a source of sustenance but as the matrix of their culture (Speck 1940). Penobscot Governor Barry Dana and Passamaquoddy Governor Rick Doyle addressed the Maine legislature on water and sovereignty issues in a historic March 19, 2002 State of the Tribes speech, the first by Native chiefs since the early nineteenth century. During his speech, Governor Dana told the story of Gluskabe, a Wabanaki epic hero, who noticed that the river was drying up. Investigating the source, he found that a giant frog was swallowing the water up at its source. Gluskabe struck the frog with a giant white pine, breaking the frog open into a thousand pieces and restoring the flow of the Penobscot river. Dana then explained to the legislature that the Penobscot see themselves as the descendants of Gluskabe, stewards and protectors of the river. He said that "our waters are not just a resource, they are us" (Maine Tribal 2002, A-5). Chief Dana's identification with Gluskabe in his legislative address emphasizes that the Wabanaki's bureaucratic fight for clean water is part of Wabanaki culture and mythic history.

In some ways, the Wabanakis have been successful in influencing the environmental regulations pertaining to their lands. As Penobscot Darren John Ranco explains in his recent Harvard anthropology dissertation, the Penobscots successfully convinced the EPA to nearly double the daily fish consumption factor that they used to calculate their health risk analysis for a 1997 permit given to the Lincoln Pulp and Paper Company (63–4). Ranco worked with the tribes and EPA during the 1990s, and he details the ways Native concerns spoke to bureaucratic culture—such as the belief that Natives are more ecologically minded than other groups (81–88). Despite having their input recognized during the several-year process of issuing the Lincoln permit, the Penobscot nation eventually opposed the 1997 permit because they were dissatisfied with the EPA's bureaucratic definitions of *pollution, health,* and *acceptable risk.*

One of the Wabanakis' options in fighting pollution by the paper mills was to pursue a sovereignty argument that had serious legal obstacles facing it. The 1980 Settlement gave the Penobscots and Passamaquoddies the right to set hunting and fishing laws within their territories, but questions arose concerning what powers they had to influence environmental law that bears on their fishing stocks. According to current federal law, if an Indian nation has received treatment-as-a-state status by the EPA, it may set its own water quality standards, even if those are more stringent than the state's standards (Ranco 2001, 104; 33 USC 1377e and 40 CFR 131.8a). The Isleta Pueblo Indians' water standards were upheld by the Tenth Circuit Court of New Mexico in 1996. In 1993, the EPA denied the Penobscot Nation the authority to set water standards under treatment-as-a-state regulations, but they left open the possibility that the nation could reapply. In other words, the Maine tribes were ultimately unable to control the quality of water that flowed through their lands. In several cases since, the courts have affirmed that Maine's 1980 Settlement explicitly restricted the sovereignty of the Penobscots and Passamaquoddies to conform with that of a state municipality (*Atkins v. Penobscot Nation* 1997; *Penobscot Nation v. Cynthia Fellencer* 1999; *Boudman v. Aroostook Band of Micmac Indians* 1999).

Probably the largest political setback for the Wabanakis occurred in May of 2002, when they were forced by the courts to hand over tribal documents to paper companies under Maine's Freedom of Access Act (Groening 2002, 1; Murphy 2002). The controversy began in 1999 when the Maine Department of Environmental Protection applied to the U.S. EPA for the authority to issue National Pollution Discharge Elimination System (NPDES) permits to companies that dump treated wastewater into Maine rivers (Young 2000). At that time, forty-four state environmental agencies had been given authority to act in lieu of the EPA to speed the permit-granting process. Wabanaki leaders protested the state's application, arguing that state officials were too easily influenced by state business interests. The Maine paper companies, who were preparing a lawsuit against the EPA to push it toward compliance, sought water quality information from the Wabanakis in May 2000 (Murphy 2002). The Wabanakis refused, claiming sovereignty. In November 2000, a state judge threatened to have three Wabanaki governors jailed for contempt and fined $1,000 a day (Murphy 2002). The Wabanakis appealed to the Maine Supreme Court, which ruled on May 1, 2001, that they had to surrender the documents because they were not sovereign "when they interact with other governments or agencies in their municipal capacities" (*Great Northern Paper v. Penobscot Nation* 2001).

Despite state success thwarting Wabanaki claims to sovereignty in the courts, Maine Governor Angus King sought to resolve the water permit situation more amicably by convening negotiations between the state, the Wabanakis, and the paper companies in February 2002. At that point, the EPA had already granted to the state Department of Environmental Protection (DEP) the authority to issue NPDES waste water permits on all but the Indian territories of the St. Croix and Penobscot rivers. The negotiations appeared to be successful, and by April, Wabanaki councils had voted to support a state DEP compromise agreement. During this process, however, the paper companies maintained that they would not withdraw their EPA lawsuits until the state DEP was given licensing authority. Furthermore, Native leaders were concerned that the compromise reduced their role to mere consultants, weakening the input of Indian representatives with the words *may*, rather than *will* (Young 2002). On May 10, the day the EPA was to decide whether to grant authority to the state DEP, the Wabanakis withdrew from the compromise, citing undue influence and bad-faith negotiations by the paper companies (Young 2002). On May 23–24, 2002, the Wabanakis organized a thirty-three-mile protest march to the state capitol in Augusta. At the capitol, they pledged to continue defending Maine's waterways and protested the court's insult to their sovereignty, but they consented to release information to the paper companies (Groening 2002; Murphy 2002). As of September 2002, the EPA had still not decided if it would grant to the state DEP the authority to issue NPDES permits concerning Native territory, forwarding the issue to the Department of Justice for further review.

## CASINOS AND PUBLIC RELATIONS

Tom Tureen, the Wabanakis' principal lawyer during the 1980 settlement, was aware that the provisions of MICSA would cede many types of regulatory authority to the state, particularly concerning gambling (Benedict 2000, 111–12). MICSA was approved by traditionalists like Passamaquoddy John Stevens, who imagined that the act would protect Wabanaki folkways and culture, like building sweet grass baskets and birch bark canoes. Unlike the Pequots, the desire to build a gambling operation was not foremost in their minds. Rather, they imagined that MICSA would allow them to develop a diversified Native economy. During the 1980s and 1990s, the Penobscots built a hockey rink and secured a contract for a factory that molded tape cassettes (Ranco 2001, 6). The Passamaquoddies ran a very successful concrete business which they later sold. They also continue to run blueberry and cranberry businesses (Scully 2002). The Penobscots are presently in negotiations to start a bottled water business as well as a windfarm for electricity in Alder Stream Township (Dana n.d.). In general, however, Wabanaki businesses have not yet brought much economic relief, particularly in poor areas such as Washington county. Forty-two percent of Pleasant Point Reservation residents were unemployed in 1999, with residents observing that selling drugs is one of the few jobs around (Young and Graettinger 2002). In Indian Township, the per capita income in 1990 was $6,165, less than half the state average (Young and Graettinger 2002). Although there are Natives who don't want to pursue gambling as an economic stimulus, poverty is making a strong case for the creation of a gaming industry in northern Maine. As in their fight to preserve clean water, however, the Wabanakis' sovereignty arguments have not been sustained by the courts on the casino issue.

Since the passage of the Indian Gaming Regulatory Act (IGRA) of 1988, which classifies gambling into three levels, many Indian nations have begun to pursue class III, or casino gambling (Mason). In the early 1990s, the Passamaquoddies attempted to start a casino in Calais and acquired a small parcel of new land on which to build it. The state legislature eventually approved use of the land for a casino if the tribe could get the support of the city council and the state's governor, or, lacking the governor's consent to negotiate a gaming contract, the ruling of a court of competent jurisdiction. The Passamaquoddies, represented by Tom Tureen, pushed for the commencement of gaming negotiations in 1995 and lost. In 1996, the

U.S. Court of Appeals upheld the 1995 Maine decision in *Passamaquoddy v. Maine* that the 1988 Indian Gaming Regulatory Act did *not apply* to the Passamaquoddies. The appeals court argued, as did the Maine courts, that the federal Settlement Act of 1980 stipulated that no federal Indian laws would effect or preempt Maine law unless made "specifically applicable" to Maine.

The Passamaquoddies' loss in this appeal had stunning consequences because they thought they had found a way to get around the "specifically applicable" clause that blocks them from the benefit of some federal Indian laws. Like the Wabanakis, the Narragansetts of Rhode Island had also negotiated a land claims settlement in the late 1970s. When they ran into state opposition to their gaming business, they successfully argued in the U.S. Court of Appeals that the federal gaming law of 1988 *implied* the repeal of the gaming provisions of their own 1978 Settlement Act (*Rhode Island v. Narragansett Indian Tribe* 1994). Similarly, the Passamaquoddies had attempted to argue that the Congress's 1988 IGRA laws had also implied the repeal of the 1980 Maine Settlement Act. If successful in their argument, the Passamaquoddies stood to gain precedent to benefit from the passage of other federal laws since 1980, too. The federal appeals court quashed this hope, however, by responding that their previous ruling in *Narragansett* merely removed a specific "incoherence" between federal gaming laws and state ones in favor of the federal laws, a situation which did not apply to the general principals of the Maine Settlement Act (*Passamaquoddy Tribe v. State of Maine* 1996).

Maine's opponents of casino gambling often invoke moralistic language—the influx of a bad element, corruption, false prosperity (Shanahan 2002)—but the more likely reason for their opposition is simply a fear of Native power. Wenona Lola, a Wabanaki editorialist in the April 4, 2002, *Bangor Daily News,* suggested that allowing the Wabanakis to develop their economy through casinos would upset the power relations between the state and the tribes. Long comfortable with keeping the Native voice in state politics silent and marginalized, Lola argued that the state of Maine feared a stronger Indian presence in its affairs. With more money at their disposal, the Wabanakis might be able to fund more formidable environmental challenges to the state's timber and paper industries. A financially powerful Wabanaki confederacy could completely rearrange state lobbying politics.

Chastened by recent court rulings against their sovereignty, however, the Wabanakis have begun to pursue casino gambling by including the state as a prospective partner, rather than an opponent. Sensing that they might get more with a carrot than a stick, the Wabanakis have turned to public relations and the conventional politics of deal-cutting. They have supported several recent referenda on gaming issues. In May of 2002, they resoundingly lost a city referendum in York by a ratio of 5 to 1, which asked if residents favored casino gambling in southern Maine, but the referendum, and seven others held in June, nonetheless has kept their agenda well-advertised and in public view (Associated Press 2002; Graettinger 2002). Also, polls indicate that state-wide opinion seems to be split, with poorer districts favoring casino gambling ("Casino Study" 2002, 8). Further, during the spring of 2002, the Wabanakis convinced the legislature to fund a study of the impact of casino gambling in Maine. In a spring 2002 editorial in the *Bangor Daily News,* Governor Angus King repeated his opposition to casino gambling in Maine, but the *Bangor Daily News* itself strongly supported legislative research into the casino question (Lola). Even the former governor, Kenneth Curtis, has agreed to serve on the board of directors of a tribal casino (Casino Study 2002, 8). In July 2002, Chief Dana proposed a plan to bring in the state as a partner in a $400–600 million casino-resort in the Kittery area in 2003, and several Republican legislators seem to be warming up to the idea (Murphy 2002; Dana n.d.; Higgins 2002).

## EDUCATION AND TRUST

In the past decade, the Wabanakis have not been successful in advancing their claims to sovereignty in court (the Aroostook Micmacs are an important exception). In fact, the courts have consistently chosen to interpret the Implementing Act in its narrowest sense, giving the Penobscots, Passamaquoddies, and Maliseets very little authority in the large business and environmental issues that their nations face. As long as provision 6204 of the Maine Implementing Act (municipality status), and sections 1725 and 1735 of the federal Settlement (excluding Maine Indians from some kinds of federal Indian legislation) remain unchanged, there seems to be very little potential for improvements in the degree of their sovereignty, even in the limited sense that federal law recognizes it in other Indian nations (Cohen 1971, 122–26).

Despite these restrictions, and perhaps *because* of them, the Wabanakis nonetheless have found several ways to advance their interests in Maine. First, the invitation to share profits with the state in the casino business may have a fruitful political yield in years to come. Second, the Wabanaki still have compelling arguments to make to the state of Maine and the U.S. government act upon their needs as *trustees* (Pevar 1992, 26). As Darren Ranco has shown in his study of Wabanaki-EPA relations, the trust obligation has been an effective legal and political tool on behalf of Native environmental concerns (111–22). If the state is going to deny the Wabanakis the sovereignty necessary to protect themselves, then the state and government need to bear that responsibility for their care. Finally, according to the recent statements made at the annual Assemblies of Chiefs and Governors, the Wabanakis see civic education as an important long-term avenue toward their political and economic advancement in Maine. By educating their peers about Wabanaki history, and by sponsoring educational and antiracist legislation, the Wabanakis hope to defuse the prejudice and xenophobia that has biased Maine's reaction to their existence for years.

## REFERENCES

*Aroostook Band of Micmac Settlement.* Pub. L. 102-71. Nov. 26, 1991, 105 Stat. 1143. http://www4.law.cornell.edu/uscode/25/1721.notes.html.

Assembly of Governors and Chiefs, Minutes. December 7, 2001; December 1, 2000. December 3, 1999. Maine Indian Tribal-State Commission.

Associated Press. 2002. Maine town rejects casino idea. *Boston Globe,* May 20. http://n19.newsbank.com.

*Atkins v. Penobscot Nation.* 130 F. 3d 482 (1st Cir. 1997).

*At Loggerheads—The state of Maine and the Wabanaki: Final report of the task force on tribal-state relations.* January 15, 1997. Revised, June 2000. 46 pp.

Benedict, J. 2000. *Without reservation: How a controversial indian tribe rose to power and built the world's largest casino.* New York: HarperCollins.

*Boudman v. Aroostook Band of Micmac Indians.* 98-174B. 1999. http://216.239.35.100/search?q=cache:bb0G9_9l_TIC:www.med .uscourts.gov/Site/opinions/brody/1999/mab_1-98cv174_boudman_v_ aroostook_doc14_jun.pdf+boudman+v+aroostook&hl=en&ie=UTF-8.

Brodeur, P. 1985. *Restitution: The land claims of the Mashpee, Passamaquoddy, and Penobscot Indians of New England.* Boston: Northeastern University Press.

Casino study. Editorial. 2002. *Bangor Daily News,* April 2, 8. http://www .penobscotnation.org/articles/study040202.htm.

Chavaree, M. 1998. Tribal Counsel, Penobscot Nation. Tribal sovereignty. *Wabanaki Legal News* (Winter): 10 pp. http://www.ptla.org/wabanaki/ sovereign.htm.

*Cherokee Nation v. Georgia.* 30 U.S. 1 (1831). http://odur.let.rug.nl/~usa/D/ 1801-1825/marshallcases/mar06.htm.

———. Telephone Interview. August 27.

Cohen, F.S. 1942/1971. *Handbook of federal Indian law.* Albuquerque: University of New Mexico Press.

Dana, B. *Chief's report,* n.d. http://www.penobscotnation.org/notes/chiefreport.htm.

Dewan, S.K. 2002. After 5 days, Oneida deal is unraveling. *New York Times,* February 22. Sec. 2, p. 1.

Gagnon, D. 2002. HoltraChem woes similar to sister plant. *Bangor Daily News,* July 15, 1.

Graettinger, D. 2002. Education next step in casino bid. *Bangor Daily News,* June 18, 1.

*Great Northern Paper v. Penobscot Nation.* 2001 ME 68. May 1, 2001. http://www.courts.state.me.us/opinions/documents/01me68gr.htm.

Groening, T. 2002. Thirty-three mile trek protests state's control. *Bangor Daily News,* May 24, 1. http://www.penobscotnation.org/articles/trek052402.htm.

Higgins, A.J. 2002. Chief Dana makes case for casino "The bottom line in life is improved," he says. *Bangor Daily News,* June 6, 1. http://www.bangornews.com.

Lola, W. 2002. What are the real issues about casino? *Bangor Daily News,* April 4. http://www.penobscotnation.org/articles/wenona_lola.htm.

Maine tribal leaders give historic speeches to state legislature: Excerpts from state of the tribes addresses. March 11, 2002. *Indian Country Today,* April 10, A-5.

Manley, H.S. 1950. Red Jacket's last campaign, and an extended bibliographical and biographical note. *New York History* 31(2): 149–68.

Mason, W.D. 2000. *Indian gaming: Tribal sovereignty and American politics.* Norman: University of Oklahoma Press.

McKinley, J.C., Jr. 2002. Pataki works out deal with Indians for upstate land. *New York Times,* February 17, 1.

MITSC (Maine Indian Tribal-State Commission). 1995. Maine Indian land claims case. February 14, 22 pp. http://www.wabanaki.com/land%20Claims%20Settlement.htm.

Murphy, G. 2002. Tribes' march to protest court order. *Portland Press Herald,* May 21. http://www.penobscotnation.org/articles/march052002.htm.

*Passamaquoddy Tribe v. State of Maine.* 1st Cir. Appeals. No. 95-1922. February 9, 1996. http://www.law.emory.edu/1circuit/feb96/95-1922.01a.html.

*Penobscot Nation v. Cynthia Fellencer* 98-1326 (1st Cir 1999). http://www.law.emory.edu/1circuit/jan99/98-1326.01a.html.

Pevar, S.L. 1992. *The rights of Indians and tribes: The basic ACLU guide to Indian and tribal rights.* 2nd ed. Carbondale: Southern Illinois University Press.

Phillips, W. Chief, Aroostook Micmacs. Telephone interview. August 27, 2002.

Prucha, F.P. 1994. *American Indian treaties: The history of a political anomaly.* Berkeley: University of California Press.

Ranco, D.J. 2001. *Environmental risk and politics in eastern Maine: The Penobscot Indian nation and the Environmental Protection Agency.* Diss. Harvard University.

*Rhode Island v. Narragansett Indian Tribe.* 19 F. 3d 685 (1st Cir. 1994).

Royster, C. 1999. *The fabulous history of the dismal swamp company: A story of George Washington's times.* New York: Knopf.

Scully, D. Telephone Interview. August 13, 2002.

Shanahan, M. 2002. Cash cow or sin city? *Portland Press Herald,* March 17. http://www.penobscotnation.org/articles/cashcow031602.htm.

Speck, F.G. 1940. *Penobscot man.* Philadelphia: University of Pennsylvania Press.

Stevens, S. Statement. Behind the scenes of the Maine Indian land claims settlement. N.d. http://www.geocities.com/CapitolHill/9118/history5.html.

Taylor, A. 1995. *William Cooper's town.* New York, Knopf.

Young, S. 2002. Tribes reject water compact. *Bangor Daily News,* May 11, 1. http://www.penobscotnation.org/articles/051102rejection.htm.

———. 2000. Maine Indian tribes gain nationwide support. *Bangor Daily News,* November 17, 1. http://www.wabanaki.com/Tribe/rep/news/maine_indian_tribes_gain_nationw.htm.

Young, S., and D. Graettinger. 2002. Gambling on the future of casinos may help tribal economies, but face legal, philosophical battles. *Bangor Daily News,* May 4, 1. http://www.bangornews.com.

# 3

# The Treaty of Canandaigua (1794): Past and Present

*Robert W. Venables*

The United States recognized the independent status of the Six Nations of the Iroquois Confederacy in the Treaty of Canandaigua, signed on November 11, 1794. From 1794 to the present day, the treaty has been the legal keystone of relations between the United States and the Six Nations of the Iroquois Confederacy. The treaty is at the center of any of the Six Nations' land claims and their rights to govern their own reservations. The Six Nations are also known as the Haudenosaunee. The Haudenosaunee ("Ho-dee-no-show-nee") are "the People of the Longhouse." The six member nations are the Mohawks, Oneidas, Onondagas, Cayugas, Senecas, and Tuscaroras. Their reservations are in what is now New York, Quebec, Ontario, Wisconsin, and Oklahoma. At the time of first European contact, the core of their homeland stretched across what is now the State of New York and northward into the St. Lawrence River Valley. During the "colonial period" of U.S. history, Haudenosaunee political power reached westward to the Mississippi and Lake Superior, southward to the Gulf of Mexico, east to the Atlantic, and northward into the northern tributaries of the St. Lawrence River. By 1850, after centuries of pressures by Europeans and Euro-Americans, they were dispersed to their present locations (Jemison and Schein 2000, xi–xv:1–83).

The Treaty of Canandaigua was negotiated in the Seneca town of Canandaigua, located at the northern end of Canandaigua Lake in what is now western New York State approximately twenty-five miles southeast of the city of Rochester. Canandaigua translates as "place selected for a settlement," "town set off," or "chosen town" (Beauchamp 1907, 155–56). The treaty was negotiated on behalf of the United States by Timothy Pickering, the commissioner appointed by President George Washington.

The Canandaigua treaty possesses strong pro-First Nation terms because the United States desperately wanted the Haudenosaunee to remain neutral during the United States' war of conquest against the Indian nations north of the Ohio River Valley. The United States also needed the treaty so that it could reassert federal rights over states' rights in Indian issues. From 1781 (the American Revolution ended in 1783) until 1789 (the implementation of the United States Constitution), the new United States was governed by the Articles of Confederation, a political construction that failed to define precisely how Indian affairs were to be controlled by the central government. The states, including the State of New York, exploited this political limbo. In New York, land speculating companies and the state itself made various treaties with the Haudenosaunee that had questionable legal status but which nonetheless opened lands up for white settlement. With white surveyors and actual settlers constantly moving in, New York created "new facts" that could only be reversed if the federal government under President George Washington wanted to risk alienating a state that had come perilously close to rejecting the new Constitution. The Treaty of Canandaigua was therefore a federal compromise with the State of New York: the federal government recognized New York State's treaties but promised to assert federal authority thereafter. Whether or not this compromise with New York State was also a fraud perpetrated against the Haudenosaunee is one of the issues raised today by the Treaty of Canandaigua (Hauptman 1999, 1–23 and passim).

At least 395 treaties were made after 1775 by the United States with Indian nations (Deloria and DeMaillie 1999, I:203–7). Among all these treaties, the Treaty of Canandaigua defines the strongest rights of American Indian sovereignty recognized by the United States. The treaty is *not* a treaty of conquest, nor does it end a war. Peace had been already been established between the United States and the Haudenosaunee at the Treaty of Fort Stanwix in 1784 (Kappler 1904/1972, 5). Overall, the Treaty of Canandaigua is a treaty between two sovereigns: the Six Nations on the one hand and the

United States on the other. In addition to setting limits for each sovereign, the treaty defines reciprocal obligations.

Although the treaty names "the Six Nations," the Mohawk nation's representatives were not present. While Mohawks lived among the other nations of the Iroquois Confederacy, most Mohawks were in Canada, having either migrated there during the colonial period or taken refuge there after the American Revolution. Thus, the Mohawk Nation was not officially represented at the treaty as a separate entity. In 1871, in the Treaty of Washington, nearly eighty years after Canandaigua, the United States and Great Britain finally agreed on a final border along the St. Lawrence, defining among other issues the exact border between Canada and the State of New York. This border officially placed some of the Akwesasne Mohawks (also known as the St. Regis Mohawks) on the New York side of the border while other Akwesasne Mohawks were defined as living on the Canadian side. In 1888, the Haudenosaunee recognized the Akwesasne Mohawks as the official representatives of the Mohawk Nation in any negotiation with the United States, and the United States recognized this designation in 1892 (United States 1995, 32; New York State 1889, 514).

About 1,600 Haudenosaunee men, women, and children eventually gathered in and around Canandaigua to attend the treaty proceedings. In addition to Timothy Pickering and his staff, four Quakers attended the negotiations as official representatives of the Friends in Philadelphia and were welcomed by the Haudenosaunee. Other Quakers and dozens of other white settlers were either in official attendance or present simply as interested observers. Also present was an outspoken evangelist, Jemima Wilkinson. She and her followers had decided to establish a white Christian colony in the midst of Haudenosaunee country to escape the corruption of the eastern seaboard (Savery 1873, 95–97, 105, 109–110, 112).

During the early stage of the negotiations, on October 21, the four Quakers read an address to the Haudenosaunee from the Quakers of Philadelphia. One of the Quakers, William Savery, recorded how Jemima Wilkinson suddenly thrust herself upon the proceedings:

> Immediately after we had read our speech, Jemima and all her companions kneeled down and she uttered something in the form of prayer, after which she desired to speak, and liberty not being refused, she used many texts of Scriptures, without much similarity or connection. (Savery 1873, 110)

Customarily, Haudenosaunee women rarely addressed councils. The Haudenosaunee were polite, and such an intrusion was accepted, but it did not go unnoticed. Two days later, on October 23, three Haudenosaunee women asked to speak, pointing out that the whites had allowed Jemima Wilkinson to speak. The three Haudenosaunee women were given permission to speak, and William Savery summarized what they said:

> The white people had been the cause of all the Indians' distresses; that they had pressed and squeezed them together, until it gave them great pain at their hearts, and that the whites ought to give them back the lands they had taken from them. That one of the white women had yesterday told the Indians to repent; and they now called on the white people to repent, for they had as much need as the Indians, and that they should wrong the Indians no more. (Savery 1873, 112)

On the same day the three women spoke, October 23, a British observer and translator, "Johnson"—perhaps George Johnson, one of the children of Molly Brant and the late Sir William Johnson—arrived in the Haudenosaunee camps from Canada. On October 25, Pickering refused to admit him to the council, vehemently accusing him of being a spy. The Haudenosaunee were shocked by Pickering's behavior, because it clearly meant that Pickering was limiting the points of view to be expressed. William Savery noted:

> The Indians appeared in amazement at the warmth with which the commissioner delivered himself, and said, when he sat down, the council fire grows warm, and the sparks of it fly about very thick. (Savery 1873, 114–17)

Nevertheless, Johnson returned to Canada.

A major aspect of Haudenosaunee diplomacy is patience, for the Haudenosaunee do not force deliberations to move forward until all parties agree that another step should be taken. Thus, on October 31, they told Pickering to take his time when he said he wasn't ready with a response.

> They delivered us seven strings of wampum, and we desired them to call on us about three o'clock for an answer. We felt it to be a weighty and delicate matter to answer their

request in our situation. They returned about the time fixed, but finding us not entirely prepared to give them an answer, told us not to hurry ourselves, and they would come to-morrow morning; for they are never in haste. (Savery 1873, 129–30)

The next day, November 1, William Savery visited one of the Haudenosanee temporary camps outside Canandaigua, that of the Seneca leader Farmer's Brother:

After dinner, John Parrish [a translator] and myself rode to view the Farmer's Brother's encampment, which contained about five hundred Indians. They are located by the side of a brook, in the woods; having built about seventy or eighty huts, by far the most commodious and ingeniously made of any that I have seen; the principal materials are bark and boughs of trees, so nicely put together as to keep the family dry and warm. The women as well as the men, appeared to be mostly employed. In this camp, there are a large number of pretty children, who, in all the activity and buoyancy of health, were diverting themselves according to their fancy. The vast number of deer they have killed, since coming here, which they cut up and hang round their huts, inside and out, to dry, together with the rations of beef which they draw daily, give the appearance of plenty to supply the few wants to which they are subjected. The ease and cheerfulness

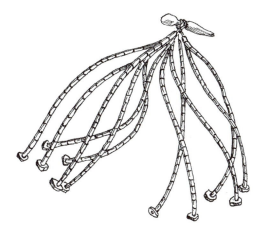

Wampum strings. *(John Kahionhes Fadden)*

of every countenance, and the delightfulness of the after-
noon, which these inhabitants of the woods seemed to enjoy
with a relish far superior to those who are pent up in
crowded and populous cities, all combined to make this the
most pleasant visit I have paid to Indians; and induced me to
believe, that before they became acquainted with white people and were infected with their vices, they must have been
as happy a people as any in the world. (Savery 1873, 130–31)

On November 11, 1794, the treaty—a preamble and seven articles—
was signed. How important is the treaty? Even the Haudenosaunee's
political opponents have conceded the treaty's importance. In 1892,
the U.S. government published a special report, entitled *The Six Nations
of New York: The 1892 United States Extra Census Bulletin*. The authors of
that official United States report concluded that no unilateral action
could be taken by either New York State or the federal government
with regard to the Haudenosaunee, and these authors reluctantly
admitted Haudenosaunee sovereignty. One of the authors, Thomas
Donaldson, noted:

> The conclusion is irresistible that the Six Nations are
> nations by treaty and law, and have long since been recog-
> nized as such by the United States and the state [sic] of New
> York, and an enlightened public will surely hesitate before
> proceeding to divest these people of long-established rights
> without their consent—rights recognized and confirmed in
> some cases by the immortal [George] Washington and by
> more than a hundred years of precedents and legislation.
> (United States 1995, 4)

Among the "rights recognized and confirmed" by George Washing-
ton are those in the 1794 Treaty of Canandaigua, negotiated during
Washington's second administration as President of the United States.
In the 1892 report, Thomas Donaldson also noted:

> If the Iroquois, native or foreign (i.e. Canadian) born, want
> to become citizens of the United States they must renounce
> allegiance to their own people . . . The several reservations
> belong to them, and neither the state of New York nor the
> United States can break them [the reservations] up without
> the Indians' consent, or through conditions analogous
> to those of war. They have always been recognized as
> nations. . . . (United States 1995, 3)

Toward the end of this 1892 U.S. government report, the other major author, General Henry B. Carrington, noted that "The alleged absurdity of the Six Nations of New York being a 'nation within a nation' does not change the fact or nullify the sequence of actual history" (United States 1995, 79).

Remarkably, Carrington calls upon the United States to accept the Haudenosaunee claim to "independence," and goes on to suggest that international law take precedence over *both* United States and Haudenosaunee law:

> Accepting all that the most technical advocate of the Indians' claim to prolonged independence can advance, a higher and equally consistent principle of international law supplies the wholesome remedy. As contiguous nations must have political intercourse, and upon a basis of mutual benefit, so there must be, on the part of each, some representative authority to adjust conflicting issues between them. (United States 1995, 79)

Thus Carrington was calling for two permanent liaison authorities, one authorized by and representing the Haudenosaunee, and the other authorized by and representing the United States. This proposal would have created a formal structure to enforce Article VII of the Treaty of Canandaigua, which calls for communication between representatives of the United States and the Haudenosaunee whenever there is an immediate crisis. However, the proposal has never been implemented.

An analysis of the provisions of the Treaty of Canandaigua reveals the complexity of the treaty.

> **Preamble:** The preamble clearly states that the initiative for the treaty had originated with the United States, "the President of the United States having determined to hold a conference with the Six Nations of Indians, for the purpose of removing from their minds all causes of complaint, and establishing a firm and permanent friendship with them." (Kappler 1904/1972, 34–35)

**Article I** consists of one brief sentence: "Peace and friendship are hereby firmly established, and shall be perpetual, between the United States and the Six Nations" (Kappler 1904/1972, 35).

**Articles II and III** define the lands of the Oneidas, Onondagas, Cayugas, and Senecas and promises that "the United States will never claim the same, nor disturb them or either of the Six Nations, nor their Indian friends residing thereon and united with them, in the free use and enjoyment thereof." The term "their Indian friends" refers to the Indian nations such as the Stockbridges (formerly of Massachusetts) that had been adopted by the Confederacy. Another of these adopted nations is that of the Tuscaroras. The Tuscaroras, fleeing North Carolina because of white slave hunters, were adopted into the Confederacy by 1722 and are officially represented by the Oneida Nation. The Tuscaroras are also known as the "sixth nation." They are thus paradoxically defined in the treaty as one of the Haudenoaunee "Six Nations" and as one of the adopted nations that are "their Indian friends residing . . . and united with them" (Kappler 1904/1972, 35).

As noted previously, the Haudenosaunee had been victimized by land speculators and by the state of New York in treaties of questionable legality made under both the Articles of Confederation and the United States Constitution. In Articles II and III, the United States federal government tacitly conceded its inability to enforce centralized sovereignty over land speculators and the State of New York. The United States, however, in this article, also proclaimed that henceforth the lands that remained under Haudenosaunee control are the "property" of the Haudenosaunee "until they choose to sell the same to the people of the United States" (Kappler 1904/1972, 35). This last phrase was and is significant, because it asserted that the United States, not the State of New York, would negotiate any future land cessions. The State of New York broke these treaty provisions the very next year by making illegal treaties with the Cayugas on July 27, 1795, with the Onondagas on July 28, 1795, and with the Oneidas on September 1 and 15, 1795 (New York State 1889, 224, 199, 242, 244). The legal arguments that evolved continue to shape today's land claims and other Haudenosaunee treaty rights (Hauptman 1999, passim).

**Article IV** notes that in exchange for federal recognition of the lands that "belong to the Oneidas, Onondagas, Cayugas, and Senecas," the Six Nations would in turn "never claim any other lands within the boundaries of the United States" (Kappler 1972, 35–36). This confirmed vast amounts of land that the Haudenosaunee had ceded in 1784 (Second Treaty of Fort Stanwix) and 1789 (Treaty of Fort Harmar), including northwestern Pennsylvania and all claims to Ohio and the other lands west of Pennsylvania.

**Article V** recognizes two very important elements of Haudenosaunee rights, the first with regard to Haudenosaunee concepts of land, and the second related to Haudenosaunee sovereignty.

*Land.* All territories not occupied by towns are regarded as "The Woods." The towns and their agricultural fields are "The Clearings." While The Clearings are under the control of one of the member nations, The Woods are under the control of both the whole Confederacy and the individual member nation in the immediate locale of the lands. Because the Haudenosaunee responsibility for the land is framed within a duality not a hierarchy, this Haudenosaunee perception of land does not have an equivalent in United States real-estate law. The United States recognizes the unique Haudenosaunee definition of land in the wording of Article V, which defines a cession of land that will allow the United States to maintain a road bypassing Niagara Falls and its rapids. These lands were regarded by the Haudenosaunee as The Woods, simultaneously within the jurisdiction of the local Seneca Nation and the entire Confederacy. The United States recognized that both the Seneca Nation and the entire Confederacy had to agree to this cession: "The Seneca Nation, all other of the Six Nations concurring, cede to the United States the right of making a wagon road from Fort Schlosser to Lake Erie, as far south as Buffalo Creek" (Kappler 1904/1972, 36).

*Sovereignty.* Article V also includes a provision that at first glance seems to undermine, rather than reinforce, Haudenosaunee sovereignty: "the Six Nations, and each of them, will forever allow to the people of the United States a free passage through their lands, and the free use of the harbors and rivers adjoining and within their respective tracts of land, for the passing and securing of vessels and boats, and the liberty to land their cargoes where necessary for their safety" (Kappler 1904/1972, 36). First, the phrase "the Six Nations, and each of them" reinforces the concept of The Woods, wherein both the Confederacy and local member nations have a simultaneous responsibility for the land. More subtly, however, the entire statement, in which the Haudenosaunee promise that U.S. citizens can have "free passage" through their territories, implies that until this provision was made, the Haudenosaunee had the right to make such restrictions. If the United States had been the single "sovereign" over these lands, this provision would not have been necessary, because the United States could have enforced the right of its citizens to travel without Haudenosaunee consent.

Furthermore, this provision basically defined a non-Indian's right to travel and trade as a balance to the provision in the various state treaties with the Haudenosaunee, in which the State of New York had already guaranteed to the Haudensaounee "the free right of hunting in every part of the said ceded lands, and of fishing in all the waters within the same" (New York State 1889, 190). Since the Treaty of Canandaigua confirms the New York treaties, the treaty confirms the Haudenosaunee right to hunt and fish throughout the lands ceded to New York State.

**Article VI** promised an annual payment to the Haudenosaunee of clothing, domestic animals, and other goods totaling "four thousand five hundred dollars" (Kappler 1904/1972, 36). No provision was made for inflation. While this was not a "fair" price for the Treaty of Canandaigua's federal confirmation of the lands ceded to New York State and for the lands ceded in the United States treaties of Fort Stanwix in 1784 and Fort Harmar in 1789, it became increasingly unfair as inflation reduced the value of this already small sum to a pittance. Only cheap muslin cloth is now presented to the Haudenosaunee by the world's richest nation for its occupation of New York, the Empire State.

**Article VII** defines how difficulties arising between the two sovereigns, the Haudenosaunee and the United States, will be resolved by representatives of each. For the United States, the representative will be either "the President of the United States, or the Superintendent by him appointed." For the Haudenosaunee, the negotiators would be "the principal chiefs of the Six Nations, or of the nation" immediately involved in the difficulty (Kappler 1904/1972, 36).

## TERMINOLOGY

Definition of limits and obligations in the Treaty of Canandaigua raises some problems of terminology. In this context, the Supreme Court decision *Worcester v. Georgia* (1832) specifically addressed the issue of conflicting interpretation:

> The language used in treaties with the Indians should never be construed to their prejudice. If words be made use of which are susceptible of a more extended meaning than their plain import, as connected with the tenor of the treaty, they should be considered as used only in the latter sense. . . . How the words of the treaty were understood by this unlettered [i.e., preliterate, not illiterate] people, rather than their critical meaning, should form the rule of construction. (Washburn 1973, IV:2637)

Thus the U.S. courts must use the interpretation presented by a First Nation, an American Indian nation—provided that the Indian nation can *prove* that its interpretation has a historical basis. That, of course, is the trick, because most of the treaty records acceptable in court just happen to be documents written by white people.

With this Supreme Court case in mind, it is interesting to examine Article II of the Treaty of Canandaigua, which defines lands reserved "to" the Haudenosaunee by the State of New York. Non-Indians, especially U.S. government lawyers, often contend that this implies that the United States is granting lands "to" the Haudenosaunee, which in turn implies that the United States is the sovereign. This non-Indian interpretation is contradicted in the very next two articles, because both Articles III and IV state that the United States will never "claim" the Haudenosaunee lands set forth in the treaty. If the United States was sovereign, it clearly *would* claim these lands. Instead, Articles II and III define a more limited right, a right known as the "right of preemption." Preemption means the right of purchase is exclusively established for one particular European or Euro-American nation. Thus Articles II and III use the same wording and define preemption as follows: Haudenosaunee lands "shall remain theirs, until they choose to sell the same to the people of the United States, who have the right to purchase" (Kappler 1904/1972, 35).

"Pre-emption" referred only to land, and did not alter Indian political systems on that land. Preemption was originally a European concept, which competing European powers used to settle which European power would have the right to negotiate with a specific Indian nation in order to purchase or otherwise obtain some or all of the lands of that Indian nation. Preemption was not an assertion of sovereignty over Indian nations, their societies, and/or their political systems.

In addition, preemption does not mean that the United States can force a sale of lands. In fact, preemption regarding lands only means that if and when an Indian nation decides to sell lands, the Indian nation—by agreeing to preemption—must approach the United States first. The United States has to be the first nation to which the Indians offer to sell their land. The right to preemption on land does not give the United States other jurisdictional powers, for the simple reason that the land retains its status as Indian territory until the Indians agree to sell it, and only then do those lands pass into the jurisdiction of the United States. Preemption affected Haudneosaunee sovereignty only in the sense that it "pre-empts" another non-Indian power such as British Canada from entering into land negotiations with the Haudenosaunee. Preemption is a mutual agreement regarding a single, specific *future* action. The Indian nation has a legal, contractual obligation to sell to only one other nation, such as the United States.

The right of preemption also depends on its recognition by other European or Euro-American powers. British Canada, for example, maintained that it had preemption rights in Canada even as the United States claimed preemption rights south of the Great Lakes. By respecting each other's rights of preemption, both Euro-American nations avoided conflict. This reciprocal recognition between the United States and British Canada of its own particular rights of preemption is dealt with in the last sentence of the treaty: "the United States do not interfere with nations, tribes or families, of Indians elsewhere resident" (Kappler 1904/1972, 36). This was an assertion both the United States and the Haudenosaunee recognized in the treaty. The immediate reason for the inclusion of the right of preemption was to restrict annuities only to those members of the Six Nations who resided south of the Great Lakes, thereby excluding those of the Six Nations who lived in Canada. The fact that the treaty ends with the overall statement of preemption, however, indicates that the United States was clearly declaring that in matters of land it would not deal with any Haudenosaunee who lived in Canada. By extension, the treaty implies that no state within the United States has the right to deal with any Haudenosaunee living in Canada with regard to land. The full text of the last paragraph of the Treaty of Canandaigua thus reads:

> NOTE. It is clearly understood by the parties to this treaty, that the annuity stipulated in the sixth article, is to be applied to the benefit of such of the Six Nations and of their Indian friends united with them as aforesaid, as do or shall reside within the boundaries of the United States: For the United States do not interfere with nations, tribes, or families, of Indians elsewhere resident. (Kappler 1904/1972, 36)

Preemption meant Haudenosaunee lands are not on an "open market." If Great Britain in Canada had had an equal right or access to the purchase of Haudenosaunee lands, for example, the United States feared that Britain could buy up lands on the western frontier of the United States and prevent the United States from expanding.

If the United States had sovereignty over the Haudenosaunee, or if it had plenary rights under the 1787 United States Constitution, it would have been totally unnecessary to state the right of preemption. Thus the larger context of Article III follows:

> The United States will never . . . disturb the Seneca nation, nor any of the Six Nations, or of their Indian friends residing thereon and united with them, in the free use and enjoyment thereof: but it [that is, the lands] shall remain theirs, until they choose to sell the same to the people of the United States, who have the right of purchase. (Kappler 1904/1972, 35)

Preemption as it was understood at the time of the Treaty of Canandaigua is reviewed in an 1815 Senate speech by Rufus King during the Senate's discussion of the Treaty of Ghent, the peace that would end the War of 1812 with Great Britain. King stated that the right of preemption, and not sovereignty, was the claim the United States could make against Indian nations. King noted that the United States:

> hold that Discovery gives them the exclusive right [preemption] to extinguish the Indian title of occupancy by purchase or conquest, possessing such a degree of Sovereignty, as the rights of the natives will allow them to exercise, the U.S. have an absolute right to the soil, subject to the Indian right of occupancy, and also the absolute right to extinguish that right. This division includes a complete title to the soil either in the U.S. or the Indians. The sovereignty of the U.S. is therefore limited not absolute. (King 1894–1900, V:553)

This last sentence deserves emphasis:

> The sovereignty of the U.S. is therefore limited not absolute.

In 1831, a decade and a half after the Treaty of Ghent, statesman Henry Clay (one of the U.S. negotiators at the Treaty of Ghent) described what he believed was absolutely certain with regard to Indian rights under the Treaty of Ghent. He noted that Indian nations had the right "Quietly to possess and enjoy its lands, subject to no other limitation than that, when sold, they can only be sold to the United States" (Seager and Hay 1959–1992, VIII:358).

Clearly, the fact that the United States claimed only the right of preemption is a major proof in the non-Indian records that

Haudenosaunee oral tradition is correct: the Haudenosaunee are a free and independent nation.

The issue of sovereignty is indeed complicated with semantic arguments. If that is the case, how would the Haudenosaunee have perceived treaty provisions when they were translated into their own languages? How did the Haudenosaunee perceive phrases such as "the lands reserved to," "to be their property," and "the United States will never claim the same [lands], nor disturb them [the Six Nations]?" Such questions cannot be answered with total certainty, but there is a provocative clue. One of the signers of the Treaty of Canandaigua was Handsome Lake. Beginning in 1799, Handsome Lake was inspired by messages provided to him by spiritual messengers from the Creator. Until his death in 1815, Handsome Lake shared these messages with the Haudenosaunee through teachings known as the "Gaiwiio." One of these teachings reviewed a vision Handsome Lake had had of George Washington in the afterlife, living in a special place provided by the Creator because Washington had been responsible for the United States' acceptance of the terms of the Treaty of Canandaigua, terms which included Haudenosaunee freedom and independence. The teachings of Handsome Lake assisted the Haudenosaunee as they created a spiritually-motivated and spiritually-guided renaissance and reformation, and these teachings—based on spiritual messages and therefore of unquestioned credibility—clearly indicate that the Haudenosaunee perceived themselves, in the years immediately following the Treaty of Canandaigua, as a free and independent people (Venables 1980, 108–9).

If United States citizens, and their elected officials, ever begin to appreciate the position of sovereignty taken by the Haudenosaunee in the Treaty of Canandaigua, it may depend upon first casting aside a powerful stereotype imbedded in the American culture: the stereotypical Western Indian, especially the Plains Indian, as the Indian "standard," the Indian "Everyman." Native American cultures are all different, and each First Nation's internal political system is different. Just as important, however, not all treaties are the same. That is, the terms of treaties vary from decade to decade, and vary according to which First Nation the United States is negotiating with. Generally, as United States history progressed through the decades of the nineteenth century, the more power the United States amassed, and the more the United States was able to impose its own agenda. In this context, the Treaty of Canandaigua is clearly a treaty between sovereigns. For example, an important phrase in the Treaty of Canandaigua is the recognition by the United States in Articles Three and Four that the United States will never "disturb . . . any of the Six Nations, or their Indian friends residing thereon and united with them, in the free use and enjoyment" of Haudenosaunee lands. This is a recognition of the sovereign right of the Haudenosaunee to determine who could live within their borders. After all, a long-established tradition among the Haudenosaunee was the adoption of other Indians into their midst. This U.S. recognition in 1794 is in stark contrast to the provisions the United States imposed upon the Crow Nation, a western Indian *ally* of the United States, in 1868:

> set apart for the absolute and undisturbed use and occupa-
> tion of the Indians herein named, and for such other
> friendly tribes or individual Indians as from time to time
> they may be willing, with the consent of the United States,
> to admit amongst them. (Kappler 1904/1972, 1008)

It is significant that the United States imposed this provision requiring "the consent of the United States" on one of its Indian allies, because similar restrictive provisions which required the consent of the United States were imposed upon First Nations which had resisted United States expansion such as the Lakotas and Navajos in treaties that same year, 1868 (Kappler 1972, 998, 1016, 1021). Yet three quarters of a century earlier, at Canandaigua, no such restrictions applied. In fact, the Haudenosaunee are recognized by the United States as having the complete freedom to determine who lived within their territories.

To indicate further that there is no such legal entity as a generic Indian treaty, and to emphasize that the Treaty of Canandaigua has terms that are different from other treaties, it can be noted that the various 1868 treaties with the Crows, the Lakotas, the Navajos, and other First Nations also imposed a provision that the United States could unilaterally alter the internal property rights of these Indians, forcing them from communal land base onto individually-owned plots of land (Kappler 1904/1972, 1009, 1013, 1017). No such provision exists in the Treaty of Canandaigua. In fact, in Articles Three and Four, the Treaty of Canandaigua specifically notes that the United States will *not* disturb the Haudenosaunee in "the free use and enjoyment" of their lands.

In this context, another term used in the Treaty of Canandaigua in both Article II and Article III is especially significant: the United States

Haudenosaunee (Iroquois) symbols: The Great Tree of Peace, eagle, buried weapons, and five nations wampum belt. (*John Kahionhes Fadden*)

recognizes Haudenosaunee lands "to be their property." At the time, in 1794, these lands were controlled communally, and both Articles II and III define a recognition by the United States that the Haudenosaunee have the sovereign right to continue their communal use of land.

One of the most significant aspects of the Treaty of Canandaigua is the recognition by the United States that the Haudenosaunee are indeed a Confederacy of Six Nations. This acknowledgment by the United States of Confederacy sovereignty, rather than a recognition of separate sovereignties for *each* of the Six Nations, is vital to an understanding of the renaissance of the Confederacy following the devastation of the Sullivan campaign during the American Revolution.

An issue raised in the records of the negotiations that led to the Treaty of Canandaigua is the Haudenosaunee right to hunt in *all* of their territories, including those now within United States jurisdiction. William Savery, a Quaker observer at the 1794 Treaty of Canandaigua, noted how these rights had been acknowledged both in the 1794 treaty negotiations and in previous treaties:

> The commissioner [United States negotiator Colonel Timo-
> thy Pickering] observed . . . that the Indians shall have the
> right of hunting on . . . those [lands] ceded at the treaty of
> Fort Stanwix [in 1784]; and on all other lands ceded by
> them since the peace [of 1783]. (Savery 1873, 124)

The right of the Haudenosaunee to travel and hunt even across
ceded lands seems to have been assumed. Although Colonel Pickering
voluntarily reiterated this right when he orally reviewed the treaty in
the presence of the Haudenosaunee, the final text of the Treaty of
Canandaigua does not include this provision. Of course, the omission
from the final text may have been intentional on the part of the
United States negotiators. On the other hand, the treaty reiterated the
New York State treaties, and these include Haudenosaunee hunting
and fishing rights. The fact remains, however, that none of the participants representing the Confederacy could read English well enough
to critique its legal contents, and one of the negotiators, "Farmer's
Brother," noted his unease at the end of the negotiations: "as we cannot read, we are liable to be deceived" (Savery 1873, 151).

The importance to the Haudenosaunee of their hunting rights
cannot be overemphasized, given the spiritual and political worldview of the Haudenosaunee.

## THE HAUDENOSAUNEE CONCEPT OF SOVEREIGNTY AND THE TREATY OF CANANDAIGUA

Haudenosaunee sovereignty was defined succinctly just before
the outbreak of the American Revolution. General Thomas Gage, the
commander in chief of all British forces in North America, was also
in charge of Indian affairs. On October 7, 1772, Gage wrote to Indian
superintendent Sir William Johnson:

> As for the Six Nations having acknowledged themselves
> Subjects of the English, that I conclude must be a very gross
> Mistake and am well satisfied were they [the Hau-
> denosaunee] told so, they would not be well pleased. I know
> I would not venture to treat them as Subjects, unless there
> was a Resolution to make War upon them, which is not very
> likely to happen, but I believe they would on such an
> attempt, very soon resolve to cut our Throats. (Sullivan et al.
> 1921–1965, XII:995)

General Gage's clear separation of the non-Indian colonists on the one hand and the sovereign Haudenosaunee on the other is the "world" that the United States inherited in 1783 at the end of the American Revolution in the Treaty of Paris.

## PARADOX OR FRAUD? NEW YORK STATE CLAIMS AND HAUDENOSAUNEE LANDS

One of the issues raised by the Treaty of Canandaigua that remains significant today is the treaty's federal validation of New York State treaties. This issue in turn raises several questions. Was New York State simply acting illegally, or did New York State have at least some jurisdictional rights to Haudensaunee lands based on their colonial precedents? Was the United States federal government acting in good faith when it clearly reasserted its federal rights over the State of New York while at the same time conceding that it could do nothing about the treaties the State of New York had already made with the Haudensaunee? What, exactly, were the rights of the United States federal government when it negotiated with the Haudenosaunee at the Treaty of Canandaigua compared to the "claims" of the State of New York? Did the federal government have more rights than it was willing to assert? If there was confusion between what the federal government claimed and what the State of New York claimed, are *any* of these treaties—state or federal—valid? Future courts will no doubt have to deal with these questions, but a review of the facts indicates why any interpretation of the Treaty of Canandaigua must depend in turn on a clear understanding of New York's colonial past, especially the 1768 Treaty of Fort Stanwix made between the Haudenosaunee and Great Britain. Placing the Treaty of Canandaigua within the context of the Treaty of Fort Stanwix of 1768 is vital, for this treaty marked the boundary of colonial New York and hence what land was considered within the colony of New York when it was transferred to the United States at the end of the American Revolution in the 1783 Treaty of Paris.

The legal facts are clear: at the beginning of the American Revolution, in 1775, New York's western border was a line that began at present-day Rome, New York, and moved southward to the present border of Pennsylvania. The northern border had not yet been determined, but the Adirondack Mountains were entirely within Haudenosaunee boundaries. These facts demonstrate that the treaties made by the State of New York, affirmed in the Treaty of

Canandaigua, were illegal assertions of boundaries that bore no relationship to New York's colonial precedents. Originally, after the English seized the Dutch colony of New Netherlands in 1664, the colonial grant to the Duke of York that defined the Duke's "New York" colony had a western boundary that left two-thirds of the Mohawk River in the sole possession of the Haudenosaunee (O'Callaghan and Fernow 1856–1883, II:296; Adams and Jackson 1984, 46).

Thereafter, New York colonists expanded their claims westward into all of the Mohawk Valley by dubious purchases, angering the Haudenosaunee and frustrating colonial officials. To settle the issue, in 1768 the western boundary of New York was established at the first Treaty of Fort Stanwix, negotiated by the Haudenosaunee and Sir William Johnson, Britain's superintendent of Indian affairs for the northern colonies. The line was clearly intended to define New York's western boundary. Initially, officials in London did not realize the importance of this (lobbyists for the colony of New York assisted in this convenient misperception). Thus London originally proposed an open frontier west of the Mohawk River. To correct this mistake, General Sir Thomas Gage, Sir William's superior, wrote to the Earl of Hillsborough on August 17, 1768:

> The Congress with the Six Nations, and Indians of Ohio, for the Settlement of the general Boundary, is expected to be held sometime next Month: Sir William Johnson . . . observes likewise, that the Boundary Line, as marked in the Map, transmitted by your Lordship, beginning at Owegy [Owego, near the southern border of New York] on the East-Branch of Susquehanna, does not include any Boundary, between the Province of New-York and the Indian's lands; and unless the Line is continued Northerly from Owegy [which it was in the final treaty], so as to form Limits between the Six Nations, and Province of New-York, the Indians will not be Secure, and the Affair of the Boundary defeated, in its principal Object. (Carter 1931 and 1933, I:185)

In the 1768 Treaty of Fort Stanwix, the line was drawn from Owego northward to Fort Stanwix. The title of the record of the Treaty of Fort Stanwix reported to London makes the treaty's intent clear: "Proceedings at a Treaty . . . for the settlement of a Boundary Line between the Colonies and the Indians, pursuant to His Majesty's orders" (O'Callaghan and Fernow 1856–1883, VIII:111).

The Haudenosaunee made their signing of the Treaty of Fort Stanwix conditional upon British acceptance of a very strong statement by the Haudenosaunee. Sir William Johnson reported their position as the following:

> We do now agree to the Line we have marked upon your Map, now before you on certain conditions on which we have spoken and shall say more and we desire that one Article of this our agreement be, that none of the Provinces [such as New York, Massachusetts, New Jersey, Virginia, and Pennsylvania, all of whom had "claims" on the Haudenosaunee lands] or their People shall attempt to invade it under color of any old Deeds, or other pretences [such as charters] what soever [sic] for in many of these things we have been imposed on, and therefore we disclaim them all. (O'Callaghan and Fernow 1856–1883, VIII:127)

Following the successful negotiation of the Treaty of Fort Stanwix, an official map was drawn which clearly notes that the western boundary of the colony of New York was the line drawn during the negotiations. The map is entitled "Map of the Frontiers of the Northern Colonies with the Boundary Line established Between them [i.e., the Northern colonies] and the Indians at the Treaty held by S Will Johnson at Ft. Stanwix in Novr. 1768" (O'Callaghan and Fernow 1856–1883, VIII: following 136).

The official British understanding of the boundaries between the Haudenosaunee and the colony of New York are clearly indicated in a map showing that the Haudenosaunee also had complete control of the Adirondack Mountains east of Lake George. These lands, lying to the north *and east* of Fort Stanwix, are described in a 1771 map drawn by Guy Johnson, Sir William Johnson's assistant superintendent (United States 1995, following 24). This map defines the line drawn at the 1768 Treaty of Fort Stanwix as "the Boundary Settled with the Indians." The lands north of Fort Stanwix and directly above Oneida Lake, is defined on the 1771 map as follows: "This Country belongs to the Oneidas." The lands north of the northern reaches of the Canada River, in the southern Adirondacks, is defined as "The Boundary of New York not being Closed this part of the Country still belongs to the Mohocks."

Furthermore, the 1771 map specifically defines two examples of where Haudenosaunee lands are in fact with the limits of New York.

The map text states that no label for the Mohawk Nation appears on the map, whereas the other four founding nations are clearly labeled in their territories: "The Mohocks are not mentioned as they reside within the limits of New York at Fort Hunter and Canajohare [;] part of the Oneida Country lies also within that Province" (United States 1995, following 24).

Guy Johnson clearly wrote in the space occupied by the Adirondack Mountains, immediately to the east of Lake George, "The Boundary of New York not being Closed [determined], this part of the Country still belongs to the Mohawks," and in the western Adirondacks above Oneida Lake Guy Johnson wrote: "This Country belongs to the Oneidas" (United States 1995, following page 24). There is no doubt that New York was separate from the Six Nations, for Guy Johnson titled his map of the Six Nations noting "the Adjacent Colony" in his map title: "Map of the Country of the VI. Nations Proper, with Part of the Adjacent Colony" (United States 1995, following page 24). There were pragmatic reasons the British wished to separate the colonies from the Indian nations and define the Indian national lands as Indian property. Describing these reasons, General Sir Thomas Gage wrote to the Earl of Hillsborough on November 10, 1770:

> I know of nothing so liable to bring in a Serious Quarrell with Indians, as an Invasion of their Property. Let the Savages enjoy their Desarts in quiet, little Bickerings that will unavoidably sometimes happen, may soon be accomodated [sic]. And I am of opinion, independent of the Motives of common Justice and Humanity, that the Principles of Interest and Policy should induce us rather to protect than molest them. Were they drove from their Forrests, the Peltry Trade would decrease, and not impossible that worse Savages would take Refuge in them; for they might then become the Azylum of fugitive Negroes, and idle Vagabonds escaped from Justice, who in time might become formidable, and subsist by Rapine, and plundering the lower Countrys. (Carter 1931 and 1933, I:278)

Given this evidence, did the United States, by conceding the claims of New York State treaties in the Treaty of Canandaigua, fail to assert all its rights and, more importantly, mislead the Haudenosaunee? At the Treaty of Canandaigua, Pickering conceded that at the Treaty of Paris in 1783, the only lands transferred as the property of the United

States were those already obtained from the Indians prior to the American Revolution: "What the British had obtained of the Indians . . . before the peace [in the Haudenosaunee case, this meant only the lands east of the 1768 Treaty of Fort Stanwix line], was transferred by that treaty to the United States (Savery 1873, 146).

The Seneca war leader Cornplanter and many other Haudenosaunee were convinced that the Treaty of Canandaigua was just another fraud perpetrated by the United States (Savery 1873, 144). If the Haudenosaunee were the victims of fraud, are any of the land cessions defined at the Treaty of Canandaigua legal? Perhaps during the twenty-first century there will be some interesting court cases dealing with this issue.

## PREEMPTION AND THE TREATY OF CANANDAIGUA

Another major issue at the Treaty of Canandaigua was the right of "preemption," allowing a non-Indian government to exclude all other non-Indian governments from claiming or purchasing specific Indian lands. Timothy Pickering clarified this at Canandaigua. With regard to the lands not yet "obtained of the Indians," he said that the British and the United States had only agreed to a transfer of preemptive rights. A line was drawn between British Canada and the United States, and it was "agreed that the British not interfere with the land on this side of that line, nor were we to interfere with the land on their side of the line" (Savery 1873, 146). Pickering's words are a classic definition of preemption.

Pickering was speaking under the authority of the U.S. government because the issue already had been clarified within the U.S. government in 1789. Secretary of War Henry Knox reviewed the circumstances and then clarified the issue in his letter to President George Washington on June 15, 1789:

> The time has arrived, when it is highly expedient that a liberal system of justice should be adopted for the various Indian tribes within the limits of the United States.
>
> By having recourse to the several Indian treaties, made by the authority of Congress since the conclusion of the war with Great Britain, excepting those made January 1789, at Fort Harmar, it would appear, that Congress were [sic] of opinion, that the Treaty of Peace, of 1783, absolutely invested them [sic, meaning Congress, not individual states]

with the fee [fee simple] of all the Indian lands within the limits of the United States; that they had the right to assign, or retain such portions as they should judge proper.

But it is manifest, from the representations of the confederated Indians at the Huron village, in December, 1786, that they entertained a different opinion, and that they were the only rightful proprietors of the soil; and it appears by the resolve of the 2d of July, 1788, that Congress so far conformed to the idea, as to appropriate a sum of money solely for the purpose of extinguishing the Indian claims to lands they had ceded to the United States, and for obtaining regular conveyances of the same. This object was accordingly accomplished at the treaty of Fort Harmar, in January, 1789.

The principle of the Indian right to the lands they possess being thus conceded, the dignity and interest of the Nation will be advanced by making it the basis of the future administration of justice towards the Indian tribes. (Lowrie and Clarke 1832, 13)

## TREATY OF CANANDAIGUA NOT RATIFIED BY THE U.S. SENATE

One of the curious aspects of the Treaty of Canandaigua is the fact that it was not ratified by the U.S. Senate. This was because the British colonial precedent was followed by the United States whereby a treaty was regarded as effective immediately upon its signing. This was clarified in an exchange between President George Washington and the U.S. Senate in 1789:

> *Gentlemen of the Senate:*
> It doubtless is important that all treaties and compacts, formed by the United States with other nations, whether civilized or not, should be made with caution, and executed with fidelity.
>
> It is said to be the general understanding and practice of nations, as a check on the mistakes and indiscretions of ministers or commissioners, not to consider any treaty, negotiated and signed by such officers, as final and conclusive, until ratified by the Sovereign or Government from whom they derive their powers. This practice has been adopted by the United States, respecting their treaties with European nations, and I am inclined to think it would be

advisable to observe it in the conduct of our treaties with the Indians: for though such treaties, being on their part made by their chiefs or rulers, need not be ratified by them [conveniently for whites eager to defraud whole nations with the signatures of a few], yet, being formed on our part, by the agency of subordinate officers, it seems to be both prudent and reasonable, that their acts should not be binding on the nation [i.e., the United States], until approved and ratified by the Government.

It strikes me that this point should be well considered and settled, so that our national proceedings in this respect may become uniform, and be directed by fixed and stable principles.

The treaties with certain Indian nations, which were laid before you with my message of the 25th May last, suggested two questions to my mind, viz: 1st. Whether those treaties were to be considered as perfected, and consequently as obligatory, without being ratified; if not, then 2dly. Whether both, or either, and which of them ought to be ratified; on these questions, I request your opinion and advice.

You have indeed advised me *"to execute and enjoin an observance of,"* the treaty with the Wyandots, &c. You, gentlemen, doubtless, intended to be clear and explicit, and yet, without further explanation, I fear I may misunderstand your meaning; for if, by my *executing* that treaty, you mean that I should make it (in a more particular and immediate manner than it now is) the act of Government, then it follows, that I am to ratify it. If you mean by *executing it,* that I am to see that it be carried into effect and operation, then I am led to conclude, either that you consider it as being perfect and obligatory in its present state, and, therefore, to be executed and observed; or, that you consider it as to derive its completion and obligation from the silent approbation and ratification which my proclamation may be construed to imply. Although I am inclined to think that the latter is your intention, yet it certainly is best that all doubts respecting it be removed.

Permit me to observe, that it will be proper for me to be informed of your sentiments relative to the treaty with the Six Nations, previous to the departure of the Governor of the Western territory; and, therefore, I recommend it to your early consideration. (Lowrie and Clarke 1832, 58)

Senator Charles Carroll of Maryland replied on behalf of the Senate to George Washington on September 18, 1789:

> The signature of treaties with the Indian nations has ever been considered as a full completion thereof; and that such treaties have never been solemnly ratified by either of the contracting parties, as hath been commonly practised among the civilized nations of Europe: wherefore, the committee are of opinion, that the formal ratification of the treaty concluded at fort Harmar, on the 9th day of January, 1789, between Arthur St. Clair, Governor of the Western territory, on the part of the United States, and the sachems and warriors of the Wyandot, Delaware, Ottawa, Chippewam Pattiwatima, and Sac Nations, is not expedient or necessary; and that the resolve of the Senate, of the 8th September 1789, respecting the said treaty, authorizes the President to enjoin a due observance thereof.
>
> That, as to the treaty made at Fort Harmar, on the 9th of January, 1789, between the said Arthur St. Clair, and the sachems and warriors of the Six Nations, (except the Mohawks) from particular circumstances affecting a part of the ceded lands [meaning perhaps the 1784 Treaty of Fort Stanwix] the Senate does not want to admit its legality OR illegality and so says nothing, the Senate did not judge it expedient to pass any act concerning the same. (Lowrie and Clarke 1832, 59)

## A NEW YORK STATE DEFENSE?

The State of New York claims that its state constitution existed in 1777, prior to both the Articles of Confederation (1781) and the United States Constitution (1789). Therefore, the state claims that issues related to the Haudenosaunee are its responsibility. In matter of historical fact, however, the 1783 Treaty of Paris, which ended the war, was negotiated between Great Britain and the United States as a single nation, albeit one that was a confederacy of states. Great Britain did not make thirteen separate treaties with each of the thirteen states. It also was the responsibility of the Congress of the United States to ratify the Treaty of Paris. Furthermore, no state boundaries were defined in the 1783 Treaty of Paris; only national boundaries were defined. Of equal importance, the treaty refers only to the transfer of claims to lands and boundaries, not to a transfer of direct jurisdiction over Indian nations. Thus, Article I of the Treaty of Paris states clearly that Great Britain "relinquishes all claims to the Government, proprietary and territorial rights of the same [that is, the United States], and every part thereof [that is, every part or state within the United States]" (Commager 1973, 117–18).

The fact that the Treaty of Paris includes only two parties also is clearly evidenced in Article II ("the said United States" with no mention of individual states); Article III ("the people of the United States"); Article IV ("either side" implying only two parties); Article V (regarding the treaty's terms regarding property confiscated from Loyalists, "the Congress" has the initiative to deal in turn with the states); Article VI ("America"). Article I does not transfer jurisdiction, only "claims." This transfer of claims is essentially a transfer from Great Britain to the United States of the right of "preemption." Preemption is not the same as jurisdiction. Preemption was a concept defined by the European powers when they colonized North America to clarify which European nation would have the right to negotiate over specific areas with the Indian nations whose political systems preceded European contact. (That every Indian nation was absent from the Paris negotiations was a travesty, but in retrospect is also a further indication that what was transferred was preemption, not jurisdiction.)

If the United States actually had sovereignty over the Haudenosauee, no treaties would have been necessary after the 1783 Treaty of Paris. The Haudenosaunee treaties that followed the American Revolution refer to cessions of land, but not to the cessation of Haudenosaunee government or society and the absorption within the United States of Haudenoaunee people. No Haudenosaunee governments were dissolved. The 1794 Treaty of Canandaigua defines a clear separation of the United States on the one hand and the Haudenosaunee on the other.

## THE TERMS OF THE TREATY OF CANANDAIGUA REAFFIRMED IN THE 1815 TREATY OF GHENT

The terms of the Treaty of Canandaigua were not regarded as temporary and were among those Indian rights recognized by both Great Britain and the United States in the Treaty of Ghent (1815), which ended the War of 1812. In Article IX, both nations guaranteed to Indian nations "all the Possessions, Rights, and Privileges, which they may have enjoyed, or been entitled to in 1811" (Israel 1967, II:357).

Under the Treaty of Ghent, the United States gained no new rights with regard to the Haudenosaunee or other Indian nations. Under the treaty's call for a return to the antebellum Indian rights, the United States still possessed only the right of preemption, which it had already possessed prior to the War of 1812. This right of preemption, however, was never to be imposed unilaterally. The right of preemption had to be exercised through the mutual agreement by treaty between the U.S. government on the one hand and each Indian nation on the other. Even the notorious 1830 Indian Removal Act stated that Indians could not be removed from their lands if they did not make a treaty with the United States agreeing to exchange their lands east of the Mississippi for lands west of the Mississippi (Washburn 1979, III:2169).

Attempting to define the status of the Indian nations within the Constitution (which defines Indians who still live within their nations as "not taxed"), the Supreme Court under the leadership of John Marshall invented the term "domestic dependent nation" in the 1831 case *Cherokee Nation v. Georgia* (Washburn 1979, IV:2556). During the next year, 1832, the Marshall court outlined these nations' rights in *Worcester v. Georgia* that a weaker power does not surrender its independence—its right to self-government—by associating with a stronger power and taking its protection. A weak state, in order to provide for its safety, may place itself under the protection of one more powerful, without stripping itself of its right of self-government, and ceasing to be a state. Examples of this kind are not wanting in Europe. "Tributary and feudatory states," says Vattel [prominent Swiss legal authority Emmerich de Vattel (1714–1767)] "do not thereby cease to be sovereign and independent states, so long as self government and sovereign and independent authority are left in the administration of the state" (Washburn 1979, IV:2622).

After the American Revolution, one of the most important opinions with regard to American Indian sovereignty and United States Indian policies was voiced by Rufus King, a United States Senator representing New York State. He defined his learned opinions in 1815 during the Senate's consideration of the Treaty of Ghent. King had been born and raised in Massachusetts. During the American Revolution, King had been in combat as an officer in the Patriot army. King was a Harvard-educated lawyer who, in the decades following the Revolution, was continually in a position to understand the legal reality of United States Indian policy and its ramifications. In 1786, Rufus King had been one of the Massachusetts negotiators who settled the conflicting land claims of Massachusetts and New York to Haudenosaunee lands.

In 1787, at the age of 32, King represented Massachusetts at the Philadelphia Convention, where he was regarded as one of the convention's most outstanding orators. (King's notes in the Philadelphia Convention describing the formation of the new U.S. Constitution today are a widely respected scholarly resource.) King moved to New York and was elected by the legislature as one of the first two U.S. Senators representing New York (his Senate colleague was another figure long familiar with Haudenosaunee issues, Philip Schuyler). King served in the Senate during all the negotiations with the Haudenosaunee that led to the Treaty of Canandaigua in 1794. Then, beginning in 1796, he served as the United States ambassador to Great Britain under Presidents George Washington, John Adams, and Thomas Jefferson (Ernst 1968, passim).

In his 1815 Senate speech, King reviewed Indian policy within the context of the Senate's debate over the Treaty of Ghent. King, a conservative Federalist, surveyed the history of United States-American Indian relations. (The internal structure and the ideas within John Marshall's 1832 Supreme Court decision *Worcester v. Georgia* indicate that Marshall may have used a copy of King's speech when he researched and wrote his decision. In any case, Marshall agreed with much of what Rufus King had already outlined in 1815.)

As noted earlier, King concluded that the sovereignty of the United States, with reference to Native nations, is limited, not absolute (King 1894–1900, V:553). In a recital of European diplomatic relations with the Indians, King declared that Europeans, including Great Britain and the United States, did not have absolute sovereignty over Indian people because of the existence of "the rights of the primitive Inhabitants" which "were not overlooked, tho' they were somewhat impaired." King even maintained that the United States only had "such a degree of Sovereignty, as the rights of the natives will allow them [the United States] to exercise." As a Senator and lawyer, he maintained that various European nations' claims to land on the basis of "discovery" were intended to exclude other European nations and were not claims "against the native inhabitants" (King 1894–1900, V:552–53).

Rufus King had served in Great Britain as the U.S. ambassador under Washington, Adams, and Jefferson, so he was entirely familiar with Britain's viewpoint. In his Senate speech, King told his colleagues that in 1713 Britain had asserted the exclusive right of purchase, but no dominion over the Haudenosaunee people or Haudenosaunee government. In this speech, he also defined the historic—and limited— meaning of *dominion* as it applied to relations with Indians. In this context, he concluded that in the United States there is "a complete title to the soil either in the U.S. or the Indians. The sovereignty of the U.S. is therefore limited not absolute" (King 1894–1900, V:553).

As a dedicated Federalist, Rufus King was a pragmatic fiscal conservative who took an interest in human rights issues because he believed that ethics were logical and that violations of the human rights of Indians and blacks would weaken the social and political fabric of the United States. This point is significant, because King's conclusions regarding the United States' relationships with Indian nations were based on a strong pragmatic and political basis. King had no patience for ideological extremes of any shade, and followed the Enlightenment's guide of reason (Ernst 1968, 53–54, 86, 93, 100–101, 217, 222, 291, 308, 361, 369–81, 405–12).

Thus Rufus King's statements on the political status of Native Americans are not those of a romantic, but of a calm, objective observer who most often either sat in the Senate or was representing his country's policies to Great Britain. One point the British had raised was that "the Indians must in some sort be considered as an independent people" (King 1894–1900, V: 549). King's response was that the Indians' status was unique because the Indians about which the British were concerned all lived within the internationally recognized boundaries of the United States. Determined to blunt British interference in U.S.-Indian relations, King reviewed the history of Indian-white relations. His major theme was that the Indians were independent nations in laws, government, and custom who, nevertheless, had signed treaties that gave one European power or another, and then the United States, the exclusive right to purchase the title of the Indians' lands. Granting specific European or European-American nations the exclusive right of purchase was a limitation on Indian sovereignty, but this was the only limit that King regarded as significant.

King declared that the European right of "Discovery gave no dominion over the Indians, except in cases of conquest" and that titles to American soil were defined among various European countries to minimize conflict among the Europeans: the right of discovery, therefore, was intended and exerted by the various European governments "not against the native inhabitants, but against each other" (King 1894–1900, V:552).

Interestingly, this description is virtually the same as that given by Lord Dorchester, Governor of Canada, in 1791 to the Six Nations and other Great Lakes Indians. This similarity indicates that this concept was widely understood. At Quebec, on August 15, 1791, Dorchester strongly affirmed that

> The Kings rights with respect to your territory were against the Nations of Europe . . . the King never had any rights against you but to such parts of the Country as had been fairly ceded by yourselves with your own free consent by Public convention and sale. (Dorchester 1791)

At a time when the United States was busy settling all the lands to the Mississippi and also had purchased from France in the Louisiana Purchase lands west of the Mississippi as well, Rufus King stated that [italics in the original]:

> Indians [east of the Mississippi] *are not citizens of the U.S., but perpetual inhabitants living in Tribes independent of each other,* and possessing by occupancy title to the soil where they inhabit. Those natives west of the Mississippi [who were not yet within the boundaries of any new state, as the Louisiana Purchase was still in territorial status] are now, as they probably were at the discovery by Columbus, independent Tribes. (King 1894–1900, V:552)

In his 1815 Senate speech, Rufus King stated that the Indians were [italics in original:]*the rightful occupants of the soil, with a just claim to retain and use the same,* according to their own discretion (King 1894–1900, V:552–53, emphasis added).

Thus the Indians could retain and use their lands at their own discretion and not at the discretion of the whites. Even though Indians were "independent nations," the Indians' "right to the soil, as independent nations, was diminished by the denial to the natives the power to dispose of the soil at will to whomsoever they pleased" (King 1894–1900, V:553).

That Senator King did not lightly regard the interdependency of the United States and Indian nations is illustrated by his opinion regarding a crucial subtlety in treaty negotiations which is applicable to an examination of British policy as well. The question was When Indian lands were set aside as "reservations," did the Indians reserve this part of their original homelands unto themselves, or did the United States claim all of their lands and *return to the Indians*—reserve for the Indians—the reservation lands?

King maintained that the Indians reserved the lands to themselves. Otherwise, if the Indians received *back* their reservations from the United States, any total transfer ended the United States' government's preemptive right of purchase—a principle which is a cornerstone of the 1815 Senate speech quoted previously. King explained his firm view on this in a letter from Washington, DC, February 12, 1818, to his son, Edward King. Rufus King, then serving in the Senate, wrote the letter to explain why the Senate had rejected a treaty drawn up by General McArthur and General Lewis Cass with the Great Lakes Indians, forcing a reconvening of the negotiators and the Indians, and a postponement of the sale of acquired lands to white settlers. King defended Indian rights because they were intertwined with the rights of the national federal government against the governments of the states and more importantly those individual citizens who wished to make purchases of Indian land directly from the Indians:

> The late commissioners [McArthur and Cass] departed from all former examples. They required the Indians to cede their whole territory to the U.S., and then by an article for that purpose, the U.S. are made to *retrocede* or grant in fee simple a portion of these lands to the Indians; the effect of such measure is to deprive the U.S. of their pre-emptive Right to obtain a future grant of these lands, so conveyed to the Indians. Other parts of the Treaty, which confirmed to the individuals of the Indian Tribes such grants in severalty as the chiefs of the Tribes might make to them, with authority or power to such individual Indians to sell their shares, or several grants to any person, Indian or white man, is reprehensible; is inserting our Laws relative to property so as to affect the Indians and their regulations. Our policy has been to leave the Indians to manage these lands as they pleased; to assign portions of it to portions, or individuals, of their Tribes, and not to meddle with these dispositions and regulations. Under the proposed Treaty, Ohio would have been embarrassed with ejectments, trespasses, covenants, and all sorts of real Contracts, between Indians & whites, and confusion, as well as fraud, would have been the consequence,

had the Senate confirmed the Treaty. It is as true in managing Indian affairs, as in attending to those of the Church, that we shd. be careful "stare (supra) vias antiquas" [consider above all the old ways]. (King 1894–1900, VI:114–16)

King then gave another example, noting how some Cherokee mixed bloods, having heard of the McArthur-Cass treaty provisions, had asked to have a recent Cherokee treaty retroactively include similar provisions:

> Before this Treaty had reached the Senate, a Deputation of Cherokee Indians, whose tribe have lately made a cession of Lands to the U.S., having heard of this Treaty, applied to have the Treaty made with their Tribe, reformed and settled on the Plan of Genl. McArthur's and Cass' Treaty.
>
> The halfbreeds among the Tribes would all prefer the new project, as it wd. enable them to make money out of it; and the novelty of the U.S. granting *in fee,* instead of the Indian Tribes reserving their unceded lands, wd. have put an end to the preemptive Rights of the U.S., and not only been the means of preventing their acquiring future and profitable cessions; but would have opened a scene of fraud, speculation and Indian controversy of the most immoral and dangerous character. (King 1894–1900, VI:115–16)

## HAUDENOSAUNEE EXPECTATIONS AT THE TREATY OF CANANDAIGUA

Regarding sovereignty, what did the Haudenosaunee expect as a result of the 1794 Treaty of Canandaigua? Speculation is exactly that, especially from this Anglo-American author. In all probability, because the Haudenosaunee viewed treaties as a part of a diplomatic continuum, the Treaty of Canandaigua would have been an extension of the premise of the "Guswenta" or "Two Row Wampum Belt" (Jemison and Schein 2000, 22–24, 36, 69–70). Symbolically, the primary elements of the Guswenta are two parallel rows made of purple wampum, separated by three rows of white wampum. This belt refers to a diplomatic concept of Haudenosaunee-European/Euro-American relationships that had been ongoing since the seventeenth century.

The Guswenta represents the two separate but parallel rivers (or paths) along which each society, Haudenosaunee and European, have each promised the other to perpetually follow. The Two Row Wampum vividly asserts the Haudenosaunee commitment to independence. At the same time, it also affirms an intention, evident since the seventeenth century, to communicate with, rather than confront, non-Indian governments. These are parallel and thus continually distinct developments. The symbolism of separate rivers or paths is not intended to be adversarial. So long as there are no attempts to force the ways of one people upon the other, neither path becomes blurred and useless, and each path remains viable. The three rows of white beads which intervene between the parallel paths simultaneously represent both the physical space that will forever remain between peoples and the method by which these separate people should communicate: the three rows of white wampum beads symbolize mutual communication based on truth, justice, and spiritual thinking.

The concepts of the Guswenta are, in turn, a part of the Haudenosaunee worldview. The goals of the Guswenta are certainly reflected in Articles II, III, and IV in which the United States promises not to "disturb" the Haudenosaunee and in Article VII that provides for a resolution of conflicts that is to be followed by both the United States and the Haudenosaunee: "the United States and Six Nations agree, that . . . complaint shall be made by the party injured to the other." Another detail of the Guswenta and the Haudenosaunee worldview it represents may also apply to the Treaty of Canandaigua: one end of the wampum belt remains unfinished to symbolize the fact that the belt must be continually renewed by both peoples, a concept promised in Article I ("Peace and friendship are hereby firmly established, and shall be perpetual between the United States and the Six Nations") and, in Article VII, in the procedure for resolving conflicts.

Other suggestions of Haudenosaunee perceptions at the time the Treaty of Canandaigua was negotiated in 1794 include the importance placed on continuation of hunting and fishing guaranteed by U.S. negotiator Timothy Pickering during his discussions with the Haudenosaunee at Canandaigua (also discussed earlier):

> The commissioner observed . . . that the Indians shall have the right of hunting on these lands, as well as on all those ceded at the treaty of Fort Stanwix [1784]; and on all other lands ceded by them since the peace; and their settlements thereon shall remain undisturbed. (Savery 1873, 124)

This concept is paramount, and closely related to the Haudenosaunee concept of The Woods as common to all. During the 1780s and 1790s, even the manipulative officials representing the State of New York had guaranteed that the Haudenosaunee would be able to maintain continuous hunting and fishing rights throughout *all* of what is now New York State. At the Eastern Door of the geopolitical Longhouse, the Mohawks had lived and cooperated with Dutch, English, German, and other European colonists for three-quarters of a century. Occasional disputes aside, this diverse population had used the same Mohawk River and the same streams, and had all hunted in the same forest. To a lesser extent, the Oneidas, Onondagas, Cayugas, Senecas, and Tuscaroras also had lived interdependently with non-Indians, especially through the Covenant Chain of trade. Perhaps the Haudenosaunee also saw that the new United States was simply another layer of political complexity that would be added to the already complex duality of The Woods. Perhaps the Haudenosaunee envisioned a future with the United States and its member states simply as the most recent addition to this Haudenosaunee concept of The

Longhouse interior. (*John Kahionhes Fadden*)

Woods—Woods that had always been simultaneously both the lands of a particular nation within the Confederacy and simultaneously the domain of the entire Confederacy.

There was perhaps an expectation on the part of the Haudenosaunee in 1794 that the Treaty of Canandaigua would reestablish the Covenant Chain of peace and mutually beneficial economic relations. After all, the Covenant Chain had more than a century of history before the American Revolution had disrupted it, and that disruption had lasted less than a decade, from 1775 to 1784. The Confederacy itself had frequently faced disruptive internal challenges and had survived. There was no reason to suspect that the English-speaking people of the United States would, in the long run, be any less or more difficult to live among than the Dutch, English, and other European colonists who had preceded these Americans of 1794.

## CONCLUSION

Today, the Haudenosaunee continue to maintain their rights under the Treaty of Canandaigua. What expectations of the Treaty of Canandaigua can be held by non-Indians? At the start of the twenty-first century, the reality of global politics is that we are all interdependent peoples. The successful maintenance of that interdependence will depend upon all of our abilities, throughout the globe, to work with each other as sovereign peoples. What if the citizens of the United States cannot persuade their government to uphold the principles of the Treaty of Canandaigua? What if the United States fails to take actions which recognize the sovereignty of the Haudenosaunee, our immediate neighbors? The answers to such questions may reveal how successfully the United States is likely to understand other cultures and nations in the global economy of the twenty-first century. The answers may also reveal who will dare to believe our word and trust us.

## REFERENCES

Adams, J. T., and K. T. Jackson, eds. 1984. *Atlas of American history.* 2nd rev. ed. New York: Charles Scribner's Sons.

Beauchamp, W. M. 1907. *Aboriginal place names of New York.* Bulletin 108: Archaeology 12 of the New York State Museum. Albany: New York State Education Department.

Bemis, S. F. 1962. *Jay's treaty: A study in commerce and diplomacy.* Rev. ed. New Haven: Yale University Press.

Carter, C. E., ed. 1931 and 1933. *The correspondence of General Thomas Gage, 1763–1775.* 2 vols. New Haven, CT: Yale University Press.

Commager, H. S., ed. 1973. *Documents of American history.* 9th ed. Englewood Cliffs, NJ: Prentice-Hall.

Deloria, V., Jr., and R. J. DeMaillie. 1999. *Documents of American Indian diplomacy.* 2 vols. Norman: University of Oklahoma Press.

Dorchester, L. 1791. Archives of Ontario. August 15, Speech to the Confederated Indian Nations. F47, A-1, Letterbook 17.

Ernst, R. 1968. *Rufus King: American Federalist.* Chapel Hill: University of North Carolina Press.

Hauptman, L. M. 1999. *Conspiracy of interests: Iroquois dispossession and the rise of New York State.* Syracuse, NY: Syracuse University Press.

Israel, F. I., ed. 1967. *Major Peace Treaties of Modern History, 1648–1967.* 4 vols. N Y: Chelsea House Publications.

Jemison, G. P., and A. M. Schein, eds. 2000. *Treaty of Canandaigua 1794: 200 years of treaty relations between the Iroquois Confederacy and the United States.* Santa Fe, New Mexico: Clear Light Publishers.

Kappler, C. J., ed. 1904/1972. *Indian treaties.* New York: Interland Publishing.

King, C., ed. 1894–1900. *The life and correspondence of Rufus King.* 6 vols. New York: G.P. Putnam's Sons.

Lowrie, W., and M. St. C. Clarke, eds. 1789–1815. *American State Papers. 1832. Class II. Indian Affairs. Documents, Legislative and Executive, of the Congress of the United States, From the First Session of the First to the Third Session of the Thirteenth Congress, Inclusive: Commencing March 3, 1789, and Ending March 3, 1815.* Washington, DC: Gales and Seaton.

New York State. 1889. Special committee to investigate the Indian problem of the State of New York. In *Report of special committee to investigate the Indian problem of the State of New York.* Albany, New York: Troy Press.

O'Callaghan, E. B., and B. Fernow, eds. 1856–1883. *Documents relative to the colonial history of the State of New York.* 15 vols. Albany: Weed, Parsons and Company.

Savery, W. 1873. *A journal of the life, travels, and religious labors of William Savery.* Ed. Jonathan Evans. Philadelphia: Friends' Bookstore.

Seager, R. II, and M. P. Hay, eds. 1959–1992. *The papers of Henry Clay.* 11 vols. Louisville: University of Kentucky Press.

Sullivan, J., A. C. Flick, A. W. Lauber, M. W. Hamilton, and A. B. Corey, eds. 1921–1965. *The papers of Sir William Johnson.* 14 vols. Albany: University of the State of New York.

United States. Eleventh Census. 1892/1995. Donaldson, T., H. B. Carrington, and T. W. Jackson, *The Six Nations of New York: The 1892 United States extra census bulletin.* Ithaca, New York: Cornell University Press.

Venables, R. W. 1980 "Iroquois environments" and "We the people of the United States." *American Indian environments,* ed. Christopher Vecsey and Robert W. Venables. Syracuse, New York: Syracuse University Press, 81–127.

Washburn, W. E., ed. 1973/1979. *The American Indian and the United States: A documentary history.* 4 vols. Westport, CT: Greenwood Press.

*Worcester v. Georgia,* 31 U.S. (6 Pet.) 515 (1832).

# 4

# The Iroquois Land Claims: A Legacy of Fraud, Politics, and Dispossession

*John C. Mohawk*

The age of imperialism and the struggle for European hegemony entered a new era in 1607 with Samuel de Champlain's voyages of exploration and the foundation of the Virginia colony. At the beginning of this period, the Iroquois (who called themselves Haudenosaunee) were united in a formal league consisting of the Mohawk, Oneida, Onondaga, Cayuga, and Seneca Nations. (A sixth nation, the Tuscarora, joined the Confederacy around 1721.) The arrival of Europeans bearing trade goods in exchange for furs intensified long-standing rivalries and competitions among the Indian Nations wherever beaver were found. From earliest contact, the French established a relationship between trade and armed conflict.

One of Champlain's first actions, and one of his most serious mistakes, was to lead a Huron war party against the Mohawk in a battle near present-day Lake Champlain. This action initiated hostilities between the Iroquois Confederacy and France that lasted intermittently until 1701. Competition over furs and warfare ebbed and flowed and reached a high point among Native combatants at mid-century. The Iroquois warriors, armed with some 400 firearms obtained from the Dutch, experienced a series of conquests of Indian Nations allied with France (Mohawk 2001, 102). In 1651, they attacked and overran a Neutral town, capturing most of the people and incorporating them into Seneca towns. In 1654, the Seneca attacked and defeated the Erie, and absorbing most of their population (White 1978, 416).

According to Arthur C. Parker, ". . . Many of the later Seneca frontier settlements west of the Genesee had a large proportion of Erie" (Parker 1926, 48). At that point, the Seneca had effective possession and control over an area extending at minimum from the western shore of the Niagara River to the southeast shore of Lake Erie. Marian E. White notes the presence of an historic Neutral archeological site on Grand Island in the Niagara River (White 1978, 407). The Wenro, who had lived east of the Niagara River, were the first to abandon their aboriginal territory in 1638. Shortly thereafter, Neutral towns appeared east of the Niagara River. In less than a decade (1648 to 1656), the population of the Iroquois League grew from 10,000 to more than 25,000. The Seneca Nation acquired possession of these territories, including lands adjacent to the Niagara River and islands in the river, at that time.

Land claims by Native Americans to areas of western, central and northern New York State have roots in unresolved issues that arose prior to the American Revolution. The seventeenth century had seen devastating wars involving Indian Nations, France, and Holland, but a peace treaty in 1701 brought an end to war throughout most of the northeast woodlands. From 1701, the French and the English recognized the sovereignty of the Six Nations and the ownership by the Seneca Nation of the Niagara country, including the islands in the Niagara River (Hauptman 2000, 127; Findings of Fact 1974, 194).

One of the legacies of warfare was the existence of towns of refugee Indians driven from their original homelands. These included populations of people from nations that had been either wholly or partly dispossessed and included Mingoes, Delawares, Shawnees, Wyandots, and others. Some of these had settled in the Ohio River country. In 1754 the French, in an attempt to build a ring around the English colonies and isolate them from Indians in the Mississippi watershed, established a post—Fort Duquesne—at the confluence of the Allegheny, Monongahela, and Ohio Rivers at present-day Pittsburgh. England reacted by sending an expeditionary force under General Braddock to drive the French from Fort Duquesne and to build roads through the wilderness to facilitate English expansion to western Pennsylvania and beyond.

Whether conquest of France was initially intentional, the attack on the French and the subsequent defeat and rout of the British under

Braddock led to a broader war—often described as the first world war—between France and England, which resulted in France's defeat and the beginning of her retreat as a colonial power from North America. Following this final episode of the "French and Indian Wars," the Indians no longer enjoyed a role in the balance of power between England and France and faced growing encroachment into their lands by English colonists. In 1763, as English land companies invaded the country of the Delaware Nation in Pennsylvania, Ottawa Chief Pontiac organized a war to expel the whites from the Indian country.

Pontiac's Rebellion consisted of attacks on a number of British forts, which fell to Indian hands, and a siege of Detroit, which lasted five months. During a siege at Fort Pitt, Sir Jeffrey Amherst, commander of British forces in North America, ordered smallpox blankets distributed among the Delaware, an incident of biological warfare. The war officially ended in October 1763. The British subsequently issued a Proclamation of 1763 that guaranteed there would be no further encroachment west of a line drawn at Fort Stanwix (present-day Rome, New York), but encroachments were inevitable. The western Senecas allied themselves with the western Indians and on September 14, 1763, about 500 of them attacked a contingent of British soldiers, driving them into the Niagara Gorge at a place called Devil's Hole. The commander of the British armed forces in North America, Sir Jeffrey Amherst, was furious and threatened a campaign of annihilation against the Geneseo Seneca, but Sir William Johnson, the British Indian agent, urged the Six Nations and those Seneca who had remained friendly to England to pressure the western Senecas to seek peace. The result was a Preliminary Articles of Peace, signed on April 3, 1764, which contains language ceding a four-mile-wide strip of land on each side of the Niagara River to Sir William Johnson. The Proclamation of 1763 did not end white encroachment into Indian country, and English settlers continued to build squatters' settlements even though these were illegal under British law. In 1773, Lord Dunmore of Virginia claimed land on both sides of the Ohio River. There followed a series of murders and assassinations on both sides, culminating in a fierce battle at Pleasant Point, Ohio, on October 10, 1774. The war for the Ohio country preceded the American Revolution, continued through it, and was unresolved and ongoing in 1783 when Great Britain capitulated.

The American Revolution ended with a victory for the revolutionaries, which was something of a military miracle involving some innovative tactics and the assistance of French arms. The Treaty of Paris, which ended the war between the United States of America and England, failed to mention the rights or interests of those seen by both as England's Indian allies.

The ensuing treaty between the United States and the Haudenosaunee, or Six Nations, produced at Fort Stanwix, left the Six Nations angry over land cessions the negotiators were not authorized to make. The Six Nations government on numerous occasions expressed a sentiment that the Haudenosaunee (Six Nations) had lost lands through coercion or deceit. In the Mohawk Valley, some Indians who had fled during the confusion of war returned to find their homes and farms occupied by supporters of the Revolution, and they tried using the courts to regain their property. These two types of complaint—Indian warriors and government complaining to officials and individual Indians seeking return of assets through the courts and petitions to the legislature—were the earliest Indian land claims following the Revolution. The Indians, for their part, have never missed an opportunity to press their claims.

The new republic had won the war but was now immersed in a sea of problems that had arisen even before the hostilities had ceased. A very significant problem was that the English military continued to occupy a string of forts at Fort Stanwix, Fort Oswego, and Fort Niagara and in present-day Ohio and Michigan, from which they encouraged resistance to encroachment into Indian country. The new United States was in many ways exhausted, its currency inflated, and its ability to enforce its laws challenged on every side internally. It did not want another war with England. The United States government, the states, and private land companies viewed the western lands—a euphemism for Indian lands—as a source of dollars to repay their debts and to finance their needs, and these three sectors approached Indian Nations with offers of money and other assets in exchange for land cessions. Some states, including New York State, began selling parcels of land in areas long recognized as belonging to Indian Nations even before negotiating a sale or other conveyance from them. During the years following the Revolution and while the United States government operated under the Articles of Confederation, it was not clear how such transactions would be handled, which ones would be legal and which not legal, or what could be done in the event of incidents of fraud or disagreement. Under the Articles of Confederation, the central government had little or no power to organize enforcement of its laws, and the states sometimes acted as though they had little or no obligation to act in the interest of the whole, especially when that interest conflicted with their own. The test of whether the central government would be able to survive and the union flourish came on two fronts: Indians and taxation. (The taxation issue would be settled in a conflict known as the Whiskey Rebellion.)

Indians had lived side by side with non-Indians in the Mohawk Valley for more than a generation. Problems had arisen because in incidents of conflict the courts were not available to the Indians. Indians were not permitted, for example, to bring suit or give testimony against an Englishman. The only workable peaceful solution was in the form of government to government agreements—treaties, and this reality greatly enhanced the influence of men such as Sir William Johnson, the British Indian agent who skillfully represented the interest of the Crown prior to the Revolution in negotiations with the Indians and settlers. With the defeat of England, the Indians turned to negotiations with Albany and Washington in search of a way to expel squatters and other intruders without resorting to violence and ultimately war. Some officials at Albany talked about expelling all Indians from New York, but this was not realistic because of the British forts that guarded British and Indian interests in central and western New York.

Encroachment into Indian country was one of the earliest issues confronting Congress. Unauthorized settlement on or purchase of Indian land by anyone other than Congress was addressed in the Proclamation of the Continental Congress, September 22, 1783: ". . . Congress assembled . . . [does] hereby prohibit and forbid and prohibit all persons from making settlements on land inhabited or claimed by Indians." In 1787, the United States government, operating under the Articles of Confederation, passed the Northwest Ordinance, an historic step toward asserting central control over lands not yet part of existing states, to create rules in anticipation of the admission of new states, and to raise money to pay the national debt. The Ordinance, however, had the effect of offering for settlement lands that had not been purchased or otherwise obtained from the Indians. When settlers moved to occupy these lands, Indians attacked and harassed them.

In 1768, the "Line of Property" had been established, running south from a point about seven miles west of Rome, New York. No

English settlement could be made west of the line without a formal cession by the Indian owners. By acts passed in 1783 and 1784, New York State created a commission to obtain cessions of land from the Indian Nations. The Six Nations, as a Confederacy, responded to the first message from the commission, saying the Six Nations desired to make peace with the United States as a whole. Nevertheless, the state proceeded with plans to deal with each of the Six Nations separately. The so-called "treaties" that resulted have never been accepted as valid by the Indian Nations. The strategy the state used was to nego-tiate with the individual Indian Nations. In the case of the Oneida Nation, when white settlers encroached on their lands, the state announced they would not expel the intruders but would hold the Oneida responsible for any violence that occurred should the Oneida try to do so (Harden 2000, 5). Using this strategy of coercion, in 1784 New York State obtained cessions of five million acres of land for $2,000 in cash, $2,000 in clothing, $1,000 in provisions, and $600 in annual rent.

A similar strategy was applied with the Onondaga Nation. When white settlers encroached on their lands, the state asserted that it was powerless to protect the land unless it had a stake in the land. They persuaded the Onondaga to sign lands over to the state under the pretension that the state would protect them. Ultimately, the state had no intentions of doing so and in this way effected what amounted to a swindle of a large amount of Onondaga land.

In 1789, the United States adopted a constitution that concen-trated much more power in the hands of the federal government, compared with the earlier Articles of Confederation. U.S. forces, including local militias, moved to punish the Indians in the Ohio region for the raids that had caused property damage, injuries, and death on disputed lands. At this time, President Washington and Congress resolved to conduct a fair treatment policy in regard to the Indians and to retreat from bribery and coercion toward offering market value for the land. At this point, it is possible to observe that the federal government was in favor of fair treatment of the Indians and that the states were not in favor of fair treatment. The history of the Indians' subsequent attempts to regain lands lost through fraud or coercion or other unfair means would confirm that while fair treatment occasionally was reborn as a federal policy, it was rarely invoked in Albany or other state capitals. This is essentially why Indian land claims have lingered for some two centuries.

American forces suffered two military defeats during this period, including a defeat of General Harmar's forces in 1790 and a disastrous loss of an army under General St. Clair in 1791. President Washington asked General "Mad Anthony" Wayne to create an army to defend U.S. interests in the Ohio region. Wayne was to march into the Miami River country to engage the Indians while avoiding military conflict with the British who had built a fort there.

At this point, the states, including New York, had interests that were distinct from those of the United States but also had the potential to interfere with federal policy. In 1790, George Washington invited a delegation of Six Nations chiefs to Philadelphia. They complained bitterly about fraudulent treatment of Indians at the hands of the states, including, obviously, New York State. Washington promised to do what he could, and Congress subsequently passed what is now called the 1790 Trade and Intercourse Act, a promise that the federal government would guarantee that Indians would not be cheated by the states in dealings over land:

> And be it enacted and declared, that no sale of lands . . . shall be valid to . . . any state, whether having the right of preemption or not, unless the same shall be made and duly executed at some public treaty, held under the authority of the United States. (Prucha 1975, 15)

By the summer of 1794, Wayne's army was marching toward the Indian towns in Ohio, and President Washington's envoy, Timothy Pickering, was assembling a treaty conference at Canandaigua, New York. Wayne's victory at Fallen Timbers, the first victory of the U.S. army in the field, placed the federal government in a position of power in relation to the states.

The Canandaigua Treaty was one of the seminal documents in U.S. history because it confirmed the federal triumph over state assertions of rights to land transactions with Indians. Had state militias defeated the Indians in Ohio and had the states been able to assert control over the future of land dealings in the territories to the west, U.S. history might have been very different. This is especially visible when we think about the future: the Louisiana Purchase, the Indian resistance organized by Tecumseh, the War of 1812 with England, the Mexican War, and the Civil War.

The 1794 treaty was also a defining document for the Indian Nations because it established a federal responsibility to guard the rights of the Indians against the ambitions and abuses of the states. It would not be lost on the Indians that this historically arises as a government-to-government arrangement, not one engineered by lawyers in courts.

Nevertheless, in the decades following this treaty, New York State aggressively followed a policy of dealing with individual nations of the Six Nations and even with unauthorized individuals and obtaining land sales and cessions in defiance of the 1790 Trade and Intercourse Act. The only recourse against abuses open to the Indians was in the form of appeals for justice to the federal government, but the United States was on a path dominated by warfare with Indian Nations across the continent.

First, in 1838, the U.S. Senate ratified a treaty quickly found to be fraudulent (the Buffalo Creek Treaty), and a long line of Indian law cases affirmed that claims could not be brought against the United States without a special act of Congress. Second, the courts will not

Cornplanter. (*Smithsonian National Anthropological Archives*)

question the validity or fairness of a treaty that has been legally signed and ratified by the United States. The courts were not open to Indian Nations for claims against New York. As a result, there was no court open to the Six Nations for their most important claims. The Indians had no realistic recourse to assert their claims that their lands had been taken—most Americans two generations ago acknowledged that the Indians' lands were "stolen"—through political or judicial means. The first case under the Trade and Intercourse Act was decided in 1920 and is known as *United States v. Boylan.* This involved 32 acres of Oneida land that was being seized for nonpayment of a loan and that the court held could not be seized because it was protected under federal law. This revelation led the New York Legislature to create the Everett Commission to study the question of Indian title to lands in New York. Assemblyman Edward Everett concluded the Indians had been subjected to very serious abuses, but his final report was rejected by the Legislature, and Everett was treated as an outcast.

In *Deere v. St. Lawrence River Power Co.,* another case brought under the 1790 Trade and Intercourse Act, the Court ruled that such cases were barred, because they did not technically arise under federal laws. This ruling was overturned in 1974 by the increasingly conservative U.S. Supreme Court in the first Oneida land claim to reach the U.S. Supreme Court, *Oneida Nation v. County of Oneida.* This decision and the 1985 Supreme Court decision in the same case made it possible at last for Indian Nations to seek justice for their land claims in the U.S. legal system.

In 1946, Congress passed the Indian Claims Commission Act, which authorized certain Indian Nations to bring claims against the United States. There was some dissatisfaction with the Act because claims could only be brought for money and not land recovery, and the amount of recovery was limited to the dollar value of the land *at the time of taking.* Because the law limited the lawsuits to actions against the federal government, it was not applicable to a whole category of cases in which the states or county or individual landowners would rightfully be the defendants. Such cases exist in New York State.

The Indian Nations in New York, including the Onondaga, Cayuga, Seneca, Tuscarora, Mohawk, and Seneca Nations, had never, until 1974, had a realistic opportunity to pursue claims for lands illegally taken beginning two centuries ago and occurring well into this century. These modern land claims are merely the latest attempt by the Haudenosaunee Nations to secure the fair treatment that

Washington had promised. History will judge this country as to whether or not it can finally fulfill this promise to be fair.

The Cayuga Nation, which lost all its lands in New York State and whose surviving population in the state resides primarily among the Seneca in western New York, brought suit in 1980. The suit cited treaties in 1795 and 1807 between the Cayuga Nation and New York State under which New York acquired 64,027 acres of Cayuga land. There was no federal presence, and the treaties were argued to be in violation of the 1790 Federal Trade and Intercourse Act. U.S. District Judge Neal McCurn concluded that the Cayuga had lost their lands in violation of the 1790 Act, and the jury subsequently awarded the Cayuga $36.9 million. This was considerably less than the $1.7 billion urged by a witness for the Cayuga Nation, but more than the $12.1 million proposed by state experts. The U.S. Justice Department arrived at a figure of $527.5 million. In October 2001, Judge McCurn handed down an award of $247.9 million. Fierce opposition to any settlement with the Cayuga arose among a right-wing white rights group calling itself United Citizens for Equality (UCE). This group has held rallies urging that the state should take the case to the increasingly conservative U.S. Supreme Court which they felt would overturn any settlement favoring Indians. The case is continued on appeal to the U.S. Court of Appeals.

The Mohawk Nation at Akwesasne functions with a traditional Haudenosaunee Council of Chiefs; a Band Council created under Canada's Indian Act, which functions on the Canadian portion of the reserve in Ontario and Quebec; and the St. Regis Tribal Council, which exists as an elective system tribal government under New York State law. All three governments brought suit in 1982 to recover claims against 15,000 acres around Akwesasne in Franklin and St. Lawrence counties; plus one square mile in Fort Covington, New York; one square mile in Massena, New York at Alcoa Point; land on the Grasse River; and Barnhart, Croil, and Long Sault Islands in the St. Lawrence River. The lawsuit is based on the 1790 Federal Trade and Intercourse Act and attacks a 1796 agreement that had no federal presence. Negotiations started in 1987, and in 1998, the U.S. Justice Department intervened on behalf of the Mohawk. Negotiations have been complicated and heated, and at one point, in 1998, New York State broke off the talks.

The Onondaga Nation began talks with officials of New York State in 1998. Their claim involves lands transferred to the State in treaties in 1790, 1793, 1795, 1817, and 1822. New York State has claimed all of the Onondaga Nation's land except the 7300-acre territory they now occupy. None of these treaties was attended by or held under the authority of the United States, and the Onondaga Nation is making its claim as a violation of the 1790 Federal Trade and Intercourse Act. The Onondaga claim is potentially the largest and most involved of all the claims against New York State, even though some of the illegal land transactions precede the 1790 Federal Trade and Intercourse Act. Other aspects of the claim, however, can be brought under the Act. As of early 2003, the Onondaga were continuing to negotiate their claim and had not filed a lawsuit. None of the five treaties mentioned are recognized as legal by the Six Nations (Haudenosaunee) Confederacy. The Onondaga Nation's position is that the Supreme Court of the United States has recognized that the state treaties are null and void, and the land transfers were illegal. The Supreme Court has also ruled that the statutes of limitation, which would rule out such lawsuits or other legal actions, do not apply to these kinds of claims by Indian Nations.

The Seneca Nation of Indians brought suit in 1993 to recover land and damages to land including a taking on the Cattaraugus Indian Reservation for construction of the New York State Thruway, fifty acres taken on the Oil Spring Reserve by New York State, and recovery of Grand Island. The Seneca Nation in New York State is composed of the Seneca Nation of Indians who occupy the Allegany, Cattaraugus, and Oil Springs Territories, and the Tonawanda Seneca, who occupy the Tonawanda Territory. The Tonawanda Seneca joined the lawsuit as it pertains to Long Island.

On August 3, 2001, New York's Governor Pataki announced that the Justice Department had filed to drop the residents of Grand Island from the lawsuit. The Seneca had sued the residents of Grand Island for monetary damages and ejectment. At the time of the Justice Department's motion, Judge Arcara offered to entertain a motion by the Justice Department to dismiss the suit, but the Justice Department did not act on this offer. On June 21, 2002, U.S. District Court Judge Richard Arcara dismissed the lawsuit. In the dismissal, the judge raised questions about whether the Seneca ever had aboriginal title to the land, a question which had been decided in a previous finding of fact in an Indian Claims Commission proceeding in 1968. A second point of the decision raised the issue of whether the federal government had the authority to enter into a treaty with an Indian Nation in 1794, which in effect, put to rest any ambiguity of the Seneca Nation's ownership of Grand Island.

The Seneca Nation has taken steps to appeal this decision. Governor Pataki, who had recently negotiated a casino compact with the Seneca Nation, appealed to the U.S. Justice Department to abstain from joining the appeal. If the Justice Department withdraws from the case, New York will invoke its sovereignty immunity from lawsuit and, under current rules, also will be dropped from the case. Should that happen, the rest of the defendants will claim that New York State is a necessary defendant and, in its absence, the case cannot go forward. The case would then be dropped, not on its merits, but on procedural grounds.

The current wealth that is enjoyed in New York and the United States as a whole was built on a foundation of illegally taken land and stolen natural resources. These claims test whether this theft will be acknowledged and at least partially paid for. The Empire State was created when the state government violated federal law and illegally obtained 98 percent of the native lands and forced 95 percent of the Haudenosaunee people to flee from their aboriginal land. They were subsequently subjected to coercion and sometimes outright fraud, and the result was that the nations lost all but a tiny fraction of their original homelands. The Cayuga and Oneida lost practically all their lands. Over the ensuing two centuries, they were barred from seeking redress in the courts, mostly through tactics involving legal maneuvering.

The Nations of the Haudenosaunee have persevered through many decades, sustained by the words of the Seneca prophet Handsome Lake who, in the early nineteenth century, predicted that although times will be difficult, the nations will survive. They have survived awaiting the fulfillment of a policy advocated by the United States' first president, George Washington. Fair treatment, the first order of the new country's business, has been a very difficult path to follow. The initial Supreme Court ruling in the Oneida decision in 1985 which found that the 1790 Federal Trade and Intercourse Act continued to be valid opened the door to a generation of pursuit of these claims. Should it happen that the claims, or some of the claims, are quieted through procedural tactics once again, the Haudenosaune seem destined to wait for another opportunity.

## REFERENCES

Findings in Fact. Indian Claims Commission. 20 In D Cl Comm. 177. December 30, 1968. In *Iroquois Indians II: Indian Claims Commission* 388 (1974): 194.

Harden, P. 2000. *Whose land: An introduction to the Iroquois land claims in New York State.* Syracuse, NY: American Friends Service Committee.

Hauptman, L. 2000. Who owns Grand Island? In *Treaty of Canandaigua 1794: 200 years of treaty relations between the Iroquois Confederacy and the United States,* eds. G. Peter Jemison and Anna M. Schein, Santa Fe, NM: Clear Light Publications, 127.

Mohawk, J. 2001. Unambiguous conquests: Haudenosaunee warfare 1603–1673, In *Aboriginal people and the fur trade: Proceedings of the 8th North American Fur Trade Conference, Akwesasne,* ed. Louise Johnston, Ottawa: Akwesasne Notes Publishing, 102.

Parker, A. C. 1926. *An analytical history of the Seneca Nation.* Rochester: New York State Archaeological Association.

Prucha, F. P. 1975. *Documents of U.S. Indian policy.* Lincoln: University of Nebraska Press.

White, M. E. 1978. Erie. In *Handbook of North American Indians.* Vol. 15 of *Northeast,* ed. Bruce G. Trigger, 412–417. Washington, DC: Smithsonian Institution.

———. 1978. Neutral and Wenro. In *Handbook of North American Indians.* Vol. 15 of *Northeast,* ed. Bruce G. Trigger. 407–411. Washington, D.C.: Smithsonian Institution.

# 5

# The New York Oneidas: A Business Called a Nation

*Bruce E. Johansen*

O ne of the most important—and, often, most vexing—questions in Indian Country today concerns the creation of reservation economic bases that produce necessary cash income while being culturally appropriate and sustainable. Casinos, the reservation cash cow *du jour,* sometimes produce mountains of money as they transform parts of reservations into annexes of the non-Indian economy, with all of their imported artifices and vices.

Thirty years ago, the New York Oneidas' landholdings were down to thirty-two acres east of Syracuse, with almost no economic infrastructure. Three decades later, the New York Oneidas own a large casino, the Turning Stone, which has incubated a number of other business ventures. Many of the roughly 1,000 Oneidas who reside in the area have received substantial material benefits.

Amidst the prosperity, however, a substantial dissident movement exists among Oneidas who assert that Ray Halbritter, "nation representative" of the New York Oneidas, was never voted into such an office. This group, centered in the Shenandoah family (which includes the notable singer Joanne Shenandoah and her husband Doug George-Kanentiio) believe that the New York Oneidas under Halbritter have established a business, called it a nation, and acquired the requisite approvals from New York State and the U.S. federal government to use this status to open the Turning Stone. The dissidents' tribal benefits were eliminated after they took part in a "march for democracy." To regain their benefits, those who had "lost their voice" were told that they would have to sign papers agreeing not to criticize Halbritter's government, not to speak to the press, and pledge allegiance to Halbritter and his men's council.

The New York Oneidas have appointed a "men's council," (a body unheard of in traditional matrilineal Iroquois law or tradition) that issued a zoning code to "beautify" the Oneida Nation. This code enabled his fifty-four-member police force (patrolling a thirty-two-acre reservation) to "legally" evict from their homes Oneidas who opposed his role as leader of the New York Oneidas, which was solidified by the acquisition of a number of other businesses, a phalanx of public-relations spin doctors, several dozen lawyers, and ownership of *Indian Country Today,* a national Native American newspaper.

The story of the New York Oneidas is a particularly raw example of conflicts that beset many Native American nations that have attempted to address problems of persistent poverty and economic marginalization by opening casinos. Supporters of the casinos see them as "the new buffalo," while opponents look at them as a form of internal colonization, an imposition of European-descended economic institutions and values upon Native American peoples.

In few areas is the conflict as sharp as among the Haudenosaunee, or Iroquois Confederacy, where New York State governor George Pataki recently announced plans to open as many as six new Native-sponsored casinos in an attempt to jump-start a state economy badly damaged by the attacks of September 11, 2001. On various Internet sites and chat rooms, supporters of Halbritter accuse the Shenandoah family of supporting antitreaty groups, while opponents of the Oneidas' corporate structure routinely call Halbritter "the king" and "the despot."

The recent experience of the Oneidas of New York raises several significant questions for Indian Country as a whole. Is the Oneida model of an economic powerhouse key to defining the future of Native American sovereignty in the opening years of the twenty-first century, as many of its supporters believe? Materially, the New York Oneidas have gained a great deal in a quarter century, including repurchase of 16,000 acres of land by the end of 2002. Have these gains been offset by an atmosphere of stifling totalitarianism and a devastating loss of traditional bearings, as many Oneida dissidents attest? This conflict also has an important bearing on the pending solution of an Oneida land claim that is more than two centuries old.

## ONEIDA HISTORICAL CONTEXT

By the time European Americans encountered the Oneidas and other Iroquois, this confederacy was a major economic and political power among Native American peoples of eastern North America. The Oneidas enjoyed a commanding position astride the only relatively flat passage between the Hudson River and the Great Lakes. In the nineteenth century, this country would be traversed by the Erie Canal, a major economic lifeline between the East Coast and interior before the spread of railroads a few decades later (Campisi and Hauptman 1988; Richards 1974).

"Oneida" is probably an anglicization of this people's own name for themselves, *Ona yote ka o no,* meaning Granite People or People of the Standing Stone. The Oneida, one of the five original Nations of the Iroquois Confederacy (with the Mohawks, Onondagas, Cayugas, and Senecas) occupied an area in upstate New York near present-day Syracuse, adjacent to the Mohawks on their east and the Onondagas on the west.

The first European to visit Oneida country who left a historical record was a Dutch surgeon, Harmen Meyndersten van den Bogaert, who traveled westward from Fort Orange (Albany) in 1634 and 1635. The Oneidas sheltered the Dutchman during the winter and fed him venison, salmon, bear meat, cornbread baked with beans, baked squash, and beaver meat. The fact that the Oneidas could bring such a feast out of winter storage spoke volumes about the abundance of their economy at the time. Van den Bogaert described storehouses of beans and maize; he estimated that one of these contained 300 bushels of corn stored for the winter.

During the early 1660s and continuing into the 1690s, Oneida and other Iroquois populations were sharply reduced by a series of epidemics, principally smallpox. By the late 1660s, according to estimates by French observers (which may have been inflated), two-thirds of the Oneida population was comprised of adopted Wyandot (Huron) and Algonquian captives (Richards 1974, 25). Alcohol beverages already were taking a toll on the Oneidas as well. At about the same time, the European religious frontier reached the Oneida, as the Jesuits arrived. By 1690, the new English government at Albany was approving purchases of native land in Iroquois country. Oneida population and economic base continued a protracted decline, mitigated somewhat by continued adoption of war captives.

The Oneidas, unlike a majority of other Iroquois, supported the patriots during the American Revolution. The Oneidas' corn surplus, an asset in peace-time trade, was put to use in 1777 feeding General George Washington's hungry troops during their desperate winter at Valley Forge. An Oneida, Polly Cooper (who also was called Polly Cook), served as Washington's cook for much of the war, at his specific request. Washington asked his staff to employ a Native American cook because of the commander's fondness for meals made from corn.

During the mid-eighteenth century, the Oneidas lived on roughly 5.3 million acres in central New York. Despite their aid in the American Revolution, New York Oneida lands were steadily eroded after United States independence was formalized in the Treaty of Paris (1783). During the mid-nineteenth century, within less than twenty years, Oneida landholdings were reduced from several hundred thousand to about 60,000 acres (Johansen and Mann, *Encyclopedia* 2000, 226).

Several land purchases around 1800 sharply reduced the Oneida territory. These treaties were written to the advantage of several land companies with the assistance of New York State, lacking federal approval required by several federal "Non-Intercourse acts" passed during and after 1790. Facing disenfranchisement in New York State, during the 1820s and 1830s, about 700 Oneidas emigrated to the present-day state of Wisconsin, settling on land purchased from the Winnebagos and Menominees (Johnson 1995, 19).

By 1930, New York Oneida landholdings were down to about 1,000 acres. Various land dealings continued to erode even that amount of land. By the late twentieth century, the Oneida Reservation in New York was down to thirty-two acres east of Syracuse. Some investment capital was provided in 1974, with a $1.2 million award (including accrued interest) from the Indian Claims Commission. Economic stimulus also was provided late in the 1980s by construction of casinos in both New York and Wisconsin. By the late 1990s, Oneida landholdings in New York State had been increased by about 4,000 acres, largely through investment of casino profits (Kates 1997, 25).

On January 21, 1974, the U.S. Supreme Court sustained the Oneidas' position that the Non-Intercourse Acts applied to takings of their lands by New York State. This decision opened the way for other New England tribes, most notably the Passamoquoddy and Penobscot of Maine, to sue for recovery of lands lost in violation of the Non-Intercourse Acts, passed between 1790 and 1834, which required that all sales of Native American lands be approved by the federal government.

The New York Oneidas' present surge of economic development began during the early 1990s. The Turning Stone Casino, twenty-five miles east of Syracuse, produced 1,900 jobs and has become, according Halbritter, the fifth most popular tourist attraction in New York State. By 1997, the casino and other Oneida businesses were employing 2,600 people, making the Oneida Nation the second largest employer in central New York. By the late 1990s, 2.5 million people were visiting the Turning Stone annually.

In addition to land purchases, the Oneida Nation has used some of its gambling profits to start other businesses, such as the Oneida Textile Printing Facility in Canastota, the New York Oneidas' first effort at diversification outside of gambling. Oneida Textile, located in a renovated 6,000-foot structure, prints and markets T-shirts, sweatshirts, and other items of clothing. A 285-room luxury hotel was opened in September 1997, adding 450 jobs. Casino profits also have been used to build a council house; a health-services center; a cultural center and museum; a recreational center (with a swimming pool, a gymnasium, and lacrosse box, et al.); scholarship programs; medical, dental, and optical facilities; job training; legal assistance; Oneida language and music classes; meals for elders; and day care (Kates 1997, 22).

## DISSENT AMONG THE NEW YORK ONEIDAS

The burgeoning business climate has been attended by some controversy from Oneidas who assert that the New York Oneidas have built a business empire on an illegitimate claim to a political base that does not exist in treaty, law, or Iroquois custom. Two reporters writing for the *New York Times* characterized the situation in Oneida: "The root of the Oneida story is a bitter dispute between the traditionalist aunt who resuscitated the Oneidas and her modernist nephew who built the casino" (Chen and LeDuff 2001, A-29). The *New York Times'* first error in this piece was its characterization of the conflict as a family squabble. It's more than that. Factually, the *Times* did worse in this piece; before a correction was published, its report placed the Onondagas' reservation "near Buffalo," when it is south of Syracuse, New York, roughly 150 miles away (Chen and LeDuff 2001, A-29).

The family conflict is a single, albeit superficial, dimension of the Oneidas' story. Maisie Shenandoah, a Wolf Clan mother among the Oneidas, has certainly spoken out against her nephew Ray Halbritter. She called Halbritter "an overfed despot with a taste for Italian suits, ruling from a white palace near the New York State Thruway"—an office at the Turning Stone casino that overlooks the championship-caliber Shenadoah Golf Course. "He's a petty tyrant," she said (Chen and LeDuff 2001, A-29; Schenandoah 2001).

Halbritter, who attended Harvard, does not apologize for having helped to create an economic juggernaut that has helped to build housing, a health clinic, and other programs, as well as per capita payments for individual Oneidas (from which Maisie Shenandoah and others who oppose his methods have been excluded). According to Christiansen Capital Advisors, a Manhattan consulting company that maintains a database of gambling statistics, the Turning Stone Casino Resort in Verona takes in an estimated $167 million in annual revenue, with a profit margin as high as 50 percent (Chen and LeDuff 2001, A-29). From these profits, each enrolled Oneida member (except the dissidents) was receiving a quarterly check of $1,100 late in the year 2001.

Halbritter, who first moved from the Syracuse suburbs to the trailers of the "32 acres" with his mother, Gloria (Maisie Shenandoah's older sister) believes that his aunt Maisie remains chained to a past that may be rich with tradition, but little else. "Sometimes, people are sort of imprisoned in poverty so long that they begin to believe that the bars are there for their own protection," he said (Chen and LeDuff 2001, A-29). Late in the 1990s, most of Halbritter's most vocal opponents still lived on "the 32 acres" when the Oneida Nation government enacted a new housing code meant to evict them from their trailer homes.

According to the *New York Times* account, "After a decade-long power struggle marked by occasional violence, [Ray Halbritter] ultimately prevailed, and in 1987 was endorsed by Maisie Shenandoah as Wolf Clan representative. By the early 1990's, the Oneida leaders representing the two other clans had died, leaving Halbritter as the sole representative. In 1993, he signed a casino compact with Gov. Mario M. Cuomo without formal consent from his people. By then, he and his aunt had had a falling out" (Chen and LeDuff 2001, A-29). The falling-out soon hardened along familiar lines in Indian Country: assimilationist versus traditionalist. "Our nation is run like a corporation," said Vicky Shenandoah, one of Mrs. Shenandoah's daughters. "But I would not trade my Indianness for money wealth. That won't be here tomorrow" (Chen and LeDuff 2001, A-29).

Many Haudenosaunee (Iroquois) traditionalists believe that Halbritter is operating under self-assumed authority, in defiant opposition to the structure of the thousand-year-old confederacy, as well as the 200-year-old beliefs of the Seneca prophet Handsome Lake, who abhorred four things that he said would doom his people: whiskey, the *Bible,* the fiddle, and gambling (Schenandoah 2001). Rick Hill, Sr., a Tuscarora leader, has warned that gambling has translated into the three G's: greed, guns, and grief. From Seneca promoters of new casinos, cut-rate cigarettes and gasoline without off-reservation taxes, to Mohawks who "buttleg" untaxed smokes across the border with Canada, Hill has said that young Iroquois are being seduced. "They all want to be the next Halbritter," he said derisively (Chen and LeDuff 2001, A-29).

In the meantime, Halbritter seems to regard the confederacy mainly as a toothless (and largely moneyless) debating society. "Our revenue has enabled us to take control of our own destiny more than any political or theoretical speech can make," he has said. "While people meet and make speeches, we're actually doing things" (Chen and LeDuff 2001, A-29).

## WHO GOVERNS THE NEW YORK ONEIDAS?

In May 1993, the Haudenosaunee (Iroquois Confederacy) Grand Council at Onondaga refused to recognize Halbritter's authority as a representative of the New York Oneidas. Halbritter earlier had been selected by the Grand Council as a message carrier or "eyes and ears" from the Oneidas to the Grand Council, to serve alongside Lyman Johns and Richard Chris-john, a position which, according to Diane Schenandoah, a faith-keeper of the Oneida Wolf Clan (and daughter of Maisie) "did not carry any legislative or administrative authority but did secure for the Oneidas a presence at the Grand Council" (Schenandoah 2001).

As Barbara A. Gray, who is Mohawk (and a Ph.D. candidate in Justice Studies at Arizona State University) points out, "Halbritter was appointed by Wolf Clan Mother Maisie Shenandoah to be a sub-chief. By Haudenosaunee traditional law, a sub-chief is to be the eyes and ears of the Nation. In effect, he is a bench-warmer keeping the spot filled, until such time that he is removed or condoled. Halbritter was never condoled, i.e., officially raised to be a full chief, which takes agreement and ceremonial procedures from the Grand Council of the Haudenosaunee Confederacy" (Gray 2002, 13).

The Onondaga Grand Council's decision was affirmed by the Bureau of Indian Affairs in August 1993, only to be reversed twenty-four hours later when a New York congressman, Sherwood Boehlert, an avid supporter of commercial gambling, persuaded Bill Clinton's White House to reinstate Halbritter's federal recognition. To those who assert special-interest politics, Halbritter's supporters replied that the reversal was obtained with affidavits supporting the action from a majority of New York Oneidas.

Following the deaths of the other two men, and without further consultation with the matrilineal Oneidas' clan mothers, Halbritter created a body calling itself the "Men's Council," whose members served at his pleasure, much like a corporation's board of directors. Halbritter then created a corporate body that he and the Men's Council called "The Oneida Indian Nation of New York." This government disregarded the traditional clan-based leadership structure of the Oneidas, which is unincorporated and unrecognized by New York State. In a belated effort to express a modicum of support for a tradition in which women make many key decisions, Halbritter later attempted to balance his Men's Council by selecting a number of elderly women to act as "clan mothers" in his governance structure. None of the "clan mothers" so selected were chosen according to traditional criteria, under which such a position is hereditary, not elective. They were not clan mothers by tradition or custom, but a female counterpart of the Men's Council.

According to Diane Schenandoah, "If we were to honor our obligations as *Onyota'a:ka*, [Oneida people] and as Haudenosaunee, we had to seek a replacement for Halbritter while fulfilling a long-standing Confederate request to appoint *rotiiane* [leaders] and clan-mothers in accordance with the Great Law" (Schenandoah 2001). To do so placed traditional Oneidas in a bind, because by exercising their freedom of expression they risked their standing as Oneidas and stood to lose all tribal benefits, placing their homes and livelihoods in serious jeopardy. During May 1995, the traditional people held a "March for Democracy." Many Oneidas lost all tribal benefits, including health insurance, tribal stipends, access to all tribal buildings and events, as well as their tribal jobs, for expressing their opposition to Halbritter openly by taking part in this march (Patterson January 2, 2002).

As a severe critic of the Haudenosaunee Grand Council, Halbritter labeled traditional Oneidas as "dissidents" who have lost their voices. Wrote Schenandoah, "Without a trial or hearing we have been found to be guilty by the 'men's council' of conspiring with the Confederacy, meeting with Wisconsin-based Oneidas and being in the company of unnamed, but apparently dangerous, 'Canadians.' Halbritter has taken away our benefits while denying us, at risk of arrest, access to our Oneida facilities, including the longhouse. He has punished Oneidas for speaking to the press, enacted ordinances which are unknown to residents and passed laws which he can change on a whim" (Schenandoah 2001; Patterson June 22, 2002).

On March 20, 1995, according to the traditionalists, members of the Oneida Wolf Clan gathered to meet at their longhouse, only to find that the locks had been changed. The police officers were instructed to arrest anyone trying to enter (Patterson 2002). The Men's Council also raised the ire of the traditionalists by holding meetings in the longhouse, a place heretofore devoted to the Handsome Lake religion, which is strenuously antigambling (Patterson January 2, 2002).

According to Schenandoah, the Men's Council then created an Oneida Nation Court over which Halbritter had veto power. She said that Halbritter and the Men's Council held themselves above the verdicts of the court, and that they enforce its decisions with "one of the largest 'Indian' police agencies in the United States, now estimated to consist of over 50 officers not one of whom is Native or has any training in Iroquois laws or customs" (Schenandoah 2001).

## THE PRICE OF OPPOSITION

By the year 2000, the Men's Council had enacted a housing code and then began using its provisions to evict from their homes several of the corporate structure's most severe critics. Most of them lived in trailer homes on the "32 acres." The housing code and bulldozing of homes was presented not as an attempt to silence his opponents, but as a way to "beautify" the reservation. The evicted people were told to apply for newly constructed "Oneida homes." Schenandoah, speaking for the traditionalists, commented:

> Yet we, the traditional Oneidas, did not qualify for the proposed homes since our membership was suspended. We suspect the housing plans are a way to remove us from our homes on the only undisputed land retained by the Oneidas: the 32 acres south of the city of Oneida. (Schenandoah 2001)

Most of the twenty-two families who were living on the thirty-two-acre territory in the spring of 2000 agreed to inspections. Every home entered by the Oneida Nation Police was condemned and subsequently bulldozed. By the fall of 2001, only seven families remained (Schenandoah 2001). Many of the homes previously demolished were in excellent condition, according to their owners (Oneida Nation Clanmother 2001). According to Schenandoah, "When we tried using our own resources to improve our homes we were threatened with arrest by the Oneida Nation Police for violation of ordinances unknown to us" (Schenandoah 2001).

One of the traditionalists, Danielle Schenandoah Patterson, a single mother of three children who was 31 years of age in 2002, flatly refused to move. Faced with an Oneida Nation condemnation order, Patterson had been trying to repair her home on her meager income from doing beadwork. The Oneida Nation had refused to comply with a 1998 Madison court order to garnish the paycheck of her ex-husband, who was an Oneida Nation employee, because of Patterson's political views. Patterson is among the Oneidas who were stripped of their "rights" as Oneidas because they opposed Halbritter's management of the Oneida Nation (Oneida Nation Clanmother 2001).

Traditionalist observers said that Arthur Pierce, Oneida Nation public-safety commissioner, threatened to take away Patterson's children (Jolene, 8; Clairese, 10; and Preston, 12; as of 2002) because the home had no central heating, then wrote a letter to Stoneleigh Housing, ordering workers there not to deliver a furnace that Patterson had obtained until after the Oneida Nation Police carried out their inspection. Traditionalist observers then watched Oneida Nation Police cars patrol the thirty-two acres twenty-four hours a day to prevent delivery of the furnace (Oneida Nation Clanmother 2001). In the meantime, Mark Emery, an Oneida Nation public-relations spokesman, said that the mobile home's condemnation was necessary "for the sake of the children" (aged 7, 8, and 10 at the time) who lived there with Patterson (Murphy 2001b).

On November 16, 2001, Patterson was confronted by Oneida Nation Police at the entrance to her residence after she refused them entry to conduct an inspection that she believed was an excuse to bulldoze her home. Patterson feared that if she allowed the inspection, her home would face the fate of eleven others on the Oneida Indian Territory that previously had been inspected, condemned, and immediately demolished. Several of the traditionalists gathered at Patterson's home. Patterson's sister, Diane Schenandoah, said, "Physically, if they come in with bulldozers, they're going to have to flatten a few of us," she said. "They're going to have to run over us" (Murphy 2001b).

Joe Hernandez, a general contractor from Sparta, New Jersey, helped make some repairs to the home. Hernandez gave reporters a quick tour of the mobile home. "This trailer's insulated pretty well," Hernandez said. "It's a darn good trailer." Hernandez said he saw nothing to merit condemnation. "I mean, it does need a couple repairs, but it's a sound house," said Hernandez, who carries a wallet full of cards certifying him to work in various construction fields. "Everything that I've seen so far is reparable and can be repaired in a reasonable amount of time" (Murphy 2001b).

Accounts of Patterson's arrest on November 16 varied widely, according to press reports. Patterson said she was driving away from her home Friday evening with her mother, Maisie Shenandoah, and her daughter Jolene, 7, when she saw about twenty cars head toward her home, carrying about thirty police. Patterson said that she turned her vehicle around and returned to the mobile home, only to find the cars, which included Oneida Nation Police cars and unmarked vehicles, blocking her driveway. One report said that "She said Arthur Pierce, the nation's public safety commissioner, approached her carrying a long, metal wrecking bar and a piece of paper from the Oneida Tribal Court granting legal permission to enter her home" (Murphy 2001a). After Patterson told the intruders to leave, according to her account, "Pierce and four other officers then grabbed her arms and jacket and pulled her away from her door" (Murphy 2001a). For confronting the officers on her doorstep, Patterson was charged with resisting arrest and assaulting a police officer, offenses for which conviction could cost her as much as a year in prison.

Emery said that the Oneida Nation had obtained an emergency inspection order from Stewart Hancock, a nation tribal judge. Emery said Patterson refused to allow police inside. Police attempted to arrest her for defying the court order, and she attacked them, Emery said. Nation police charged Patterson with second-degree criminal contempt and resisting arrest, according to Emery (Murphy 2001a). According to a report in the Syracuse *Post-Standard*, "During the inspection, Patterson was arrested on accusations of refusing to allow officers inside and kicking a police officer during a scuffle on her porch" (Coin 2001). Patterson also was injured in the scuffle.

According to traditionalist eyewitnesses, five to seven officers slammed Patterson against the door of her home. They yanked Maisie Shenandoah, who was 69 years of age, off the porch. Eyewitnesses said the police grabbed Patterson from all sides, forced her off her porch, and pulled out chunks of her hair. According to the same eyewitnesses, as one of the officers announced that Patterson was being taken into custody for resisting arrest, her glasses were broken and a heavy silver bracelet she was wearing was bent out of shape as she was handcuffed. When Patterson screamed that they were hurting her and that she was not provoking them, one of the officers threatened her by shoving a can of mace in her face before she was hustled into one of the police cars.

The traditionalists said that once Patterson was removed, one of the police officers pried open the door of the house with a crowbar, breaking it beyond repair, as several police swarmed into the home. During the inspection, according to the same witnesses, police ripped open her bedroom drawers, throwing her clothes all over the floor; broke a lamp; dismantled her kitchen pipes, and ripped out a triangular door in the bathroom (Oneida Nation Clanmother 2001).

Patterson said that her children were traumatized because of constant harassment by the Oneida Nation Police. The children had been living with Patterson's sister since Pierce's threat to remove them. One of the children, 7-year-old Jolene, fully witnessed the November 16 police "inspection" (Oneida Nation Clanmother 2001).

Following her confrontation with Oneida police November 16, hospital reports said that Patterson was treated for "multiple contusions" at Oneida Health Care Center. According to another report, Patterson went to the Oneida City Emergency Room and was treated for severe bruising, neck and back injuries, as well as emotional trauma resulting from the arrest (Oneida Nation Clanmother 2001). Patterson suffered serious bruises and emotional trauma following a scuffle with several of the police.

The same day, Patterson was interrogated for several hours by an Oneida Nation judge and police during which, according to one account, she was told she faced three weeks in jail without legal representation. "I was sitting there with blood on my face, big chunks of hair falling from where they [had] pulled hair out of my head. And the judge told me to get a good lawyer and he laughed" (Steinberger 2002).

Speaking for the Oneida Nation, Emery said that "Patterson attacked nation police, not the other way around, and that her mobile home was treated respectfully" (Murphy 2001a). Oneida City Police Chief David Meeker, who was present at the arrest, said "Patterson resisted arrest and that he did not see nation officers use excessive force in subduing her" (Murphy 2001a).

The Oneida Nation inspection report of Patterson's home, issued after the incidents of November 16, asserted that it was badly deteriorated and "in such an overall dilapidated condition that it is not fit for human habitation." The report described holes in the ceiling and floor, broken doors, boarded windows, and a sink not connected to the drain, among reasons for the condemnation (Murphy 2001b). According to an account in the Syracuse *Post-Standard,* "The notice also said the mobile home has no heating system. It states that the home is condemned for demolition because the violations cannot be corrected. Pierce . . . signed the order" (Murphy 2001b).

Patterson said that when she returned to her home a day after the November 16 inspection, she found it trashed. A back door had been ripped open and plumbing had been taken apart and not put back together. Several people camped at Patterson's home scoffed at the condemnation notice. Jerry Shenandoah, Patterson's brother, said that much of the damage cited on the inspection report was inflicted on the house during the inspection. He referred to some broken doors and damage to sink pipes (Murphy 2001b).

As the Oneida Nation condemned her home, Patterson protested, "The most current violations committed by Halbritter and his Casino Cartel include creating a housing/beautification project as a guise to eject all Natives from their homes and the land completely . . . In one year, 11 families were evicted and their homes demolished. The Nation police lost their deputization agreement with the State of New York and the surrounding counties. Further illegal surveillance and spy reports of the Nation police were publicly exposed. This occurred in the beginning of the housing/beautification project when a secret ordinance was created, and allowing the theft of private boat and vehicle owners' property" (Patterson January 2, 2002).

"On November 16, 2001," Patterson continued, "I was violated at my home, along with my mother, the Oneida Wolf Clan Mother Maisie Schenandoah, who was 69 years old at the time, and my seven-year-old daughter who witnessed the entire incident. As the police performed their forced-armed entry of my home that I own, I vocally refused the entry of my home; knowing that it was intention for eviction, which led to police brutality upon me and then my arrest" (Patterson 2002). Patterson said she was not read her Miranda rights until she had been taken to the police station seven miles from her home.

## THE CONFRONTATION GRINDS ON

On December 2, 2001, word was carried on the Internet that Oneida Nation Police had banned photographers from entering the thirty-two acres. The same reports said that reporters who visited the thirty-two acres without advance permission risked arrest (Oneida Iroquois 2001). The traditional Iroquois invited observers and cautioned about the risk of arrest. As of December 7, 2001, Danielle Patterson's furnace had been repaired and a new carbon-dioxide-detection system installed in her trailer.

As Patterson refused to leave her home, in mid-December, the Oneida Indian Nation announced that it had offered her a four-bedroom rental house. Nation officials said that they wrote to Patterson to tell her the house was available for her and her three children. Patterson could live in the rental house, in the nation-owned Village of the White Pines, six months for free, and then pay rent according to her income. Clint Hill, a Men's Council member, said that Patterson was offered the house over people on a waiting list because she and her children needed safe housing (Coin 2001).

"I spent my life savings on my home," said Patterson, who paid $18,000 for the trailer, purchased in 1985. "I have no money . . . and now I am going to be thrown in the street. I'm going to be forced to submit to the Halbritter administration and to pay rent at the Village of White Pines" (Bilodeau September 7, 2002).

Patterson appealed the demolition order in tribal court. She told the Syracuse *Post-Standard* that she hadn't received the letter offering the rental house, and in any event, she didn't want it. "That's ridiculous," she told a Syracuse *Post-Standard* reporter. "Why would I pay rent to them for a house that I could never own? Why would I pay rent to them if I already own my own home?" (Coin 2001).

On December 30, 2001, dissident Oneidas held a protest outside an Oneida Council meeting presided over by Halbritter in the longhouse. During the course of the protest, the dissidents asserted that the Oneida Nation Police assaulted twenty-four protesters. According to one account from the scene, "Clint Hill of Halbritter's council hit Joe Hernandez with his truck." Hernandez was not seriously injured (Oneida Protest 2002).

Danielle Patterson watched the altercation at about 10 A.M. from her house. "I held a open house the same time as Halbritter's meeting," Patterson said. "I put a huge sign on my house that said 'YOU CAN BREAK MY DOORS BUT NOT MY SPIRIT!!!' Halbritter's mother Gloria . . . tore our signs up and assaulted the protesters as well. Halbritter and his Nation prosecutor told the Oneidas in his meeting that he has big plans for this land and he's going to do whatever it takes to evict all remaining families off this land" (Oneida Protest 2002).

The Oneida Nation's public-relations office called the protest "a blatant attempt to intimidate members and disrupt the proceedings of a Nation government activity." A press release said protesters were wearing Nazi swastikas and compared them to the Taliban (Bilodeau January 3, 2002). The Nation Police were filming the protest, Emery said, as "police evidence" (Bilodeau, January 3, 2002). "That's such a lie," Diane Schenandoah said of the swastika accusation. She said that one protester wore a Nazi swastika with a line through it on his shirt, and the shirt read "No More Hitler," comparing Halbritter's regime to the Hitler regime in Nazi Germany (Bilodeau January 3, 2002).

The Men's Council's statement compared the protesters to the Taliban terrorist regime in Afghanistan. "They had their faces covered, looking for all the world like the Taliban," the statement said. "If they feel strongly about an issue, why must they hide their faces in shame?" (Bilodeau January 3, 2002). "The Shenandoah family today showed just how much disrespect they have for Oneida members, not just the government," the statement said. "They invited these trained trouble-makers to Nation lands in the hope of inciting violence" (Bilodeau January 3, 2002). The statement continued:

> Sunday's little stunt proves that people like Joanne Shenandoah and Danielle Patterson are not interested in justice, fair play and making peace. All they want is to disrupt the peace and tranquility of the Nation and are willing to use professional agitators and innocent children to achieve their misguided ends. All they accomplished was to defile the Nation's lands . . . It takes more than a few out-of-state trespassers and a handful of greed-driven malcontents to interrupt the business of the Nation. (Bilodeau January 3, 2002)

By January 2002, the *Onyota'a:ka* (traditional Oneida) had organized a series of social events to raise awareness and support. Diane Schenandoah made the following statement:

> We know our struggle is far more than a simple family dispute but involves every right and freedom held sacred to all Haudenosaunee. We are opposed to trading our ancestral lands for casino compacts; we want traditional leadership, and seek a return to our ancestral democratic heritage. Anyone who dismisses the *Onyota'a:ka* situation as a "family" matter not only belittles the suffering of the Oneidas but demonstrates contempt for the decisions of the Grand Council itself. For many, it is all too convenient to trivialize the Oneida struggle since it provides them with a weak excuse not to get involved when they know it is time to make a unified stand before the situation at the 32 acres degenerates to a point where more people are injured. What the *Onyota'a:ka* are to all Haudenosaunee is a conscience, an opportunity to do what is good and right. For those who cannot rouse themselves to action when the issues are so crystal clear this is the time to step aside and let the courageous ones restore freedom to the People of the Standing Stone. (Schenandoah 2001)

In early February 2002, the Oneida Indian Nation court's appeals judge upheld forced inspections of homes on nation land. The judge, Richard Simons, said the nation possesses the legal power to inspect homes under nation ordinances. "While the interest of property owners to be free from searches from their homes is substantial, it necessarily must be outweighed by the community's need to protect itself by identifying and abating conditions dangerous to its citizens," Simons wrote (Coin February 10, 2002).

The decision was rendered in the case of Ray and Elizabeth Roberts, who had refused to allow inspections required by nation ordinances. Simons said the nation had proven that the home inspections were reasonable. He said the nation's Redevelopment Ordinance "addresses a particular and localized problem on Territory Road" (Coin February 10, 2002).

Danielle Patterson, who continued to occupy her trailer home against the nation's expressed wishes, criticized Simons' decision and the entire nation court system. "This whole ridiculous court system is in violation of the Great Law," Patterson said. "They are a foreign government imposing their laws on our land" (Coin February 10, 2002).

By mid-February 2002, only eight traditional families remained on the thirty-two acres, as construction crews continued to lay industrial-sized sewer and water pipes in the area, preparing for a thus-far undisclosed project.

## CONTROVERSY OVER A PROPOSED LAND SETTLEMENT

As the New York Oneidas' government applied pressure to the last of the traditionalists on the thirty-two acres, it also was moving toward a settlement of the Oneidas' centuries-old land claim involving more than 270,000 acres in and near Madison and Oneida counties. The claim had been adjudicated in the Oneidas' favor by the U.S. Supreme Court in 1974, with particulars to be negotiated (Oneida Indians 1974; County of Oneida 1985).

Three groups of Oneidas (New York, Wisconsin, and Canada) are parties to the suit, in which the Oneidas and the U.S. Justice Department contend that from 1795 to 1840, state and local governments signed twenty-six illegal treaties and several other "purchase agreements" with the Oneidas.

None of those transactions were approved by Congress as required under the Non-Intercourse Acts. These acts, which were passed to prevent just the kind of fraud by states and individuals that cost the Iroquois much of their land base, required federal approval for land transactions that was not obtained. In the late eighteenth century, as at the turn of the millennium, the law often was incidental to moneyed power. The Oneidas' land claims were upheld by the U.S. Supreme Court a quarter-century ago, but as of the year 2002, no land had yet been awarded.

During mid-February, Governor Pataki, Halbritter, and a number of local officials announced a proposed settlement of the long-stalled land claim. Notable by their absence at the announcement were representatives of roughly 20,000 Oneidas living in Wisconsin and Canada.

In the proposed agreement, the Oneida Indian Nation of New York agreed to reacquire no more than 35,000 acres of reservation land, 5,000 of which was required to be "forever wild." The New York Oneida Nation also agreed to purchase no more than 5,000 acres of land during the first ten years after the agreement. In effect,

Halbritter's Oneidas relinquished a claim to 215,000 acres that had been adjudicated by the U.S. Supreme Court.

The proposed agreement contained a major political problem: it excluded from land claims the Oneidas now residing in Wisconsin and Canada, groups much larger in numbers than the New York Oneidas. The Oneidas represented by Halbritter represented less than 5 percent of those who asserted rights in the land claim. While the New York Oneidas asserted a membership of about 1,000 (not counting expelled dissidents), the Oneidas of the Thames, in Ontario, have roughly 5,000 enrolled members, and the Wisconsin Oneidas have 15,000 members. Governor Pataki, in other words, was attempting to settle a 200-year-old claim with the consent of roughly 5 percent of the aggrieved parties.

The agreement offered Oneidas outside of New York State some monetary compensation, although no one seemed certain how much, under what conditions, or whom would pay. The proposed settlement included a proposed payment of $500 million purportedly to be funded by the State of New York and the federal government. Of that amount, $50 million was earmarked for Madison and Oneida counties, with $450 earmarked for the Oneida Indian Nation. To protect the counties, a $100 million fund also would be created by the Oneida Nation and the state to reimburse local governments for lost property and sales taxes as the Oneidas purchased land and took it off the tax rolls. According to a report from Turtle Island Native Network, "If the other two plaintiffs in the land claim suit (the Wisconsin and the Canadian Oneidas) choose to participate in the settlement, they will share in a portion of the remaining $450 million" (Agreement 2002). The exact amount to be shared was open to dispute, ranging from half (an amount cited by the governor's office) to substantially less than that (the New York Oneidas' preference).

The proposed agreement's explicit exclusion of any out-of-state Oneida group from acquisition of any land in New York State infuriated the Wisconsin Oneidas. The Wisconsin Oneidas' General Manager, Bill Gollnick, said, "Our tribal council has said there would be no settlement without an agreement on land. We are talking about our ancestral lands. . . . The majority are here [in Wisconsin] because the state of New York took our land and we have been seeking retribution for seven generations" (Anderson and Corbett 2002). Arlinda Locklear, an attorney for the Wisconsin Oneidas, said that courts had ruled that all of the three surviving branches of the Oneidas have a legitimate claim to the more than 270,000 acres in dispute. The New York Oneidas cannot negotiate for the other two groups, she said. "The cases are not over" (McKinley 2002).

Within a week, the Wisconsin Oneidas had filed twenty federal lawsuits seeking private lands in central New York, all meant to derail the proposed agreement. As the year 2002 progressed, the Wisconsin Oneidas filed several dozen other, similar lawsuits in waves of twenty at a time. By the end of March 2002, sixty such lawsuits had been filed, seeking about 2,000 acres of land. Locklear said that the Wisconsin Oneidas wanted land, but do not intend to establish a reservation in New York. "We are deeply troubled to pursue this course," the Wisconsin tribe said in a written statement. "At the same time, however, we must establish the legal foundations that support our position" (Oneidas File 2002).

Halbritter himself quickly alienated the rest of the Oneidas by calling them "greedy outsiders" (Carter 2002). Halbritter's New York Oneidas further accused the Wisconsin tribe of seeking a New York casino, caring only about money, and showing no interest in their homeland since leaving it many years ago. Halbritter was quoted on the front page of his own newspaper, *Indian Country Today,* as asserting that the Wisconsin Oneidas had been away from New York so long that they had forgotten the location of their homeland, a profound insult (Oneidas File 2002).

On March 28, 2002, Locklear said that the Wisconsin Oneidas would drop the sixty lawsuits if New York State allowed them back into negotiations. "The state has not contacted us since we filed the lawsuits," Locklear said. "The tribe is currently discussing filing more lawsuits." "We believe their demands are unreasonable," replied Suzanne Morris, speaking for Pataki. "We fully expect a dismissal. They have no standing to sue. These cases are frivolous and are a waste of time" (McKinley 2002; Bilodeau March 29, 2002). Within a week of Pataki's assertion that the Wisconsin Oneidas had no standing to sue, a seventy-page decision handed down March 29, 2002, by Judge Lawrence E. Kahn in the Northern District of New York held the opposite. Kahn ruled that both the Wisconsin and Ontario Oneidas had standing to sue. The judge threw out New York State's assertion that the passage of time had erased their ability to sue for land in New York State (McKinley April 3, 2002). During the summer of 2002, a New York judge threw out the Wisconsin Oneidas' suits, agreeing with Pataki's assertion that they had no right to sue individual landowners. The Oneidas appealed.

As controversy continued regarding the Halbritter government's legitimacy, Onondaga Sid Hill was sworn in April 14, 2002, as the new Tadadaho (speaker) of the traditional Haudenosaunee Confederacy council. Chiefs and clan mothers from as far away as Wisconsin crowded into the Onondaga longhouse to witness the eight-hour ceremony. Halbritter and his Men's Council (including his half-brother, Clint Hill) were pointedly not invited (McAndrew 2001).

Early in October 2003, the federal government refused to pay $250 million toward the Oneida Indian land claim, a move that essentially killed a highly publicized settlement agreement announced in 2002. In a one-page letter sent to the land claim mediator, federal negotiators said that they have no plans to put up the money (Coin, October 5, 2003). That money was the foundation of the agreement announced in February 2002 by state and New York Oneida leaders. Gov. George Pataki had said at that time that the three Oneida tribes would be paid $500 million to end the land claim lawsuit. Half of that money was to come from the state, and the other half from the federal government (Coin, October 5, 2003). Federal Department of Justice officials issued a statement shortly after the press conference, saying Pataki had never contacted them before publicly committing the federal government to the settlement.

## DANIELLE PATTERSON'S STRUGGLE CONTINUES

The Oneida Nation's attempts to demolish Danielle Patterson's trailer home on the thirty-two acres continued throughout the summer and into the fall of 2002. Speaking for the Nation, public safety director Arthur Pierce on June 21 told a closed hearing of the Oneida tribal court that Patterson's trailer was "a fire trap," with no smoke alarms, plywood blocking a window in a child's bedroom, and piles of clothing blocking walkway, warmed by electric space heaters (Coin June 22, 2002, n.p.). Pierce was the only witness at the hearing that had been convened to decide whether Patterson's home should be condemned and demolished. Pierce testified that an inspector hired by the Nation had found numerous violations in Patterson's trailer that could not be repaired without completely rebuilding it. These included, according to a report in the Syracuse *Post-Standard,* lack of "a permanent foundation, windows were knocked out, doors [that] didn't fit properly, the heating system [that] didn't work, the kitchen sink . . . not connected to the drain, the roof was leaking, and the floors were rotting" (Coin June 21, 2002, n.p.). "It was obvious," said Pierce, that "the trailer was dangerous unsafe and not suitable for human habitation" (Coin June 22, 2002, n.p.).

Patterson did not attend that hearing. Her lawyer, Barbara Olshansky of the Center for Constitutional Rights in New York City, said she was angered that Judge Stewart Hancock III had held the hearing on the condemnation order without her present. After the hearing, Patterson said, through Olshansky:

> I will not defend a country that has no honor when it comes to their own citizens. I am appalled that the President of this country can spout his anger at terrorism and allow it to run rampant under his nose. . . . God Bless America? United We Stand? For this? For extermination? For loss of human, civil and constitutional rights in the land of the free? Well, maybe the powers that be in Washington D.C. need to wrap themselves in that flag and march to Yankee Doodle Dandy because that means as much as their words. Shame on you United States Government. (Patterson June 22, 2002)

Judge Hancock on August 21 ruled to uphold the demolition order against Danielle Patterson's home, to be carried out no later than September 15. Previously, an appeal hearing in defense of Patterson's home had been scheduled in the same court for September 23, eight days after the deadline of the demolition order. By the legal logic of the court, she faced the possibility of defending her right to live in a demolished home.

The day after the demolition order was made public, Patterson described, via the Internet, squad cars of Oneida police cruising around the house like hungry sharks, with her children in a panic.

> I was called on the telephone yesterday by media and asked for a statement on the . . . appeal of the eviction of my family and destruction of our home. Halbritter's tribal court ordered the demolition of my home to be executed by no later than September 15, 2002. I was shocked, as I was unaware of this decision. I immediately went to Halbritter's legal office to obtain my paperwork on this order. I was denied the demolition order, even though it's publicly accessible.

My three children's and my inherited birthrights of this country are being violated. Although my home meets and exceeds all New York State safety and housing codes, we are going to be made homeless with no financial means as we have to seek all future accommodations at our own expense. I have been a prisoner, unable to leave my home unattended in fear of when the demolition and eviction will occur. There is no justice in this tribal court since Halbritter has final decision over any and all appeals. Because I do not recognize this illegal dictatorship under Ray Halbritter, "whatever it takes" measures are being used against me and the remaining families to remove us from our inherited birthrights to live as Haudenosaunee free people upon our indigenous land. (Patterson August 22, 2002)

By the first week of September, Christian Peacemakers had pitched about a dozen tents in Patterson's yard, answering a call by her to witness the anticipated demolition. The Peacemakers specialize in obstructing violence; they are a project of the Mennonite churches of the United States and Canada and the Friends United Meeting. In addition to their Oneida camp, during the late summer of 2002 the Peacemakers maintained teams in Hebron in the West Bank and in Colombia.

Reports from the scene described "Multi-colored pup tents . . . springing up around the condemned trailer of Danielle [Shenandoah] Patterson at the end of Territory Road" (Peace Camp 2002). As the tent village grew, Oneida Nation spokesman Mark Emery said, "It's never helpful for outside agitators to be part of any situation." Of the characterization that they were "outside agitators," one of the Quakers joked: "Are they afraid we are going to throw oatmeal at them or something?" (Quakers 2002).

Patterson was adamant that the gathering remain peaceful. Mike Running Horse, a participant in the Oneidas for Democracy chat page on the Internet asked, at one point, "Can we bring our weapons and stuff to help out and have a stand off with the Goons like the good ole days? Or are we going to serve cup cakes and cookies to them? Time is getting short ya know. We have AIM [American Indian Movement] friends already up there in the area with weapons who will help if needed . . . even if not needed" (Oneidas for Democracy August 31, 2001).

To rumors of weapons, Danielle Patterson replied:

> Dear people,
> I have stated clearly for all those who have been following this situation that if attending our peaceful stand here the rules clearly stated on every e-mail, letter, and request for legal observers: NO DRUGS! NO ALCOHOL! NO WEAPONS!!!. Our weapon is the truth, and their weapons against us is guns, so who do we think is in the right????? WE need no bullets because the truth is piercing enough!! I have asked everyone to keep on this and flooding the places and people that are able to not only bring attention to end this thing, but so everyone will be able to find out this truth. (Patterson September 1, 2002)

On September 4, advocacy on behalf of the Oneidas by M. Brooke Helman paid off when New York Senator Hilary Clinton ordered the Bureau of Indian Affairs to investigate the situation at Oneida. The same day, Lawrence Kahn, a U.S. District judge dismissed Wisconsin-based Oneidas' land-claims suits. "The time has come to put an end to the tactics long employed by the Oneida plaintiffs in these land-claim actions that are meant only to scare the local population and delay resolution of the ultimate issues," Kahn said in his decision (Judge Rules 2002). The judge's was loudly applauded by Governor Pataki, who said, "This lawsuit was nothing more than an outrageous and frivolous attempt to scare the people of central New York. Judge Kahn has made clear that individual homeowners have nothing to fear as we continue our efforts to resolve the centuries-old land-claim issue" (Judge Rules 2002).

On September 13, with the Oneida Nation's self-imposed deadline for demolition of her home two days in the past, Diane Schenandoah and Danielle Patterson issued an Internet invitation to "all Indigenous peoples and friends" to "a peaceful 'sit-in' and social dance" on Saturday evening [September 14]. "We ask for peaceful witnesses with cameras and camping equipment, food, etc. NO weapons, NO drugs, NO alcohol. This is very urgent and we are praying that people of good minds will join us in our community struggle to maintain our homes" (Schenandoah September 13, 2002).

During the weekend of September 14–15, residents of the camp around Patterson's home prepared to form a human chain, anticipating the arrival of bulldozers. Some of the Christian Peace-makers compared Patterson's situation to that of Palestinians on the West Bank whose homes were demolished by the Israeli Army. "I was in Hebron in a so-called time of peace in 1997," said Anne Herman of Binghamton, New York. "People's houses were being demolished because they didn't have a permit to build, or they didn't have a permit to add on or repair. The same thing is happening here." Herman also said that the Oneida Nation Police resembled Mexican security forces in Chiapas, Mexico, as they put down a rebellion of Mayan farmers who sought land reform and equal rights (Coin September 14, 2002).

The court's self-imposed September 15 deadline came and went without incident, as the Patterson family and roughly 200 guests waited for the bulldozers. They were still waiting for the bulldozers the following Friday when supporters of the traditional Oneidas marched in front of the State Capitol at Albany.

Carrying signs and banging drums, demonstrators gathered out-side the New York governor's mansion in Albany on September 20 on behalf of Patterson's right to her home. About fifty people heard Patterson's sister, Diane Shenandoah, criticize Halbritter as a "dicta-tor" (Kriss 2002). "Acts of terrorism, in the name of 'beautification' and 'sovereignty,' are being committed against the peaceful residents of the Oneida Indian territory by the Oneida Nation police," Shenan-doah said. "Governor [George] Pataki and state leaders need to be made aware of the dictatorship they are supporting by keeping him in this position," Schenandoah said (Kriss 2002). Pataki missed the demonstration; He was in Syracuse to announce $5.5 million for manufacturing jobs and to attend a fund-raiser. Shenandoah said that patrons of the Turning Stone should boycott it. "So you," she said in a reference to Turning Stone patrons, "have the real power to bring about change" (Kriss 2002).

On September 24, the Oneida Tribal Court brought Patterson to trial for alleged assault and contempt of court. Oneida Nation prose-cutor Peter Carmen contended that Patterson had violated a tribal court order by refusing to allow an inspector into her home last November. He has also charged Patterson with assault for kicking a Nation police officer as he tried to restrain her. Carmen asked the judge to sign a warrant for Patterson's arrest and have her brought to court, Heath said. "They clearly planned to end this standoff . . . by bringing her in on that warrant, no matter what it took," Joe Heath, representing Patterson, said (Coin September 26, 2002, n.p.).

Judge Richard Simons refused to sign the warrant and postponed the trial until October 14 after Heath questioned the legality of a contract between the Oneida Nation and the Lewis County Jail. The Nation has no jail of it own. "Lewis County has no authority to receive inmates from the Oneida tribal court," said Scott Steinhardt, spokesman for the state Commission of Corrections (Coin September 26, 2002, n.p.).

Patterson's sister Diane Schenandoah and their mother, Maisie Shenandoah, also refused to testify during August 2002 in the tribal court trial of Oneida Nation Men's Council member Clint Hill, who was accused of harassing them. Hill was acquitted after the two women refused to testify (Coin September 24, 2002, n.p.).

October dawned with Patterson still in her home and roughly three-dozen observers still camped outside. Appeals circulated over the Internet for winter camping supplies. Shortly after 3 P.M. Friday, October 18, 2002, however, Patterson was arrested by approximately a dozen, well-armed non-Indian Oneida Nation Police on a warrant for criminal contempt and assault issued the same day by the Oneida Nation Tribal Court. The warrant's stated intent was to force her attendance at tribal court hearing the following Monday. She was first taken to tribal headquarters where she was denied bail at an impromptu hearing with no legal representation present. She then was transported to a jail 325 miles away in Cambria County, Pennsylvania, 50 miles from Pittsburgh. (The Cambria County jail in Pennsylvania also houses inmates for the Mashantucket Pequot tribe of Connecticut.) Patterson's three children were cared for by her sisters.

"This is an outrage," said Joe Heath, Patterson's lawyer. "Once you have a lawyer in a criminal proceeding you can't have a hearing without that lawyer being notified" (Coin October 19, 2002). Nation Police Chief John Folino said that the hearing that ordered Patterson's arrest was closed. He ordered a Syracuse *Post-Standard* reporter to leave the Nation police headquarters in Canastota where the hearing was held (Coin October 19, 2002). Heath said the hearing should not have been closed. "They like to do things behind closed doors and they don't like to be questioned," Heath said. "They're going to show everybody who's boss" (Coin October 19, 2002). On Monday, October 21, Oneida Nation Police transported Patterson back to the Oneida territory and compelled her to stand trial. Before jury selection began for an ordeal that Patterson was sure would convict her of anything the prosecution requested, she consented to a plea bargain, in which she pleaded guilty to one count of criminal contempt, a

Oneida Nation police officer observes Danielle Patterson-Schenandoah's home on Oneida Territory before demolition, October 22, 2002.

misdemeanor. The agreement freed Patterson of the felony assault charge but compelled her to leave her home within twenty-four hours. She also agreed not to interfere when crews come to demolish the home. Patterson's lawyer said she was forced to submit to the "brute force" of the Nation. "She had no choice," said Heath. "When you hold a gun to somebody's head and say, 'I'm the boss,' what are they going to say? Leadership does not come from raw power being imposed on your people. It comes from compassion for your people" (Coin October 22, 2002).

Oneida Nation Prosecutor Peter Carmen praised the plea bargain as "an important resolution for law enforcement purposes because it ensures a peaceful, nonviolent end to this case" (Coin October 22, 2002). Heath replied that the Oneida Nation's assertion that it is simply trying to ensure safe housing is "a farce" (Coin October 22, 2002). He pointed out that Halbritter's Oneidas employ a large police force but has no fire department. "They claim to be concerned about housing and fire safety of Danielle and her children. But if we look at the result of all this, she is now homeless, they have locked her up

Crane owned by Oneida Nation begins demolition of Danielle Patterson-Schenandoah's home, October 22, 2002. (*Joe Hernandez*)

over the weekend and they have caused her children trauma," Heath said (Coin October 22, 2002).

Shortly after 1 p.m., Tuesday, October 22, heavy equipment crushed Danielle Patterson's trailer on Territory Road. The demolition occurred behind a cordon of Oneida Nation Police who brandished cans of pepper spray and shoved several people, including a teenage girl, away from their police line.

The Oneida Police ordered all media representatives away from the scene before the trailer was demolished. According to Doug George-Kanentiio, who videotaped the demolition, "The police then formed a line with yellow police tape, and kept the supporters and observers about 60 feet away from the trailer." Some family members and Christian Peacemakers stood outside the line and protested the demolition. George said that supporters started singing and verbalized their opposition to the house being demolished. "The supporters got into a shouting match with the Oneida Indian Nation Police, and there was a minor scuffle," George said. "A teenage girl was thrown to the ground" (Bilodeau October 24, 2002). Diane

Schenandoah, Danielle's sister, said that girl was 16-year-old Mary Jean Schenandoah, Danielle's niece. Schenandoah said that the girl was singing and was grabbed by a Nation Police officer and slapped and thrown to the ground (Bilodeau October 24, 2002).

Patterson had moved to an emergency shelter pending location of a permanent home, George said. Schenandoah said Danielle was staying in a "safe location" and would seek to rebuild a home on the thirty-two-acre territory for herself and her three children. Patterson was forbidden to talk with the media as a condition of her release by the Oneida Tribal Court. Patterson did speak privately as bulldozers rolled over her home: "They took my house but they didn't take my spirit," said Patterson, huddled in a blanket on the back deck of the home of her sister, Oneida folksinger Joanne Shenandoah, in Oneida Castle. "I see the demolition of my home as a foundation of our victory, for all these illegal actions will be seen for the world's review" (Coin October 23, 2002, n.p.). Patterson said she doesn't know where she and her children will live. Nation officials have cut off her tribal benefits, so she will not receive $50,000 in housing assistance provided to Oneida members who have not criticized the Halbritter regime. "My first cousin, Ray Halbritter, uses unlawful and inhumane tactics against our people who will not bow to his illegitimate leadership and his casino cartel," Patterson said (Coin October 23, 2002, n.p.). "I was in the house. The house was not a firetrap," said Russell Perler, one of about thirty people who watched the demolition. "It needed some work as lots of houses do, but there was nothing unsafe about where they were living" (Coin October 23, 2002, n.p.).

Coincidentally, one week after Danielle Patterson Schenandoah's trailer home was demolished, the Oneida Nation's business developers announced details describing an expansion of its gambling-based activities, including two championship-caliber golf courses, a 20-story hotel, a separate 100-room luxury hotel, 70,000 additional square feet of gaming space, a spa, and a convention center "capable of hosting thousands" (Corbett 2002).

In the meantime, Joanne Shenandoah was voted "Artist of the Year" by music customers for the Native American Music Awards (nicknamed the "Nammys"), her ninth "Nammy" award. Following a large monetary contribution from the Oneida Nation, the stage presentation of Artist of the Year was stripped from the annual awards program September 7 in Milwaukee, akin to presenting the Oscars without "Best Actor" or "Best Actress" (Schenandoah November 1,

2002). Two months after the awards ceremony, Shenandoah was waiting for her trophy to arrive in the mail.

During mid-November, Halbritter's police served inspection orders on the last five families living on the thirty-two acres. In the meantime, nineteen Oneidas who had been evicted (or faced eviction) filed a federal civil-rights complaint against Halbritter and his associates on grounds that the guise of housing "beautification" project was being used as a cover to suppress political dissent. The suit sought Habeas Corpus and injunctions to prohibit the arrest or detention of the Oneida people or the deprivation of property and denial of their civil rights in violations of the Indian Civil Rights Act. The suit asserted that Danielle Patterson's guilty plea in tribal court was illegally coerced (Oneida Families 2002).

While the last of the families on the thirty-two acres were being evicted, the Oneida Nation filed financial reports required by a bond offering to expand its casino operations. For the first time, the size of the operation was detailed, with some omissions. Annual profits from Turning Stone, Inc., were put at about $70 million. The casino also paid $1.56 million in the fiscal year ending September 30, 2002, to Ray Halbritter's brother Barry for cleaning, trash pickup, and construction. Halbritter's wife Jane headed a company that was paid $233,000 during the same period. The amount paid Halbritter himself was not disclosed (Coin December 19, 2002).

## REMAINING HOMES "INSPECTED" ON THE THIRTY-TWO ACRES

During May 2003, the Oneida Nation issued inspection orders for the remaining trailers on the thirty-two acres, many of which were occupied by members of the Shenandoah family. Five residents (plus Danielle Schenandoah, evicted earlier) also filed a federal lawsuit alleging violation of their civil rights before they protested the inspection orders, which they said amounted to eviction orders. A four-page statement signed by Diane Schenandoah, Vicky Schenandoah-Halsey, Monica Antone-Watson, Elwood Falcon, and Lawrence Thomas said that "Our houses are condemned already." Said Vicky Schenandoah, who lives in one of these houses with her two sons, "It's a charade, a farce" (Coin May 9, 2003, n.p.).

Oneida Court Judge Richard Simons granted the Oneida Nation's inspection orders May 12. The residents said that they were being treated "in the same manner as the Jews of Germany [under Adolf Hitler]." "We have been forced to wear the bright Yellow Star of members not in good standing, which was used to identify and target only us to suffer homelessness under ordinances being enforced against us," they said. The Oneida Nation's prosecutor, Peter Carmen, himself Jewish, said he "deeply resented" the comparison. The Oneida Nation, he said, "Is trying to create better housing" (Coin May 13, 2003, n.p.).

On May 22, 2003, Danielle Schenandoah-Patterson, having outlined her situation at the United Nations Permanent Forum on Indigenous Peoples, asked it to grant her political asylum from the U.S. government and its sanctioned officeholders in the Oneida Nation of New York. She said that the Halbritter government had made her and her family homeless refuges. "I and other families of the Oneida Indian Territory have suffered and are facing further oppressive abuse of civil and human rights including arbitrary arrest, imprisonment and demolition of our privately purchased and owned homes, all as punishment for speaking out against those placed into power by the U.S.," she said (U.S. Citizen 2003).

During the first week of June, Danielle Patterson won custody of her children from the state of New York. The children had been removed from her custody after her home was demolished. Patterson also was offered a new home, a 110-year-old farmhouse in need of repairs in Canastota, eight miles from the thirty-two acres.

A few days after that, during the morning of June 11, a Wednesday, fourteen Oneida Police broke down the door of Dianne Schenandoah's home on the thirty-two acres, to perform an "inspection." According to Schenandoah, the incursion "Took all of two minutes, I had my son follow them around to make sure they didn't break anything I sure hope they didn't plant any bugs or anything illegal. We all feel so violated! We truly don't have any rights, so I called 911 to tell them the rent-a-cops were breaking into my home. It appeared they already knew about the forced inspection when I called" (Schenandoah 2003). The Oneida police also tacked notices on the doors of homes belonging to Vicky and Maisie Shenandoah at the same time. By the final days of June, the remaining dissidents on the thirty-two acres were awaiting eviction orders that they regarded as a *fait accompli.*

The "inspections" continued through the late spring and early summer of 2003. At 9 A.M., Wednesday, June 18, eight Oneida Police broke down the door of a trailer belonging to Victoria Halsey, one of the last dissidents on the thirty-two acres, as she showered. Kathleen Bell

(Owl Dancer) of the Eastern Delaware Nation was sitting in Halsey's kitchen when the door was busted open and Nation Police streamed in with video and still cameras for their "housing inspection." She said, "I've never witnessed such violations of humans rights to privacy and absolute disregard for [the] sanctity of one's home before this day. No effort was made to properly inspect the safety of the Halsey's home" (E-mail 2003). Wesley Halsey, 13, was in his bedroom when Nation Police rushed in. He said he was very afraid and afraid for his mother "since he knows their home is going to be next on the demolitions list, knowing they have no place to go when they become homeless like all the other families and children he grew up [with] in this community that are now gone" (E-mail 2003). The "inspection" took only two minutes as the officers walked through the house.

Seventy-one-year-old Maisie Shenandoah's home was invaded and inspected during the day of July 2, 2003. On Wednesday at 4:15 P.M. Sonny Falcon called to say that the police from Oneida Nation, Inc., had just inspected the home that he and Maisie Shenandoah have lived in for more than thirty years on the thirty-two-acre Oneida Territory. Their home was the last on the thirty-two acres to be inspected. Art Pierce has issued an order that Maisie's large, well-built house had failed inspection and that she must immediately vacate her premises. The notice was posted Friday, July 25, 2003. Her trailer/home is to be demolished and removed by August 20, 2003.

Maisie's was one of the last four dissidents' homes slated for demolition. The families set to be evicted included Diane Shenandoah (single mother, five children), Vicky Shenandoah (single mother, three children), Maisie Shenandoah and the Thomas family (Mohawks). "The sad thing is that every one of the members of the Men's Council, including Ray, has come to my mother for help over the years," said Diane Schenandoah, who lives with four of her five children. "She has never refused to help. For her to be treated like this is a disgrace. I am ashamed of each and every one of them" (Coin July 30, 2003, n.p.).

Oneida Nation officials who inspected the four houses on Territory Road cited numerous problems, including faulty wiring, leaking roofs, and no foundations, Diane Schenandoah said. The family of Maisie Shenandoah and others on Territory Road said that the nation deliberately wrote its housing laws to ensure that their homes would not pass inspection. For example, houses must have foundations, but residents are not allowed to put foundations under mobile homes already on the Territory, Diane Schenandoah said (Coin July 30, 2003).

Vicky Shenandoah, the sister of Diane and Danielle, said that she expected to receive her eviction notice. She said Nation leaders are improperly using profits from the Turning Stone Casino Resort in Verona. "The casino was created to benefit our Oneida people for jobs, education, homes, and better housing, but in our case the casino money has been used to consolidate power by the use of a police force and to make us homeless," she said (Coin July 30, 2003).

During July and August, Danielle Patterson was renting and repairing an old farmhouse in Canastota, New York, eight miles from the site where her former home had been demolished. Several people were volunteering their construction skills to bring the house up to code, painting, installing wiring, and laying a new floor in the kitchen. Danielle's children, Jolene, Clarice, and Preston (who had recently been returned to her from state custody) were painting their own bedrooms. Jolene was eagerly painting her room purple. The volunteers lived in a cluster of tents as they worked on the house.

Eight months after the residents' civil-rights suit requested a preliminary injunction and a writ of *habeas corpus,* Judge Mordue, on August 8, denied their request to stop the evictions. Despite a long history of federal adjudication regarding Native reservations, Mordue asserted that he lacked authority to act on the suit. Furthermore, he ruled that the plaintiffs did not show "severe actual or potential restraint on their liberty," as required for a writ of *habeas corpus* (Judge Won't Stop 2003). Attorney Donald Daines, speaking for the families, said they would appeal to the Second Circuit U.S. Court of Appeals in Manhattan. "We disagree with the holding and the finding and hope the Second Circuit Court will agree with us," Daines said (Judge Won't Stop 2003). The scheduled August 20 demolitions were postponed pending the appeal.

During the third week of October, rumors began to circulate around the thirty-two acres that the Oneida Nation's Court had met in secret days earlier and decided to evict the remaining residents of the Territory. The four remaining families awoke October 22 to find notices taped to their doors, giving them until Sunday, October 26, to vacate their homes. No compensation or housing alternative was offered by the Oneida Indian Nation of New York. The eviction notices were posted despite the pending appeal of the residents' civil-rights suit in the Second Circuit Court in New York City. The

Oneida Nation thus reneged on its prior promise to wait for the court's ruling before moving to evict.

During the ensuing days, the evictions were postponed while lawyers negotiated. In the meantime, bulldozers and backhoes were drawn up nearby. "It's snowing out as I'm speaking here, and they're going to tell me they're going to destroy my house and make me homeless," said Vicky Shenandoah, "Where are my children supposed to go?" (Coin October 24, 2003, n.p.).

Lawyers for the families convinced the Oneida Nation that moving against the families as their appeal was pending would not sit well with the courts, so the bulldozers were withdrawn. The dispute is not about safety or economic consequences but about "the [Nation's] exercise and abuse of power . . . to legislatively enact laws targeting [the families] for punitive treatment not shared or suffered by others of the Nation," lawyer Donald Daines wrote in documents filed with the Second U.S. Circuit Court of Appeals (Kates 2004, n.p.).

As all parties awaited a ruling in the civil-rights suit, the Oneida Nation during January 2004 tried to fire a local public-school teacher who had criticized Halbritter in her classroom.

Stockbridge Valley Central Schools Superintendent Randy Richards said that the district will have to make budget cuts, which could affect programs or personnel, because the Oneida Indian Nation revoked a $120,000 "Silver Covenant" grant, which had been paid in lieu of property taxes. The Oneida Nation revoked the grant after the school district refused to fire Monica Antone-Watson, a teacher's aide at the Stockbridge Valley School, Antone-Watson runs a Native American program at the school. She mentors Native American students, working with them academically and teaching them Native American culture, giving them lessons in nature, and taking them on field trips. About sixty students at Stockbridge Valley are Native American; more than forty of them participate in the program (Rinaldo 2004).

Residents of the Stockbridge Valley School District said that they were willing to make up the loss of a $120,000 grant from the Oneida Indian Nation, even if that meant raising taxes. "If it's not a binding contract, don't accept the money anymore . . . If you don't know you're going to get this money, don't put it in the budget," resident Rick Papa said. "It's troubling that our children's education is being held hostage, in a way, and our board is being blackmailed" (Kollali 2004). Antone-Watson and the school district said that the Oneida Nation is trying to exercise punishment for her political views on Nation leadership. After an internal investigation into the Oneida claim, the board refused to fire Antone-Watson. "We don't intend to budge from our position," Board President Michael Oot said (Kollali 2004).

## CONCLUSION

Like many contemporary conflicts involving economic development in Indian Country, the current contest of wills in Oneida Country presently lacks a firm resolution or conclusion. As this account was being prepared, the remaining traditionalists on the thirty-two acres continued to stand their ground, as the Wisconsin Oneidas continued to file suits against property owners in the area to protest their exclusion from the land deal. The slots at the Turning Stone Casino continued to turn, and money continued to flow. The Shenandoah family continued to raise questions about the Oneida Nation's political legitimacy.

The recent events in Oneida Country take place in a struggle over gambling that has wracked the People of the Longhouse for many years. The debate over gambling as an economic-development tool has been especially sharp in Iroquois country in part because of the two-century-old antigambling tradition of the Handsome Lake religion.

The casino issue has divided the Senecas for several years. Supporters and opponents clashed in 1995, with gambling a major issue in a Seneca Nation presidential election that was decided by three votes. Opposing groups encamped for several months in adjacent Seneca government buildings; the confrontation climaxed with a gun battle that killed three men. The same factional differences were evident seven years later as the Senecas debated plans for as many as three new casinos under their jurisdiction under Gov. Pataki's economic-development plans. The Akwesasne Mohawks, who probably will open at least one casino in the Catskills under the same plans, have been beset by tensions along the same lines. Two men died in factional violence there during 1990 (Johansen 1993).

Dean Howard Smith, writing in *Modern Tribal Development* (2000) erects a theoretical context in which he seeks reservation economic development consistent with "the cultural integrity and sovereignty of the Native American Nations . . . leading to cultural integrity, self-determination, and self-sufficiency" (Smith 2000, x.). Instead of being assimilated into an industrial capitalistic system, Smith believes that Native American traditions can be used to design "a new type of system that incorporates competitive behavior, social compatibility and adaptation, and environmental concerns" (Smith 2000, 77).

The Oneida Nation of New York under the leadership of Ray Halbritter has created a powerful economic motor, but one that has left many traditionalists feeling like strangers in their own land, as they have been evicted from their homes, watched by non-Indian police, and cut off from tribal benefits because they exercised their rights to dissent. Many of them have come to ask: "What kind of sovereignty is this?" Any resolution of this conflict must consider the traditionalists' rights to live in the security of their own homes and their freedom to express their points of view with full benefits of Oneida Nation membership. Only under such conditions will economic development be taking place in a culturally appropriate context.

## REFERENCES

Agreement in principle reached to settle land claim. 2002. Turtle Island Native Network. February 16. http://www.turtleisland.org.

Anderson, T. and R. P. Corbett. 2001. "Oneidas rip offer for land: Wisconsin tribe rejects New York settlement." (*Green Bay*) *Press-Gazette,* February 17. http://www.greenbaypressgazette.com/news/archive/local_2367879.shtml.

Bentwell, M. 2002. Personal communication via Internet from Kahanawake. January 28.

Bilodeau, M. 2002. Protest at nation sparks more controversy. *Oneida Daily Dispatch,* January 3. http://www.zwire.com/site/news.cfm?Newsid= 2886439&BRD=1709&PAG=461&dept_id=68844&rfi=6.

———. 2002. State: Land claims left to courts. *Oneida Daily Dispatch,* March 29. http://www.zwire.com/site/news.cfm?newsid=3697175&BRD= 1709&PAG=461&dept_id=68844&rfi=6.

———. 2002. Home to be demolished soon. *Oneida Daily Dispatch,* September 7. http://www.zwire.com/site/news.cfm?newsid=5279651&BRD= 1709&PAG=461&dept_id=68844&rfi=6.

———. 2002. Patterson's mobile home leveled. *Oneida Daily Dispatch,* October 24. http://www.zwire.com/site/news.cfm?newsid=5803138&BRD= 1709&PAG=461&dept_id=68844&rfi=6.

Campisi, J., and L. M. Hauptman. 1998. *The Oneida Indian experience: Two perspectives.* Syracuse, NY: Syracuse University Press.

Carter, D. L. 2002. Outside tribes dispute talk of land claim deal. Gannett News Service in *Ithaca* (*New York*) *Journal,* March 19, n.p.

Chen, D. W., and C. LeDuff. 2001. Bad blood in battle over casinos; Issue divides tribes and families as expansion looms. *New York Times,* October 28, A-29.

Coin, G. 2003. Court slow to act on eviction appeal; lawsuit was filed in November by lawyer for four Oneida Nation families. (*Syracuse*) *Post-Standard,* August 1, n.p.

Coin, G. 2003. Feds refuse to pay $250M; Oneida land claim pact fails. *Syracuse Post-Standard,* October 5, http://www.syracuse.com/news/poststandard/index.ssf?/base/news-0/1065342930173820.xml.

———. 2001. Nation offers rental house as option. (*Syracuse*) *Post-Standard,* December 19. http://www.syracuse.com/news/syrnewspapers/index.ssf?/newsstories/20011219_rnnatio.html.

———. 2002. Ruling upholds forced inspections: Judge says Oneida Nation's ordinances allow for checks of homes on Indian territory. (*Syracuse*) *Post-Standard,* February 10. http://www.syracuse.com/news/syrnewspapers/index.ssf?/newsstories/20020210_rnrule.html.

———. 2002. No settlement, but Governor, Oneidas and counties to announce "a big plus". (*Syracuse*) *Post-Standard,* February 16, A-1.

———. 2002. Hearing focuses on safety of trailer. Oneida Nation official testifies mobile home had numerous hazards. (*Syracuse*) *Post-Standard,* June 22, n.p.

———. 2003. Oneidas evict four families: Those forced to leave include the aunt of Nation leader Ray Halbritter. *Syracuse Post-Standard,* July 30.

———. 2002. Lawyer says Danielle Patterson doesn't plan to appear at her assault trial. (*Syracuse*) *Post-Standard,* September 24, n.p. http://syracuse.com/news/poststandard/index.ssf?/base/news-2/1032856565100493.xml.

———. 2002. Oneida Nation called unjust: Peacemakers liken Oneida woman's plight to that of Palestinians, Mayans. (*Syracuse*) *Post-Standard,* September 14. http://www.syracuse.com/news/poststandard/index.ssf?/base/news-2/103199253112290.xml.

———. 2003. Tribal court delays eviction; Four families told to leave their homes on the Oneida Nation may remain for now. (*Syracuse*) *Post-Standard,* October 24, n.p.

———. 2002. Tribal jail deal violates state law; Housing of Oneida Nation prisoners in Lewis County forbidden, officials say. (*Syracuse*) *Post-Standard,* September 26, n.p.

———. 2002. Nation jails woman in trailer dispute; Danielle Patterson is ordered held through weekend. Her trial is set to begin Monday. (*Syracuse*) *Post-Standard,* October 19. http://www.syracuse.com/news/poststandard/index.ssf?/base/news-2/103501301360180.xml.

———. 2002. Deal lets nation tear down trailer; Danielle Patterson admits one count in tribal court. Sentencing is Wednesday. (*Syracuse*) *Post-Standard,* October 22.

———. 2002. Nation demolishes trailer; Danielle Patterson agreed to vacate it in plea bargain. (*Syracuse*) *Post-Standard,* October 23, n.p.

———. 2002. Turning Stone's one-year profit: $70 Million. (*Syracuse*) *Post-Standard,* December 19, n.p.

———. 2002. Tribe to ask to inspect five homes. (*Syracuse*) *Post-Standard,* May 9, n.p.

———. 2003. Nation opponents' letter criticized. (*Syracuse*) *Post-Standard,* May 13, n.p.

Cook, R. W. 2002. When "scholars" pour vinegar on Indian wounds. *Indian Time,* February 21, 4.

Corbett, R. P. 2002. Casino, Vernon Downs: The gambling connection. Harness track hopes to cash in on Turning Stone's success. *(Utica) Observer-Dispatch,* October 27. http://uticaod.com/archive/2002/10/27/news/8195.html.

*County of Oneida, New York, et al. v. Oneida Indian Nation of New York State, et al.* 470 U.S. 226 (1985).

E-mail (personal communication) from Victoria Halsey, Oneida 32 Acres, NY June 19, 2003.

Gray, B. A. 2002. The eagle's cry: A warning for native American Indians concerning political trials. A paper presented at the School of Justice Studies, Arizona State University, Tempe.

Hauptman, L. M., and L. G. McLester III, eds. 1999. *The Oneida Indian journey: From New York to Wisconsin, 1784–1860.* Madison: University of Wisconsin Press.

Johansen, B. E. 1993. *Life and death in Mohawk country.* Golden, CO: North American Press/Fulcrum.

———. 2000. Oneida: Historical sketch. In *The encyclopedia of the Haudenosaunee (Iroquois Confederacy),* Johansen and Barbara Alice Mann, eds. Westport, CT: Greenwood Press.

———. 2002. Halbritter, Inc.: A business called a nation. Part 1. *Indian Time,* January 17, 8; Halbritter, Inc.: A business called a nation. Part 2. *Indian Time,* January 31, 8–9; Halbritter, Inc.: A business called a nation. Part 3. *Indian Time,* February 6, 8–9; Halbritter, Inc.: A business called a nation. Part 4. *Indian Time,* February 13, 7. Johansen, B. E., and Barbara Alice Mann, eds.

Johnson, T. 1995. The dealer's edge: Gaming in the path of Native America. *Native Americas* 12:1 & 2(Spring/Summer):16–25.

Judge rules against Wisconsin tribe's claims against homeowners. 2002. Associated Press in *Boston Globe,* September 5. http://www.boston.com/dailynews/248/region/Judge_rules_against_Wisconsin_:.shtml.

Judge won't stop demolitions; Request denied for injunction to keep Oneida Nation from tearing down four homes. 2003. *Syracuse Post-Standard,* August 9.

Kates, W. 2004. Lawyer: Oneidas distort dispute; eviction case is more about abuse of power than safety, families' attorney says. Associated Press in *Syracuse Post-Standard,* January 5, n.p.

———. 1997. Oneidas' enterprises bolster struggling central New York. *(Omaha) World-Herald,* November 5, 22,25.

Kollali, S. 2004. School district won't fire teacher; Stockbridge Valley must now search for money to replace lost $120,000 grant. *(Syracuse) Post-Standard,* January 14, n.p.

Kriss, E. 2002. Halbritter protest held in Albany; Supporters of Oneida Nation woman rally at the Governor's mansion. *(Syracuse) Post-Standard,* September 21, n.p.

McAndrew, M. 2001. Iroquois Nations install leader. (*Syracuse*) *Post-Standard*, April 15, n.p.

McKinley, J. C. 2002. Wisconsin Oneidas vow to persist in their lawsuit, jeopardizing Pataki's settlement. *New York Times*, February 18. http://www.nytimes.com/2002/02/18/nyregion/18ONEI.html?todaysheadlines.

———. 2002. Judge rejects many defenses by New York State in Oneida lawsuit. *New York Times*, April 3. http://www.nytimes.com/2002/04/03/nyregion/03CLAI.html.

Murphy, T. 2001. Nation's home condemnation disputed; Contractor says residence needs some repairs but none that require tearing it down. (*Syracuse*) *Post-Standard*, November 24. http://www.syracuse.com/newsstories/20011124_rmevict.html.

Murphy, T., and G. Coin. 2001. Tension mounts in home dispute; Oneida claims nation police assaulted her; Nation says she attacked police. (*Syracuse*) *Post-Standard*, November 20. http://www.syracuse.com/news/syrnewspapers/index.ssf?/newsstories/20011120_cfonida.html.

Oneida families file federal suit to prevent eviction from reservation homes. Press Release. November 14, 2002.

*Oneida Indians Nation of New York, et al. v. County of Oneida, New York, et al.* 94 S. Ct. 772 (1974).

Oneida Iroquois urgently need legal observers, December 2, 2001. http://mytwobeadsworth.com/OneidaPet3.html.

Oneida Nation Clanmother assaulted by Oneida Nation Police. In personal Communication, Barbara Gray (Kanatiyosh). November 17, 2001, from Oneida Indian Territory, Oneida, NY. http://207.126.116.12/culture/native_news/m19480.html.

Oneida protest: Letter from Danielle Patterson. January 2, 2002.

Oneidas file 20 lawsuits seeking private land. 2002. Associated Press in (*Syracuse*) *Post-Standard*, February 21. http://www.syracuse.com/newsflash/regional/index.ssf?/cgi-free/getstory_ssf.cgi?n0611_BC_NY—OneidaLandClaim&&news&newsflash-newyork-syr.

Oneidas for Democracy chat page, August 31, 2002. oneidasfordemocracy@yahoogroups.com.

Patterson, D. S. 2002. Statement Given at Oneida Indian Territory, Oneida, New York 13421. January 2. http://www.oneidasfordemocracy.org.

Patterson, D. 2002. Personal communication. June 22. oneidasfordemocracy@yahoogroups.com.

———. 2002. Personal Communication. August 22. oneidasfordemocracy@yahoogroups.com.

———. 2002. Personal Communication. September 1. oneidasfordemocracy@yahoogroups.com.

———. 2003. Personal communication via Oneidas for Democracy. July 1.

"Peace camp" grows around condemned trailer in Oneida Nation homelands, N.Y. 2002. Knight-Ridder Business News. August 30. via oneidasfordemocracy @yahoogroups.com.

Quakers at peace camp. 2002. Personal Communication, August 31. oneidas fordemocracy@yahoogroups.com.

Richards, C. E. 1974. *The Oneida people.* Phoenix: Indian Tribal Series.

Rinaldo, E. 2004. SVCS faces budget cuts in wake of grant loss. *Oneida Daily Dispatch,* January 12, n.p.

Schenandoah, D. 2001. Oneida struggle not a "family dispute." Oneidas for Democracy, December. http://www.oneidasfordemocracy.com.

———. 2002. A plea from *Onyota'a:ka* Oneida Indian Territory. September 13. Via Oneidas for Democracy. http://www.oneidasfordemocracy.com.

———. 2003. Personal communication. November 1.

———. 2003. Personal communication. June 11, via e-mail.

Smith, D. 2000. *Modern tribal development: Paths to self-sufficiency and cultural integrity in Indian country.* Walnut Creek, CA: AltaMira Press.

Steinberger, R. 2002. Traditional Oneida fight tribal police to stop demolition of mobile homes. *Lakota Journal,* May 3–10. http://www.lakotajournal.com/Oneida%20Series%20pt%201.htm.

U.S. citizen asks United Nations for asylum from U.S. Government. 2003. Press Release. Oneidas for Democracy, May 22.

# 6

# The Greenville Treaty of 1795: Pen-and-Ink Witchcraft in the Struggle for the Old Northwest

*Barbara Alice Mann*

The Greenville Treaty of 1795 was the culmination of half a century's worth of dedicated efforts by Euro-American settlers to grab the excellent farmland of Ohio. From 1747, when the Ohio Company was formed, through the French and Indian War (1754–1763), Lord Dunmore's War (1774), the American Revolution (1776–1783), the Harmar Campaign (1790), the St. Clair Campaign (1791), and the Wayne campaign (1794), land-greedy settlers had their eyes steadily fixed on fertile Ohio.

War was not the only strategy for seizing the land. The newly formed United States also launched a series of fraudulent "Indian Treaties," always with Ohio in view. Arguably starting with the 1783 Treaty of Paris, which ended the Revolutionary War, these dishonest documents included the second Fort Stanwix Treaty (1784), the Fort McIntosh Treaty (1785), the Mouth of the Great Miami Treaty (1786), and the Fort Harmar Treaty (1789). All of these treaties pressed for concessions that the United States was finally able to wrench from the defeated Union of Ohio Natives in the Greenville Treaty (1795).

There was a good reason that, in 1791, the famed Ottawa speaker Egushawa dubbed these dubious instruments *"pen and ink witchcraft"* (italics in the original, McKee 1792, 11), for they made *reading* truth among the settlers of what was never the *speaking* truth among the

Natives of Ohio. Worse for students of history, pen-and-ink witch-craft continues in Western scholarship today through inertia, since the method of collecting and listing "Indian Treaties" for the standard text, compiled in 1904 by Charles Kappler, was quite haphazard and even self-contradictory. Kappler exercised but minimal care to ensure that only Native-ratified treaties were included (Deloria and DeMallie 1999, 1:181). As a result, to this day, unratified and even heatedly disavowed treaties appear in Kappler as legally clean, while problematic treaties, such as the Greenville Treaty, appear as if no questions ever surrounded them.

In the present instance, despite the fact that they are included in Kappler, *every treaty* waved aloft by speculators and politicians from 1784 to 1789 as supporting the American claim to Ohio had been *specifically repudiated* as spurious by the Native nations involved. These treaties had either been negotiated by duplicitous federal agents with Natives who were not authorized speakers or imposed upon people who later claimed having signed under duress, in literal fear for their lives should they demur. In addition, translators were often inept, so that Natives were told they were signing something quite different from what they ultimately found foisted upon them. U.S. officials were well aware of these failures at the time, explaining why those treaties, though often cited, were never enforced. In the end, it was the very high-handedness of those counterfeit treaties that led to war in the Old Northwest from 1784 to 1794, as squatters, settlers, and speculators, confident in the pen-and-ink witchcraft of their government, attempted to seize Ohio under the terms of invalid accords.

Another facet of pen-and-ink witchcraft concerns the Native presence in Ohio. For too long, old settler propaganda portraying Ohio as open territory or, at best, a common "hunting grounds," has framed discussion of the fraught years from 1747 to 1795. The claim that Ohio was unpopulated was clearly false at the time. Indeed, Ohio was so heavily populated by Native nations that even the deliberate distribution of smallpox blankets in Ohio by order of Lord Jeffrey Amherst in 1763 failed to wipe out its Native population, as intended, despite the fact that *at least* 100,000 Ohio Natives died (Churchill 1997, 154). Had any one of the thirteen colonies lost 100,000 people in 1763, it would have reeled into ruin—the most populous, Virginia, boasted only 120,000 in 1774—yet Ohio continued to be well populated by Natives long after 1763.

Neither was Ohio a mere "hunting ground," for the living space of the various agricultural groups was well known to all Natives of

Ohio, with each respecting the other's boundaries, as is very clear in minutes of councils talks (e.g., Aupaumut 1998; McKee 1792; American State Papers (ASP) 1998, 1:576, 577). As Anthony Wayne, himself, conceded at the Greenville Treaty council concerning homelands in Ohio, "You, Indians, best know your respective boundaries" (ASP 1998, 1:577). It is, therefore, well past time to explode what was, in fact, simply the sales pitch of duplicitous land speculators of the day, who, seeking customers, were eager to assure them that no Native group had anything like prior dibs on Ohio (Clark 1977, 2).

There is also the ridiculous settler contention, still popular, that, historically and prehistorically, there were "no native Ohio Indian tribes" (e.g., Leidy 1929, 4). The Lenape, Cherokee, and Iroquois all anciently claimed Ohio as their homeland, with the Miami and Shawnee moving in later, but still well before the Europeans. In particular, Ohio had been Cherokee, Iroquoian, and Lenape since almost the beginning of their traditions. The keepings of all three say that they started out far to the west and migrated east, in a long-ago time. The Cherokee were the first Iroquoian group to travel east, around four thousand years ago (based on linguistic calculations) settling in Ohio among the "Moon-Eyed" people they found already there (Barton 1798/1976, 9; Haywood 1823, 226, 236–37; Duncan 1998, 199). The Cherokee were still in Ohio two thousand years later, when the Lenape and Iroquois came to stay (Mann 2003, 127–68).

Ohio became the first named homeland of the Iroquois and the Lenape, who were separate but allied peoples. A tradition that the settlers well knew and often recorded states that the Iroquois, along with the Lenape, migrated into Ohio from a distant point west, forcing the Cherokee south to Tennessee in the process (e.g., Lafitau 1974, 1:86; Heckewelder 1876/1971, 50; Schweinitz 1870, 36–37; Clinton 1811–1859, 92; Beatty 1768, 27). Having taken Ohio, the Lenape and Iroquois spent considerable time, a millennium perhaps, in Ohio before an over-population problem occasioned by the great fertility of the area encouraged the Lenape to continue east to Dawnland (Heckewelder 1876/1971, 50). Although some Iroquois likewise went east or south shortly thereafter, an Iroquoian presence always remained in Ohio, namely, the Seneca. The Erie, or Cat People, for whom the great lake of Ohio was named, were western Seneca, as not only tradition but also the *Jesuit Relations* of 1648–1649 make clear (for tradition, Cusick 1892, 31; Johnson 1881–1978, 176; Thwaites 1959, 33:63). Rumors that Iroquoian rights to Ohio were "nebulous" (Horsman 1961, 38) are, therefore, unfounded in anything other than the wishful thinking of eighteenth- and nineteenth-century land speculators.

Under the much later pressure of European invasion, the Lenape were incorporated into the Iroquois League circa 1660 and, for their own safety, moved back into Ohio from eastern Pennsylvania in 1763 (Heckewelder 1818/1971, 120–22). The Miami then occupying their old lands moved over, allowing the Lenape to reestablish themselves along the Muskingum River Valley (ASP 1998, 1:696), because they recognized the tradition that the Lenape had originally lived there, before any Miami or Shawnee had arrived (Brinton 1885/1999, 144).

Notwithstanding these easily checked facts, Western historians have not only accepted the speculators' fabrication of an empty Ohio but also collaborated with it to the extent of gratuitously changing Iroquoian national names from Seneca, Cayuga, and Wyandot to the umbrella slur-term *Mingo* (Mann 2000, 17–18), while determinedly speaking of the Lenape as if they were independent agents, instead of League adoptees speaking through the Cayuga. Ohio Leaguers were not, however, distinct from the New York Leaguers, nor were the Ohio Lenape disassociated from the League. So much a part of the League were both that, even after the Revolution, when wretched-ness in New York slimmed down the focus of the League to one coerced concession treaty after another, the still vigorous Ohio com-ponent complied. Dragged along by the momentum of misery in New York, they attempted to keep faith with League policies that no longer kept faith with them until 1791, when it became clear that the spine of the League was broken. At that point, they saw that their only sane path led to the new "Union" formed by the Ohio nations to defend their homeland.

A formal league created by the allied nations of Ohio to resist a U.S. take-over of the Old Northwest, the Union consisted of the following groups:

1. The Miami peoples, including the Wea and Piankashaw
2. The Shawnee
3. The Ohio Cherokee, misleadingly called "outcast Cherokee" in most documents of the time, although they were, in fact, a legally incorporated group of the Ohio Shawnee (ASP 1998, 1:10)
4. The Three Fires Confederacy, comprised of the Pottawatamie, Chippewa, and Ottawa of southeastern Michigan and northwest-ern Ohio

5. The Haudenosaunee, or Iroquois League, whose nations in Ohio included, primarily, the Seneca, Wyandot, and Lenape, although, for political purposes of dividing and conquering, U.S. commissioners at the time insisted upon separating the Wyandot and Lenape peoples from the League proper and treating with them individually

Each of these nations and confederacies had its own internal policies toward and analysis of events then current, but all shared a clear-eyed recognition of the threat looming on their eastern door: ever-encroaching settlers whom the Natives dubbed "Virginians," "Long Knives," or "Big Knives" (Heckewelder 1818/1971, 179; Aupaumut 1998, 128–29; McKee 1792, 17). None of these appellations was a compliment. The Long Knives were well known to Natives as "a barbarous people" (Heckewelder 1818/1971, 131), who were wont, on the slightest provocation, to congeal into death squads they called "militias." The Long Knives would "in their usual way, speak fine words to you, and at the same time murder you!" (Heckewelder 1818/1971, 219). Natives soon realized that colonial and later U.S. governments covertly used the militias as advance guards of land-grabbing, snuffing out the terms of newly negotiated treaties so that, once a "council fire begins to be kindled, and burn a little bright and clear, *they send the Virginians to kick it out!*" (italics in the original, McKee 1792, 17).

The Long Knives first came fire-kicking in Ohio in 1747, when the wealthiest families of Virginia pulled together into a speculative land venture they christened the Ohio Company. In 1749, George II of England granted the first Ohio Company 500,000 acres west of the Alleghenies for the purpose of encouraging European settlement and trade with the Native nations of Ohio (Kutler, 2003, 6:175). Not to be outdone, in 1748, the jealous Pennsylvania legislature entered into a treaty with the Iroquois, also seeking access to Ohio valley land (Morris and Morris 1996, 75).

Among the first families of Virginia involved in the Ohio Company land speculation were the Washingtons, who had had a vested interest in it since 1747, with a youthful George Washington often acting as their point man (Clark 1995, 22, 27–28). Even in the 1750s, there were allegations that Washington's forays into Ohio in 1753–1754 were not for the advertised purposes of aiding the British empire during the French and Indian War, but for the private purposes of aiding the Ohio Company in its land deals (Clark 1995, 37–40; Fitzpatrick 1925, 1, 43–46, 77, 416, 449). These charges were justified, and after the war, Washington's trip into Ohio in 1770, under cover of surveying it for soldiers' claims after the French and Indian War, was actually for the purpose of surveying lands he wished to stake out for Ohio Company speculation (Clark 1995, 174–76).

This early attempt to seize Ohio was stymied by a massive outcry from the Ohio Natives, who did not at all agree that anyone but themselves had the right to grant—let alone, to sell—Ohio. A distant king who was nothing to them in 1749 certainly had no power over their lands. Thus, the Natives watched Washington's repeated entries in Ohio with foreboding and realized that Amherst, in ordering smallpox blankets handed out, quite literally meant to carry through on his threat to "extirpate" them (Churchill 1997, 154), the better to ready Ohio for European settlement. Protesting loudly enough that the British Crown heard them, the nations of Ohio seeded fears of a bloody backlash should the settlers not desist. The British consequently entered into the Treaty of Fort Stanwix in 1768, effectively denying Ohio Company claims to the land (Clark 1995, 168), as well as the claims of all other Ohio land speculators.

This First Treaty of Fort Stanwix (situated at modern-day Rome, New York) was in the talking stages as early as 1766, when the official speaker of the Six Nations, in an address at Fort Pitt, on May 6, 1766, complained that "it is not without grief that we see our country settled by you, without our knowledge or consent, and it is a long time since we first complained to you of this grievance." The Six Nations demanded that the "settlers must be removed from our lands, as *we look upon it, they will have time enough to settle them, when you have purchased them, and the country becomes yours*" (italics in the original, Butler 1834, 380–81).

After hemming and hawing about, making excuses for having been unsuccessful in rooting out squatters (although it is questionable how hard they tried), the Crown's agents came up with a likely response in October 1768. Sir William Johnson, the King's lead Indian Agent, presented the problem of settler encroachment as springing from a *Native* failure to establish fixed boundaries, as did the Europeans. "You know, brethren," said Johnson,

> that the encroachments *upon your lands* have always been one of your principal subjects of complaint; and, so far as it could be done, endeavors have not been wanting for your obtaining redress. But it was a difficult task, and generally unsuccessful; for, although the provinces have bounds

between each other, *there are no certain bounds between them and you;* and thereby, not only several of our people, ignorant in Indian affairs, have advanced *too far into your country,* but also many of your own people, through the want of such a line, *have been deceived in the sales they had made,* or in the limits they have set to our respective claims. (italics in the original, Butler 1834, 385)

Johnson then proposed a line on a map, formally delineating the boundaries of the Six Nations.

The implication that the Six Nations did not know their own boundaries was just insulting, so that, when their Speakers agreed to some sort of line, they insisted that the line be what Haudenosaunee counselors already saw as the boundary between themselves and the British settlers, based on where Iroquoian territory was well known to lie (Butler 1834, 387). Their line was accepted, with the signed treaty giving it as

> beginning at the mouth of the Cherokee or Hogohege river [the Tennessee River], where it empties into the river Ohio [at Paducah, Kentucky]; and running from then upwards along the south side of the said river to Kitanning [Pennsylvania, on the Allegheny], which is above Fort Pitt [now Pittsburgh, Pennsylvania]; from thence by a direct line to the nearest fork of the west branch of the Susquehanna [in mid-New York, Clearfield County]; thence through the Allegany mountains, along the south side of the said west branch, till it comes opposite to the mouth of a creek called Tiadaghton; then across the west branch, and along the south side of that creek, and long the north side of Burnet's hills, to a creek called Awandae; thence down the same to the east branch of Susquehanna, and across the same, and up the east side of that river to Owegy; from thence east to Delawore [*sic*] river, and up that river to opposite to where Tianaderha falls into Susquehanna; thence to Tianaderha, and up the west side thereof, and the west side of its west branch to the head thereof; and thence by a direct line to Canada creek, where it empties into Wood creek, at the west end of the carrying place beyond Fort Stanwix [Rome, New York], and extending eastward from every part of the said line, as far as the lands formerly purchased, so as to

> comprehend the whole of the lands between the said line
> and the purchased lands or settlements, except what is
> within the province of Pennsylvania. (Butler 1834, 392)

This treaty was really a bill of sale, with the territory ceded in New York the most minutely defined and the Six Nations receiving for it "ten thousand four hundred and sixty pounds seven shillings and three pence sterling" (Butler 1834, 392). Although land farther west was more hazily defined, for all intents and purposes, the Fort Stanwix Treaty of 1768 set the Ohio River as the boundary between the settlers and the League, with all land north of the Ohio River reserved to the Natives. This treaty was signed on November 5, 1768, for the British, by the Governor and Chief Justice of New Jersey, the Commissioner of Virginia, and two Councilmen of Pennsylvania; and, for the Six Nations, by Tyahanesera (Mohawk), Saquarisera (Tuscarora), Conahquieso (Oneida), Chenaugheata (Onondaga), Tagaaia (Cayuga), and Gaustarax (Seneca) (Butler 1834, 393).

It should be stressed that, although all Six Nations of the Iroquois League were present at Fort Stanwix for this treaty, *no other Native nation* was represented or consulted in creating this treaty, nor did any other nation sign it. It is likely that all the Six Nations meant to establish was the line behind which *their* territory lay, on the assumption that the British would negotiate with other nations for any land outside of their agreed-upon boundaries. This was not necessarily the spin put on the treaty by the settlers, however, particularly the Virginians, who instantly interpreted it as conceding all land south of the Ohio River to them.

This generous interpretation was highly questionable. Although the Iroquois did have claim to parts of West Virginia, by 1768, those parts were fast becoming home to a disaffected faction of the Ohio Seneca that had seceded from the League, preferring pure democracy to the League's representative democracy (Mann 2001, 120). In finding their land suddenly unprotected by the League proper, these Seneca were, perhaps, being punished for their gall, but the League could not have intended to sell Kentucky, let alone points south, for it was Cherokee, Shawnee, and Miami country that had never belonged to the Six Nations in the first place. It was not theirs to sell.

Certainly, none of the non-League nations ever agreed, or intended to agree, to the supposed 1768 concession of land south of the Ohio River. Egushawa summed up the non-League view of the matter in 1791, when he pointedly asked Shawnee, Cherokee, and Miami counselors,

> Pray when, or where, . . . did you give or sell your hunting country on the south side of the Ohio? You may perhaps be told, *at Fort Stanwix about twenty-three years ago!* What ignorance!—These unwise chiefs [the U.S. negotiators] must have been children at that time, or been asleep, or they must not have listened to their wise men, whose business it is to relate what has passed in the councils of their fathers! . . . Where did you ever meet the United States in council, on any business whatever! Have you ever yet entered into a covenant of friendship with them? no; you have not. How then have you given them your hunting country? (italics in the original, McKee 1792, 13)

Nevertheless, on the certain premise that all Indians looked alike, eager Virginians rushed into Kentucky and, forthwith, set about trying to grab Ohio, as well. The upshot of the post-Stanwix race for Ohio was Lord Dunmore's War in 1774 (Tanner 1974, 90–94), a direct result of illegal settlement and frenzied speculation in Ohio lands by factions from Virginia and Maryland (Sosin 1969, 11–14), as well as by Crown agents, including Lord Dunmore, himself, then governor of Kentucky (Carter 1987, 55). This speculation resulted in brutal attacks on Ohio Natives by land-grabbers, "in which, as it became well known, the white people were the aggressors" (Heckewelder 1818/1971, 130). Virginians, who "settled on choice spots of land, on the south side of the river Ohio" (Heckewelder 1818/1971, 130), worked to goad the Seneca, Lenape, and Shawnee north of the river into retaliatory violence, which could then be construed as an excuse to attack Ohio, seizing it by right of conquest. Thus it was that

> some, careless of watching over their conduct, or destitute of honour and humanity, would join a rabble, (a class of people generally met with on the frontiers) who maintained, that to kill an Indian, was the same as killing a bear or buffalo, and would fire on Indians that came across them by the way;—nay, more, would decoy such as lived across the river, to come over, for the purpose of joining them in hilarity; and when these complied, they fell on them and murdered them. (Heckewelder 1818/1971, 130–31)

Sanguinary though they were, the Long Knives lost this round, for the Crown could not afford to alienate its League allies, especially since the colonists were clearly gearing up for their Revolution. The 1768 Fort Stanwix boundary of the Ohio River was, therefore, reaffirmed by the 1775 Treaty of Pittsburgh, the last legitimate treaty regarding Ohio.

The next round of attempted invasion came during the American Revolution. Contrary to the popular perception, the Natives of the Old Northwest did not flock to the British at the outset of the Revolution. Wary of this squabble between Europeans, they suspected that the British were professing more enmity than they felt for the colonists and that, should push come to shove, the British were more likely to protect American than Native interests. As the Lenape Speaker, Hopocan, voiced Native doubts in 1781,

> while I [the League] am in the act of rushing on that enemy of yours [the Americans], with the bloody destructive weapon you [the British] gave me, I may, perchance, happen to look back to the place from whence you started me, and what shall I see? Perhaps, I may see my father [the King] shaking hands with the *long knives,* yes, with those very people he now calls his enemies. I may, then, see him laugh at my folly for having obeyed his orders. (italics in the original, Heckewelder 1876/1971, 135)

The British and the Americans were, the Lenape said, like a pair of scissors, whose "two sharp edged knives" looked as if they would "strike together and destroy each other's edges" in closing, but which ultimately cut only what came between them. Thus, the sharp blades of the American and British sides of the Revolution would not destroy each other, but "us, poor Indians, that are between them" (Heckewelder 1876/1971, 104).

It was not trust in the British but disgust with the militias that ultimately turned some Natives to the British. The Long Knives had a bad habit of attacking Ohio Natives without provocation and a worse habit of skinning Natives alive for "hide" from which to make their "leatherstockings," behaviors that incurred the undying animosity of the Natives (Churchill 1997, 185; Mann 2000, 47). Egushawa recounted some of the perfidious horrors visited upon Ohio peoples during the Revolutionary War, especially the premeditated attacks on towns whose men were away, to kill defenseless women and children

(McKee 1792, 17), a profound violation of woodlands law (Mann 2001, 154–55). Egushawa particularly instanced what happened at Fort Randolph near the Ohio River, early on in the Revolution.

The Shawnee had made peace with the militia "shut up" in Fort Randolph, promising to send word, should they notice the English or their allies advancing. As good as their word, the Shawnee sent a delegation under Colesqua with such a warning, urging the "Virginians" to stay put because the English were about. One of the officers decided to sally forth, however, to see the enemy for himself. His foolhardiness led to his being taken, killed, and scalped, as his cohorts looked on from the safety of their fort. In "revenge," the militiamen fell upon their Shawnee allies inside the fort, murdering them all. Not content with simple murder, however, the enraged militia skinned the poor counselors, taking special care to ensure that Colesqua was alive while the operation was performed on him (McKee 1792, 17). Such events as these (and there were many more) turned the Natives from neutrals into allies of the Crown. It was a matter of self-preservation.

General Washington certainly did his level best to seize land that the Ohio Company had been eyeing greedily for thirty years. His plan was to starve out the Iroquois Leaguers and the Shawnee, even as he had starved the League in New York, through massive, murderous assaults on their bread-baskets (Mann 2001, 148, 150). As many Natives as possible were killed in these forays, and not a few skinned, as towns and fields were burned, so that the Haudenosaunee began to call the Americans, "the town destroyers" (ASP 1998, 1:140). By 1781, scarcity had reduced the Ohio defenders to walking skeletons, left to "creep about looking for Food," too weak even to drag out of town the carcasses of animals that had fallen dead of starvation in the village streets (Wallace 1958, 188). The people thus weakened, Washington closed in for the kill, drawing up a "Memorandum" on May 1, 1782, outlining his plans to assault and seize "Canada," as he termed Ohio and southeastern Michigan (Fitzpatrick 1938, 24:198).

As the war was drawing to a close with Ohio no more in the bag than it had been in 1776, General Washington authorized an attempt to wipe out the Lenape, who were sitting on some of the finest farmland available, in the Muskingum River valley (Fitzpatrick 1938, 24:48; Mann 2001, 158). Leading the Pennsylvania militia on March 8, 1782, Colonel David Williamson seized 98 starving women, children, and old folks—90 of them Christian converts—as they attempted to alleviate starvation at Upper Sandusky by retrieving the previous fall's harvest, which the women had hidden in pits around their capital of Goschochking (modern-day Coshocton, Ohio). Clubbing, scalping, and burning to death ninety-six of the harvesters, the militia rampaged back to Pittsburgh, crowing up its great victory over the "warriors" of the mighty League in the pages of the *Philadelphia Gazette* (Johansen and Mann 2000, 118–22). In fact, the mission had had a strong motive of piracy from the outset, for the militia was after the food and goods held by the Lenape. It was, however, for purely personal profit that militiamen later sold, as "souvenirs," shaving strops they had made from the tanned hides of skinned Lenape (Heckewelder 1876/1971, 342). Due to such crimes against humanity (and there were many more), the Seneca named Washington's campaign of terror, fire, and famine "the Hollocaust [*sic*]," long before that word became identified with another genocide in the twentieth century (Parker 1926/1970, 126).

Signed in 1783, the Treaty of Paris officially ended the mayhem of the American Revolution, and in a way highly satisfactory to the former colonists, for, in one of the most boneheaded moves in the annals of Western diplomacy, Great Britain blithely handed over to them the Old Northwest (modern-day Ohio, Indiana, Illinois, Michigan, and Wisconsin). Apparently, the British negotiators were working from a bad map, the John Mitchell map of 1755, which seriously underrepresented the size of the territory they thus conceded (Sword 1985, 11; Berkeley and Berkeley 202; for reproduction of map, see Berkeley and Berkeley 1974, 204–5). Soon recognizing their blunder and the weakness of the colonists' United States under the Articles of Confederation, the British dragged their feet in evacuating their forts in the Old Northwest. Instead, intent upon continuing their control of the lucrative fur trade around the Great Lakes, they set about looking for excuses to invalidate the Treaty of Paris, touching off a cold war with the United States that continued until 1812, when it burst into open hostilities (Walsh 1977, 4).

The British map-mistake was exceeded only by the British snub to their Native allies at the Paris conference. Not even the Iroquois League, which had so valiantly exhausted itself in the war, was invited to sit down at the treaty table in Paris, so that no Native interests whatsoever were represented in the talks. Had Native counselors been present, they would never have conceded the Old Northwest, especially since the Natives had actually *won* the war in the west, out-generaling George Washington at every turn in Ohio, largely under the military leadership of the Wyandot war chief, Katepakomen ("Simon Girty") (Johansen and Mann 2000, 111, 114).

Consequently, news of the terms of the Treaty of Paris left the Natives "thunderstruck," as Sir Frederick Haldiman reported back to the Crown in 1782 (Sword 1985, 17). When the British assured the Natives that the Old Northwest was, indeed, to be given to the settlers, they erupted in fury, charging the British with a treacherous alliance by which they had inveigled the Natives into their "own ruin" (Sword 1985, 17). In fact, the Ottawa flatly refused to believe the terms of the Paris Treaty as read to them at a council in 1783, accusing the British of "telling us lies" (Sword 1985, 17).

The Natives were as strident with the Americans, when they tried to press their claims to the Old Northwest under the treaty. Egushawa bespoke the outrage of Ohio Natives at the presumptuous arrogance of U.S. agents in claiming "to be *the sole and absolute sovereigns* of all the territory ceded to them" by the Paris Treaty (italics in the original, McKee 1792, 14). This vast "territory" extended from the Upper Great Lakes in the north to Spanish Florida in the South, and all included lands from the Atlantic coast west to the Mississippi River. "Here are bounds for you, my friends," Egushawa jeered, "for *these sole and absolute sovereigns!*" (italics in the original, McKee 1792, 14).

In 1786, the Six Nations, Cherokee, Three Fires, and Miami banded together, in what was the first act of their budding Ohio Union, to send an official protest against the Treaty of Paris to the new government of the United States. In their letters of November 28, 1786, and December 18, 1786, the "United Indian Nations" announced that they were "disappointed, finding ourselves not included" in the Paris treaty talks and complained that both the British and the Americans had misled them as to the content of the talks at the time (ASP 1998, 1:8). They demanded that any further talks be conducted with "the general voice of the whole [Native] confederacy, and carried on in the most open manner, without any restraint on either side," particularly as concerned "any cessions of our land" (ASP 1998, 1:8). Requesting a conference including the entire Union in the spring of 1787, they demanded that, in the meantime, the United States "prevent your surveyors and other people from coming upon our side the Ohio river [*sic*]," the boundary as set by the only treaty they recognized, the 1768 Fort Stanwix Treaty (ASP 1998, 1:9).

If they were not answered directly, these forthright letters of grievance were not ignored, either. They motivated the United States, on October 26, 1787, to order Arthur St. Clair, Governor of the Old Northwest, "carefully to examine the real temper of the Indian tribes" in Ohio. Supposing he should find that temper "hostile" to the settlements "forming in that country," he was to hold "as general" a council as possible with "all the tribes." He was also instructed that, even though "the purchase of the Indian right of soil is not a primary object of holding this treaty, yet you will not neglect any opportunity that may offer, of extinguishing the Indian rights to the westward, as far as the river Mississippi" (ASP 1998, 1:9).

This was not necessarily the response that the Union had hoped to garner with its complaints, and the blatant attempts by the United States to forward its unwavering goal of land seizure had, by 1790, hardened Native resentment into an eyeball-to-eyeball confrontation with the Americans over the Paris treaty. The Seneca chiefs, Shinnewaunah ("Cornplanter"), Half-Town, and Great-Tree, flatly informed the United States that New York, western Pennsylvania, and Ohio "belonged to the Six Nations; no part of it ever belonged to the King of England, and he could not give it to you" (ASP 1998, 1:142). Egushawa took the argument a step beyond simple rejection of British rights in 1791, by reasoning that, since the settlers could not have inherited land that the Crown had not owned in the first place, all that the United States had acquired at Paris was the duty to keep the terms of treaties previously negotiated by the British—in particular, the 1768 Treaty of Fort Stanwix, which set the Ohio River as an inviolable boundary line between settlers in the south and Natives in the north:

> If they [the U.S. agents] tell you that they have conquered the right of our father, the King of England, I say then they have only conquered his right, and can claim no more than that treaty at Fort-Stanwix gave to him: and if they claim all the rights which that treaty gave to the king of England, let me ask you whether they are not equally bound by all the conditions of the treaty? If they are so bound, let me ask them further, whether they have complied with those conditions? You know they have not, and they know they have not! (McKee 1792, 13)

Despite St. Clair's continual pooh-poohing of the Union, statesmen and Congressional leaders feared its complaints and its gathering strength. Both left them struggling for policy tacks that would ultimately yield the lands they sought without calling upon an exhausted American populace for renewed military action. They were all agreed that Ohio could not be foregone. Land was of utmost importance to the shaky settler government, if it was to enjoy any stability, for Ohio was vital to seeding the economic and political base of the new country. Veterans of the Revolution had been promised land in payment for their services, yet no land was free in the older, settled states. Without Ohio, the house of cards that was the United States under the Articles of Confederation was set to crumble. The government felt, therefore, that it had no choice but to defend the Treaty of Paris. The only question was how to do so effectively.

In 1783, Congressman James Duane, Chairman of the Indian Affairs Committee, not to mention a major land speculator in the Mohawk Valley, recommended a peace council or councils to establish just boundaries with Northwestern Natives. This was to be accomplished by forcefully informing them that they had lost their lands at the Paris treaty table. Duane's idea of a just boundary transferred most of Ohio to the United States, on the excuse that Natives owed the United States reparations for having vigorously defended their homeland from invasion during the Revolution (Horsman 1961, 36)—a rationale ultimately written into Article III of the Greenville Treaty (Kappler 1904/1973, 40). Duane also reasoned that Ohio could be used to pay off Revolutionary veterans. His policy would, incidentally, do no harm to the prospects of the Ohio Land Company.

George Washington noticed as much. In 1783, he showed that he, too, had given considerable thought to how the Ohio country might be obtained through sly and shifty means rather than through bloodshed. In a letter of September 7, 1783, that was later used as a policy instrument by the United States, Washington replied to Duane's request for policy thoughts on the taking of Ohio. Primarily alert to rivals of the Ohio Company, Washington recommended preventing stray "land jobbers, speculators, and monopolizers" from rushing in "to aggrandize a few avaricious men" (Sparks 1855, 8:477). Instead, Washington proposed that the land be taken in a methodical way.

First, Natives of the Old Northwest were to cough up all their "prisoners" (Sparks 1855, 8:478), i.e., adoptees, many of whom had no wish to return to "civilization." The repatriation demand had the surreptitious effect of reducing the muster of troops that the Union could raise to resist new invasion. Next, Washington suggested that the Americans make it clear to the Natives that, as the losing party in the Revolution, they could "be compelled to retire" with the British "beyond the [Great] Lakes," as Duane had recommended, but that, being compassionate, Americans looked upon the Natives "as a deluded people" whose "true interest and safety must now depend upon *our* [settler] friendship" (italics in the original, Sparks 1855, 8:478).

This friendship would be evinced by agreeing upon a "boundary line between them and us," a line, cautioned Washington, that should neither "yield" nor "grasp at too much," but strive to look conciliatory to the affected Natives (Sparks 1855, 8:478–79). He urged that no overt effort be made to remove the Six Nations from New York, as it would certainly lead to war, for he believed that the land could more easily be taken through treaty concessions, a tactic just as fruitfully pursued in points west (Sparks 1855, 8:479). Such a strategy would allow for the land to be seized "upon legal and constitutional ground" instead of through the hasty, shady, and illicit means then being used by the lower classes (Sparks 1855, 8:480). This, Washington felt, was "the cheapest, as well as the least distressing way of dealing" with the Natives (Sparks 1855, 8:480). He even gave a rough set of boundaries that anticipated the actual boundary lines drawn by the Greenville Treaty, twelve years later, showing how long and how consciously plans to grab Ohio had been afoot (Sparks 1855, 8:483).

Grasping the drift, if not the intricacies, of the budding American position on the Old Northwest, settlers began pushing into eastern Ohio, demanding protection that they were not receiving from the government, due to its lack of money and military might. The insecure situation of these earliest settlers left them open to the blandishments of the Spanish who, from their colonial seats in Florida and the Mississippi delta, were encouraging the more westerly settlers to separate from the United States, to become an independent sovereignty under Spanish rule. The Spanish had, or at least pretended to have, sufficient influence over Natives to ward off attack. Under these pressures, some settlers in the west began pushing for secession from eastern rule, a matter of deep concern to U.S. officials (Walsh 1977, 8–9).

Swift action was required to retain the loyalties of these western settlers, and it came in a famous series of laws called the Northwest Ordinances, passed in 1784, 1785, and 1787. The 1784 Ordinance (the handiwork of Thomas Jefferson) tried to set up a gaggle of self-governing districts with Congressional representation. The Ordinance of 1785 set up the "Seven Ranges" in southeastern Ohio, sections of land to be sold in small parcels, to the enrichment of eastern land companies. (It became the model of the later Homestead Act of 1862.)

A reborn Ohio Company was deeply involved in the writing of the third and final Ordinance of 1787. Since the rights of the original Ohio Company had been based on a grant from the Crown, the company fizzled after 1783, for the new United States had no interest in recognizing Crown actions, especially as they dealt with the Old Northwest. The demise of the first required the birth of a second Ohio Company, which occurred in 1786. This second Ohio Company enjoyed the specific charge of selling and settling the Seven Ranges in eastern Ohio, its primary act being to found Marietta, Ohio, in 1788 (Morris and Morris 1996, 571–72).

Superseding that of 1784, the Ordinance of 1787 set up a territorial government that allowed sections of the Old Northwest to enter the Union as new states once they hit a population of 60,000. Although the 1787 Ordinance is justly renown for outlawing slavery in the Old Northwest and for establishing the precedent of new states entering the union on an equal footing with the original states, the Ordinance set another, less worthy precedent of never questioning the right of settlers to occupy the land. A consequent flood of illicit immigration was loosed, adding to the influx that had been growing steadily since 1783, without any honest treaties or negotiations with the Native proprietors of the land. Instead, illicit treaties seeming to hand over Ohio were coerced, cajoled, and created out of whole cloth.

The first of these fraudulent treaties sought to quiet the Native demand that the 1768 Fort Stanwix treaty line be observed. The simple method was to create a second Treaty of Fort Stanwix, which would set boundaries more to the liking of the United States. Accordingly, Article III of the 1784 Treaty of Fort Stanwix fixed the western boundary of Pennsylvania as the border of Iroquois, belying the League's full extent through Ohio, "so that the Six Nations shall and do yield to the United States, all claims to the country west of the said boundary," i.e., Ohio (Kappler 1904/1973, 6). The loss of Ohio was the dire retribution visited upon the League for its resistance during the Revolution, and it made the Seneca chiefs, Shinnewaunah, Half-Town, and Great-Tree, cry out, "What have we done to deserve such severe chastisement?" (ASP 1998, 1:140).

The consistent Native account of the 1784 treaty talks was one of American threats and intimidation. In a letter of grievance officially filed with the U.S. government in 1786, chiefs Shinnewaunah, Half-Town, and Great-Tree made it clear that the treaty had been thrust upon the Leaguers in New York. Having seen how utterly the British had sold out Native interests at the Paris conference, League counselors "made haste" to a council fire, which the Americans had "kindled" at Fort Stanwix (ASP 1998, 1:140). Once there as a captive audience, the chiefs charged, the United States

> told us that we were in your hand, and that, by closing it, you could crush us to nothing, and you demanded from us a great country, as the price of that peace which you had offered us; as if our want of strength had destroyed our rights; our chiefs had felt your power, and were unable to contend against you, and they therefore gave up that country. (ASP 1998, 1:140)

Egushawa characterized the matter in almost identical terms in 1791, claiming that the American negotiators told the League that *"the United States were mighty and powerful! That all the Indian nations, compared to them, were but as one child to an hundred warriors! That they held all our nations in their hand, by closing of which they could crush us to death!"* (italics in the original, McKee 1792, 13). The chiefs' and Egushawa's statements accord well with the American delegation's own account of the matter. Negotiators did not hide their having informed the League chiefs that they held "sole power" over them (Sword 1985, 24).

Accession to this treaty could be coerced by the United States because the League counselors at Fort Stanwix were little other than hostages of the government at this point, forced into signing whatever was placed before them, however much their League brethren in Ohio might protest. Cowed though they were, the New York counselors resisted stealthily. Ever the weapon of the dispossessed, sabotage appeared in the scanty count of counselors who showed up for the Stanwix treaty talks (ASP 1998, 1:141; Sword 1985, 23, 24). Some who did appear did not necessarily support the treaty. The Seneca Sagoye-watha ("Red Jacket") urgently and courageously opposed it, beseeching the Ohio Iroquois to continue the fight (Galbreath 1925, 1:241).

Nevertheless, the kangaroo council went along with the extortion, so that, after the talks, the signatories came in for harsh criticism. New York Leaguers were shocked at "how great a country" they had been "compelled" to give (ASP 1998, 1:140). Neither was it just other League peoples who rebuked "those chiefs with having given up that country," for the "Chippewas, and all the nations who lived on those lands westward, call to us, and ask us, Brothers of our fathers, where is the place you have reserved for us to lie down upon?" (ASP 1998, 1:141). The Americans had, indeed, as Egushawa announced, been able to "make dogs of our relations, the Shawanese, Delawares, Wiandots [sic], and six nations" (McKee 1792, 16). Chiefs Shinnewaunah, Half-Town, and Great-Tree obliquely agreed, recording their humiliation that the United States "compelled us to do that which has made us ashamed" (ASP 1998, 1:141).

These grievances did not go unattended: The League formally disavowed the Fort Stanwix Treaty of 1784. When it was finally submitted to a legitimate Six Nations council at Buffalo in 1786, the counselors impatiently repudiated it, stating that none of the Natives present had been deputed to negotiate (Sword 1985, 26). Realizing that it could not enforce the treaty, should matters come to a fighting head, the United States quietly laid it aside. Nevertheless, the 1784 Treaty of Fort Stanwix appears to this day in Kappler as a legitimate instrument (Kappler 1904/1973, 5–6).

Bogus as it was, the Fort Stanwix treaty had the far-reaching effect of splitting the Iroquois League. Thoroughly disgusted with what U.S. negotiators had been able to extract from browbeaten and spurious delegates, the Mohawk Chief Thayendanegea ("Joseph Brant") negotiated a tract of land in Ontario, Canada, as a reward from the British for his people's services during the late Revolution. There, he set up what he considered the true, undefeated Six Nations. Gathering like-minded Iroquois to his new League in Canada, he then set about rallying all the Iroquois, particularly those in Ohio, to join in a fight against the Americans. To press this end, he traveled to a major council on the Great Lakes in 1785, at the same time that he prevailed upon his high position with the British to feel out Crown support for Ohio resistance (Wilson 1909, 40–41).

The 1784 Fort Stanwix Treaty was also important in forging a tactic thereafter regularly employed by the United States to ease Natives off their land, i.e., negotiating individually with the Natives, rather than as a collective. The Ohio Union strongly protested this strategy in 1786, noting that those of its nations present had done "everything in our power" at the 1784 treaty of Fort Stanwix "to induce" the United States to consult with the entire Union at all councils, rather than picking nations off, one by one (ASP 1998, 1:9), but to no avail. Instead, the United States consciously used League loyalties of the Iroquois in Ohio to drive a wedge between the Iroquoian and Miami factions of the Ohio Union. In 1788, Arthur St. Clair, first governor of the Old Northwest, specifically stated that he deliberately treated separately with the "more westerly tribes" (the Shawnee and Miami) and "the Six Nations" (with whom he correctly included "the Wyandots"). On the one hand, he did this to fan the flames of "a jealousy that subsisted between them" and, on the other hand, to resist the precedent of "appearing to consider them as one people" (ASP 1998, 1:10).

The next fraudulent treaty took place at Fort McIntosh in 1785. Built in 1778 thirty miles northwest of Fort Pitt, Fort McIntosh had been used throughout the Revolution as a staging ground for military action against Ohio Leaguers holed up at the impregnable Wyandot capital of Upper Sandusky, Ohio (Wilson 1894, 19). Although they never took Upper Sandusky, Revolutionary militias did inflict considerable damage on the countryside. Partly for its intimidation factor, then, the United States chose Fort McIntosh as the site of its next treaty council.

In attendance were the League nations of the Lenape and Wyandot, along with the Chippewa and Ottawa, two of the three nations of the Three Fires Confederacy. Since no hostages were taken from the Ottawa or the Chippewa as surety against the repatriation of their "white prisoners" (Kappler 1904/1973, 6–7) and since the third nation of the Confederacy was absent, there is every reason to believe that the Three Fires representatives were there merely as observers, and not as participants. Signed on January 21, 1785, the Treaty of Fort McIntosh ceded to the United States all land east and south of Cuyahoga River in northeastern Ohio and west to the Big Miami in southwestern Ohio, where it ran into the Ohio River—in other words, all but the northwestern portion of modern-day Ohio (Kappler 1904/1973, 7). (Northwestern Ohio was the Great Black Swamp, land that the settlers did not figure was worth much.) Not in payment for the land, but simply "in pursuance of the humane and liberal view of Congress," the treaty pledged to deliver "goods," unspecified in type or amount, to the "different tribes," equally unspecified (Kappler 1904/1973, 8).

Well might the Three Fires wish to distance themselves from such a concessionary treaty. So outrageous was its cession of nearly all of Ohio that, when the Union discovered the treaty's terms (no doubt, from the Three Fires observers), it determined to put the Wyandot and Lenape negotiators to death as traitors. The Union did not carry through with this plan solely because the Lenape and Wyandot explained the duress they had been under at the treaty talks. They had signed the treaty "to *save* their lives," they told the Union (italics in the original, McKee 1792, 9). Terror had been the main negotiating tool of the Americans at this council, with the U.S. negotiators assuring the Wyandot and Lenape "that every nation should be destroyed who would not enter into the like agreement" (McKee 1792, 9). The Iroquois had seen enough of American-led genocide during the Revolution to believe that threat credible. The majority of the Union kicked these threats aside, however, and frightened that any attempt to force the terms of the McIntosh Treaty would result in a war it was unprepared to wage, the United States laid this pen-and-ink witchcraft by, for the time being. Although the United States had more sense than to attempt to enforce it and whereas the Union immediately repudiated it, the Fort McIntosh Treaty of 1785 is also listed in Kappler as legitimate (Kappler 1904/1973, 6–8).

The Shawnee and their incorporated Cherokee clans were clearly in no happy mood over the U.S. attempt to write them out of existence in the Fort McIntosh Treaty, as though none of the entailed lands had ever been theirs. Interestingly, as pressed as they had been at the Fort McIntosh council, the Wyandot agreed with their neighbors, contending that the Shawnee and Cherokee must be guaranteed their traditional lands. So insistent was this demand that the Wyandot actually received a codicil to the treaty (Kappler 1904/1973, 8), prepared and inserted by Arthur St. Clair, himself.

Officially termed a "Separate Article," this codicil was pure pen-and-ink witchcraft on St. Clair's part. Although he made it clear in his letter of May 2, 1788 to President Washington that the "claim of the Wyandot nation to lands reserved to the Shawanese, was strongly insisted upon by them," St. Clair had it merely "inserted at the bottom" of the Treaty, "by way of memorandum," so that is was not technically part of the treaty (ASP 1998, 1:10). St. Clair acknowledged to Washington that this land claim of the Shawnee had "always been held up," but he felt so little bound by his own codicil as to propose that the President order forts erected on the self-same lands (ASP 1998, 1:10). The codicil was clearly a sop to quiet down the Shawnee and Cherokee, who were otherwise disposed to defend their lands vigorously.

George Washington was surprised that the Wyandot and Lenape acquiesced to the Fort McIntosh Treaty, and many Western historians have since echoed his wonder (Sword 1985, 28). The signing of the treaty by Ohio Leaguers cannot evoke exclamation from any who understand the workings of the Iroquois League, however. Being members of the Iroquois League, the Ohio Lenape and Wyandot observed the Great Law, or Iroquoian Constitution, under which it is unconstitutional for member nations of the League to negotiate at cross purposes with its official policies (Parker 1916, Article 25, 37). Although Thayendanegea was actively courting the Ohio Iroquois to join his rival League in Ontario throughout this dilemma, they were not at that time prepared to help him weaken the U.S. League by negotiating a treaty that contradicted the terms to which their New York kin had already agreed.

Consequent of their Constitution and their loyalties to their New York brethren, the Lenape and Wyandot of Ohio believed that they had no choice but to cut an agreement in 1785 at Fort McIntosh, Ohio, analogous to that signed by their relatives at Fort Stanwix, New York, in 1784. To have done otherwise would have been to dismember the League. By the same token, once the Buffalo council repudiated the 1784 Fort Stanwix Treaty, the Ohio League believed that its contingent Fort McIntosh Treaty was simultaneously dissolved.

The despised treaties of 1784 and 1785 were followed in 1786 by a third, the Treaty of Mouth of the Great Miami River, negotiated with the Shawnee. This treaty was an effort to seize from the Shawnee land that had been guaranteed to them in the codicil to the Fort McIntosh Treaty. Egushawa scoffingly characterized talks at the Great Miami as further extortion, in the style of the Forts Stanwix and McIntosh debacles, born of "more gracious papers, writing, belts, and messages; ordering you to repair to their forts under the pretext of entering into a covenant of friendship with you; but in reality to treat *you*, as they did those whom they frightened at fort McIntosh, on Beaver-creek, to sign what they call *a deed*" (italics in the original, McKee 1792, 8–9).

Legitimate Shawnee counselors were enticed to the Mouth of the Miami treaty talks, to see whether the proffered peace "were to be done consistently with the safety of their women and children" (McKee 1792, 9). They soon found that it could not. By the Union account, "The commissioners of the United States came, as though to frighten our relations; and repeated to them the old stories" of

England's defeat requiring the forfeiture of Native lands. They "required the Shawanese nation to sign an acknowledgement [sic] thereof, and to give hostages!," a gentle demand hotly declined by Kekewepellethy, the appointed speaker of the Shawnee. Indignant at the high-handed tactics and the degrading terms, Kekewepellethy stormed, "I tell you brothers, what you say is not true! you never conquered any of us" (McKee 1792, 9). To the hostage demand, Kekewepellethy replied that "you do this no doubt to insult us, because you know that we are poor, defenceless [sic], and ignorant; and because you are, as you say, strong and mighty, and that you have all our nations within your hand; by closing which, you can crush us all to death! and that all our nations are but as one child compared to an hundred [sic] warriors! and you tell me you have a million of warriors!" (McKee 1792, 9).

When the United States continued to press its demands, Kekewepellethy defiantly stood his ground: "I will give you no hostages! neither shall you have our lands!" (McKee 1792, 10). Looking about, then, at the hardening faces on the American side of the table, he continued, "I suppose now, you will strive in earnest to conquer our lands; and to conquer me! I tell you brothers that unless you come to your senses these rivers must run with blood, for we will never submit to be your dogs!" Kekewepellethy then offered peaceful and honorable co-existence, instead, "on proper terms," reiterating that "I will neither give nor sell you my lands; nor shall you take them from me" (McKee 1792, 10).

With this, Kekewepellethy slapped down black (war) wampum, and in such a way as to cover up the American map that was splayed across the council table. Richard Butler, "a Virginian," promptly and "*contemptuously*" whisked the wampum off "with his cane" (italics in the original, McKee 1792, 10; Sword 1985, 30). The angered Commissioner barked back that the U.S. government would supply the Shawnee counselors with "ten days provision of flour," enough to see them "beyond the immediate reach of the tomahawk of the United States" but that, thereafter, government forces would attack the Shawnee at will (McKee 1792, 10). This response was profoundly hostile. Ten days was barely enough time for the Shawnee delegates to get home, while threatening to attack Emissaries of Peace was a major violation of woodlands law, which granted automatic safe passage to all counselors, regardless of how a council turned out (Mann 2001, 39).

Outraged as much that their status as Messengers of Peace was ignored as that the United States had proven intractable, the authorized Shawnee delegates retired from the council and headed home in high dudgeon. A few older chiefs stayed behind, however. They were headed up by the elderly chief Moluntha, who took over as speaker. Although he was emphatically *not* the Shawnee's designated negotiator—Kekewepellethy was—and regardless of the fact that *none* of the remaining chiefs was an authorized delegate, Moluntha and his cohorts signed the mortifying treaty on January 31, 1786 (Kappler 1904/1973, 17). Belying what had transpired, the Commissioners falsely affixed the name "Kakawipilathy" (Kekewepellethy) to the treaty, as though he, too, had signed (Kappler 1904/1973, 17), a spiteful act of pen-and-ink witchcraft. This treaty, too, is listed in Kappler as pristine (Kappler 1904/1973, 16–17).

Moluntha and his cronies paid dearly for their presumption, not because the Union took revenge but because the towns of those signatory chiefs were *the very first ones* brutally attacked by the militias, barely eight months after the treaty was signed (McKee 1792, 11; Sword 1985, 38–39). In fact, as recently as May 1786, the signatory Shawnee chiefs had received a reaffirmation of U.S. friendship (Sword 1985, 38). Notwithstanding, on a mission of trumped-up vengeance in the fall of 1786, the Kentucky militia charged headlong through their "friendly" Shawnee towns, all north of the Ohio River, burning, looting, scalping, and killing. Foolishly certain that his part in the Treaty of the Mouth of the Great Miami afforded him and his town protection, on October 6, 1786, Moluntha went forward to meet the militia under a white flag. For his trouble, he found the sword of Captain Hugh McGary embedded in his head and his scalp lifted forthwith by the same gentleman (Sword 1985, 39), in pursuit of the U.S. bounty on Native scalps.

This trio of fraudulent treaties—the 1784 Fort Stanwix, the 1785 Fort McIntosh, and the 1786 Mouth of the Great Miami River—hardened Native resolve into the self-defensive political action of forming an Ohio Union committed to stopping invasion. Confederacies were no new thought among woodlanders. As the Mahican Aupaumut pointed out on August 2, 1791, the "good Ancestors" of the Lenape and Mahicans had "many, many years ago" entered into such a Union (Aupaumut 1998, 101). Similarly, the Iroquois League had been formed in 1142, and it was modeled on a still older confederacy of Iroquois north of the St. Lawrence (Mann and Fields 1997, 105, 142–46; Johansen and Mann 2000, 269–70).

In historical Ohio, a wampum alliance had long been maintained by the Iroquois League, but with the outcome of the Revolution and, worse, the Fort Stanwix Treaty of 1784 and the Fort McIntosh Treaty of 1785, the League lost its leadership role, sending its old alliance network into limbo. Between 1783 and 1786, therefore, Ohio Natives floundered, yanked from one outrageous treaty council to the next, until the wanton attacks on the signatory Shawnee instilled a new resolve. In November and December 1786, the Iroquois League (including the Wyandot and Lenape), the "Twichtwees" (i.e., Miami), the Shawnee and Cherokee, the Three Fires Confederacy, and the "Wabash Confederates" (i.e., the Wea and Piankashaw, both Miami peoples) pulled together at an initial meeting near the mouth of the Detroit River (ASP 1998, 1:8). There, they sketched out their common cause, issuing a ringing grievance statement in all their names to the new United States (ASP 1998, 1:8–9).

Between 1786, when it was conceived, and November 1791, when the Ohio Union was ratified in an historic council, the Natives of Ohio hashed matters over among themselves, and not always cordially. Early bickering erupted, with some bitter words directed toward the League nations by the Shawnee, Cherokee, and Miami. Since the League had dragged them into Revolution against the Americans, other Ohio nations held the League accountable for the disastrous turn of the Treaty of Paris and the handover of the Old Northwest. It was the "Five Nations and the English" that "did lay a foundation for our ruin," they charged; it was these two that "gave us the tomahawk, and the English" had been "at the bottom of this war" to retain their homelands "ever since" (Aupaumut 1998, 115). Ideally, the Shawnee, Cherokee, and Miami wanted to "throw the hatchet back to the English and to the Five Nations," to let them slug out the difference. Bitterly, they suggested that true justice called for the League and the English to "lose their lands," rather than themselves (Aupaumut 1998, 115). However, they recognized that, consequent of the ill-fated Revolution, they had been left holding the bag as much as the League, leaving them struggling in its aftermath to "retain all our lands just as much as before the war" (Aupaumut 1998, 115).

It is commonly alleged in Western histories of this period that the British were largely behind the Native resistance to the U.S. invasion of the Old Northwest, with the Crown egging the Union on, fanning the flames of its resentment into war (e.g., Horsman 1961, 40; Sword 1985, 231). This is, however, a facile and insulting caricature of Native counselors as naive puppy-dogs, panting to go fetch for their master. It owes more to the white supremacy of the period, untested for bias in the present, than to any actual research into Native analysis at this critical juncture. Such arguments simply assume that the portrait of brutal savages attacking innocent bystanders at the British behest is correct, whereas the brutal, mindless attacks on innocents mainly happened the other way around. As Egushawa indignantly rebutted the stereotype, "I declare them [the settlers] to be the aggressors, notwithstanding their pen and ink work!" (McKee 1792, 14).

The British-made-them-do-it argument also relies heavily upon depictions of Joseph Brant, Simon Girty, and Alexander McKee as "British agents," allowing historians to glide all too easily past the fact that Thayendanegea ("Joseph Brant"), Katepakomen ("Simon Girty"), and Wampomshawuh ("Alexander McKee") were *Native Americans*— Mohawk, Wyandot, and Shawnee, respectively—working for *Native* causes (for Katepakomen's Wyandot identity, see Johansen and Mann 2000, 112; for Wampomshawuh's Shawnee identity, see Aupaumut 1998, 105). It was not the British who were using the Natives to further Crown causes, but Thayendanegea, Katepakomen, and Wampomshawuh who were using the British to further Native causes.

Indeed, far from a slavish dependence on the Crown, in the wake of British treachery at the Treaty of Paris, Union nations were acutely aware that they could not depend upon British promises, and said as much in their speeches. They even looked for diplomatic ways to maneuver the British into action on their behalf. For example, Deunquat, a lineage chief of the League Wyandot of Ohio, who was to become a revered leader of the Ohio resistance well into the 1820s (Mann 2000, 312–13), proposed to the Union that it "apply to your father the king of England for his mediation" between the Union and the United States "making known to him the preliminaries, on which you wish for peace with the United States," i.e., that it ask the King to demand that the United States recognize British treaties, including the 1768 Fort Stanwix accord. This step would "authorize and justify his [the King's] interference" (McKee 1792, 21–22). In other words, Deunquat cleverly proposed using English rhetoric of support to force the British into the fray, necessarily on the Native side, a move sure to give the United States something to think twice about before opening fire in Ohio.

It does not require British intrigues, deeply laid, to explain the Union. The intransigence of the new Union had been entirely brought on by the injudicious posturing of the U.S. Commissioners at earlier treaty talks followed by the wanton attacks of militias on peoples at treaty peace with them. In particular, Union members were incensed by the arrogant U.S. claim to be their "sole and absolute sovereigns," by the intimidating habit of calling councils at military forts, and by the duplicitous dealings of pen-and-ink witch-craft resulting. The Union advised its members to

> let them know, whenever you do enter into a covenant chain of friendship with them, that *you and the southern nations* are the sole and absolute sovereigns of all the lands within the limits described, which they have not acquired by *honest purchase*—and you must let our elder brethren [the United States] know that you will prescribe the mode of sale, if ever you make any; and that *your* united councils, within your own country, *distant from their forts,* shall be the place where all future agreements shall be made; and that too in the presence of those who will not suffer *pen and ink work,* to cheat or deceive you. (italics in the original, McKee 1792, 14)

Incredibly, Arthur St. Clair remained oblivious of the analysis, mood, and even the existence of the Ohio Union. In 1788, he deluded himself so extravagantly regarding the force of the rapidly coalescing Union as to assure President Washington that he was "persuaded their general confederacy is entirely broken" (ASP 1998, 1:10). This foolish conviction emboldened him to push through the final straw by way of pen-and-ink witchcraft, the 1789 Treaty of Fort Harmar. Had St. Clair truly had his plump finger anywhere near the pulse of Native Ohio, it would have been singed by the fire he was playing with.

The Fort Harmar treaty purportedly went forward with the authorized participation of the Iroquois (Seneca, Wyandot, Lenape), the Three Fires Confederacy (Ottawa, Chippewa, and Pottawattamie), and the Sac nations. However, St. Clair knew—or certainly ought to have known—what John Heckewelder pointed out, that only four of the twenty-seven "chiefs" who supposedly signed the treaty were, in fact, recognized lineage chiefs (Sword 1985, 74). Furthermore, only two of the Three Fires were present, the Ottawa being absent (McKee 1792, 11), meaning that no accord could be struck with them. Finally, those non-League peoples who attended did so in violation of the express councilmanic directives of their respective nations (McKee 1792, 11). Nothing about the Fort Harmar Treaty was legal, yet this heatedly disavowed "treaty" is still listed in Kappler as legitimate (Kappler 1904/1973, 18–23).

The Native account of the Fort Harmar treaty talks asserts that those few from "several nations" who "undertook to attend" the Fort Harmar council did so "although their chiefs forbad them; knowing well that our elder brethren [The Euro-Americans] would require more of that *pen and ink witchcraft,* which they can make to speak things we never intended, or had any idea of, even an hundred years hence; just as they please" (italics in the original, McKee 1792, 11). Furthermore, contrary to the pen-and-ink witchcraft that had twenty-seven "chiefs" in attendance, tradition recalls, aside from League counselors, only eleven men present at most, none of them chiefs, and all of them self-appointed: two Sac, three or four Pottawatamie, three or four Chippewa, and one Shawnee. By Native account, these men *"went to look at the treaty,* but without any authority whatsoever from their respective nations" to sign (italics in the original, McKee 1792, 11). Egushawa remarked of the matter, "Here was no doubt fine work, although we knew little or nothing of the matter, except that it completed the evil deeds of our elder brothers [the U.S. Commissioners]; for since that time we have heard of nothing but threats to chastise us all! even those whom they cajoled to sign their papers, have not escaped!" (italics in the original, McKee 1792, 11).

Notwithstanding the completely unauthorized embassy of the supposed "chiefs" at the Fort Harmar council, St. Clair rushed the treaty through, from talks beginning on December 15, 1788, to signature on January 9, 1789. In essence, this new treaty did little more than repeat, almost verbatim, the purported land cessions of the 1784 Fort Stanwix, 1785 Fort McIntosh, and 1786 Mouth of the Great Miami Treaties. Worse, so self-deluded were the American authorities regarding actual Native sentiment on the Fort Harmar Treaty, that General Josiah Harmar actually lauded it as having had the salutary effect "at last to divide the savages in their councils" (Sword 1985, 75). St. Clair and Harmar even congratulated themselves on having checkmated Thayendanegea and his Canadian League with the Harmar treaty, an estimate of the situation so spectacularly wide of the mark that it could only have led to the total destruction that both men met with at the hands of the not-so-divided "savages." The only possible outcome of so much pen-and-ink witchcraft was war.

The United States was unready to wage war in 1789, however, despite the policies tending in that direction that were being eagerly hatched by President Washington and his Secretary of War, Henry Knox. A main concern on the part of the United States was to organize the attack in such a way as not to appear to be the aggressor. On October 6, 1789, George Washington admitted that war against the Union could only be sold as "just on the part of the United States" should the Union thumb its nose at U.S. demands for so-called peace treaties. Unfortunately for this rationale, some few Natives always showed up for the treaty councils. Another possibility did loom, however. Washington pinned his hopes for a just war on continued "incursions" by Ohio Natives against the settlers, for then the United States would be "constrained to punish them with severity" (ASP 1998, 1:97).

The matter was equally fraught for Henry Knox, who elegantly reasoned in his Report of June 15, 1789, that two alternatives were before the United States: "raising an army, and extirpating the refractory tribes entirely;" or "forming treaties of peace with them" that the settlers would supposedly be forced to observe (ASP 1998, 1:13). Peace treaties were really political cover, however, allowing the United States to establish "its character on the broad basis of justice," while covertly waiting for illegal settlers to push the Natives into retaliation (ASP 1998, 1:97). Then, should the Natives "persist in their depredations, the United States may with propriety inflict such punishment as they shall think proper" (ASP 1998, 1:97). Military action was, unfortunately, a lengthy and costly option.

Knox frankly acknowledged that cost was the true stumbling block to outright genocide: "the finances of the United States," were unequal either to removing the "Wabash Indians" farther west or to mounting a military campaign against them. Knox personally favored removal over extirpation as the cheaper solution, reasoning that removal would "have nearly the same effect" on the Natives as direct genocide. Were they "removed from their usual hunting grounds, they must necessarily encroach on the hunting grounds of another tribe, who w[ould] not suffer the encroachment with impunity—hence they destroy each other" (ASP 1998, 1:97). In other words, the more westerly nations would do the United States's dirty work for them.

For some reason, Western scholars doggedly insist upon interpreting these genocidal policy statements as genuine if halting attempts at peace. At most, they view them as confused, as did

William Walsh in 1977, when he termed the peace/war policy "schizophrenic" (Walsh 1977, 27). These statements were neither confused nor schizophrenic, however, but profoundly cynical, calculating, and devious. They coolly weighed the monetary costs of genocide against the time costs of fraud, to decide which combination of approaches might best seize Ohio at the lowest price, at the same time that it maintained a veil of rectitude over the naked face of greed. Moreover, both Washington and Knox knew full well what Egushawa so tartly observed in 1791, that the series of bogus treaties from 1784 through 1789, promulgated through "necessity and compulsion," could "never bind either side longer than convenient" (McKee 1792, 12). Everyone involved understood that the treaties were merely a holding action until the United States could find the money to wage all-out war.

As it turned out, the "frontier" settlers resolved the matter for the United States by provoking just those "incursions" the United States needed to justify war. Kentuckians were especially forward in the endeavor, while promulgating hysterical war propaganda about bloodthirsty savages mercilessly attacking poor, blameless settlers. St. Clair was a handy messenger at this stage, forwarding the endless demands that the United States smite the Union, lest the settlers take matters into their own hands. "It is not to be expected, sir," he ominously informed President Washington on September 14, 1789, "that the Kentucky people will or can submit patiently to the cruelties and depredations of those savages; they are in the habit of retaliation, perhaps, without attending precisely to the nations from which the injuries are received; they will continue to retaliate, or they will apply to the Governor of the Western Country (through which the Indians must pass to attack them) for redress." A failure to respond, warned St. Clair, would undermine settler loyalty to the United States (Smith 1882, 2:123–24).

St. Clair then asked Washington to revive an earlier Congressional resolution to allow him to "call upon Virginia and Pennsylvania" for their militias to add to his regular troops, thus showing the Kentuckians that he was neither impotent nor careless of their concerns (Smith 1882, 2:124). The Union's push against illegal settlement was precisely the "just" cause that Washington and Knox had sought, so that, on September 16, 1789, Washington complied with St. Clair's request by asking Congress to reactivate the July 21, 1787, and August 12, 1788, resolutions calling up the Pennsylvania and Virginia militias (Smith 1882, 2:124 [n1]).

Washington specifically instructed St. Clair to take stock of whether the Union was inclined to peace and, if not, to make ready for war (Smith 1882, 2:125–26). St. Clair responded with his hope to use the League Wyandot to influence other Ohio natives to peace, investing, as he did, "great confidence" in their "friendly disposition." He assured Knox that "their influence over many of the tribes" was considerable," although the "Miamis, and the renegade Shawanese, Delawares, and Cherokees, that lay near them" were, he feared, "irreclaimable by gentle means. The experiment, however, is worth the making," he continued. Once more, St. Clair directly identified the true reason behind the peace overtures, the fact that, "at any rate, I do not think we are yet prepared to chastise them" (Smith 1882, 2:132).

By now undeceived as to the true mood of resistance brewing in Ohio, Knox rather desperately engaged eastern Natives to send emissaries ("friendly Indians") to the Ohio Union, in an attempt to cool its call for war (ASP 1998, 1:139). Among the ambassadors thus dispatched was the eminent League speaker, Sagoyewatha ("Red Jacket"). St. Clair's hopes for the Wyandot aside, the League had by that time lost much of the respect that the United States was counting on. At a Union council in 1791, one Shawnee chief sarcastically demanded that Sagoyewatha explain to everyone just "what was [the League's] business with the white people these several years" (Aupaumut 1998, 121), clearly hinting at League collaboration with the United States against the Natives of Ohio. This insinuation must have been galling to Sagoyewatha who, privately, cheered on the Ohio Union (Parker 1926/1970, 136–37). Unfortunately, when he attended the Ohio councils of 1791, it was in his official role as the Speaker of the Seneca Clan Mothers, who had instructed him to argue for peace, so that he could not present his personal point of view on the matter. Thus, he swallowed many acrid taunts, without making any noticeable headway for peace among Unionists.

Accompanying Sagoyewatha were several emissaries of the Seneca, Cayuga, and Onondaga. The Shawnee speaker next turned scornfully on them, accusing them of spying for the United States: "We have acquainted you of our Business with the western nations [the Union]. Now you may return home, and tell your white people all what you have heard." Noting that the United States had "laid these troubles" and could, therefore,"remove these troubles," the Shawnee speaker explained the only terms of peace acceptable to the Union, an immediate withdrawal of the United States from

Ohio: "if they take away all their forts and move back to the ancient line [of 1768], then we will believe that they mean to have peace, and that Washington is a great man—then we may meet the U.S. at Sandusky, or kausaumuhtuk [*sic*], next spring" (Aupaumut 1998, 121).

Hendrick Aupaumut ("Captain Hendricks"), a Mahican who had fought for the Americans in the Revolutionary War, was also dispatched by the U.S. government on this mission to carry its message of "peace" to the Ohio Union. Like the League emissaries, he was utterly unsuccessful in trying to coax the people into peace talks. Throughout his embassy to the Union, his efforts were undermined by the continual lifting of the "alarming voice," that is by messengers rushing headlong into town and, after they "breathe little," giving news of yet more depredations and massacres perpetrated by settlers and militias (Aupaumut 1998, 97, 98, 102, 104, 107, 124). Given Egushawa's maxim "never to treat of peace with an enemy advancing and holding his tomahawk over our heads," it was generally considered "not a time then to talk, or to think of peace!" It was "only a time to act like men and warriors!" (McKee 1792, 19).

Well might Knox watch developments closely—and the Shawnee were correct that many of his emissaries were spies—for these Union actions allowed him to certify that his conditions for a "just war" had been met. On December 8, 1790, Knox transmitted to Congress increasingly frantic pleas for military aid that he had been gathering up from settlers in Virginia, Kentucky, and Ohio since the spring of 1789 (ASP 1998, 1:84–92). One-sided accounts all, they failed to detail the depredations of the settlers against the Natives, even though Knox had openly acknowledged in his report of June 15, 1789, that "the injuries and murders have been so reciprocal, that it would be a point of critical investigation to know on which side they have been the greatest" (ASP 1998, 1:13). The pure imbalance in the 1790 transmissions showed that the ultimate policy intention of the United States was never an evenhanded assessment of the situation. They were merely intended to justify the orders soon forthcoming to General Josiah Harmar and Governor St. Clair to proceed militarily against the Union forces.

The precipitating reason for the U.S. military incursions into Ohio was that the Miami peoples, in collaboration with the Shawnee and Cherokee, had set up a headquarters along the Wabash and Scioto Rivers. From this access point to the Ohio River, they were able to "make attacks upon every boat which passes, to the destruction of much property, the loss of many lives, and the great annoyance of all intercourse from the northward." The situation had gotten so extreme by the spring of 1790, that the settlers generally held that "if this party is not dislodged and dispersed, the navigation of the Ohio must cease" (ASP 1998, 1:91).

In authorizing action in 1790, Knox conveniently forgot something else he had freely admitted in his 1789 report, that "the United States have not formed any treaties with the Wabash [Miami] Indians; on the contrary, since the conclusion of the war with Great Britain, hostilities have almost constantly existed between the people of Kentucky and the said Indians" (ASP 1998, 1:13). It was these very Miami, with whom the U.S. had no treaties, who were shutting off travel along the Ohio River, the better to staunch the flow of illegal settlers and speculators into their lands. Since no treaties had been coerced from them ceding their lands, they were well within their rights to turn the squatters away.

To get around this conundrum, the United States went to doublespeak, labeling the Union troops guarding the Ohio River "*banditti,*" an eighteenth-century term for petty criminals. (To confuse the issue further, the term *banditti* was as equally applied to lumpen settler elements as to problematic Natives. See, e.g., Sparks 1855, 8:481.) Having thus redefined the Union as a criminal enterprise bent upon mugging lawful settlers, the government could treat the Union soldiers as outlaws not armies, thus allowing it to fight a police action without declaring open war in Ohio.

In May of 1790, operating on poor intelligence from St. Clair, Knox downplayed the strength of and support for the so-called banditti, identifying the "bad people" as Shawnee, Cherokee, and Miami desperados and asserting that the entire cadre "may not exceed two hundred" (Smith 1882, 2:146), a picture that conflicted seriously with settler claims of huge casualties and significant property losses suffered at the hands of at least a thousand "warriors." Egushawa found this contradiction comical and scoffed at the inconsistency of featuring a crazed, blood-thirsty banditti who—although only about 200 in number and presumably on the lam, even from their own people— still somehow managed to have "killed and taken prisoners, fifteen hundred men, women, and children, from Kentucky alone, beside [sic] as many more from other quarters, with two thousand horses, and goods to the value of fifty thousand dollars" (McKee 1792, 15). If the settler reports of grievous damages were true, however. Egushawa rejoiced, counting them as encouraging news, for "If a despised *banditti* can do thus," how much more could a disciplined, righteous, and consolidated Union army do? (italics in the original, McKee 1792, 15).

Based on St. Clair's ludicrous underestimate of the strength of the Union at 200 men, on May 27, 1790, Knox authorized a force of "about one hundred Continental troops and three hundred picked militia, mounted on horseback for the sake of rapidity" to put them down (Smith 1882, 2:146). In further orders, on June 7, 1790, Knox authorized General Harmar "to extirpate, utterly, if possible, the said banditti" of Ohio, taking care not to injure the "friendly, or even neutral" Natives (ASP 1998, 1:97, 98). The frenzied war preparations that followed seemed to belie the supposed strength of the "banditti" at a mere 200, for Harmar gathered up 1,453 men (Sword 1985, 96). To cover, St. Clair quietly upped his estimate of Union strength to a more likely "1,100 warriors," with more in the wings, should the Wyandot, Lenape, and "St. Joseph and Illinois Indians" have chosen to join in, thus making Harmar's recruitments appear more reasonable (Smith 1882, 2:182).

To St. Clair's further suggestion that new forts be set up north of the Ohio River to awe the Natives, Knox cautioned that the United States was in no position to supply or defend forts that would have little other effect than to drag the British into the fracas, a widening of the war that the United States was not prepared to face. Instead, Knox authorized an expedition into Ohio to "punish" Natives holding up along the Wabash for their attacks on settlers and for "conniving" to attack others and for "refusing to treat with the United States when invited thereto" (Smith 1882, 2:181).

Thus it was that, on September 26, 1790, Brevet General Josiah Harmar invaded north into Ohio from Fort Washington, just outside of Cincinnati, to attack the Miami, while Major John Francis Hamtramck went to attack the Shawnee on Wabash (Walsh 1977, 19–20). The upshot was that both men were driven back. Hamtramck blamed his failure on the ostensibly poor discipline of his militia and a shortage of supplies (Walsh 1977, 21–22), but it actually stemmed from a stiff Native resistance, which kept supplies cut off while demoralizing the militiamen. Harmar was also stifled, in this instance, by the strategic genius of Meshikinoquak ("Little Turtle"), who trapped and then decimated Harmar's militiamen, under the command of Colonel John Hardin, at Eel River, near Kekionga, on October 19, 1790 (Sword 1985, 106–8; Perry 42–43). Next, on

Meshikinoquak (Little Turtle). (*Smithsonian National Anthropological Archives*)

October 21, 1790, instead of retreating like a sane General, Harmar allowed Hardin to talk him into another foolish raid, with Hardin again at its head. This one turned out just as disastrously for Hardin as his first foray. Once more, the nemesis of the U.S. Army was Meshikinoquak (Sword 1985, 111–15; Perry 44–46).

Rather than admit that Harmar had sustained a humiliating defeat, St. Clair sent a gussied up report back to Knox on October 29, 1790, claiming that a great victory had been won over the Union (Sword 1985, 120). Then again, on November 6, 1790, after he certainly knew the truth, St. Clair sent Knox yet another sanitized report, claiming that "the savages have got a most terrible stroke" (Smith 1882, 2:190). For his part, despite admitting that he had suffered "heavy" losses—183 killed and 31 wounded—Harmar also reported back to Knox on November 4, 1790, as though his mission had been a success (ASP 1998, 1:104, 106). News of the actual state of affairs did eventually filter back east, however, probably courtesy of the literal exodus of deserters skedaddling away from Harmar's pitiful excuse for an army (Sword 1985, 120).

Unable to concede that a Native American commander had beaten the stuffing out of a Euro-American commander in a fair fight, the United States brought Harmar up on charges of failure of leadership, in an inquiry technically requested by Harmar (ASP 1998, 1:178). Although Harmar was eventually acquitted, to this day, Western historians attempt to lay Harmar's smashing defeat to desertions in his ranks, poor supply lines, bad militias—*any*thing but the real reason, the tactical genius of the Miami chief, Meshikinoquak.

In a froth over Harmar's disgrace, Knox set about estimating the cost of raising an army sufficient to gain a final victory over the Union. He placed it at about $100,000 for an army 2,128 strong (ASP 1998, 1:113, 118–20), which based on St. Clair's revised estimate of 1,100 Union men, gave the United States a numerical advantage of almost two to one. In further preparation for hostilities, on March 4, 1791 St. Clair was made Major General of the U.S. Army and appointed to head up this ambitious campaign (St. Clair 1812/1971, 1).

Disdaining to take the field himself at first, in May of 1791, St. Clair sent Brigadier General Charles Scott araiding, with 750 Kentucky militiamen (Smith 1882, 2:213). Although ordered to attack the Miami at the Wabash River, Scott detoured to the northwest, there to attack undefended Wea (Miami) towns. This sudden change of plans owed to Scott's discovery that 2,000 Union troops were waiting for him along the Wabash. Realizing that the Wea men were all at the Wabash, Scott knew there would be only women, children, and old folks in the towns. These, he proceeded to massacre on June 1, 1791, a deed he covered up in his report by referring to his victims as "warriors" (Sword 1985, 139–40). St. Clair was no more discriminating in his accounts, crowing over Scott's supposed victory over the Union army and congratulating the Kentucky militia (Smith 1882, 2:222–23).

Next, on July 31, 1791, St. Clair sent Major General Wilkinson, to "assault" Miami and Kickapoo villages along the Wabash River in "surprise" raids (Smith 1882, 2:227–29). Wilkinson rather quickly and literally bogged down, because he refused to place faith in the perfectly accurate directions of his guides (ASP 1998, 1:134). Stubbornly selecting his own route, arrived at by guesswork, he got his troops gloriously lost, as he led them slogging through swamps, "which injured several of [his] horses exceedingly" and left him dismounted, "to the arm-pits in mud and water" (ASP 1998, 1:134). Other than muddying his men, Wilkinson managed very little, besides killing six men, two women, and a child, while capturing thirty-four more Natives at the Eel River and taking one Lenape prisoner, even though the United States was supposedly at peace with the Lenape. Since the towns he came across were mainly evacuated before he could enter, he satisfied himself with burning them and the people's crops (ASP 1998, 1:134), before finally straggling home in August, fairly bedraggled. For all the boastful tone of his report to St. Clair, Wilkinson did little more than lame his horses and galvanize Union resistance by his indiscriminate killing and imprisonment of noncombatants (ASP 1998, 1:134; Smith 1882, 2:236, 237–39). Ineffectual as this foray was, it, too, was cried up as a victorious campaign.

Finally, St. Clair attempted an assault, himself. He commissioned 1,150 troops, although he did not expect, or even want, more than 750 to show up. Despite the government's obvious impatience that he be underway yet that summer, before the weather turned cold and wet, he piddled about so that it was not until late September 1791 that he began massing and moving his troops out of Fort Washington and not until October that he was finally in the field (St. Clair 1812/1971, 25–26; Smith 1882, 2:243, 244). To allow for successful invasion, he was supposed to create a series of forts to "curb and overawe" Union members, starting from his home base at Fort Washington (right outside of Cincinnati) and proceeding north to the Miami town that formerly stood where Fort Wayne, Indiana, is today (ASP 1998, 1:112; Wilson 1909, 56). Instead, he moved just outside of Fort Washington to build Fort Hamilton, where he then dawdled for another month, blaming the usual culprits: desertion, slow or no supplies, difficult progress, and personal illness (Smith 1882, 2:245–46; 249–51).

The Union heard the war drums at Fort Hamilton and beat a few of its own in reply, coalescing into a unified, militant front that finally brought the Ohio League on board. It did this by turning the face of the Ohio Leaguers from New York to Ontario. On October 2, 1791, the Shawnee Speaker to the unified council complained that the Union had been in the works "these four years past" and needled Sagoyewatha to get the New York League off the dime and into collaboration with the Ohio Union (Aupaumut 1998, 116). When Sagoyewatha could or would not, Thayendanegea stepped to the fore. On October 11, 1791, he boldly bid the Ohio League peoples to enter into the Union as members of the *Ontario* League, to which they might just as reasonably belong as to that in New York. The Ohio Leaguers were at last persuaded to throw in their lot with their Canadian kin. Aupaumut witnessed the outcome with dismay: "At this time I saw the warriors of Shawenese and Wyondots [sic] divide ammunition, which Colonel McKee sent to them. Then I see them set out for war" (Aupaumut 1998, 122).

It was at this time that the Union was formally consummated at a major meeting at the Council Grounds along Maumee River, a site now located in downtown Toledo, Ohio. The council was twice recorded for posterity. The first record was made by one of the Shawnee representatives in attendance, Wampomshawuh, in a pamphlet published in Philadelphia in November 1791. The second record of this momentous event was Aupaumut's *Narrative of an Embassy,* although scholars have been behindhand in recognizing as much. This is partly because Aupaumut's hesitant English confounds hasty readers, but more because, understanding neither the diction nor the conventions of traditional councils, western readers have dismissed the account as "a rambling manuscript" (Sword 1985, 213).

There is also a confusion surrounding its date. The year of Aupaumut's visit to Ohio, as detailed in his *Narrative of an Embassy,* is uncertain, since the title page that once contained it was lost as early as 1827 (Aupaumut 1998, 65). What is certain is that Aupaumut was in Ohio on official business in the late summer and fall of 1791. His embassy was mentioned in an entry for August 4, 1791, by St. Clair, in the apologia for his failed campaign (St. Clair 1971, 24). Similarly, the U.S. treaty commissioner to whom Aupaumut was assigned, Timothy Pickering, stated that he discussed the disappointing embassy with Aupaumut in 1791 (Aupaumut 1998, 69). Aupaumut was again in Ohio in 1792, under orders from Henry Knox (ASP 1998, 1:233), with Rufus Putnam mentioning that he would be at a council at Au Glaize council grounds in Ohio, late in August (ASP 1998, 1:237).

Based on these latter references, Wiley Sword placed Aupaumut's *Narrative* in 1792 (Sword 1985, 213). I believe, however, that the *Narrative* leads up to and highlights the crucial council of 1791. It was there that the Union was ratified by all Ohio nations, a step of supreme importance, as Aupaumut would have instantly realized. There is, moreover, the second version of this council to consider. Both accounts record identical arguments in favor of resistance, right down to their examples and analogies. It was, furthermore, those very arguments that convinced Aupaumut of the folly of all

U.S. attempts to entice the Union into peace talks, as he confided to Pickering in 1791 (Aupaumut 1998, 69). Most significantly, the Union council was gearing up to meet St. Clair's expedition, an event that occurred in 1791. Natives would not have held a council to do this in 1792.

There were five ascendant reasons that the Ohio Union refused to dicker with the United States:

1. Aupaumut recorded the Union's "principal" charge against the United States as one of treachery, "that the white people are deceitful in their dealings with us Indians." They "have taken all our lands from us, from time to time, until this time, and that they will continue the same way" (Aupaumut 1998, 126). Egushawa's entire speech, as recorded by Wampomshawuh, sought to prove the same point, belaboring the lethal deceits of land-grabbing, the *"Frauds, murders,* and *massacres"* they entailed (italics in the original, McKee 1792, quotes respectively, 7, 16; whole speech, 6–20).

2. The Union told Aupaumut that Christianity was a ruse, under cover of which the settlers planned genocide: "the Big knifes [*sic*] use learning to Civilize Indians; and after they Christianize number [*sic*] of them so as to gain their attention, then they would killed them [*sic*]" (Aupaumut 1998, 126). As proof, Aupaumut recorded the specific accusation that the Virginians had "killed of such [converts] 96 in one day, at Cosuhkeck, few years ago," a direct reference to Williamson's destruction of the Moravian Lenape and Mahicans at Goschoschking on March 8, 1782 (Aupaumut 1998, 126). For his part, Egushawa defined Christianity as "an opinion, *called religion,* which they inculcate on the minds of their children, that they please God by exterminating us *red men,* whom they call *heathen"* (italics in the original, McKee 1792, 8). In an arch aside, Egushawa remarked that "This sentiment of theirs has . . . cost many of our relations their lives! And, they who murder with this sentiment, will lye [*sic*], to find an excuse for that murder!" (McKee 1792, 8). The same proof of the Moravian converts murdered at Goschoschking was expressly offered by Egushawa, in Wampomshawuh's record (McKee 1792, 16).

3. Aupaumut recorded the charge that no treaty was honored by the United States, in particular instancing the treaty signed by the Shawnee chief, Moluntha. "But soon after this agreement was

made, the Big knifes came in the town of this Chief; some of the Indians could not trust the Big knifes and run off; but the Chief [Moluntha] have such confidence in the words of the Big knifes he hoisted up his flag; but the Big knifes did not regarded [sic], but killed the Chief and number of his friends" (grammar in original, Aupaumut 1998, 126). This same allegation of treaties dishonored, as supported by the instance of Moluntha was made by Egushawa, as recorded by Wampomshawuh (McKee 1792, 11).

4. Union speakers told Aupaumut that words of peace always preceded actions of war with the United States, so that "every time the Big knifes get ready to come against us, they would sent [sic] message to us for peace—then they come to fight us—and they know how to speak good, but would not do good towards Indians" (Aupaumut 1998, 127). Egushawa's lengthy remarks elaborated, in excruciating detail, the same complaint of U.S. peace councils' being used as a smoke screen for war, as Wampomshawuh recorded (McKee 1792, 8, 14, 15, 16, 17, 19). With peace in their mouths, Egushawa charged, U.S. forces "invade your country with their warriors! build forts in it without asking or obtaining your leave!" (McKee 1792, 8).

5. The Union alleged to Aupaumut that the U.S. government allowed the state militias to "always have war with the Indians. If the United States could govern them, then the peace could stand sure. But the Big knifes are independent, and if we have peace with them, they would make slaves of us" (Aupaumut 1998, 127–28). Again, Egushawa repeatedly made this same allegation against the "Virginians" as people who "kicked out" peace fires, as recorded by Wampomshawuh (McKee 1792, 11, 13, 15, 16–17). "I ask again," Egushawa thundered, "by what authority is it that the Virginians have possessed themselves of our hunting country, on the south side of the Ohio! They know, and we know, they never obtained our permission!" (McKee 1792, 13).

In closing his lengthy remarks to the 1791 council, the appointed speaker for war, Egushawa advised his fellow Union members to "listen to no proposals for peace, unless your elder brethren of the United States, shall send some of their wise men to this council fire; fully impowered [sic] to agree upon such terms of peace, as shall be *your* and *their* interests to observe inviolably. When they do this, but not until then, I will be among the foremost to advise you to melt down your tomahawks into stretching needles" (italics in the original, McKee 1792, 20). Following councilmanic rules, Egushawa then turned the floor over to the appointed peace speaker, Ab, beth, din, Wyrosh, Yeshivo, who briefly—*very* briefly—enumerated the main arguments in favor of an immediate, concessionary treaty. After perfunctorily addressing the long, difficult haul it had been to weld the many nations into a Union (McKee 1792, 21), he added that (McKee 1792, 20–21):

1. The Americans vastly outnumbered the Natives;
2. It was unwise to count on the British for any aid, regardless of their fine speeches to the contrary;
3. By fighting the Americans, the Union would actually be teaching them its own art of war;
4. It was necessary to remember the right of women and children to peace and safety; and
5. Since the Union had been so difficult to create, it was delicate enough to fold under the pressures of any prolonged war with the United States.

In fact, Ab, beth, din, Wyrosh, Yeshivo, actually endorsed war, an unusual step for a peace speaker. Notwithstanding the eminently rational arguments he had just ticked off in favor of conciliation, he flatly conditioned a peace council on good-faith actions by the United States, including an immediate withdrawal from Native lands and guarantees that it would negotiate honestly in the future instead of cheating "as they have done." If, however, the United States "Will not do this, then I say, Be strong, and let us war on, like men, for ever [*sic*]" (McKee 1792, 21).

Blithely unaware of the depth, determination, and—most importantly—unity of the Ohio Natives that October, St. Clair continued his plodding campaign. After his unaccountable dillydallying about Forts Washington and Hamilton, just outside of the relative safety of Cincinnati, St. Clair finally pushed north, albeit slowly, with the intention of taking the seat of Harmar's ignoble defeat, Kekionga. Instead, upon reaching Kekionga on November 4, 1791, St. Clair and the whole U.S. Army found themselves trapped in a dawn attack coordinated by Meshikinoquak. Other Native generals included Wayapiersenwah of the Shawnee, Buckongahelas of the Lenape, Katepakomen of the Wyandot, Black Eagle, and Blackstaffe (Wilson 1909, 71).

Quickly thrown into disarray, the militia hightailed it back to base camp for cover, thereby exposing the camp followers, women and children all, to extreme danger from the pursuing Union troops. Now in a thorough panic, having watched their officers deliberately picked off, one by one, the U.S. army simply ran for it, full tilt, leaving many of the wounded and all of the camp followers behind to certain death. During this disgraceful retreat, the U.S. Army dropped clothing, supplies, and weapons in its frantic wake, the better to run, as recorded in the diaries of Winthrop Sargent and Major Ebenezer Denny, St. Clair's aide-de-camp, as well as in St. Clair's own, chagrined report back to Knox on November 9, 1791 (Denny's Diary, Smith 1882, 2:258–62; Sargent 1924, 237–82; St. Clair's report, Smith 1882, 2:262–67).

Fewer than 500 of St. Clair's complement of 1,400 men escaped. Even so, as Sargent noted, had Meshikinoquak's army given chase, it could easily have killed every U.S. soldier on the field that morning (Sargent 1924, 261). Sargent's head count of casualties listed 647 dead and 263 wounded (Sargent 1924, 260), a tally that did not include the 100 camp followers, who were all killed (Edel 1997, 89). By contrast, the Union suffered very few casualties. Native losses were conventionally put at about 150 by Western sources, but they were guessing (Wilson 1909, 71; Rafert 1996, 52). Scholars turning to oral tradition report much lower numbers. According to Alan Eckert, the Natives sustained sixty-six dead and nine wounded, with all but one of the injured recovering (Eckert 1995, 568). James Perry and Alan Axelrod put Union losses even lower, at twenty-one confirmed dead, and forty wounded (Perry 58; Axelrod 1993, 125). Whatever the true number of Union casualties, proportionally speaking, Kekionga was the worst loss that *any* U.S. general *has* ever suffered in *any* campaign (Axelrod 1993, 125).

This remarkable fact notwithstanding, as Wilbur Edel noted in 1997, "No reference to the battle at Kekionga can be found in any standard American history text" (Edel 1997, xii). Indeed, throughout most of the twentieth century, the historiographical habit was to gloss over the two overwhelming Native victories at Kekionga, as did Edgar Leidy in 1929, by lumping together Harmar's and St. Clair's defeats and calling them collectively "incidents in the attempt to conquer the Northwest" (Leidy 1929, 15).

Primary sources aid in the glossing. Mincing around the truth in his own reports back to Henry Knox, St. Clair set up a rationale that all subsequent authors used to excuse his rout: Besides St. Clair's own illness that day, it was the "want of discipline" on the part of his inexperienced troops, the loss of all his important officers, and the fact that he was outnumbered which must account for the defeat (Smith 1882, 2:264, 265). Although, in its "Report of the Special Committee," March 27, 1792, Congress also fingered "gross and various mismanagements and neglects," it carefully avoided laying these problems at St. Clair's door, thus letting him off the hook (Smith 1882, 2:299). Official whining and whitewashing aside, the simple fact was that St. Clair (and Harmar before him) had been outflanked and outwitted at Kekionga by Meshikinoquak.

Due to the debacle of Kekionga, on March 26, 1792, St. Clair informed the President that he would be resigning his command of the U.S. Army. He simultaneously requested an inquiry to clear his name, asking only that he be allowed to keep his commission as a Major-General until the inquiry was completed (Smith 1882, 2:282–83). On April 7, 1792, however, under investigation in the Capitol and under derision everywhere, St. Clair was pressured into resigning his commission as Major-General (Smith 1882, 2:285–86).

The Congressional Inquiry—America's first—was not the only inquiry into St. Clair's conduct (Smith 1882, 2:286–99). So angry as to be stupefied, President Washington also commissioned Knox to investigate and report back to the executive branch. Knox's report, "The CAUSES of the existing HOSTILITIES between the UNITED STATES, and certain Tribes of INDIANS North-West of the OHIO," went beyond simplistic whitewashing to prevaricate heavily, portraying the Natives of the Northwest as perversely bent on war, despite all benevolent attempts on the part of the United States to "establish a liberal peace with them" (Carter 1934, 360).

Having thus falsely framed the issue, Knox declared that it did "not appear that the right of the Northern and Western Indians, who formed the several before mentioned treaties to the lands thereby relinquished to the United States ha[d] been questioned by any other tribes; nor d[id] it appear that the present war ha[d] been occasioned by any dispute relatively [sic] to the boundaries established" by the treaties of Fort Stanwix (1784), Fort McIntosh (1785), The Mouth of the Great Miami (1786), and Fort Harmar (1789) (Carter 1934, 361). *Au contraire,* Knox cried, it appeared "that the unprovoked aggressions of the Miami and Wabash Indians upon Kentucky and other parts of the frontiers, together with their associates, a banditti, formed of Shawanese and outcast Cherokees, amounting in all to about one thousand two hundred men, [we]re solely the causes of the war" (Carter 1934, 361). As evidence, he conjured up the statistic of 1,500 settlers "on the Ohio, and the frontiers on the south side thereof" killed between 1783 and 1790 as conclusive proof of Native perfidy (Carter 1934, 363).

No summary of events in Ohio could have been farther from the truth, and unless he had slept through every dispatch from 1785 to 1791, Knox knew it. His report was never intended as an impartial inquiry, however, but as a propaganda tool. It had the dual job of, first, minimizing the U.S. war drive against the Union and, second, establishing that, indeed, "just cause" now existed for an all out assault upon Ohio.

At this juncture, an attempt was made to remove a legal thorn long in the federal side, namely, that the Miami peoples had never signed any treaty with the United States. This boded ill for a "just war" against them, since the United States lacked the excuse of their having violated a treaty. Consequently, Knox ordered General Rufus Putnam to negotiate a peace treaty with the Miami, a commission that the mild Putnam took so much to heart as to discharge honestly.

Throughout the summer of 1792, Putnam strategized to emplace the desired treaty by assuring the Miami that the United States had no wishes for land, but only for the best for the Miami peoples (ASP 1998, 1:238). Finally, on September 27, 1792, Putnam met with the "Wabash Indians" to sign a treaty "solemnly" guaranteeing to the Miami and Illinois peoples "all the lands to which they have a just claim," stipulating that "no part" of it would "ever be taken from them, but by a fair purchase, and to their satisfaction." The government openly acknowledged that the land "originally belonged to the Indians; it is theirs, and theirs only. They have a right to sell, and a right to refuse to sell." The United States promised to "protect them in their said just rights" (ASP 1998, 1:338). The Putnam Treaty, ratified by the Miami and Illinois peoples, appears nowhere in Kappler.

This is because, when he saw the final product, President Washington was seriously displeased with Putnam's promises and guarantees: They included no counteractive pen-and-ink witchcraft, under which the United States might unilaterally preempt the treaty lands at will, a feature of all acceptable treaties. Consequently, when the Putnam Treaty went to the Senate for ratification, Washington arranged that a vote on it be stalled until a new article, more to the government's satisfaction, could be negotiated into it (Prucha 1994, 91).

The official U.S. story behind the failure to manage this was that a new council could not be called, because many of the signatory chiefs had since died of smallpox (Prucha 1994, 91). The Native truth was that, already having the treaty they wanted, the Miami and Illinois were unavailable for trickery. They well recalled a prior council on May 1791, which was a blind, "to give the great Virginia warriors, an opportunity to steal to the Wabache [*sic*] to strike the women and children there, whilst their warriors were at *this* council fire!" (italics in the original, McKee 1792, 19).

Miami suspicions were founded. Even before it initiated Putnam's peace negotiations with the Miami, the government was preparing for war. On March 5, 1792—two-and-a-half months before Putnam was commissioned to treat for peace (ASP 1998, 1:234)—Congress passed "An Act for Making Farther and More Effectual Provisions for the Protection of the Frontiers of the United States," authorizing President Washington's request to (Peters 1853, 1:241–43):

1. Double the existing army (two infantry regiments and an artillery battalion) by adding three additional regiments of 960 men each, plus officers for a total military strength of 5,120 men;
2. Give the President the ability to call up the cavalry (militias) and appoint their officers; and
3. Appropriate $20,000 to hire Indian scouts.

On April 12, 1792, still a month before Putnam's peace commission, President Washington appointed Major-General Anthony Wayne commander of the reconstituted Army (Carter 1987, 124).

The next U.S. onslaught in Ohio finally yielded the results that had been yearned for by the settlers since 1747. Beginning in 1793, Anthony Wayne whipped his dismal U.S. recruits into something resembling a disciplined army, and in the summer of 1794, led 3,500 troops into Ohio against some 2,000 troops of the Union (Edel 1997, 104). The final confrontation occurred the morning of August 20, 1794, at Fallen Timbers, Ohio—a field littered with trees tossed about like match sticks by a probable F-5 tornado. Along the Maumee River, not far from the shores of Lake Erie, Wayne took the field with 2,000 men of four sublegions (Pratt 1997, 5) against perhaps 1,300 Union men (Pratt 1997, 10). Wayne's well-known triumph followed, the only engagement with the Ohio Natives from 1783 to 1794 that is typically covered in the textbooks, for it was the only engagement from which the United States emerged victorious.

Wayne's success at Fallen Timbers is typically portrayed in Western histories as a brilliant achievement of generalship, but in fact, it was more of a lucky stroke than anything else. Not only was it begun and finished in fewer than two hours, but also, contrary to the information of most published accounts, it was not prosecuted by Wayne, himself, but by his subordinates. Two weeks prior to the encounter, Wayne had been gravely injured when a large tree fell across his tent, nearly crushing him to death and inflicting internal injuries so serious that he was copiously excreting blood. He could barely rise at times and needed to be set upon his horse by others (Pratt 1997, 7–8). In extreme pain at Fallen Timbers, he was mounted too far from the battle to see much of anything. Thus, the account written by Wayne really consists of secondhand reports and suppositions, which were not at all borne out by archaeological research undertaken at the battle site in June 1995 by Michael G. Pratt of Heidelberg College, Ohio. Instead, Native oral traditions of the battle proved to have been remarkably accurate, especially regarding the location of the fighting (Mann 2000, 30).

The battle was won by the U.S. Army primarily because accident concentrated all its force against a small contingent of no more than 200 Union fighters, being 100 Wyandot and another 100 "British allies," trapped in a triangle between the strewn tree trunks and the Maumee River (Pratt 1997, 19). Eventually, a skirmish line of some 400 Natives was formed but only to have been overwhelmed by a U.S. charge of 1,000 regular army troops, which eventually drove the Union forces into retreat (Pratt 1997, 20). Eight Wyandot chiefs were killed, as was the Ottawa chief, "Little Otter" (Pratt 2001, 21, 22; Carter 1987, overstated dead of Wyandot and Ottawa, 136). The Ottawa casualties included Egushawa, who had been head-shot, but not killed. Wounded, too, though again not fatally, was Tarhe, the Great Crane, lineage chief of the Upper Sandusky Wyandot (Pratt 1997, 21).

As usual, the British utterly failed to come through on their promises of aid, should the battle go awry. Instead of allowing the Union troops to regroup inside Fort Miamis, as previously arranged, when Wayapiersenwah and his Shawnee contingent arrived at the fort, with Wayne's men hard on their heels, the British commander had the gates swung shut in their faces. None of the Native troops were suffered to enter (Mann 2000, 49; Murphy 1882/1997, 1; Carter 1987, 136). British assurances were no better honored in the winter following the battle, causing the Union to send to Detroit a delegation consisting of Pacan and Meshikinoquak of the Miami, Wayapiersenwah of the Shawnee, and Buckongahelas of the Lenape to complain of the bad treatment (Carter 1987, 145).

Although Wayne technically won the Battle of Fallen Timbers, the situation was still quite restive. His army thinned considerably throughout the winter, whereas the Union remained in force. In view of Wayne's weakened status, there was considerable pressure from some Union members to continue the war, and agents of the war faction began mounting raids (Sword 1985, 325). Adding to its guerrilla sentiment was the Union's knowledge that Wayne fully intended to create a new treaty at Greenville that simply reiterated the terms of the failed Treaty of Fort Harmar; he had made as much clear in his November 1794 precouncil communications with the Wyandot, the Firekeepers of the Union (ASP 1998, 1:528, 549). Given the resistance to the Harmarly direction of the Greenville council, it was touch and go whether peace or war would prevail—not the least because a rival, long-running council was raised by the war faction at Detroit to counteract the approaching Greenville council, called for the summer of 1795.

The Miami were for war. The Three Fires Confederacy were for peace. The Shawnee were divided, with the majority for war, against a small but vocal faction for peace. Ohio Leaguers were also divided. The Lenape were for peace, while the Wyandot were split down the middle, with those of Upper Sandusky for peace, but the rest, who lived in the Toledo area, for war. On the other hand, the Iroquois League of Canada was for war. Thayendanegea even promised to bring the Canadian League into the fray, full force, with the support of the British (ASP 1998, 1:529, 548–49). Although war sentiment was running high, the recent experiences of British treachery, combined with the vivid memory of past betrayals, made some Unionists wary of new promises from the Crown (ASP 1998, 1:527–28).

The conference in Detroit did not arise from bloodthirsty motives but from the Union's clear understanding that the United States was untrustworthy. Counselors at Detroit viewed the American posturings at Greenville as "snares the Americans have formed for their ruin," anticipating that a "massacre and destruction" of signatory nations would follow the treaty, as had so often happened before (ASP 1998, 1:568). Intended as a roadblock to a dishonorable peace at Greenville, the Detroit conference slowed, and in some instances, prevented peaceminded delegates from arriving at Greenville.

For example, the largest number of Shawnee at Detroit, including the formidable Wampomshawuh, came down forcefully on the side of continued resistance. Thus, Wayapiersenwah and his smaller peace faction had literally to sneak out of the Detroit conference, since their lives might have been forfeit had they been caught departing for Greenville (ASP 1998, 1:568). Indeed, Wampomshawuh had already threatened Wayapiersenwah's life for trying to garner peace supporters. When Wampomshawuh heard that the peace faction was gone, he angrily burned up a pair of gold epaulets that had been intended for the "traitor," Wayapiersenwah (Sword 1985, 326).

Due to such firm resistance in Detroit, Wayne found himself cooling his heels, waiting for delegations to arrive, some of them a month after the official start of the Greenville council on June 16, 1795 (ASP 1998, 1:564). By June 16, a sufficient number of *bodies* from most of the desired nations had straggled in to Greenville that Wayne began his greetings, but it is doubtful how authorized any of these bodies were as "speakers" of their nations. The Shawnee were, for example, listed in the minutes as being present on June 16, although the appointed speaker of the peace faction, Wayapiersenwah, did not show up until more than a month later, on July 18 (ASP 1998, 1:564, 568). Even then, honesty constrained him to admitted that very few Shawnee supported him, and his tinny assertion that the Shawnee nation would, nonetheless, "be well represented" was little more than a tacit admission that the majority of the Shawnee were ill-disposed to the Greenville council (ASP 1998, 1:568). Similarly, the Wyandot were listed as present on June 16, yet Tarhe, their speaker—and, indeed, the Firekeeper of the whole Greenville council!—did not even arrive until July 12 (given as "Tarke," ASP 1998, 1:564, 567, 568). Again, Tarhe represented only the peace faction of the Wyandot, their war-inclined brethren remaining at Detroit.

Indeed, of all the nations listed as present on June 16, only the Three Fires Confederacy was represented by authorized delegates—almost. These did not actually arrived until June 17, bringing "prisoners" (adoptees) for repatriation, a signal that they were ready for "peace" (ASP 1998, 1:564, 565). Repatriations notwithstanding, their official Speaker, Mashipinashiwish, did not arrive until June 25 (ASP 1998, 1:565).

In addition to the question of speaker accreditation, Western readers must also understand the matters of consensus logic and Speakerhood if they are to grasp what happened at Greenville. The personal preferences of individual delegates did not determine their positions on peace. The consensus will of their authorizing councils did that. For example, the council of the Three Fires Confederacy had decided for peace. As a result, no speaker could oppose that consensus at Greenville yet remain a Three-Fires member in good standing. This was the reason that the fiery Egushawa of the Ottawa, who finally arrived in Greenville on July 4, fresh from the Detroit war council, spoke for peace (given as "Agooshaway," ASP 1998, 1:566). Although his peace stance appears in the record as a major coup for Wayne, it did not reflect Egushawa's personal preference for peace but his loyalty to the Three Fires. What the reader should notice is the tardiness of his arrival, two weeks after the designated Speaker of the Three Fires Confederacy, a sure signal of his personal displeasure at the direction in which the Three Fires had chosen to go.

By the same token, ironically flipped, Meshikinoquak arrived at Greenville promptly on June 23 but specifically to oppose the treaty (ASP 1998, 1:564). His opposition did not represent his personal preference, since he began advocating for peace as early as 1794 (Carter 1987, 134). His personal feelings were beside the point, however, because he been appointed Speaker of the Miami, and the Miami consensus viewed the Greenville council with contempt. Meshikinoquak had, therefore, no choice but to argue against the treaty, as he explained to Wayne after the council had closed (ASP 1998, 1:583).

In Western accounts of the Greenville treaty council, Wayne is often presented as having been a "perfect host," one who "applied without error his knowledge of Indian psychology" (Carter 1987, 149), but Native readers of the minutes must disagree. Wayne was rude, arrogant, deceitful, and not particularly adept at councilmanic forms. For instance, it was customary at any great council for the host liberally to provide food and drink, as well as lodgings. Before he came through on this most basic of hostelric duties, however, Wayne had to be prompted twice—first, kindly, on June 26 by Michimang of the Pottawatamie (ASP 1998, 1:565) and again, in open reproach, on June 30 by New Corn and Sun, both Pottawatamie, and Le Gris of the Miami (ASP 1998, 1:565). Wayne was probably penny-pinching, but his failure as a host was inviting serious difficulties, which realization alone pushed him to give the chiefs of each nation then present "a sheep for their use, and some drink for them and their people" (ASP 1998, 1:565). By the same token, he cruelly mocked Meshikinoquak, misrepresented the Jay Treaty to the counselors, gave a cropped and awkward "condolence" speech, and worst of all, allowed nations that had not been present to be inserted into the treaty after it had been signed, as though they had attended the council and agreed to the treaty (ASP 1998, 1:573; Stout 1974, 345, 351–56, 357–58).

With bodies, if not necessarily speakers, present on July 9 and itching to proceed before the apparent peace momentum subsided, Wayne attempted to open negotiations, but Meshikinoquak and Egushawa protested heavily, insisting that he await the arrival of the Wyandot and Shawnee, who had tarried in Detroit (ASP 1998, 1:566). Their protests did make Wayne anxiously delay opening negotiations until July 15, when the first Wyandot arrived from Detroit, probably with word that their Speaker, Tarhe, was on his way, as were the breakaway Shawnee under Wayapiersenwah (ASP 1998, 1:567).

Consequently, on July 15, Wayne went forward to stipulate the authority by which he was negotiating, telling everyone that he planned to pattern the Greenville Treaty after the "treaty at the mouth of the Muskingum," i.e., the Fort Harmar Treaty of 1789 (ASP 1998, 1:567). Knowing that this was a touchy matter, Wayne then adjourned the Council until July 18. Some of this lagtime was to await the Wyandot and Shawnee delegates, but more of it was to allow cooling-off time for those already assembled, for the Fort Harmar Treaty was heartily despised.

Immediately as the talks of the July 18 got under way, Meshikinoquak protested that the Harmar Treaty was not binding upon the Miami, since it had not been attended by any authorized counselors of the Miami. Protesting further that he was ignorant of the terms of that treaty, he asked the remaining speakers to indicate whether the Harmar treaty had been "agreeable to them" (ASP 1998, 1:567). Although the Sun made a conciliatory speech in reply, Mashipinashiwish replied that "I never heard before, what the Sun has been observing." He went on to state that he (i.e., the Michilimackinac Chippewa), from their "remote situation on Lake Michigan," were unacquainted with the Harmar Treaty and suggested that any present who had made the treaty speak to its terms, an uncomfortable suggestion for those who had been strong-armed into it (ASP 1998, 1:568).

To smooth over the animosity brewing up in these remarks, Tarhe pointed out that those Harmar counselors were not appointed speakers of their nation at Greenville, meaning that they had no authority to reply. Instead of them, Tarhe proposed that proper speakers be appointed by their respective nations to consult with their councils and "appoint a day" in the future when all might hear their remarks (ASP 1998, 1:568). Such a delay might unhinge the entire conference, especially since breakaway nations would be forced back into their main fold to consult. Tarhe's proposition, therefore, frightened Wayne sufficiently that he sought to defuse the situation by offering to enlighten the ignorant and "bring to the recollection" of those who had signed the treaty what was in it (ASP 1998, 1:568). On that sour note, he adjourned the council until July 20, two days later (ASP 1998, 1:568). The lapse of time during a council was, once more, a sure sign that everyone needed to get ahold of himself before the council met again.

Immediately as the talks opened on July 20, Wayne was challenged again on the legality of the Fort Harmar Treaty. In reply, Wayne simply read aloud and interpreted its terms (ASP 1998, 1:569). The next day, a shamefaced Masass of the Chippewa spoke for the Three Fires Confederacy, admitting that he had been at the Harmar Treaty council and that the terms were, indeed, what Wayne had explained the day before. Nevertheless, he added, "I now tell you that some words of that treaty we did not perfectly understand at the time we made it," for "at that treaty we had not good interpreters, and we were left partly unacquainted with many particulars of it" (ASP 1998, 1:569, 570). Furthermore, the Wyandot had led the Three Fires into the agreement blind, with the Three Fires never receiving the compensation promised for the lands made over. Masass concluded by saying that the Three Fires had believed themselves still be the "true owners of those lands," but given the pen-and-ink witchcraft of the treaty, he no longer knew how matters stood. Despite the underhandedness of the Fort Harmar Treaty, however, the Three Fire remained committed to peace at Greenville and would consequently honor the Harmar accord (ASP 1998, 1:569–70).

This speech threw Tarhe, along with the entire Wyandot delegation, into no little consternation, for the Wyandot had been fingered, at the very least, as dupes of deception. It had been the Ohio Iroquois, largely the Wyandot, who had facilitated the Harmar treaty and who had kept all the payments realized from it. In a clever effort at shifting the onus away from the Wyandot and onto the United States, immediately before requesting an adjournment to let tempers cool, Tarhe asked Wayne to explain to the Three Fires just how their lands had come to have been seized through the Fort Harmar Treaty (ASP 1998, 1:570). Considering the tight spot he was in, Wayne was more than willing to adjourn, but the hasty Masass jumped up to insist that "what I have said, I will never retract." At this point, the cooler Mashipinashiwish, primary speaker of the Three Fires, urged that the matter be handled immediately, as his Chippewa delegation was far from home (Michilimackinac) and longing to return (ASP 1998, 1:570). Clearly, no adjournment was to put out these fires.

At this heated point, Meshikinoquak entered the lists, pouring fuel on the fire. Again feigning ignorance of U.S. negotiations, he politely asked just which Miami lands had been handed over to the Americans and by what authority. "I expect that the lands on the Wabash, and in *this* country, belong to me and my people. I now take the opportunity to inform my brothers of the United States, and others present, that there are men of sense and understanding among my peoples, as well as among theirs, and that these lands were disposed of without our knowledge or consent." Moreover, he added his surprise at hearing from the Lenape "that these lands had been ceded by the British to the Americans, when the former were beaten by, and made peace with, the latter; because you had before told us that it was the Wyandots, Delawares, Ottawas, Chippewas, Pattawatamies [*sic*], and Sauckeys [*sic*], who had made this cession" (ASP 1998, 1:570).

Meshikinoquak had just deftly exploded the expedient duplicity of the United States, which, on the one hand, claimed to have taken the Old Northwest from Britain by conquest, but which, on the other hand, pretended to have negotiated it away from the Natives through treaties. While he was at it, Meshikinoquak had also unveiled the hidden U.S. agenda of purposely fomenting discord among Natives of the Old Northwest with spurious treaties that made one group of Natives appear to have been the culprit in the loss of lands belonging to another group of Natives. Pious postures of rectitude on this point no longer feasible, Wayne hastily adjourned the council to the next day.

On July 22, Meshikinoquak returned to the charge, even as the council opened, confessing that he was "a little astonished" to hear about all the lands included in the Fort Harmar Treaty, for "the print" of his "ancestors' houses" were "everywhere to be seen" among the lands ceded in that treaty (ASP 1998, 1:570). To embarrass the peace factions, he went on to delineate the Miami lands that the

Fort Harmar Treaty had had no business having included, laying out the "well known" boundaries of the territory claimed by the Miami, Pottawatamie, and "Wabash," a mixture of mainly Miami, including the Wea, and the Shawnee (ASP 1998, 1:570). He then blistered those who had presumed to dicker away Miami lands, in a speech that must have chagrined Wayne as well as the illicit Native participants in the Fort Harmar treaty:

> I have now informed you of the boundaries of the Miami nation, where the Great Spirit placed my forefather a long time ago, and charged him not to sell or part with his lands, but to preserve them for his posterity. This charge has been handed down to me. I was much surprised to find that my other brothers differed so much from me on this subject: for their conduct would lead one to suppose, that the Great Spirit, and their forefathers had not given them the same charge that was give [sic] to me, but, on the contrary, had directed them to sell their lands to any white man who wore a hat, as soon as he should ask it of them. (ASP 1998, 1:571)

The council was now on the point of breaking down completely. Not only had Meshikinoquak openly uttered the unspeakable truth behind the pen-and-ink witchcraft of the Fort Harmar Treaty, but he had also publicly shamed those who had acceded to a rapacious seizure of territory belonging to peoples not even represented at its council fires. Wayne said nothing at this juncture, for there was, in fact, no honest reply to be made to the allegations of double-dealing and bad faith; they were only too true. It was Tarhe, Speaker of the Upper Sandusky Wyandot, and Wayapiersenwah, Speaker of the peace faction of the Shawnee, who pulled Wayne's bacon from the fire.

Tarhe rose first to smooth down the significant wrinkles that Meshikinoquak had pushed up in the council by condoling the United States on its losses during the war for the Old Northwest (ASP 1998, 1:571). Taking the hatchet from an enemy's head and throwing it into the bottomless pit, cleaning off the blood, wiping away the tears of grief, opening the ears and the throat, and clearing up the clouds—delivered on white wampum—gathering up the bones of those fallen and burying them for eternity—delivered on white and purple wampum—are potent words to soothe and quiet troubled minds. Under condolence rules, the council *must* enter into the One Mind of Peace after such words are uttered. Whether Wayne (or later historians) understood what Tarhe had just done is unclear, but that the assembled nations understood it was indisputable. When Tarhe called, "Listen to me! We are all of one mind who are here assembled; this is a business not to be trifled with; it is a matter of the utmost concern to us" (ASP 1998, 1:571), he had their full attention.

Seizing his advantage, Tarhe argued that the counselors necessarily built upon the Harmar Treaty, however little it was to their taste. Acknowledging openly that "not so many different nations then assembled as are now present" and even supposing that boundaries set there had crept "a little towards us," he nevertheless pressed his point that the task before them was not to quarrel about the past but to "establish a general, permanent, and lasting peace, for ever [*sic*]" (ASP 1998, 1:571). Wayne seemed to have been dazed by the speeches of July 21 and 22, for, once Tarhe resumed his seat, Wayne simply said that he had "listened with great attention" and quickly adjourned the council before it had a chance to reheat (ASP 1998, 1:571).

On July 23, Wayapiersenwah of the Shawnee made a dramatic move that helped solidify Tarhe's peace thrust of the day before: He changed his seat. Previously, the Shawnee had sat among the Miami, that is, they had supported the Union in close alliance with the Miami. Now, Wayapiersenwah moved between the Lenape and the Upper Sandusky Wyandot, the two loudest voices for a concession treaty. Because the Shawnee were well known to have been the strongest advocates of the Union and the war, this gesture for peace was the stuff of gripping theater (ASP 1998, 1:571).

At this point, Egushawa added to the dramatic effect by pulling out a peace pipe that had been sent down from the Michilimackinac Ottawa to be presented to the Three Fires Confederacy for presentation, in turn, to the Wyandot, Lenape, and Shawnee—but only when "any thing good was contemplated" (ASP 1998, 1:572). Telling Wayapiersenwah, "I do not consider you as a brother; I view you as a friend," Egushawa held it out stem-first (for peace), telling the Shawnee Speaker that, should he, in turn, point it stem-first to the U.S. delegation before returning it to the Ottawa, that was acceptable. Egushawa then presented the United States with a very large peace belt. Again, theatrical gestures in favor of peace had come from a speaker well known to have been a strong advocate of Union and war.

Mashipinashiwish then rose to recite a condolence for the United States, spoken upon the proper wampum. While he was at it, he managed to blame the British for the war, a proposition that the United States and subsequent historians have been all too eager to take at face value. New Corn, Speaker of the Three-Fires Pottawatamie chimed in for peace next, although he could not resist needling Wayne a bit: "I must observe, that I [meaning the Pottawatamie] never received any part of the compensation" pledged at the Fort Harmar Treaty (ASP 1998, 1:572). Again, Wayne simply adjourned the meeting.

On July 24, the peace faction made another bid to sway the council in favor of a treaty when Wayapiersenwah forcefully reminded everyone that the Wyandot were the Firekeepers of the council, not the Miami. Under councilmanic rules of eastern Nations, Firekeeping was heavily formalized, and everyone knew that all matters properly passed through the Firekeeper, who handed them out to the rest of the council. The council could not consider a matter that the Firekeeper had not put on the agenda. This point of order, once clarified, severely undercut the ability of the Miami to steer discussions at the council, as they had been doing. Once more, it is unclear whether Wayne (or later historians) understood what Wayapiersenwah had just done, but the assembled nations certainly understood. The Miami had been arrogating the Firekeeping function to themselves, so that, by supporting the proper procedures of council, Wayapiersenwah had replaced the Wyandot in control of the agenda, tipping the balance heavily to the peace camp (ASP 1998, 1:573).

Wayne then took the floor to make an insulting and condescending speech, a piece of spin-doctoring that attempted to blacken the reputation of the British and ridicule Union grievances while denigrating the Miami. To the just complaint that the Three Fires had seen none of the compensation promised them in the Fort Harmar Treaty, Wayne alleged that the United States had already paid twice for those lands, once in the Fort McIntosh Treaty and, again, in the Fort Harmar Treaty. Side stepping the facts that the Three Fires had not been represented at either of those treaties, that their lands had been illegally negotiated away in their absence, and that they never received any compensation for the land (indicating that the United States knew they had not been party to the treaties), Wayne presented the United States as magnanimously paying a third time for the same lands. In fact, Greenville represented the first time that authorized representatives of the Three Fires had ever negotiated over those lands (ASP 1998, 1:573).

Next, Wayne sneered at Meshikinoquak's outline of Miami boundaries, stating that many nations now lived on those lands, while some of the land the Miami claimed had already been ceded to the United States (ASP 1998, 1:573). Although it was true that, by 1795, other Natives lived upon Miami lands, it was only because they had been pushed west by the concerted landgrabs of the last generation, something Wayne forbore to mention. He also omitted to mention that the ceding had never been done by the Miami, for the United States had never ratified any treaty with them.

To the claim that the Miami people were under ancient injunction never to sell their lands, Wayne sniffed that, if such were the case, the Miami had "paid very little regard to the sacred injunction," as the French and the British "are now, or have been, in possession of them all" (ASP 1998, 1:573). Therefore, Wayne concluded that "the charge urged against the Ottawas, Chippewas, and other Indians comes with a bad grace indeed, from the very people who perhaps set them the example" of land sales (ASP 1998, 1:573). Not only was his description of Miami land policy toward the French and British inaccurate, but Wayne also misstated, the more easily to deflect, the actual charges laid, to wit, that the United States had never treated with the Miami for any of the lands it claimed.

Next, Wayne dredged up the old saw that the Northwest was America's by right of conquest from the British, a dubious claim, but one on which the United States had built its legal case for land-grabbing. In the general effort to sully the British before the assembled Union, Wayne rubbed salt into the open wound of the Treaty of Paris, by remarking that, in those talks, the British "did not discover that care for your interest which you ought to have experienced" (ASP 1998, 1:573). Of course, had this omission honestly troubled the Americans, they could have refused to negotiate until Native delegates were present in Paris, but never mind: Wayne's real point was not the past treachery, but the future ineffectiveness, of the British as allies.

To convince the Union that it need not look to Britain for further aid, Wayne pulled out a copy of the Jay Treaty, reading aloud articles one and two, which called upon the British to leave their forts in the Old Northwest—Forts Michilimackinac, St. Clair, Detroit, and Niagara—by June 1796. Here was pen-and-ink witchcraft at its most nefarious, for Wayne deliberately misled the Greenville council to believe that the Jay Treaty had already been ratified. It had not. Although negotiated by November of 1794, when Wayne addressed the Greenville council on July 24, 1795, there was serious doubt that it would ever be ratified, for it had kicked up a considerable ruckus politically. Many Americans furiously disputed portions of it, while the French flew into a positive tizzy over its terms. Once partially ratified in February 1796, the Jay Treaty promptly touched off an undeclared naval war between the United States and France. The Jay Treaty was anything but the pristine piece of diplomacy that Wayne represented it to be at the council—and that, less than one month after he had assured the Native delegates that "I have never yet, in a public capacity, told a lie" (ASP 1998, 1:565).

Having thus fibbed, Wayne recited a slapdash condolence speech of his own, leaving out requisite parts in a half-baked performance that, presumably, is one of the bases on which Western historians laud Wayne's profound grasp of Native psychology. Wayne next told the council, not that he would negotiate on the morrow, but that he would "shew [sic] you the cessions you have made to the United States, and point out to you the lines which may, for the future, divide your lands from theirs" (ASP 1998, 2:573). In other words, having assured the Union that it was without hope of British allies and, therefore, in the power of the United States, Wayne would dictate the terms of the Greenville Treaty to the delegates, thus finally forcing the terms of the Harmar Treaty down the throats of the Natives of the Old Northwest.

Resuming work on July 27 (the three-day break a sure sign of the disgruntlement he had raised in many quarters), Wayne read aloud his proposed Greenville Treaty, but if he had thought it would pass unchallenged, he had reckoned without Meshikinoquak. In clear disgust, the Miami Speaker told the delegates, "I expected to have heard him deliver those words ever since we have been here, for which reason"—turning to the peace camp—"I observed that you were precipitate on your part," in agreeing so quickly to a treaty on any terms (ASP 1998, 1:574). In a clear slap at Tarhe's immediate avowal of the treaty, Meshikinoquak continued: "This is a business of the greatest consequence to us all: it is an affair to which no one among us can give an answer" for the rest (ASP 1998, 1:574). Wayne quickly adjourned, while he was ahead.

The next day, squabbling between speakers favoring the concession treaty and Meshikinoquak led to another prompt adjournment. As talks haltingly resumed on July 29, speaking for the Wyandot, Ottawa, Lenape, Six Nations at Upper Sandusky, and the peace-faction Shawnee, Tarhe requested that the United States set the boundaries among the Native nations, a ploy to secure as much

Miami land as possible for those easterly nations most likely to be soonest dispossessed by the relentless settlers. Meshikinoquak was having none of Tarhe's encroachment, however. Instead, he made a beeline for the loopholes in the recycled Harmar-cum-Greenville Treaty, read July 27. Concerning the proposed boundary in western Ohio, he noted that it encompassed "the greater and best parts" of the Miami lands, despite the U.S. assurances that it "had no such design" of seizing Native lands (ASP 1998, 1:576).

Neither had Meshikinoquak forgotten Wayne's insulting allegation that the Miami had led the way in land cessions by selling land to the French and the British (ASP 1998, 1:576). The French and British "were seen by our forefathers first at Detroit; afterwards we saw them at the Miami village," Meshikinoquak said, adding, "Brothers, these people never told us they wished to purchase our lands from us." Regarding the supposed land sale at Chicago, Meshikinoquak caustically continued that his people had "never heard of it" (ASP 1998, 1:576). Of the supposed European fort on the Maumee River in Northwestern Ohio, he said "it was a fort built by me," i.e., by the Miami people (ASP 1998, 1:576).

On July 30, Meshikinoquak returned to the issue of alleged Miami land sales, mentioning "Musquiton," supposedly in French possession. "We have lived at our village for a long time; it is very surprising that we should never know anything about" the rumored sale. Instead, the "French lived at Vincennes, where they were permitted to settle by my forefathers" on a small grant of land (ASP 1998, 1:577). Thus, none of the lands that Wayne claimed that the Miami had sold had, in fact, been sold by the Miami, or anyone else.

Having forcefully refuted the bogus claims and set the record straight on Miami boundaries, Meshikinoquak budged, ever so slightly, on the subject of land. He suggested the sharing of certain "reservations," i.e., land in Ohio set aside for the use of the United States as forts or trading posts (ASP 1998, 1:577). He thereby opened

Two historical maps of Ohio shortly after the Greenville Treaty. The first map (top), hand-drawn the same year as the treaty in 1795, shows the location of various forts. The second map (bottom), professionally drawn only seven years later in 1802, shows locations of towns as well as county lines. (*Top: Frazer Ells Wilson,* The Treaty of Greenville. *Piqua, Ohio: The Correspondent Press 1894, facing chapter head 4. Bottom: Nevin O. Winter,* A History of Northwest Ohio. *Vol. I. Chicago: Lewis Publishing Co., 1917, p. 97.*)

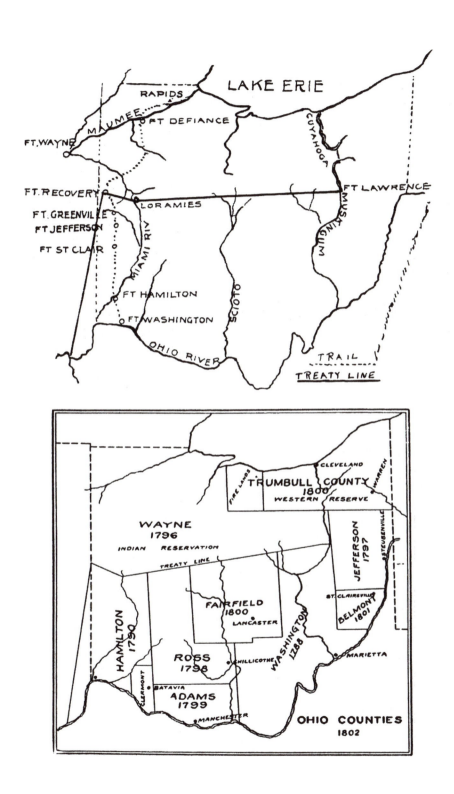

LAKE ERIE

RAPIDS

MAUMEE

FT. DEFIANCE

FT. WAYNE

CUYAHOGA

FT. LAWRENCE

FT. RECOVERY

LORAMIES

FT. GREENVILLE
FT. JEFFERSON

FT. ST CLAIR

MIAMI RIV

MUSKINGUM

FT HAMILTON

FT WASHINGTON

SCIOTO

OHIO RIVER

TRAIL

TREATY LINE

CLEVELAND

WARREN

FIRE LANDS

TRUMBULL COUNTY
1800
WESTERN RESERVE

WAYNE
1796

INDIAN RESERVATION

TREATY LINE

JEFFERSON
1797

STEUBENVILLE

FAIRFIELD
1800
LANCASTER

ST. CLAIRSVILLE

BELMONT
1801

HAMILTON
1790

WASHINGTON
1788

CLERMONT

ROSS
1798

CHILLICOTHE

MARIETTA

BATAVIA

ADAMS
1799

MANCHESTER

OHIO COUNTIES
1802

a large and unexpected window in the Miami opposition to the Greenville Treaty: The Miami would give in to peace, as long as the land division was on its own terms. Neither Wayne nor the peace factions hesitated. They dived headlong through the open window, swiftly concluding the treaty.

The shouting over, all that remained was to haggle out the details of exact boundary lines, the repatriation of "prisoners" among the Natives (most of whom were, by then, adoptees, and not all eager to return to "civilization"), and Wayne's rather offensive demand that hostages be left to secure Native compliance with the treaty (ASP 1998, 1:578). Although Meshikinoquak continued to lob flares through the holes in Wayne's position, it was clear that the council had turned conclusively to peace, a fact underscored by the very late arrival on July 31, of Red Pole, leading eighty-eight Shawnee, and Teyyaghtaw, bringing Six Nations delegates, including seven more Wyandot (ASP 1998, 1:578). With this new show that support for the war factions of the Shawnee and Wyandot was waning, all residual opposition collapsed. A relieved Anthony Wayne seized the opportunity to read aloud the terms of the Greenville treaty a final time, preparatory to its signing.

As the council wound down on August 8, the Pottawatamie New Corn, who had consistently upheld peace, showed that the peace faction did not consist of gullible, grinning yes-men, but browbeaten peoples who were leery of the accord they had just struck. Addressing Wayne as "my friend, the Great Wind," he admonished him not to "deceive us in the manner that the French, the British, the Spaniards, have heretofore done. The English have abused us much; they have made us promises which they never fulfilled; they have proved to us how little they have ever had our happiness at heart; and we have severely suffered for placing our dependence on so faithless a people. Be you strong, and preserve your word inviolate" (ASP 1998, 1:580–81).

New Corn was right to doubt the honor of the United States. The ink was scarcely dry on this latest pen-and-ink witchcraft before deceits were perpetrated with the Greenville Treaty. Not the least of these was the misrepresentation of what nations had attended the council. Western documents list the representatives thus: Wyandot delegation, 180; Lenape, 381; Shawnee, 143; Ottawa, 45; Chippewa, 46; Pottawatamies, 240; Miami and Eel River Indians, 73; Wea and Piankeshaw, 12; Kickapoo and Kaskaskia, 10 (Bowersox 1920, 1:93).

However, it appears that some of the data was fudged, especially concerning the Wea, the Kickapoo, the Piankashaw, and the Kaskaskia. It is fairly clear that Wayne willy-nilly "appointed" the Wea to speak for the Piankashaw and the Kickapoo to speak for the Kaskaskia, although the nations involved recognized no such crisscrossed offices or relationships. Furthermore, Wayne seems to have neglected to mention to the Wea and the Kickapoo that he had made them the speakers of the Piankashaw and the Kaskaskia (Stout 1974, 360).

Wayne invented these speakerships to cover another difficulty, to wit, that the Piankashaw and the Kaskaskia never attended the Greenville treaty council (Stout 1974, 345). William Henry Harrison, Wayne's aide-de-camp, wrote in 1802 and again in 1805, that neither of these groups had been present (Stout 1974, 357–58). Their signatures on the treaty were added later and falsely (Stout 1974, 346). The minutes of the Treaty council support this contention, for they carefully recorded the arrival of the other nations, by date, but never mentioned the arrival of either the Piankashaw or the Kaskaskia, nor were any representatives of these nations on record as making any of the speeches (ASP 1998, 1:564–82; Stout 1974, 348–50, 360–63). In addition, the original, handwritten copy of the Treaty clearly indicates that the Piankashaw and Kaskaskia were scribbled in, and there is much room for suspicion that these interlineations—written in a different hand from the rest of the document—were inserted *after* the signatures were affixed to the treaty (Stout 1974, 351–56).

The serious questions of the accreditation of speakers, especially from the Wyandot, Shawnee, Wea, and Kickapoo; the misrepresentation of nations in attendance, especially the Piankashaw and the Kaskaskia; and the clear document doctoring notwithstanding, the Greenville Treaty is listed in Kappler as stainless (Kappler 1904/1973, 39–45) and has been treated as such by every mainstream historian since the treaty was signed.

The Greenville Treaty handed over all but the northwest corner of Ohio to the United States, i.e., all the "good" land, since much of northwest Ohio was the Great Black Swamp. The treaty supposedly protected the Natives on the land left to them, guaranteeing farming and hunting rights thereon and promising to boot out squatters, yet it contradictorily set up twenty-eight "reservations" of land in Articles III and IV—nineteen for trading posts and military forts (Kappler 1904/1973, 40–41); five for portage rights on water passages through the lands (Kappler 1904/1973, 41); and four further "relinquishments" for forts and personal usage by settlers (Kappler 1904/1973, 41).

Worse, the Treaty retained what amounted to a right of pre-emption of land by the U.S. government, practically at will, under Article V, which stipulated that, "when disposed to sell their lands, or any part of them," the Natives must sell "only to the United States" (Kappler 1904/1972, 42). As Stewart Rafert pointed out in 1996, when the settler urge to landgrab reached a boiling point, the Native "disposition to sell could be manufactured" (Rafert 1996, 62)—and it was. In 1796, just one year after the Greenville Treaty was signed, there were already 5,000 "white" inhabitants in Ohio (Winter 1:95). Euro-American population statistics skyrocketed thereafter. By the year 1800, there were 45,365 settlers in Ohio, a whopping increase of over 40,000 people in just four years (OSR 1995).

The Greenville Treaty, with its twenty-eight reservations and sale clause, allowed for the Treaty of Fort Industry (a trading post) to be signed in modern-day downtown Toledo, on July 4, 1805 (ASP 1998, 1:695–96). Forced upon the Three Fires, the Wyandot, the Lenape, and the Shawnee (with the Miami conspicuously absent), the Fort Industry Treaty effectively moved the Greenville Treaty line far north and west, up to the southern shores of Lake Erie, and over to the Maumee River, *all* land that had been guaranteed to the Natives at Greenville a mere decade before. The Fort Industry Treaty stimulated a massive invasion of northern Ohio, with ship building taking off along southern shores of Lake Erie, as settlers poured in to yet more Native lands. In 1810, immediately before Tecumseh began his armed struggle to reunite eastern Natives against land seizure, the settler population in Ohio had lept to 230,760 (OSR 1995).

As the number of settlers soared, the official Native census plummeted. By 1816, the number of Natives whom the missionaries could lay their hands on to enumerate were Wyandot of Upper Sandusky 695; Shawnee on the Auglaize and Miami Rivers, 840; Lenape on the Sandusky and Muskingum Rivers, 161; Seneca at the cities of Upper and Lower Sandusky, 450; and Ottawa on the Maumee Bay, 450; for a grand total of 2,600 Natives recorded as living north of Greenville treaty line in Ohio (Bowersox 1920, 1:175). Although other records show this census to have been seriously understated—by that time, hundreds of Native Ohio families had slipped into hiding in the swamps of the Maumee Valley and the hills of Ohio Appalachia—the fact remains that their treaty lands were up for settler grabs.

This became painfully apparent in 1817, when even the Northwest corner of Ohio, which had been solemnly reserved to the

Native Union in 1795, was seized in de facto retribution for Tecumseh's failed resistance movement. The Treaty at the Foot of the Rapids of the Miami of Lake Erie, signed September 29, 1817, wrenched the last bit of Ohio away from the very peoples who had formed the peace faction at Greenville: the Ohio Iroquois, including the Lenape, Seneca, and Sandusky Wyandot; the Shawnee; and the Three Fires Confederacy (Kappler 1904/1973, 145; whole treaty, Kappler 1904/1973, 145–55). Notwithstanding the 1816 missionary census of 2,600 Natives, all told, in Northwest Ohio, at least 7,000 men, women, and children turned out at the rapids to watch the land, guaranteed to them by Wayne at Greenville, spirited away from their legal possession (Winter 1:194). Many more did not bother to attend a council whose end was so sadly predictable but simply dug into deeper hiding as the inundation of settlers ballooned yet again. By 1820, three years after the Foot of the Rapids Treaty, the settler population of Ohio had climbed to 581,434, more than twice what it had been a mere decade before (OSR 1995).

The boggling invasion facilitated by the Greenville Treaty was (and still is) cheerfully dubbed "the opening of the Old Northwest" by mainstream historians, but the Greenville Treaty reached far beyond this much-touted achievement. It also formed the prototype of the pen-and-ink witchcraft to follow, standing as the model for all subsequent land treaties between the United States and Native Americans up to the year 1871 (Rafert 1996, 60). It set the precedent of the United States's recognizing Natives as the owners of their land so as to be in a better position to force those same Natives into selling that land, once the United States had pressed their backs to the wall. "But," as Egushawa observed, "this is the mode our elder brethren are pleased to adopt, to evidence to us, they wish to live in peace with all nations" (McKee 1792, 11).

## REFERENCES

*American State Papers (ASP)*. 1998. Class II. Vol. 1. 1832. Buffalo, NY: William S. Hein & Co., Inc.

*American State Papers*. Class II. Vol. 1. 1832. Buffalo, NY: William S. Hein & Co., Inc.

Aupaumut, H. 1998. A narrative of an embassy to the western Indians, from the original manuscript of Hendrick Aupaumut, 1791 and 1793. *Memoirs of the historical society of Pennsylvania* 2.1 (1827): 9–131.

Axelrod, A. 1993. *Chronicle of the Indian wars from Colonial times to Wounded Knee.* New York: Prentice Hall.

Barton, B. S. 1798/1976. *New views of the origin of the tribes and nations of America.* Millwood, NY: Kraus Reprint Co.

Beatty, C. 1768. *The journal of a two months tour.* London: William Davenhill and George Pearch.

Berkeley, E. and D. S. Berkeley. 1974. *Dr. John Mitchell: The man who made the map of North America.* Chapel Hill, NC: University of North Carolina Press.

Bowersox, C. A. 1920. *A Standard History of Williams County, Ohio.* 2 vols. New York: The Lewis Publishing Company.

Brinton, D. G. 1885/1999. *The Lenâpé and their legends; with the complete text and symbols of the Walam Olum, A new translation, and inquiry into its authenticity.* Lewisburg, PA: Wennawoods Publishing.

Butler, M. 1834. Treaty of Fort Stanwix, 1768. In *A history of the commonwealth of Kentucky.* Louisville, KY: Wilcox, Dickerman and Co., 379–94.

Carter, C. E., ed. 1934. *The territorial papers of the United States.* 28 vols. Washington, DC: Government Printing Office.

Carter, H. L. 1987. *The life and times of Little Turtle: First Sagamore of the Wabash.* Chicago: University of Illinois Press.

Churchill, W. 1997. *A little matter of genocide: Holocaust and denial in the Americas, 1492 to the present.* San Francisco: City Lights Books.

Clark, J. E. 1997. *The Shawnee.* Lexington: The University Press of Kentucky.

Clark, H. 1995. *All cloudless glory: The life of George Washington, from youth to Yorktown.* Washington, DC: Regnery Publishing, Inc.

Clinton, De W. 1811–1859. A discourse delivered before the New-York Historical Society, at their anniversary meeting, 6th December 1811. In *Collections of the New-York Historical Society for the year 181.* Vol. 2. New York: I. Riley.

Cusick, D. 1892. Sketches of ancient history of the six nations. 1825. In *The Iroquois Trail or Foot-prints of the Six Nations, in Customs, Traditions, and History.* Ed. William M. Beauchamp, Fayetteville, NY: H. C. Beauchamp.

Deloria, V., Jr., and R. J. DeMallie. 1999. *Documents of American Indian diplomacy: Treaties, agreements, and conventions, 1775–1979,* 2 vols. Norman, OK: University of Oklahoma Press.

Dodge, J. R. 1859. *Red men of the Ohio Valley: An aboriginal history of the period commencing* A.D. 1650, and ending at the Treaty of Greenville [*sic*], A.D. *1795.* Springfield, OH: Ruralist Publishing Company.

Duncan, B. R. 1998. *Living stories of the Cherokee.* Chapel Hill, NC: University of North Carolina Press.

Eckert, A. 1995. *That dark and bloody river: Chronicles of the Ohio River Valley.* New York: Bantam Books.

Edel, W. 1997. *Kekionga! The worst defeat in the history of the U.S. Army.* Westport, CT: Praeger Publishers.

Fitzpatrick, J. C., ed. 1925. *The diaries of George Washington, 1748–1799.* 4 vols. New York: Houghton Mifflin.

———, ed. 1938. *The writings of George Washington from the original manuscript sources, 1745–1799.* 39 vols. Washington, DC: Government Printing Office.

Galbreath, C. B. 1925. *History of Ohio.* 5 vols. New York: The American Historical Society, Inc. Vol. 1.

Griffin, J. B. 1943. *The Fort Ancient aspect.* University of Michigan Anthropological Papers, no. 28. Ann Arbor, MI: Museum of Anthropology.

———, ed. 1952. *Archaeology of Eastern United States.* Chicago: University of Chicago Press.

Hale, H. 1883/1963. *The Iroquois book of rites.* Toronto: University of Toronto Press.

Haywood, J. 1823. *The natural and aboriginal history of Tennessee, up to the first settlements therein by the white people, in the year 1768.* Nashville: George Wilson.

Heckewelder, J. 1876/1971. *History, manners, and customs of the Indian nations who once inhabited Pennsylvania and the neighboring states. 1820.* New York: Arno Press.

———. 1818/1971. *Narrative of the mission of the United Brethren among the Delaware and Mohegan Indians from its commencement, in the year 1740, to the close of the year 1808.* New York: Arno Press.

Horsman, R. 1961. American Indian policy in the Old Northwest, 1783–1812. *William and Mary Quarterly* 18.1 (January): 35–53.

Johansen, B. E., and B. A. Mann. 2000. *Encyclopedia of the Haudenosaunee (Iroquois Confederacy).* Westport, CT: Greenwood Press.

Johnson, E., Chief. 1881/1978. *Legends, traditions and laws, of the Iroquois, or Six Nations.* New York: AMS Press.

Kappler, C. J., ed. and comp. 1904/1973. *Indian treaties, 1778–1883.* New York: Interland Publishing, Inc.

Knox, H. 1934. The CAUSES of the existing HOSTILITIES between the UNITED STATES, and certain Tribes of INDIANS North-West of the OHIO. *Territorial papers of the United States.* Ed. Clarence Edwin Carter. 28 vols. Washington, DC: Government Printing Office, 2: 359–66.

Kutler, Stanley I., ed. 2003. *Dictionary of American history.* 10 vols. New York: Charles Scribners Sons. 6:175.

Lafitau, J. F. 1724/1974. *Customs of the American Indians compared with the customs of primitive times.* Ed. and trans. William N. Fenton and Elizabeth L. Moore. 2 vols. Toronto: The Champlain Society.

Leidy, E. E. 1929. The extinction of the Indian title in Ohio beyond the Greenville Treaty line. Ph.D. Diss. Ohio State University.

Libby, D. 1974. An anthropological report on the Piankashaw Indians. *Piankashaw and Kaskaskia Indians.* Ed. David Agee Horr. New York: Garland Publishing, 27–341.

Mann, B. A. 2000. *Iroquoian women: The Gantowisas.* New York: Peter Lang Publishing.

———. *Native Americans, Archaeologists, and the Mounds.* 2003. New York: Peter Lang Publishing.

———, ed. 2001. *Native American speakers of the Eastern woodlands: Selected speeches and critical analysis.* Westport, CT: Greenwood Press.

Mann, B.A., and J.L. Fields. 1997. A sign in the sky: Dating the League of the Haudenosaunee. *American Indian Culture and Research Journal* 21. 2: 105–63.

McElwain, T. 2001. "Then I thought I must kill too": Logan's lament: A "Mingo" perspective. *Native American speakers of the eastern woodlands: Selected speeches and critical analysis.* Ed. Barbara Alice Mann. Westport, CT: Greenwood Press, 107–21.

[McKee, A]. 1792. Minutes of debates in council on the banks of the Ottawa River, (commonly called the Miami of the Lake), November, 1791. Philadelphia: William Young, Bookseller.

Morris, R.B., and J.B. Morris. 1996. *Encyclopedia of American History.* 7th ed. New York: HarperCollins Publishers.

Murphy, J.A., ed. 1882/1997. *The Greenville Peace Treaty: The Actual Speeches of the Council.* Columbus, OH: Brockston Publishing Company.

Office of Strategic Research (OSR). Ohio Department of Development. Population of Ohio and Ohio's Top Ten Cities, 1800 to 1990. Posted November 1995. Accessed 11, December 2001. http://www.odod.state.oh.us/osr/srpopu.htm.

Parker, A.C. 1926/1970. *An analytical history of the Seneca Indians.* Researches and Transactions of the New York State Archaeological Association, Lewis H. Morgan Chapter. New York: Kraus Reprint Company.

———. 1916. *The Constitution of the Five Nations, or the Iroquois Book of the Great Law.* New York State Museum Bulletin, no. 184. Albany: The University of the State of New York.

Perry, James M. *Arrogant Armies: Great Military Disasters and the Generals Behind Them.* 1996. New York: John Wiley, 1996.

Peters, R. 1853. *The public statutes at large of the United States of America.* 8 vols. Boston: Little, Brown, and Company.

Pratt, G.M. 1997. The battle of Fallen Timbers: An eyewitness perspective. *Northwest Ohio Quarterly* 67.1 (Winter): 4–34.

———. Fallen Timbers Battlefield archaeological project at Heidelberg College. Accessed 12 December 2001. http://www.heidelberg.edu/offices/chma/fallen-timbers/.

Prucha, F.P. 1994. *American Indian treaties: The history of a political anomaly.* Berkeley: University of California Press.

Rafert, S. 1996. *The Miami Indians of Indiana: A persistent people, 1654–1994.* N.c.: Indiana Historical Society.

St. Clair, A. 1812/1971. *A narrative of the campaign against the Indians, under the command of Major General St. Clair.* New York: Arno Press & The New York Times.

Sargent, W. 1924 Winthrop Sargent's diary while with General Arthur St. Clair's expedition against the Indians. *Ohio Archaeological and Historical Quarterly* 33 (July): 237–82.

Schweinitz, E. de. 1870. *The life and times of David Zeisberger, the western pioneer and apostle of the Indians.* Philadelphia: J.B. Lippincott & Co., 36–37.

Smith, D. L. 1950. *Wayne's peace with the Indians of the Old Northwest, 1795.* Fort Wayne, IN: The Public Library of Fort Wayne and Allen County.

Smith, W. H., ed. 1882. *The St. Clair papers.* 2 vols. Cincinnati: Robert Clark & Co.

Sosin, J. M., ed. 1969. *The opening of the West.* Columbia, SC: University of South Carolina Press.

Sparks, J., ed. 1885. *The writings of George Washington.* 12 vols. Boston: Little, Brown, and Company.

Stout, D. B. 1974. The Piankashaw and Kaskaskia and the Treaty of Greene Ville. *Piankashaw and Kaskaskia Indians.* New York: Garland Publishing, Inc., 343–75.

Sword, W. 1985. *President Washington's Indian war: The struggle for the Old Northwest, 1790–1795.* Norman: University of Oklahoma Press.

Tanner, H. H. 1974. The Greenville Treaty, 1795. *Indians of Ohio and Indiana Prior to 1795.* 2 vols. New York: Garland Publishing, Inc., 1: 51–463.

Thwaites, R. G., ed. and trans. 1959. *Les Relations de Jésuites, or The Jesuit Relations: Travels and explorations of the Jesuit Missionaries in New France, 1610–1791.* 73 vols. New York: Pageant Book Company.

Trowbridge, C. C. 1939. *Shawnese Traditions.* Ed. Vernon Kinietz and Erminie W. Voegelin. Ann Arbor, MI: University of Michigan Press.

Van Every, D. 1963. *Ark of empire: The American frontier, 1784–1803.* New York: William Morrow and Company.

Wallace, Paul A. W., ed. 1958. *Thirty thousand miles with John Heckewelder.* Pittsburgh: University of Pittsburgh Press.

Walsh, W. P. 1977. The defeat of Major General Arthur St. Clair, November 4, 1791: A study of the nation's response, 1791–1793. Ph.D. Diss. Chicago: Loyola University of Chicago.

Wilson, F. E. 1945. *Around the council fire: Proceeding at Fort Greene Ville in 1795 culminating the the signing of the Treaty of Greene Ville.* Greenville, OH: Frazer E. Wilson.

———. 1909. *The peace of Mad Anthony: An account of the subjugation of the north-western Indian tribes and the treaty of GreeneVille* [sic]. Greenville, OH: Chas. R. Kemble.

———. 1894. *The Treaty of Greenville.* Piqua, OH: The Correspondent Press.

Winter, Nevin O. *A History of Northwest Ohio: A Narrative Account of Its Historical Progress and Development from the First European Exploration of the Maumee and Sandusky Valleys and the Adjacent Shore of Lake Erie, down to the Present Time.* 1917. 3 vols. Chicago & New York: The Lewis Publishing Co.

# 7

# Rebirth of the Osni (Northern) Ponca

*Jerry Stubben*

> *Not like the white people who put their laws in large, heavy books and forget them. We Ponca carry our laws in our hearts, where we never live a day without them.*
>
> **—Ponca Elders 1979**

## THE TRADITIONAL OSNI PONCA

The term *Ponca* is derived from the Ponca words *Pun* (People) and *Ka* (Head) or "Head People." An Oglala Sioux skin painting sign identified the Ponca as a side view of a human head, usually facing to viewers left, with one long white feather (Powell 1886). One may surmise that the Ponca used wisdom rather than strength to defend themselves, since prior to the coming of the white man the Ponca had no more than 300 warriors at any given time. They were surrounded by over 40,000 Sioux, Pawnee, and a variety of other tribal warriors, yet they survived among these warring groups and even when the white men came, never engaging in war with them. Oral stories have reported that the Ponca clan heads would meet the Pawnee at the present-day Elkhorn River near Orchard, Nebraska, in order to exchange clan staffs with the Pawnee clan heads in order to move and hunt within the Pawnee territory and to allow the Pawnee to move and hunt in Ponca territory. As long as the hunting parties carried each others' clan staffs, they could move and hunt throughout each others' lands without fear of attack by either tribe. Thus, the Ponca utilized the art of negotiation and had treaties with other tribes prior to treaty making with the Europeans and Americans. A Ponca elder told the author nearly 40 years ago that, "We [Ponca] have the sacred wisdom to know when something is evil and when something is good, and when to move away from evil and towards good." The Trial of Standing Bear, reported later in this chapter, is further evidence of the wisdom of the Ponca people.

The Ponca are of the Degiha division of the Siouan language family, which also includes the Omaha, Osage, Kansa, and Quapaw and is further related to the Chiwere division which includes the Iowa, Oto, and Missouri (Howard 1965, 4). In language and custom the Ponca are mostly akin to the Omaha (Dorsey 1884, 211), who they separated from some time between 1390 and 1700 after moving into present-day northeast Nebraska from southern Ohio (Dorsey 1884 and 1886; Connelley 1918, 449). After separating from the Omaha, the Ponca traveled as far west as the Black Hills before establishing a village near the mouth of the Niobrara River in the early to mid-1700s (Howard 1965, 24; Wishart 1994, 6). The strategic location of the Ponca fostered trade with the Arikara, Omaha, Pawnee, the upriver Dakota, Lakota speaking Sioux, and other tribes in the region. The Ponca also obtained the horse after settling on the Niobrara sometime between 1725 and 1750, which allowed the Ponca to extend both their hunting and trade territories throughout the eighteenth and nineteenth centuries (Jablow 1974, 33). Archeological findings at the Ponca Fort site, located west of the Niobrara River's entry into the Missouri River, identify that the Ponca trade with other tribes was both extensive and lucrative. Pottery, stone mauls, mealing slabs and mullers, bone knives, hoes, tubes, shaft wrenches and picks, catlinite pipes and disks, twined mats, and strip bark in rolls have been found at the Ponca fort site from tribes as far away as the southeastern United States (Wood 1955; Howard 1965, 11–12; LeRoy 1998). Corn was a basic article of trade, and although the Ponca raised corn, they often preferred to trade robes and meat to the Omahas for corn (Jablow 1974, 40).

Socially and politically, the Ponca possessed a strict set of moral and social rules. Ponca elder Peter LeClaire (1947) offered the following moral laws as told to him by both northern and southern Ponca elders: (1) Have one god; (2) Do not kill one another; (3) Do not steal from one another; (4) Be kind to one another; (5) Do not talk about each other; (6) Do not be stingy and (7) Have respect for the Sacred Pipe (Le Claire 1947). Almost all tribal government and law was based on family relations or kinship, where family clans were central in tribal governing. Social rules were both tribal and clan based (Yerington 1985, 20). Individual violations of specific tribal laws of the Ponca were often enforced by the victims or their relatives, as was common among plains tribes. The punishment of an adulterer was left to the injured husband who might kill, scalp, or cut off the hair of a man whom he caught with his wife. A wife could kill another woman with whom her husband eloped. Ponca women also went to war and became braves, whereas Omaha women did not (Jablow 1974, 60). Killing as a form of capital punishment or in warfare was not considered murder. When murder was committed, retaliation was left to the relatives of the murdered individual and was often swift due to the belief that "the spirit of a murdered person will haunt the people, and when the tribe is on the hunt, will cause the wind to blow in such a direction as to betray the hunters" (Fletcher and La Flesche 1911, 216). Religious sanctions acted as a powerful deterrent to illegal acts. The murderer "can never satisfy his hunger, though he eat much food" (Dorsey 1894, 420).

Tribal laws in terms of property required that property belonged to either families, individuals, or the tribe as a whole. Community buildings and land belonged to the tribe. Individual property might be a man's gun and clothes. People had to ask to use one's individual property, and stealing was not tolerated. Families owned the tent or house. If a family member left, he lost his rights to the house. If a man left his wife, she kept the tipi. If she ran off with another man, he keeps the tipi (Le Claire 1965, 96). Divorce was simple in Ponca society. "If a man and wife didn't get along, or weren't satisfied, they just split up" (Le Claire 1965, 148). The children may go with their mother, her mother, or their father's mother. Should the father be unwilling, the wife cannot take the children with her. Each can remarry (Dorsey 1884, 262).

In terms of clan politics and law, each clan was responsible for a certain duty. One clan might take care of military matters, another religious duties, and another might be in charge of hunting or the harvest (Yerington Paiute Tribe 1985, 20–21). The political structure of the Ponca clans was hereditary and patrilineal. An individual's position in Ponca society depended upon his or her position in their family, and their family's position in the clan, and the clan's position in the tribe. Certain clans outranked certain others socially and had special rights and prerogatives not possessed by others (Howard 1965, 81). The terms *clan, band,* and *gente* are used synonymously throughout past literature. The Ponca like the Omaha were divided into two moieties or half-tribes, the earth and sky (Fletcher and La Flescher, 1911, 140). The Ponca had seven clans until the mid-1800s when the Wa-ge-ziga or whitemen's sons clan became the eighth clan (Ponca Census 1860, 1). The eight clans of the Ponca and their duties follow.

The Ponca camp is called Hu-thu-gah, it is round with the entrance in the east. Each of the bands has duties in the camp (Ponca Census 1860; Le Claire 1947). From the entrance left to right are the Wazaze or Wah-ja-ta (Snake or Osage) who guard the entrance and are expert trackers (Le Claire 1947). Touching snakes is taboo to members of this clan. The Nikapasna (skull or bald head) who know all about the human head and how it should be dressed. The Dixida (Blood) or *Te-xa-da* (Le Claire 1947) who perform magic, and when the camp is getting short of meats, they would get their bows and arrows out and make believe they are shooting animals saying "I'll shoot this fat one." The band in the center is the Wasabe, Washabe, or Wahshaba. The principal chief of the tribe was always selected from this clan, and members were forbidden from touching the head of an animal because they were of the head clan. The Maka or Miki (Medicine) who knew all about medicines and contained the best herbalists in the tribe. The Nuxe or Nuxa (Ice) who knew everything about water and ice. The Hisada or He-sah-da (Stretching of a bird's leg when running) were the tribal rainmakers. The Wageziga (White men's sons), which originated in the 1850s, had been founded to accommodate the sons of white traders who took Ponca wives. This clan had similar taboo with the Dixida in that they could not touch mice. Ponca subagency records identify that members of the Wageziga often were interpreters between the Ponca and the whites. Some clans had one or two subclans or subgentes who also had specific clan duties and rules.

Although, the principal chief of the Ponca came from the Wasabe, there were seven chiefs of the first order which were older chiefs, and a number of second order chiefs, ranging from five to twelve. First and Second order chiefs could be hereditary, chosen on bravery or trustworthiness to the people, or could buy their position based on acts of bravery in war, usually the number of times they counted coup in battle. Seven first order chiefs, which included the principal chief met in council to decide upon most matters. A third class of chiefs have been mentioned in past literature but were most likely younger warriors who had demonstrated that they were "not just interested in themselves, but in the tribe as a whole" (Howard 1965, 92). Each clan also had a hereditary clan head or chief and a group of subchiefs, who were appointed by the clan head. A chief of the first, second, and third order might also be a clan head (Howard 1965, 92). In most cases, clan heads and subchiefs were selected by heredity (son of clan head), which was the norm with the Omaha. Among the Ponca, however, a clan head could chose his successor or subchiefs based on trustworthiness or bravery in battle. Thus, Ponca chieftainships, unlike those of the Omaha, were both autocratic and democratic in nature (Jablow 1974, 55–58).

The clan heads and their subchiefs enforced the laws of the clan and settled conflicts within the clan. Conflicts between members of different clans were often settled by the council of seven, which was made up of the first order chiefs and the principal chief (Howard 1965, 92–93). Intragroup loyalty and cooperation required that even the clan heads must follow tribal rules. Tribal clan heads and sub-chiefs must (1) be good to the old; (2) be good to orphans; and (3) be good to the needy. Any violation could mean shame to the clan and removal as clan head (Le Claire 1965, 98). Tribal legend also indicates that women were not barred from becoming a chief. Often they were women with great supernatural power, medicine women (Le Claire 1965, 93). As a Ponca elder (1979) told me over twenty years ago, "Not like the white people who put their laws in large, heavy books and forget them. We Ponca carry our laws in our hearts, where we never live a day without them." I hope that all people will soon learn to do so.

## TREATY ERA

Treaties between the United States and over 500 tribes from 1780s to the 1870s were commonplace. The following is an example from the Ponca tribe in regards to how treaty relationships changed and the devastating toll that they took on tribal nations. The Ponca tribe entered into four treaties with the government. The Treaty of

1817 was a treaty of "peace and friendship" between the two nations. In the Treaty of 1825, the Ponca acknowledged that they lived within the "territorial limits of the United States," thereby recognizing the supremacy of the government. The Ponca also authorized the government to regulate all trade and commerce. The third treaty, signed in 1858, nullified the Poncas' title to all their lands occupied and claimed by them "except for a small portion on which to colonize or domesticate them." The fourth and final treaty signed in 1865 ceded an additional 30,000 acres of their reserved land. This final treaty provided for a reservation of 96,000 acres in the present-day Nebraska counties of Knox and Boyd. The following treaties (1817 and 1858) identify the shift in treaty policy from "peace, friendship and protection" to "domestication" and reservation life for the Ponca. Lewis and Clark visited the Ponca tribe in the fall of 1804, and Clark returned in 1817 to negotiate the following treaty and be the first to sign.

### TREATY WITH THE PONCA, June 25, 1817 | 7 Stat., 155. |

A treaty of peace and friendship made and concluded between William Clark and Auguste Chouteau, commissioners on the part and behalf of the United States of America, of the one part, and the undersigned chiefs and warriors of the Poncarar [sic] tribe of Indians, on the [their] part and of their said tribe of the other part.

The parties being desirous of re-established peace and friendship between the United States and their said tribe, and of being placed, in all things and every respect, upon the same footing upon which they stood before the late war between the United States and Great Britain, have agreed to the following articles:

ART. 1. Every injury or act of hostility by one or either of the contracting parties against the other, shall be mutually forgiven and forgot.

ART. 2. There shall be perpetual peace and friendship between all the citizens of the United States of America and all the individuals composing the said Poncarar tribe; and all the friendly relations that existed between them before the war shall be, and the same are hereby, renewed.

ART. 3. The undersigned chiefs and warriors, for themselves and their said tribe, do hereby acknowledge themselves to be under the protection of the United States of America, and of no other nation, power, sovereign, whatever.

In witness whereof, the said William Clark and Auguste Chouteau, commissioners as aforesaid, have hereunto subscribed their names and affixed their seals, this twenty-fifth day of June, in the year of our Lord one thousand eight hundred and seventeen, and of the independence of the United States the forty-first.

William Clark, [L. S.]
Auguste Chouteau, [L. S.]
Aquelaba, the Fighter, his x mark, [L. S.]
Gradonga, Fork-tailed Hawk, his x mark, [L. S.]
Shondagaha, Smoker, his x mark, [L. S.]
Kihegashinga, Little Chief, his x mark, [L. S.]
Necawcompe, the Handsome Man, his x mark, [L. S.]
Ahahpah, the Rough Buffalo Horn, his x mark, [L. S.]
Showeno, the Comer, his x mark, [L. S.]
Bardegara, he who stands fire, his x mark, [L. S.]

**Witnesses present:**

Lewis Bissel, acting secretary to the commissioners,
Manual Liea, United States Indian agent,
Benja O'Fallon, United States Indian agent,
R, Graham, Indian agent for Illinois,
Dr. Wm. J. Clarke,
B. Vasques,
Saml. Solomon, interpreter,
Stephen Julien, United States Indian interpreter,
Joseph Lafleche, interpreter.

The following treaty of 1858 established the first Ponca reservation and transferred millions of acres of land over to the U.S. government for compensation of less than $400,000 in annuity payments, agency schools, housing, and other reservation improvements, half-breed provisions, and payments to non-Indians for past losses of property attributed to the Ponca. Some have estimated that the Ponca received 2 cents an acre for their lands, which the U.S. government sold for a minimum of $2.00 an acre.

## TREATY WITH THE PONCA, 1858. Mar. 12, 1858. | 12 Stats., 997. | Ratified Mar. 8, 1859. | Proclaimed Apr. 11, 1859.

Articles of agreement and convention made and concluded at the city of Washington, on the twelfth day of March, one thousand eight hundred and fifty-eight, by Charles E. Mix, commissioner on the part of the United States, and Wa-gah-sah-pi, or Whip; Gish-tah-wah-gu, or Strong Walker; Mitchell P. Cera, or Wash-kom-moni; A-shno-ni-kah-gah-hi, or Lone Chief; Shu-kah-bi, or Heavy Clouds; Tah-tungah-nushi, or Standing Buffalo, on the part of the Ponca tribe of Indians; they being thereto duly authorized and empowered by said tribe.

ARTICLE 1. The Ponca tribe of Indians hereby cede and relinquish to the United States all the lands now owned or claimed by them, wherever situated, except the tract bounded as follows, viz: Beginning at a point on the Neobrara River and running due north, so as to intersect the Ponca River twenty-five miles from its mouth; thence from said point of intersection, up and along the Ponca River, twenty—miles; thence due south to the Neobrara River; and thence down and along said river to the place of beginning; which tract is hereby reserved for the future homes of said Indians; and to which they agree and bind themselves to remove within one year from the date of the ratification of this agreement by this Senate and President of the United States.

ARTICLE 2. In consideration of the foregoing cession and relinquishment, the United States agree and stipulate as follows, viz:

First. To protect the Poncas in the possession of the tract of land reserved for their future homes, and their persons and property thereon, during good behavior on their part.

Second. To pay to them, or expend for their benefit, the sum of twelve thousand dollars ($12,000) per annum for five years; commencing with the year in which they shall remove to and settle upon the tract reserved for their future homes; ten thousand dollars ($10,000) per annum for ten years, from and after the expiration of the said five years; and thereafter eight thousand dollars ($8,000) per annum, for fifteen years; of which sums the President of the United States shall, from time to time, determine what proportion shall be paid to the Poncas in cash, and what proportion shall be expended for their benefit; and also in what manner or for what objects such expenditure shall be made. He shall likewise exercise the power to make such provision out of the same, as he may deem to be necessary and proper for the support and comfort of the aged and infirm members of the tribe. In case of any material decrease of the Poncas in number, the said amounts shall be reduced and diminished in proportion thereto, or they may, at the discretion of the President, be discontinued altogether should said Indians fail to make satisfactory efforts to advance and improve their condition; in which case such other provision shall be made for them as the President and Congress may judge to be suitable and proper.

Third. To expend the sum of twenty thousand dollars ($20,000) in maintaining and subsisting the Poncas during the first year after their removal to their new homes, purchasing stock and agricultural implements, breaking up and fencing land, building houses, and in making such other improvements as may be necessary for their comfort and welfare.

Fourth. To establish, and to maintain for ten years, at an annual expense not to exceed five thousand dollars, ($5,000,) one or more manual-labor schools for the education and training of the Ponca youth in letters, agriculture, the mechanic arts, and housewifery; which school or schools shall be managed and conducted in such manner as the President of the United States shall direct; the Poncas hereby stipulating to constantly keep, during at least nine months in every year, all their children between the ages of seven and eighteen years in school; and that, if this be not done, there shall be deducted from the shares of the annuities due to the parents, guardians, or other persons having control of the children, such amounts as may be proportioned to the deficiency in their time of attendance, compared with the said nine months, and the cost of maintaining and educating the children during that period. It is further agreed that such other measures may be adopted, to compel the attendance of the children at the school or schools as the President may think proper and direct; and whenever he shall be satisfied of a failure to fulfil the aforesaid stipulation on the part of the Poncas, he may, at his discretion, diminish or wholly discontinue the allowance and expenditure of the sum herein set apart for the support and maintenance of said school or schools.

Fifth. To provide the Poncas with a mill suitable for grinding grain and sawing timber, one or more mechanic shops, with the necessary tools for the same, and dwelling-houses for an interpreter, miller, engineer for the mill, if one be necessary farmer, and the mechanics that may be employed for their benefit, the whole not to exceed in cost the sum of ten thousand five hundred dollars, ($10,500;) and also to expend annually, for ten years, or during the pleasure of the President, an amount not exceeding seven thousand five hundred dollars, ($7,500,) for the purpose of furnishing said Indians with such aid and assistance in agricultural and mechanical pursuits, including the working of said mill, as the Secretary of the Interior may consider advantageous and necessary for them; the Poncas hereby stipulating to furnish from their tribe the number of young men that may be required as apprentices and as assistants in the mill and mechanic shops, and at least three persons to work constantly with each laborer employed for them in agricultural pursuits, it being understood that such laborers are to be employed more for the instruction of the Indians than merely to work for their benefit. The persons so to be furnished by the tribe shall be allowed a fair and just compensation for their services, to be fixed by the Secretary of the Interior. The Poncas further stipulate and bind themselves to prevent any of the members of their tribe from destroying or injuring the said houses, shops, mill, machinery, stock, farming utensils, or any other thing furnished them by the Government; and in case of any such destruction or injury, or of any of the things so furnished being carried off by any member or members of their tribe, the value of the same shall be deducted from the tribal annuities. And whenever the President shall be satisfied that the Poncas have become sufficiently confirmed in habits of industry, and advanced in acquiring a practical knowledge of agriculture and the mechanic arts, he may, at his discretion, cause to be turned over to the tribe all of the said houses and other property furnished them by the United States, and dispense with the services of any or all of the persons hereinbefore stipulated to be employed for their benefit and assistance.

Sixth. To provide and set apart the sum of twenty thousand dollars ($20,000) to enable the Poncas to adjust and settle their existing obligations and engagements, including depredations committed by them on property of citizens of the United States prior to the date of the ratification of this agreement, so far as the same may be found and decided by their agent to be valid and just, subject to the approval of the Secretary of the Interior; and in consideration of the long-continued friendship and kindness of Joseph Hollman and William G. Crawford toward the Poncas, of their furnishing them, when in distress, with large quantities of goods and provisions, and of their good counsel and advice, in consequence of which peace has often been preserved between the Poncas and other Indians and the whites, it is agreed that out of the above-mentioned amount they shall be paid the sum of three thousand five hundred dollars, ($3,500,) and the sum of one thousand dollars ($1,000) shall in like manner be paid to Jesse Williams of Iowa, in full for his claim, as such has been admitted by the Poncas for depredations committed by them on his property.

ARTICLE 3. The Poncas being desirous of making provision for their half-breed relatives, it is agreed that those who prefer and elect to reside among them shall be permitted to do so, and be entitled to and enjoy all the rights and privileges of members of the tribe; but to those who have chosen and left the tribe to reside among the whites and follow the pursuits of civilized life, viz: Charles Leclaire, Fort Piere, N. T.; Cillaste Leclaire Pottowattomie, K. T.: Ciprian Leclaire. St. Louis, Missouri; Julia Harvey, Omaha, N. T.: Jenny Ruleau. Sioux City, Iowa; David Leclaire, Amelia Deloge, and Laura Deloge. at the Omaha mission, there shall be issued scrip for one hundred and sixty acres of land each, which shall be receivable at the United States land-offices in the same manner, and be subject to the same rules and regulations as military bounty-land warrants. And in consideration of the faithful services rendered to the Poncas by Francis Roy, their interpreter, it is agreed that scrip shall, in the like manner and amount, be issued to his wife and to each of his six children now living, without their being required to leave the nation. Provided, That application for the said scrip shall be made to the Commissioner of Indian Affairs within five years from and after the date of the ratification of this agreement.

ARTICLE 4. The United States shall have the right to establish and maintain such military posts, roads, and Indian agencies as may be deemed necessary within the tract of country hereby reserved for the Poncas, but no greater quantity of land or timber shall be used for said purposes than shall be actually requisite; and if, in the establishment or maintenance of such posts, roads, and agencies, the property of any Ponca shall be taken, injured, or destroyed, just and adequate compensation shall be made therefore by the United States. And all roads or highways authorized by competent authority, other than the United States, the lines of which shall lie through said tract, shall have the right of way through the same; the fair and just value of such right being paid to the Poncas therefor by the party or parties authorizing the same or interested therein: to be assessed and determined in such manner as the President of the United States shall direct.

ARTICLE 5. No white person, unless in the employment of the United States, or duly licensed to trade with the Poncas, or members of the family of such persons, shall be permitted to reside, or to make any settlement, upon any part of the tract herein reserved for said Indians, nor shall the latter alienate, sell, or in manner dispose of any portion thereof, except to the United States; but, whenever they may think proper, they may divide said tract among themselves, giving to each head of a family or single person a farm, with such rights of possession, transfer to any other member of the tribe, or of descent to their heirs and representatives, as may be in accordance with the laws, customs, and regulations of the tribe.

ARTICLE 6. Such persons as are now lawfully residing on the lands herein ceded by the Poncas shall each have the privilege of entering one hundred and sixty acres thereof, to include any improvements they may have, at one dollar and twenty-five cents per acre.

ARTICLE 7. The Poncas acknowledge their dependence upon the Government of the United States, and do hereby pledge and bind themselves to preserve friendly relations with the citizens thereof, and to commit no injuries or depredations on their persons or property, nor on those of members of any other tribe; but, in case of any such injury or depredation, full compensation shall, as far as practicable, be made therefor out of their tribal annuities; the amount in all cases to be determined by the Secretary of the Interior. They further pledge themselves not to engage in hostilities with any other tribe, unless in self-defence, but to submit, through their agent, all matters of dispute and difficulty between themselves and other Indians for the decision of the President of the United States, and to acquiesce in and abide thereby. They also agree, whenever called upon by the proper officer, to deliver up all offenders against the treaties, laws, or regulations of the United States, who may be within the limits of their reservation, and to assist in discovering pursuing, and capturing all such offenders, whenever required to do so by such officer.

ARTICLE 8. To aid in preventing the evils of intemperance, it is hereby stipulated that if any of the Poncas shall drink, or procure for others, intoxicating liquor, their proportion of the tribal annuities shall be withheld from them for at least one year; and for a violation of any of the stipulations of this agreement on the part of the Poncas, they shall be liable to have their annuities withheld, in whole or in part, and for such length of time as the President of the United States shall direct.

ARTICLE 9. No part of the annuities of the Poncas shall be taken to pay any claims or demands against them, except such as may arise under this agreement, or under the trade and intercourse laws of the United States; and the said Indians do hereby fully relinquish and release the

United States from all demands against them on the part of the tribe or any individuals thereof, except such as are herein stipulated and provided for.

ARTICLE 10. The expenses connected with the negotiation of this agreement shall be paid by the United States.

In testimony whereof, the said Charles E. Mix, commissioner, as aforesaid, and the undersigned delegates and representatives of the Ponca tribes of Indians, have hereunto set their names and seals, at the place and on the day hereinbefore written.

Charles E. Mix, Commissioner. [L. S.]
Wah-gah-sah-pi, or Whip, his x mark. [L. S.]
Gish-tah-wah-gu, or Strong Walker, his x mark. [L. S.]
Mitchell P. Cera, or Wash-kom-mo-ni, his x mark. [L. S.]
A-shno-ni-kah-gah-hi, or Lone Chief, his x mark. [L. S.]
Shu-kah-bi, or Heavy Clouds, his x mark. [L. S.]
Tah-tungah-nushi, or Standing Buffalo, his x mark. [L. S.]

**Executed in the presence of—**

Edward Hanrick,
E. B. Grayson,
James R. Roche,
Moses Kelly,
Joseph Hollman,
Jno. Wm. Wells,
J. B. Robertson, United States Indian agent,
Henry Fontenelle, United States interpreter,
Francis Roy, his x mark.

Ironically, it was a treaty with another group of tribes, the Fort Laramie Treaty of 1868, that forever altered the course of Ponca history. Among other things, it established the boundaries of the Great Sioux Reservation which included the 96,000 acres of land that the same government had set aside for the Ponca Reservation, established by the last treaty with the Ponca, in 1865. The Ponca thus became trespassers under U.S. law in their own aboriginal homeland. Over the next eight years, the Ponca repeatedly appealed to the government for assistance but received very little. In 1877, most of the tribe was forcibly removed to the Indian Territory in present-day Oklahoma.

## REMOVAL

In the 1870s, the United States government formulated a policy to consolidate as many tribes as possible in Indian Territory in Oklahoma. Due to continual attacks by the Sioux in the late 1860s, the Ponca as early as 1867, had considered moving in among the Omaha (Ponca Agency 1864–1870). In 1869, attacks by the Sioux increased, mainly due to the Fort Laramie Treaty of 1868 and the attempt by the Sioux to drive the Ponca from lands that they now considered theirs. White Bird was killed by a party of Brule in August (Ponca Agency 1864–1870, 0028–0035). Over 300 horses were stolen, and over two dozen Ponca were killed by the Sioux in 1870 (Ponca Agency 1864–1870). The whites in the area also suffered as a Bohemian settler, his wife, and son were killed and daughter "stolen" by the Oglala Sioux just prior to an attack on a Ponca village and the theft of several horses and supplies (Ponca Agency 1864–1870, 0081–0082). U.S. Army troops were placed at the agency near Niobrara in May 1870, but they had little impact on the continual raids and the inability of the Ponca to farm or go on seasonable buffalo hunts (Ponca Agency 1864–1870, 0090). In June 1870, the Ponca hunted with the Pawnee (Ponca Agency 1864–1870, 0105), and in July, Chief Spotted Tail came to the Ponca to negotiate a treaty between the Sioux and Ponca. The Ponca visited the Sioux on the present-day Rosebud Reservation to retrieve twenty-one horses taken by Black Kettle's band, but on August 15, bands of Sioux raided Ponca farms near Niobrara taking even more horses (Ponca Agency 1864–1870, 0151–0153). On September 15, 1870, a band of Sioux stole seven horses and shot three oxen with arrows at the Ponca agency (Ponca Agency 1864–1870, 0168).

Throughout the early 1870s, the Ponca requested arms on several occasions to defend themselves and were continually denied (Ponca Agency 1871–1873), and in 1873 only two soldiers were available to guard the agency (Ponca Agency 1871–1873, 0689–0691). On February 11, 1874, a Pawnee band head named "Peter the Great" invited the Ponca to join the Pawnee in Oklahoma (Ponca Agency 1874–1875, 0299–0302). The last major attack by the Sioux on the Ponca came on January 4, 1875 (Ponca Agency 1874–1875, 0715–0717). During 1876, the Sioux sought peace with the Ponca and only one instance of a raid by "Sioux Indians" was reported. Even though the hostilities with the Sioux over the Treaty of 1868 have diminished (Ponca Agency 1876–1877), it appears that the U.S.

government had paid special attention to the Pawnee offer and had begun to make plans to move the Ponca to Oklahoma.

In the early spring of 1876, Ponca Agent James Lawrence, requested nearly $10,000 for seed, farming supplies, and other goods for the Ponca (Ponca Agency 1876–1877, L121–L140) from the federal government, making it appear that the Ponca would plant a crop in Nebraska that year. In July, Agent Lawrence "asks permission to take 6 chiefs to Washington to make arrangements for the removal of the tribe to Indian Territory" (Ponca Agency 1876–1877, L320). Another letter, written shortly thereafter, requested "information related to the removal of the Ponca Indians" (Ponca Agency 1876–1877, M817). In August, Lawrence reported an attack by the Sioux (Ponca Agency 1876–1877, W856) and recommended that "the Ponca be removed to the Omaha reservation for their safety" (Ponca Agency 1876–1877, M580). One must wonder about the timing of these reports since the Sioux and their allies had defeated General George Armstrong Custer on June 26, 1876, and were fleeing the U.S. Army by the time Agent Lawrence's requests were sent. How could Sioux war parties have attacked the Ponca, and how could they be more of a threat to the Ponca then ever before when most were either imprisoned on their reservations, fleeing into Canada, or being pursued by federal troops across western South and North Dakota, Montana and Wyoming? Deception and dishonesty have been the norm in the U.S. government's dealing with Native peoples. I theorize that prior to the spring of 1876, the U.S. government knowingly placed the Ponca reservation within the boundaries of the land of the Sioux in the Fort Laramie Treaty of 1868, hoping that the Sioux would wipe out the Ponca. Their refusal to arm the Ponca or send adequate troops to protect is added proof to this theory. After Custer's defeat in June 1876, the Sioux were no longer a real threat to the Ponca, so the U.S. government turned to the policy of removal to the Indian Territory under the guise of protecting the Ponca from an enemy that no longer existed.

In the winter of 1876, the eight Ponca clan heads were approached by agent Lawrence who offered to take them to Oklahoma to look over several alternative reservation sites (Ponca Agency 1876–1877, C186). Prior to their departure, the agent promised the clan heads that if they didn't like the land they saw they could return to their Nebraska homeland. The Ponca clan heads made the journey to Indian Territory, visiting many different land reserves which were equally barren and unsuitable for agriculture. The clan heads agreed not to exchange their land but instead return home. Upon informing the agent of their decision, the agent threatened to withdraw all money and support, including the interpreter. The clan heads stubbornly refused to relinquish their Nebraska homeland, so the agent departed without the Ponca clan heads (Ponca Agency 1876–1877, C771). Clan heads White Eagle and Standing Buffalo telegraphed the Secretary of the Interior, requesting "assistance to return to their reservation" (Ponca Agency 1876–1877, P100). Government officials did not respond, and the clan heads, some of whom were advanced in years and ill, were forced to make the journey in the middle of winter on foot without money, food, or an interpreter, and fifty days later, near starvation, the Ponca clan heads, reached the Otoe Reservation along the Kansas-Nebraska border. The Otoe provided them with enough food and ponies to make their way back to Niobrara (Ponca Agency 1876–1877, C1089 and C1089; Howard 1965, 33). When the clan heads returned home, they found their people already preparing for the move. Appeals were made by Rev. J. O. Dorsey and other white friends of the Ponca to leave the Ponca in Nebraska (Ponca Agency 1876–1877, C1212; Howard 1965, 33). In spite of all their appeals, E. C. Kemble, U.S. Indian inspector, ordered the Ponca removal, and on April 12, 1877 the removal of the Ponca to their new home in Oklahoma, although the exact location was not yet known, had begun. (Howard 1965, 33).

E. A. Howard was appointed agent for the removal, and federal troops were called in to enforce the removal orders. About 170 Ponca members had begun the long trek in late April of 1877. Clan head Standing Bear and his brother, Big Snake, were briefly imprisoned when they urged the remainder of the Poncas to resist the removal. By May, the remaining 600 or so Poncas—including Standing Bear and his brother—were forced to join in the march, leaving behind their homes, farms, and many of their possessions. Nine persons died in the course of the journey, including a daughter of Standing Bear. The nine deaths turned out to be a grim prelude to much further hardship and death for the Poncas in their new locale. They suffered from diseases, such as malaria, which afflicted a large number of Indians transported from northern climates to the humid Indian Territory. Estimates of the number of deaths vary greatly, from 9 to 300, but even Indian Bureau reports indicate that a sizeable portion of the tribe perished in the course of the first year. Standing Bear and

Standing Bear, Ponca Chief. (*Nebraska State Historical Society*)

several other leaders went to Washington, DC, in the autumn of 1877, seeking President Rutherford B. Hayes' approval of their request to return to Nebraska. Hayes reportedly vetoed the request but allowed the Ponca leaders to select a more desirable location for their reservation within the Indian Territory. Although the Poncas eventually settled on a more favorable site 150 miles away, the ravages of disease and poverty continued. Standing Bear's last living son was among those who had died by 1878.

## STANDING BEAR AND THE RETURN OF THE OSNI PONCA

The death of Chief (Clan head) Standing Bear's eldest son set in motion events which were to bring a measure of justice and worldwide fame to the chief and his tribe. Despair over the situation of the Poncas in Indian Territory, together with the more personal desire to bury his son in the tribe's Nebraska homeland, led Standing Bear to make the move that made him famous, though it cost him the leadership of his tribe. In early January of 1879, he led a small band of thirty Poncas on a return march to Nebraska, determined to resettle on the old land or die in the attempt. Another group of nearly 150 Ponca left shortly after Standing Bear but were arrested by the U.S. Army and taken to Fort Smith, Arkansas (Ponca Agency 1878–1879). They were released on the grounds that they return to their lands in Oklahoma, so most of the roughly 600 members of the tribe were forced or chose to remain in the Indian Territory, but Standing Bear and several dozen followers arrived at the Omaha Indian agency at Decatur, Nebraska, on March 4, 1879. Even though the Omaha welcomed their kinsmen and invited them to settle there, because Indians were not allowed to leave their reservation without permission, Standing Bear and his followers were labeled as a renegade band (Howard 1965; Tibbles 1972).

The Indian Bureau had been informed of Standing Bear's flight from the Indian Territory soon after his departure. Secretary of the Interior Carl Schurz ordered General George Crook, commander of the U.S. Army Department of the Platte, at Omaha, to arrest the chief and his followers and return them to the territory in Oklahoma. Schurz and his advisers feared that if Standing Bear and his band were allowed to remain in Nebraska, it would set a precedent for all Native Americans in the Indian Territory to demand a return to their respective homelands. Although General Crook obeyed the order and arrested Standing Bear and his followers, he is said to have personally sympathized with the Poncas and believed that they had been repeatedly wronged by the government. Crook convinced Thomas Henry Tibbles, an Omaha newspaperman, to undertake a publicity campaign and institute a case in the federal district court to have Standing Bear and his group released (Wishart 1994).

With the help of Thomas Tibbles and two lawyers, John L. Webster and A.J. Poppleton, and probably General Crook, Standing Bear petitioned the court by a writ of *habeas corpus* (King 1969). He appeared before Judge Elmer Dundy (Wishart 1994). Tibbles saw to it that the plight of Standing Bear and his followers was well publicized not only in his own Omaha newspaper but in papers nationwide. The trial of *Standing Bear vs. Crook* was held from April 30 to May 2, 1879. The case was of great significance not only as a means of righting the wrongs inflicted on the Ponca tribe, but also because it raised the larger question of Native American citizenship and the rights of Indians to appear in and to sue in the courts of the nation (Tibbles 1972).

The federal district attorney, G. M. Lambertson, argued that Standing Bear was not entitled to the protection of a writ of habeas corpus because he was not a citizen or even a "person" under American law. Standing Bear spoke briefly but eloquently on his own behalf (Mardock 1979). Judge Elmer S. Dundy, in the decision he handed down several weeks later, held that an Indian was, indeed, a person within the meaning of the laws of the United States, although he avoided the larger question of what rights of citizenship an Indian might have. He also ruled that the federal government had no rightful authority to remove the Poncas to the Indian Territory by force; Native Americans, he stated, possessed an inherent right of expatriation—that is, a right to move from one area to another as they wished. Dundy, therefore, ordered the release of Standing Bear and his followers from custody (Tibbles 1972).

Thomas Tibbles and other leaders of the movement for Indian rights hoped to carry the case of Standing Bear to the U.S. Supreme Court in order to secure a more definitive statement on Indian citizenship and rights. Tibbles himself made a tour to Chicago, New York, and Boston in the summer of 1879 to publicize the case and to raise money for the Supreme Court appeal. By October of that year, he had arranged for Standing Bear to lecture in key cities in the eastern United States. As interpreters for the chief, who spoke no English, Tibbles included in the party two Omaha Indians: Susette La Flesche (better known by her Indian name, "Bright Eyes") and her brother, Francis La Flesche, both of whom had been educated in English-speaking schools. The tour generated great enthusiasm in urban social and literary circles, especially in Boston. Standing Bear, an impressive figure in his full Indian regalia, including feather headdress, related his story and that of his people in simple but emotional terms, while Bright Eyes, also in Indian dress, translated it into poignant English. A good deal of money was raised for the court appeal and for relief of the Ponca, and reform leaders were moved to become active in the cause of Indian rights. Standing Bear and Bright Eyes also testified before committees of Congress in Washington. The tour finally ended in April of 1880 (Green 1969; Mardock 1971; Tibbles 1972).

Secretary of the Interior Schurz was able to quash the proposed appeal of the Ponca case to the Supreme Court. However, the agitation over the affair did lead to both congressional and presidential investigations. On February 1, 1881, President Hayes recommended to Congress that the Poncas be allowed to live where they chose and that they be compensated for lands relinquished and losses sustained during the forced removal to the Indian Territory in Oklahoma. Congress voted the necessary legislation and funds on March 3, 1881 (Howard 1965; Wishart 1994). Although the majority of the Ponca tribe remained in the Indian Territory, Standing Bear and his group lived quietly on the old Nebraska reservation near the mouth of the Niobrara River, and the Northern (Osni) Ponca Tribe was born. Standing Bear died in September of 1908.

One previously overlooked fact is that several Ponca did not go to Oklahoma. The tribal census rolls for December 26, 1872, identify a total population of 1,090 men, women, and children (Ponca Agency 1871–1873), whereas the tribal census roll for November 19, 1874, identifies a total population of 739 (Ponca Agency 1874–1875). The tribal census of 1872 also reports eleven "bands," and the 1874 census reports eight full-blood clans and one half-breed clan (Ponca Agency 1871–1873; 1874–1875). It appears that over 300 people and three clans disappeared within two years. Government and other historical written records offer no insight into why there was this drastic reduction in the Ponca population. There is no evidence that disease or the Sioux killed those missing from the census. I theorize that prior to and definitely after the invitation by the Pawnee to the Ponca to join them in Oklahoma, that most Ponca knew of the government's intentions to move them to Oklahoma. Oral history identifies that several Ponca, moved in with the Yankton-Sioux, forty miles up the Missouri River near Ft. Randall, Dakota Territory, and others, especially the half-breeds settled among the whites in the present day Knox County area, then called "Leau-gui-court" (Howard 1965). Additional evidence that many stayed behind is the reappearance of names on the July 1, 1885, "Census of Ponca Indians of Dakota Ponca Agency" of Ponca families that were on the 1872 census but not on the 1874 census, such as the Whitecoat family. After the Poncas return from Oklahoma, the tribal census increased from 161 in 1885 to 207 in 1886, remaining at around 230 throughout the rest of the nineteenth century (Santee Agency 1885–1898). Oral history reports that on his return to the Niobrara, Standing Bear recruited many of the half-breeds who remained behind to rejoin the tribe to increase the size of the tribe.

## THE SECOND REBIRTH OF THE OSNI PONCA: ALLOTMENT AND REORGANIZATION

The Ponca who returned to their homelands on the Niobrara by the mid-1880s found that most of their farms, agency buildings, and most of the other structures, including the saw mill and school, that they had constructed in the late 1860s until their removal in 1877 were gone. Most either torn down by local whites or moved less than twenty miles to the Santee-Sioux reservation. They also encountered a new federal law, the Dawes Allotment Act of 1887. The Dawes Act sought to resolve the Indian "problem" by persuading, or forcing if necessary, Indians to abandon their traditional tribal-communal way of life for the life of independent, individualistic yeomen farmers. In order to pave the way for the elimination of the tribes as distinct, social, political, and legal entities, the Dawes Act provided for the division of community-held reservation lands into individual 160 acre holdings (*Indian Historian* 1976). The Dawes Act utilized two strategies to dissolve participation in traditional tribal government and the control over lands within reservation boundaries. First, it took away the lands over which the tribal government had previously held control through communal ownership and distributed these lands through individual Indian ownership. Second, it distributed (stole) "surplus" lands to the ever-mounting wave of white settlers who demanded such land, which totally removed tribal lands from tribal government control. Between 1887 and 1934, when allotment was ended by the Indian Reorganization Act, the land holdings of American Indians diminished from 130 million acres to 50 million acres (*Congressional Record* 1887; *Indian Historian* 1976). In 1903, nearly one-half of the Osni Ponca Reservation was owned by non-Indians. Standing Bear owned 240 acres about one mile south of the agency (*Knox County Plat Book* 1903). In 1920, although Standing Bear's allotment remained, less than 20 percent of the Osni Ponca Reservation was owned by Poncas (*Knox County Plat Book* 1920). The Depression took even more land out of the hands of the Ponca and left many destitute and left the tribal government without the resources to assist them.

Due to the onset of the Depression and mounting public criticism in the handling of Indian affairs by the federal government, Congress set out to reorganize federal Indian policy and strengthen tribal governments and landholdings. This abrupt policy change was mainly due to the Meriam Report of 1928. In 1926, Mr. Lewis

Meriam and other selected "Indian specialists" [*sic*], while on the staff of the Institute for Government Research, began a survey of the economic and social condition of Native Americans. The overall general findings of Meriam were that Indian people were in a state of severe poverty with no desire to adjust to the economic and social system of the dominant white civilization. When an Indian family obtained a small amount of wealth, they quickly distributed it among their friends and family and remained at the same socioeconomic status as everyone else, a common practice among Indian people even today. Upon publication, the Meriam Report brought into sharp focus the problems of governmental administration of Indian affairs, thereby initiating a movement toward change and the Indian Reorganization Act (Meriam et al. 1928, 3–51).

The Indian Reorganization Act (IRA) of 1934 was successful in ending the practice of allotment and the elimination of the "absolutist" executive discretion previously exercised by the Interior Department and the Office of Indian Affairs over Indian tribal governments and people. During Congressional hearings on the IRA, Commissioner of Indian Affairs John Collier revealed that not only had administrative power grown beyond control, but its exercise depended on the attitude or whim of any given commissioner. This practice was also exercised by the local agency superintendents, which led Senator Wheeler to refer to the local agent as a "czar." The IRA bill sought "to get away from the bureaucratic control of the Indian Department and give the Indian people control over their own affairs" (Canby 1981, 23–25).

The following is the corporate charter that established the Ponca Tribe of Native Americans in Nebraska and which would be a key factor in the restoration of the Ponca Tribe of Nebraska nearly sixty years later.

### CORPORATE CHARTER OF THE PONCA TRIBE OF NATIVE AMERICANS, NEBRASKA

#### Ratified August 15, 1936

A Federal Corporation Chartered Under the Act of June 18, 1934

Whereas, the Ponca Tribe of Native Americans of the Ponca Reservation in Nebraska constitute a recognized Indian tribe organized under a constitution and bylaws ratified by the tribe on February 29, 1936, and approved by the Secretary of the Interior on April 3, 1936, pursuant to section 16 of the act of June 18, 1934, (48 Stat. 984), as amended by the act of June 15, 1935 (49 Stat. 378): and

Whereas, more than one-third of the adult members of the tribe have petitioned that a charter of incorporation be granted to such tribe, subject to ratification by a vote of the adult Indians living on the reservation;

Now, therefore, I, Harold L. Ickes, Secretary of the Interior, by virtue of the authority conferred upon me by the said act of June 18, 1934, (48 Stat. 984), do hereby issue and submit this charter of incorporation to the Ponca Tribe of the Ponca Reservation to be effective from and after such time as it may be ratified by a majority vote of the adult Indians living on the reservation at an election in which at least thirty percent of the eligible voters vote.

SECTION 1. <u>Corporate Existence</u>. In order to further the economic development of the Ponca Tribe of the Ponca Reservation in Nebraska by conferring upon the said tribe certain corporate rights, powers, privileges and immunities; to secure for the members of the tribe an assured economic independence; and to provide for the proper exercise by the tribe of various functions heretofore performed by the Department of the Interior, the aforesaid tribe is hereby chartered as a body politic and corporate of the United States of America, under the corporate name "The Ponca Tribe of Native Americans."

SEC. 2. <u>Perpetual Succession</u>. The Ponca Tribe of Native Americans shall, as a Federal Corporation, have perpetual succession.

SEC. 3. <u>Membership</u>. The Ponca Tribe of Native Americans shall be a membership corporation. Its members shall consist of all persons now or hereafter members of the Tribe, as provided by its duly ratified and approved Constitution and Bylaws.

SEC. 4. <u>Management</u>. The Board of Governors of the Tribe established in accordance with the said Constitution and Bylaws of the Tribe, shall exercise all the corporate powers hereinafter enumerated.

SEC. 5. <u>Corporate Powers</u>. The Tribe, subject to any restrictions contained in the Constitution and laws of the United States, or in the Constitution and Bylaws of the said

Tribe, shall have the following corporate powers, in addition to all powers already conferred or guaranteed by the Tribal Constitution and Bylaws:

(a) To adopt, use, and alter at its pleasure a corporate seal.

(b) To purchase, take by gift, bequest, or otherwise, own, hold, manage, operate, and dispose of property of every description, real and personal, subject to the following limitations:

(1) No sale or mortgage may be made by the Tribe of any land, or interests in land, including water rights, and mineral rights, now or hereafter held by the Tribe.

(2) No leases, permits (which terms shall not include land assignments to members of the Tribe) or timber sale contracts covering any land or interests in land now or hereafter held by the Tribe within the boundaries of the Ponca Reservation shall be made by the Tribe for a longer term than ten years, except when authorized by law, and all such leases, permits or contracts must be approved by the Secretary of the Interior or by his duly authorized representative.

(3) No action shall be taken by or in behalf of the Tribe which in any way operates to destroy or injure the tribal grazing lands, timber, or other natural resources of the Ponca Reservation. All leases, permits, and timber sale contracts relating to the use of tribal, grazing or timber lands shall conform to regulations of the Secretary of the Interior authorized by section 6 of the Act of June 18, 1934, with respect to range carrying capacity, sustained yield forestry management, and other matters therein specified. Conformity to such regulations shall be made a condition of any such lease, permit, or timber sale contract, whether or not such agreement requires the approval of the Secretary of the Interior, and violation of such condition shall render the agreement revocable, in the discretion of the Secretary of the Interior.

(c) To issue interests in corporate property in exchange for restricted Indian lands or other lands of members of the Tribe, the forms for such interests to be approved by the Secretary of the Interior.

(d) To borrow money from the Indian Credit Fund in accordance with the terms of Section 10 of the Act of June 18, 1934 (48 Stat. 984), or from any other Governmental agency, or from any member or association of members of the Tribe, and to use such funds directly for productive tribal enterprises, or to loan money thus borrowed to individual members or associations of members of the Tribe: Provided, That the amount of indebtedness to which the Tribe may subject itself, except for indebtedness to the Indian Credit Fund, shall not exceed five thousand dollars, without the express approval of the Secretary of the Interior.

(e) To engage in any business that will further the economic well-being of the members of the Tribe or to undertake any activity of any nature whatever, not inconsistent with law or with any provisions of this charter.

(f) To make and perform contracts and agreements of every description, not inconsistent with law or with any provisions of this charter, with any person, association, or corporation, with any municipality or any county, or with the United States or the State of Nebraska, including agreements with the State of Nebraska for the rendition of public services: Provided, That any contract involving payment of money by the corporation in excess of $1,000 in any one fiscal year shall be subject to the approval of the Secretary of the Interior or his duly authorized representative.

(g) To pledge or assign chattels or future tribal income due or to become due to the Tribe: Provided, That such agreements of pledge or assignment, other than agreements with the United States, shall not extend more than ten years from the date of execution and shall not cover more than one-half the net tribal income in any one year: <u>And provided further</u>, That any such agreement shall be subject to the approval of the Secretary of the Interior or his duly authorized representative.

(h) To deposit corporate funds, from whatever source derived, in any national or state bank to the extent that such funds are insured by the Federal Deposit Insurance Corporation, or secured by a surety bond, or other security, approved by the Secretary of the Interior; or to deposit such funds in the Postal Savings Bank or with a bonded disbursing officer of the United States to the credit of the corporation.

(i) To sue and to be sued in courts of competent jurisdiction within the United States; but the grant or exercise of such power to sue and to be sued shall not be deemed a consent by the said Tribe or by the United States to the levy of any judgment, lien or attachment upon the property of the Tribe other than income or chattels specially pledged or assigned.

(j) To exercise such further incidental powers, not inconsistent with law, as may be necessary to the conduct of corporate business.

SEC. 6. <u>Termination of Supervisory Powers</u>. Upon the request of the Board of Governors for the termination of any supervisory power reserved to the Secretary of the Interior under sections 5 (b) 2, 5 (c), 5 (d), 5 (f), 5 (g), 5 (h), and section 8 of this charter, the Secretary of the Interior, if he shall approve such request, shall thereupon submit the question of such termination to the tribe for referendum. The termination shall be effective upon ratification by a majority vote at an election in which at least thirty per cent of the adult members of the Tribe residing on the reservation shall vote.

If at any time after ten years from the effective date of this charter, such request shall be made and the Secretary shall disapprove it or fail to approve or disapprove it within ninety days after its receipt, the question of the termination of any such power may then be submitted by the Secretary of the Interior or by the Board of Governors to popular referendum of the adult members of the Tribe actually living within the reservation and if the termination is approved by two-thirds of the eligible voters, shall be effective.

SEC. 7. <u>Corporate Property</u>. No property rights of the Ponca Tribe of Native Americans as heretofore constituted, shall be in any way impaired by anything contained in this charter, and the tribal ownership of unallotted lands, whether or not assigned to the use of any particular individuals, is hereby expressly recognized. The individually owned property of members of the Tribe shall not be subject to any corporate debts or liabilities, without such owners' consent. Any existing lawful debts of the tribe shall continue in force, except as such debts may be satisfied or cancelled pursuant to law.

SEC. 8. <u>Corporate Dividends</u>. The Tribe may issue to each of its members a non-transferable certificate of membership evidencing the equal share of each member in the assets of the Tribe and may distribute per capita, among the recognized members of the Tribe, all profits of corporate enterprises or income over and above sums necessary to defray corporate obligations and over and above all sums which may be devoted to the establishment of a reserve fund, the construction of public works, the costs of public enterprises, the expenses of tribal government, the needs of charity, or other corporate purpose. No such distribution of profits or income in any one year amounting to a distribution of more than one-half of the accrued surplus, shall be made without the approval of the Secretary of the Interior. No distribution of the financial assets of the Tribe shall be made except as provided herein or as authorized by Congress.

SEC. 9. <u>Corporate Accounts</u>. The officers of the Tribe shall maintain accurate and complete public accounts of the financial affairs of the Tribe, which shall clearly show all credits, debts, pledges, and assignments, and shall furnish an annual balance sheet and report of the financial affairs of the Tribe to the Commissioner of Indian Affairs.

SEC. 10. <u>Amendments</u>. This charter shall not be revoked or surrendered except by act of Congress, but amendments may be proposed by resolutions of the Board of Governors which if approved by the Secretary of the Interior, to be effective shall be ratified by a majority vote of the adult members living on the reservation at a popular referendum in which at least 30 per cent of the eligible voters vote.

SEC. 11. <u>Ratification</u>. This charter shall be effective from and after the date of its ratification by a majority vote of the adult members of the Ponca Tribe of Native Americans living on the Ponca Reservation, provided at least 30 per cent of the eligible voters shall vote, such ratification to be formally certified by the Superintendent of the Winnebago Agency and the President of the Board of Governors of the Tribe.

Submitted by the Secretary of the Interior for ratification by the Ponca Tribe of Native Americans of the Ponca Reservation in a popular referendum to be held on August 15, 1936.

HAROLD L. ICKES,
Secretary of the Interior.
Washington, D. C., July 18, 1936 [SEAL]

* * *

CERTIFICATION

Pursuant to section 17 of the Act of June 18, 1934 (48 Stat. 984), this charter, issued on July 18, 1936, by the Secretary of the Interior to the Ponca Tribe of Native Americans of the Ponca Reservation, was duly submitted for ratification to the adult Indians living on the reservation and was on August 15, 1936, duly ratified by a vote of 47 for and 1 against, in an election in which over thirty per cent of those entitled to vote cast their ballots.

JOSEPH J, PENISKA,
President of the Board of
Governors of the Tribe.

GABE E. PARKER,
Superintendent, Winnebago Agency.

* * *

## THE THIRD REBIRTH OF THE OSNI PONCA: TERMINATION AND RESTORATION

The Depression caused many Ponca to seek government work programs such as the Indian Civil Conservation Corps (ICCC) off the reservation and some moved to cities in order to find work. Many youth went to boarding schools in South Dakota, such as Marty and Flandreau, and those who remained behind attended public country schools or went to public school in Niobrara. World War II saw many Ponca going oversees or to other areas of the United States. Most returned to the reservation with different economic and social expectations and with a higher degree of assimilation into white culture and religion. The following interview by James H. Howard, an anthropologist at the University of Nebraska—Lincoln, of Peter Le Claire identifies one Ponca elder's life experience during this time period.

> In 1897 I went to Genoa Indian Industrial School . . . and I learned the Painting trade well enough to be in a city. I didn't follow the trade. I worked at different places doing all kinds of work. In 1924 I worked in the Homestake mine in Lead, S.D. 1925–26 I worked for Dakota Power Co. as a night watch. In 1928 I went down to Oklahoma and worked on repainting houses and buildings. I got the history of my tribe there from an old man, Ni jin ha thee. In 1932 I was appointed a Special Deputy Sheriff under Joe McFadden of Kay Co. Oklahoma. In 1936 when the northern Poncas reorganized under the Wheeler & Howard act, I was the Secretary of the Election Board. In 1949 I was elected Treasurer of the Brotherhood of Christian Unity and am President for the year 1950. (Howard 1950)

In 1945, the government formulated a policy that called for termination of Indian tribes. Many Ponca had become fully assimilated into the white culture and many had abandoned their traditional ceremonies, practices, and language. Some felt that this policy would finally get them their long overdue treaty payments and allow them to break the chains of the government agent. Peter Le Claire stated "the Ponca tribe are to be emancipated, perhaps this year, 1950. After we are emancipated the money that is coming to us from our treaty or treaties will be paid to us and my wife and I will buy a home and retire from hard work. My white friends are helping every way to find a good farm for us" (Howard 1950).

In 1953, Congress adopted House Concurrent Resolution No. 108, declaring that various Indian tribes would no longer be entitled to federal benefits and services and should be cut off at the earliest possible time. This policy affected some 109 tribes and bands, including 13,263 Native Americans and 1,365,801 acres of trust land. In 1962, the Congress of the United States decided that the Northern Ponca tribe should be terminated. The tribal council held an election in 1964 to determine if the tribe should be terminated or not. Nearly 90 percent voted for termination. Ponca elder, Bill Smith, Sr., told the author (1981) that "we voted for termination so we could get the money, which nearly everyone needed." The average payment to an adult Ponca was around $1,500. In 1966, the Northern Ponca were completely terminated, and 442 Ponca were removed from the tribal roll. All of the tribal land and other holdings were dissolved. The old Ponca Agency building, out buildings, and over 300 acres of land was purchased by a local white businessman for around $10,000. Within three years, most Ponca were dispossessed of their allotted lands, as many did not have the income to pay the property taxes now being levied on their land, which had previously been held in federal trust and exempt from such taxes. By 1969, all that was left of the old Ponca Reservation was the Ponca Cemetery and 80 some acres of allotment land held in trust by the Bureau of Indian Affairs at the Winnebago Agency or known as the Spotted Wood land. By 1970, many Ponca moved from the Niobrara area. On a personal note, I remember my surprise at the start of the 1969 fall semester at Norfolk High School meeting Greg Bear, Richard Bear, Gary Knudson, and Willis Leroy. Most of us had been at Niobrara High School the previous spring.

The termination meant that the Northern Ponca were "no longer Indians." Deb (Wright) Robinette identifies the impact of this fact: "this one time I got sick and went to the clinic in Santee and was told that I could not be seen by the doctor because I was not Indian. I was shocked because I had been getting my medical at this clinic for a long time. When we first moved to Verdigre I was hired at the nursing home because I was Indian and a few months later I was told by the Santee's I was not."

## RESTORATION: INDIAN AGAIN TO EVERYONE

During the 1970s, members of the Ponca Tribe, unwilling to accept their status as a terminated tribe, initiated the process of restoration to federal recognition. In 1986, representatives from the Native American Community Development Corporation of Omaha, Inc.; Lincoln Indian Center; Sequoyah, Inc.; National Indian Lutheran Board; and the Ponca tribe met to discuss what they needed to do to once again become a federally recognized tribe. In the spring of 1987, the Northern Ponca Restoration Committee, Inc., was incorporated as a nonprofit organization in Nebraska and was the base for the federal recognition effort. In April of 1988, the Nebraska Unicameral passed Legislative Resolution #128 giving state recognition to the Ponca tribe and their members. This was an important step in the restoration efforts. The Ponca Restoration Bill was introduced in the United States Senate on October 11, 1989 by Senators James J. Exon and J. Robert Kerry. The Senate passed the Ponca Restoration Act (#1747) by unanimous consent on July 18, 1990, and it was sent to the House of Representatives.

The passage of the bill in the House was not an easy task by any means. At the hearing on September 13, 1990, before the House Interior and Insular Affairs Committee, Bureau of Indian Affairs representatives and then 1st District Representative, Doug Bereuter, Nebraska Republican, expressed their concerns and reservations on the passage of the "Ponca Bill." The Bureau of Indian Affairs presented its testimony on Senate Bill #1747 on the following objections:

1. ***We (Ponca) did not fulfill the six criteria for Federal Restoration.*** The House Committee acknowledged that the Poncas of Nebraska presented overwhelming evidence that fulfilled restoration requirements as much as, or better than, other tribes who had been terminated and subsequently restored.

2. ***They objected to the requirement that the Secretary accept land "in trust" without geographical limitations and the language of the Bill that read that the Secretary of Interior "shall take into trust" instead of "at his discretion take into trust, land for the Ponca Tribe."*** The House Committee amended the bill to say that the first 1,500 acres of land purchased by the Ponca Tribe

shall be taken "in trust" and after that, the Secretary of Interior, "at his [the present Secretary of Interior is a female] discretion may take other land into trust for the Ponca Tribe." The geographical limitations for land to be taken in trust are from Boyd and Knox Counties in Nebraska.

3. ***The Bureau also recommended an amendment be added that stated that the Poncas not have a "residential" reservation.*** In the bill, we (Ponca) cannot have a "residential reservation," but we are still able to take land "in trust" for economic development purposes, for conducting cultural events, for building a cultural center, and for operation tribal offices.

4. ***They objected to the expansion of the service area to include Boyd, Charles Mix (South Dakota), Knox, Douglas, Lancaster, and Madison Counties.*** The House Committee decided to allow us to have these six (6) counties that we had requested for our service area.

Representative Doug Bereuter stated that he would oppose the bill on the House floor if we didn't amend the Bill excluding a residential reservation. The amendment was subsequently made that any land taken into trust for the tribe would not have reservation status and was passed by the House and signed into law on October 31, 1990, by President Bush (Ponca Tribe of Nebraska Newsletter, 1990). The Omaha *World-Herald* once again acknowledged the return of the Ponca tribe to Nebraska with the following:

> The Poncas have a proud place in Omaha history. . . . The simple, human dignity of Standing Bear and his followers and the injustice of their situation captured the attention of an Omaha *Herald* editor, Thomas Henry Tibbles, who persuaded some of the city's top lawyers to take up the Indians' case. . . . A link to that important chapter in our history was broken when the federal government erased the name of the Nebraska Poncas from its books. Now it is being restored. About 900 Poncas, descendants of the original band that broke away from Oklahoma, are eligible for enrollment. They will constitute a tribe again. They will have an

organization that can serve as a focal point for preserving the rich heritage that is so much a part of our local history. Their reinstatement adds a welcome dimension to the Midlands. (Ponca tribe's revival restores link to history, 1990)

The Following is the Ponca Restoration Act of 1990:

### United States Code
### TITLE 25—INDIANS
### CHAPTER 14
### MISCELLANEOUS

**SUBCHAPTER XLVI-A**

**PONCA TRIBE OF NEBRASKA: RESTORATION OF RIGHTS AND PRIVILEGES**

**Sec.983. Definitions.**

For purposes of this subchapter—

**(1)** The term **"Tribe"** means the Ponca Tribe of Nebraska.

**(2)** The term **"Secretary"** means the Secretary of the Interior or the designated representative of the Secretary of the Interior.

**(3)** The term **"Interim Council"** means the Board of Directors of the Northern Ponca Restoration Committee, Inc.

**(4)** The term **"member"** means a person who is enrolled on the membership roll of the Tribe of June 10, 1965, that was compiled by the Bureau of Indian Affairs or is entitled to be enrolled as a member of the Tribe under section 983e of this title.

**(5)** The term **"State"** means the State of Nebraska.

**Sec.983a. Federal recognition.**

Federal recognition is hereby extended to the Ponca Tribe of Nebraska. All Federal laws of general application to Indians and Indian tribes (including the Act of June 18, 1934 (48 Stat. 984; 25 U.S.C. 461, et seq.), popularly known as the Indian Reorganization Act) shall apply with respect to the Tribe and to the members.

## Sec.983b. Restoration of rights.

### (a) Rights abrogated or diminished.

All rights and privileges of the Tribe which may have been abrogated or diminished before October 31, 1990, by reason of any provision of Public Law 87-629 (25 U.S.C. 971 et seq.) are hereby restored and such law shall no longer apply with respect to the Tribe or the members.

### (b) Rights existing prior to restoration.

Nothing in this subchapter may be construed to diminish any rights or privileges of the Tribe, or of the members, that exist prior to October 31, 1990.

### (c) Acceptance by Secretary of real property transferred for benefit of Tribe; exemption from taxation.

The Secretary shall accept not more than 1,500 acres of any real property located in Knox or Boyd Counties, Nebraska, that is transferred to the Secretary for the benefit of the Tribe. Such real property shall be accepted by the Secretary (subject to any rights, liens, or taxes that exist prior to the date of such transfer) in the name of the United States in trust for the benefit of the Tribe and shall be exempt from all taxes imposed by the Federal Government or any State or local government after such transfer. The Secretary may accept any additional acreage in Knox or Boyd Counties pursuant to his authority under the Act of June 18, 1934 (25 U.S.C. 461 et seq.).

### (d) Effect on existing rights and obligations.

Except as otherwise specifically provided in any other provision of this subchapter, nothing in this subchapter may be construed as altering or affecting—

**(1)** any rights or obligations with respect to property,

**(2)** any rights or obligations under any contract,

**(3)** any hunting, fishing, trapping, gathering, or water rights of the Tribe or the members, or

**(4)** any obligation to pay a tax levied before October 31, 1990.

### (e) Reservation status.

Reservation status shall not be granted any land acquired by or for the Tribe.

## Sec.983c. Services.

Notwithstanding any other provision of law, the Tribe and its members shall be eligible, on or after October 31, 1990, for all Federal services and benefits furnished to federally recognized tribes without regard to the existence of a reservation for the Tribe. In the case of Federal services available to members of federally recognized tribes residing on or near a reservation, members of the Tribe residing in Sarpy, Burt, Platte, Stanton, Holt, Hall, Wayne, Knox, Boyd, Madison, Douglas, or Lancaster Counties of Nebraska, Woodbury or Pottawattomie Counties of Iowa, or Charles Mix County of South Dakota shall be deemed to be residing on or near a reservation.

### Sec.983d. Interim government.
Until such time as a constitution for the Tribe is adopted in accordance with section 983f(a) of this title and tribal officials are elected under section 983f(b) of this title, the Tribe shall be governed by the Interim Council.

### Sec.983e. Membership roll.
**(a) Accuracy pending adoption of tribal constitution.**
Until a tribal constitution is adopted in accordance with section 983f of this title, the Interim Council shall take such measures as will insure the continuing accuracy of the membership roll of the Tribe.
**(b) Eligibility pending adoption of tribal constitution; appeal of exclusion.**
**(1)** Until a tribal constitution is adopted in accordance with section 983f of this title, an individual shall be eligible for membership in the Tribe, and the name of the individual shall be placed on the membership roll of the Tribe, if—(A) the individual is living and is not an enrolled member of another Indian tribe that is recognized by the Federal Government, and (B) the individual—
**(i)** was listed on the tribal membership roll of June 18, 1965, that was compiled by the Bureau of Indian Affairs,
**(ii)** notwithstanding the application or appeal deadline dates, was entitled to be listed on the membership roll of June 18, 1965, that was compiled by the Bureau of Indian Affairs, but was not listed, or
**(iii)** is a lineal descendant of an individual, living or deceased, who is described in clause (i) or (ii).

**(2)** Any individual who is excluded from the membership roll of the Tribe by the Interim Council may appeal to the Secretary for a determination of the eligibility of the individual for membership in the Tribe. Such determination by the Secretary shall be final. The Interim Council shall include on the membership roll any such individual that the Secretary determines in such an appeal to be eligible for membership in the Tribe.

**(c) Constitution as governing.**

After adoption of a tribal constitution in accordance with section 983f of this title, the constitution of the Tribe shall govern membership in the Tribe.

### Sec.983f. Tribal constitution.

**(a) Adoption by secret ballot; absentee balloting.**

Upon the completion of the tribal membership roll and upon the written request of the Interim Council, the Secretary shall conduct, by secret ballot, an election to adopt a constitution for the Tribe. Such constitution shall be submitted by the Interim Council to the Secretary no later than 1 year following October 31, 1990. Absentee balloting shall be permitted regardless of voter residence. In every other regard, the election shall be held according to section 476 of this title.

**(b) Election of tribal officials.**

Not later than 120 days after the Tribe adopts a tribal constitution, the Secretary shall conduct an election by secret ballot for the purpose of electing tribal officials as provided in the constitution. Said election shall be conducted according to the procedures stated in subsection (a) of this section except to the extent that said procedures conflict with the tribal constitution.

**(c) Governing body treated as Indian tribal government for purposes of taxation.**

Notwithstanding any other provision of law, the governing body of the Tribe established under the constitution of the Tribe that is adopted under subsection (a) of this section shall be treated as an Indian tribal government for purposes of title 26.

### Sec.983g. Regulations.

The Secretary shall prescribe such regulations as may be necessary to carry out the provisions of this subchapter.

## Sec.983h. Economic development plan.

### (a) Establishment; submittal to Congress.

The Secretary shall—

**(1)** enter into negotiations with the governing body of the Tribe to establish a plan for economic development for the Tribe;

**(2)** in accordance with this section, establish such a plan; and

**(3)** upon the approval of such plan by the governing body of the Tribe (and after consultation with the State and local officials pursuant to subsection (b) of this section), shall submit such plan to the Congress by no later than the date that is 3 years after October 31, 1990.

### (b) Consultation with State and local officials.

**(1)** To ensure that legitimate State and local interests are not prejudiced by the economic development plan established under subsection (a) of this section, the Secretary shall notify and consult with the appropriate officials of the State and all appropriate local governmental officials in the State with respect to the proposed economic development plan. The Secretary shall provide complete information on the proposed economic development plan to such officials, including the restrictions imposed on such plan by subsection (c) of this section.

**(2)** During any consultation by the Secretary under this subsection, the Secretary shall provide such information as the Secretary may possess and shall request comments and additional information on the extent of any State or local service to the Tribe.

### (c) Required provisions.

Any economic development plan established by the Secretary under subsection (a) of this section shall provide that—

**(1)** real property acquired by or for the Tribe located in Knox or Boyd Counties, Nebraska, shall be taken by the Secretary in the name of the United States in trust for the benefit of the Tribe;

**(2)** any real property taken in trust by the Secretary pursuant to such plan shall be subject to

(A) all legal rights and interests in such land held by any person at the time of acquisition of such land by the Secretary, including any lien, mortgage, or previously levied and outstanding State or local tax, and

(B) foreclosure or sale in accordance with the laws of the State of Nebraska pursuant to the terms of any valid obligation in existence at the time of the acquisition of such land by the Secretary; and

**(3)** any real property transferred pursuant to such plan shall be exempt from Federal, State, and local taxation of any kind.

**(d) Statement regarding individuals consulted, and testimony or comments received by Secretary.**

The Secretary shall append to the economic development plan submitted to the Congress under subsection (a) of this section a detailed statement—

**(1)** naming each individual consulted in accordance with subsection (b) of this section;

**(2)** summarizing the testimony received by the Secretary pursuant to any such consultation; and

**(3)** including any written comments or reports submitted to the Secretary by any individual named in paragraph (1).

A conflict between tribal members in Niobrara and Omaha erupted into lawsuits over who was to govern the tribe until a tribal council could be elected. A group called the Niobrara faction held a meeting on February 16, 1992, at which a new chair, vice chair, and seven members were elected to the Northern Ponca Restoration Committee, Inc. (NPCRI). A lawsuit was filed in Madison County court by those disposed, know as the Omaha faction, most being from Omaha and Norfolk. The Niobrara group, which also had members from Lincoln, Norfolk, and Omaha, maintained that the terms of the board comprising the Omaha faction had expired. There were two main issues in the lawsuit, whether there is a committee membership outside the board of directors who could have held a special election, and if so, whether, that election was valid. The Niobrara faction filed a lawsuit in Lancaster County District Court in Lincoln in September 1992 and asked for an accounting of the NPCRI board's financial records (Factions of Ponca tribe in dispute 1992.) Within a year, the cases were settled. One NPCRI board was elected, and the development of the Tribal Constitution began. Chairs of that board included Raymond Smith and Deb Wright.

The Tribal Constitution was approved in October 1994, and although the restoration is legally grounded, it has a more direct impact on the Osni Ponca, as expressed by Deb (Wright) Robinette: "when we were reinstated again it meant I was Indian again to everyone. I felt good about being a Tribe again." A few others did have some mixed emotions about governmental issues that have never been settled between the federal and tribal governments. A female elder expressed concern over government control of the tribe, "government programs have killed more Indians than Custer." Another female Ponca told of how "my brothers had mixed feelings (about the reinstatement) and said we have taken care of ourselves for years why do we need the government?" Ponca elder, Clara (Peniska) Vasquez, expressed the true outcome of the restoration, "it's just good that the Ponca are home again." In November of 1994, the first council of the Ponca tribe of Nebraska under the new constitution took office. Fred Leroy was elected chairman, Alex Taylor was vice chairman, Deb Robinette was treasurer, and Pearl Laravie was secretary. The other members of the council were Sheila Bogacz, Gloria Chytka, James La Pointe, Marion Peniska, and Richard Wright.

## THE OSNI PONCA TRIBAL GOVERNMENT AND CULTURE

"A tribe without a culture is just another business venture"
(Leroy 1994).

Today, the Ponca Tribe of Nebraska's headquarters is located in Niobrara, Nebraska. The Ponca Tribe of Nebraska operates under a constitution consistent with the Indian Reorganization Act, and the tribal council governs the tribe. The tribal council consists of a chair, vice chairman, secretary, treasurer, and three additional councilmen all of whom are elected by the tribal membership. The tribal council chair serves as the administrative head of the tribe. The tribal chair, officers and council serve a term of three years at-large without regard to residence in a particular district of the reservation.

The Ponca tribe is once again rebuilding its traditional culture and land base on its ancestral lands near the Niobrara River. The Tribal Headquarters is at Niobrara, Nebraska, and the tribal service areas are in Douglas, Knox, Lancaster, and Madison Counties in Nebraska; Charles Mix County in South Dakota; and Woodbury County in Iowa. Presently, there are nearly 1,300 enrolled members with roughly 60 living on or near the old reservation in the towns of

Niobrara, Verdel, Verdigre, Creighton, and Crofton, Nebraska; 250 living in Omaha; nearly 200 in Norfolk; and around 50 in both Lincoln, Nebraska, and Sioux City, Iowa. The rest of the tribal members are spread throughout the United States as far away as Alaska.

The tribe owns 159 acres of land most in or near Niobrara and sites in Lincoln, Norfolk, Omaha, and Crofton, Nebraska, and Carter Lake and Sioux City, Iowa. Since the tribe was reinstated, new community facilities that have been developed include a new health clinic in Omaha; a transitional living center in Lincoln (which also houses the administrative offices); administrative offices, museum, and health clinic in Niobrara; the Ponca Agency Building and grounds in Niobrara (which include a community center building, powwow grounds, cemetery, and bison reserve); bingo hall in Crofton; and a multiagency use building in Carter Lake, Iowa (near Omaha). Although the tribe does have offices in Norfolk and Sioux City, the facilities are rented and are not under tribal trust ownership.

Most of the tribal members own their own homes or rent privately. The Ponca Tribe's Housing activities are managed by the Northern Ponca Housing Authority, located in Norfolk, Nebraska. Currently, there are housing development activities occurring in Lincoln, Omaha, Niobrara, and Norfolk. In each area, housing is either being developed by new construction or acquired for members use (provided that the housing unit is less than ten years old). The Ponca Tribe maintains the right and responsibility to provide environmental authority in compliance with tribal and federal law for protection of the land and resources within the exterior boundaries of the reservation through code development and regulatory mechanisms. This includes all rights-of-way, waterways, watercourses, and streams running through any part of the reservation and to such others lands as may hereafter be added to the reservation under the laws of the United States. The maintenance and protection of the land is very important to the Ponca tribe and our future generations.

Although many improvements have been made in terms of tribal government, services, landownership, and protection, perhaps the most important reason for restoration was the expansion of Ponca culture and language to future generations. By 1990, less than 3 percent of the Osni Ponca spoke their tribal language and few practiced tribal ceremonies or traditional activities. Even powwow dancing and singing were nearly gone, as no Osni Ponca drum group existed. One of the first offices developed by the tribe was the Department of Cultural Affairs, which organizes programs to reintroduce the culture and language of the Ponca people to tribal members. The Department of Cultural Affairs is in place to help tribal members research their families and tribal history, provide language restoration, and help tribal members become involved in the Ponca culture.

The Native American Graves Protection and Repatriation Act (NAGPRA) of 1990 has enabled the Ponca tribe to once again possess artifacts formerly housed in museums across the country. The return of Ponca artifacts have added a wealth of information to the history and culture of the tribe. NAGPRA also insured that the bones of the ancestors in museums across the country would be returned to their ancestral home. Information on tribal history is contained in books that have been purchased for the tribal library, as well as copies of articles that have been written and published about the Ponca (such as this book chapter) are being collected and organized for the tribal archives. This historical information is available for tribal members to utilize.

Regaining the Ponca language is a responsibility of the Department of Cultural Affairs. The reintroduction of the language to Ponca members will be a major step toward the Ponca people regaining their culture. The Department of Cultural Affairs assists in planning the annual Powwow, which includes the reintroduction of Ponca songs, drum groups, and dancers. Oral histories of the elders and history as it unfolds today are being recorded. The ancestral homeland has sites that are of significant importance to the history of the tribe. The Department of Cultural Affairs is documenting these sites and is in the process of locating related research materials from various universities and governmental departments. This information is being added to the tribal library. The Department of Cultural Affairs is responsible for working with all cultural-related committees, including the Cultural Committee, Powwow Committee, and Cemetery Committee; administering the restoration of the Old Ponca Agency Building and gaining its designation in the National Register of Historical Places; grants for the enhancement of Ponca culture; administering the tribal museum and working with other museums in the area to create exhibits relating to the Ponca people. An earth lodge is also being planned and built through the Department of Cultural Affairs and should be completed by the summer of 2003.

The tribal government and departments have made a commitment to the cultural rebirth of the Ponca people. Some traditional societies, ceremonies, and activities are being reborn among the tribal members. The following letter by Larry Wright in the Ponca Tribal Newsletter (1990) emphasized the need for the tribal members to once again be active participants in the Osni Ponca culture and traditions:

> Ponca Members:
> Just a few days ago we received some bones and artifacts back from Washington so that they could be buried in their homeland. The turnout for this was not good. Talk is cheap. Everyone says they want the tribe to bring back the customs, traditions, language, and religious beliefs.
>
> We, as Ponca members, ARE the tribe. In order to get these things done, we as the people must be the ones to do it. We must contribute our time, which we all have.
>
> We, as the tribe, must look to the people we have chosen as leaders to get these things done. Everyone can come up with excuses, but we as individuals must examine ourselves as to what is important to the making of the tribe, and to us.
>
> If you sit back and do nothing—that's what gets done— NOTHING. Bringing these bones back should mean a lot to all Ponca members because we are descendants of these people. If you don't care about this, you don't care about the Ponca Tribe.
>
> Some sacrifices have to be made. You can't be paid to be a Ponca, nor can we let our personal conflicts interfere with our support of the tribe. We must learn to pull together for the good of all.
>
> ALL AS ONE, is our wisdom.
> OUR WORD, is our honor.
> LOYALTY, HONESTY AND SUPPORT for one another, for family and our people makes OUR PONCA TRIBE. Without that we are NOTHING.
>
> Ponca Member<br>Larry Wright (Sr.)

The traditional ways are returning to the Osni Ponca with the help of other tribes in the region and Ponca from Oklahoma.

Larry Wright, Sr., a member of the Osni
Ponca Heduska Society. (*Jerry Stubben*)

The Northern Ponca Powwow was reborn in August of 1994. Today,
the Powwow draws Poncas and members of several other tribes
and races by the hundreds. It is held at the old agency grounds, west
of Niobrara, Nebraska, the third weekend of August. The Osni Ponca
Heduska (Warrior) Society has also been reborn and has nearly
30 members who hold ceremonies, sponsor an annual tribal Youth
Powwow in June, dance at powwows and gatherings, and offer assistance to tribal elders and families. Members of the Heduska Society
have also made several trips to Oklahoma to learn from the Southern Ponca, and elders from the Southern Ponca, such as Rosetta Le
Claire, have blessed the Northern Ponca with both their presence in
the ancestral homelands and knowledge. As one member of the
Heduska Society stated, "we are honoring our ancestors by sharing
our traditional ways with all Ponca and all humans."

Northern Ponca elders also have come forward to share their traditional knowledge. My family was blessed by Clara (Peniska)

Vasquez when she translated my second youngest grandson's Ponca name, given to him at birth. A few minutes after his birth, his grandmother heard the name "old soul." I told Clara of the name and she said she would translate it into Ponca. After about a week, she told me that she could not think of a translation for "old soul" and that may be due to the fact that there was no such thing as an "old" soul. Souls were ageless. She felt that he was one with a good soul. We named him "Na sha(y) ga ma Uda" or Good Soul.

Tribal and individual ceremonial sites are present in nearly every tribal service area. Members of other tribes in the region have also come forth to assist the Osni Ponca with reclaiming their traditional ways. Several pipe carriers and holy people from the Sioux have invited the Ponca to their spiritual ceremonies and held ceremonies at Ponca sites. A spiritual sign that the Osni Ponca have been reborn on their ancestral lands is the presence of a ceremonial sweat lodge in a tribal buffalo pasture. The buffalo show great respect for this sacred site and do not bother the lodge or those who come to pray.

## REFERENCES

Canby, W.C., Jr. 1981. *American Indian law.* St. Paul, MN: West Publishing Co.

*Congressional Record.* 1887. Proceeding and debates of the forty-ninth Congress, Second session, vol. XVIII. Washington, DC: Government Printing Office.

Connelley, W.E. 1915–1918. Notes on the early Indian occupancy of the Great Plains. *Collections.* Vol. 14. Kansas State Historical Society.

Dorsey, J.O. 1884. Omaha sociology. In *Third annual report of the Bureau of American Ethnology.* Washington, DC: Smithsonian Institute Bureau of Ethnology.

———. 1886. Migrations of the Siouan tribes. *American Naturalist* 20(3).

———. 1894. A study of Siouan cults. *Eleventh Annual Report Bureau of American Ethnology.* 1889–90. Washington, DC: Smithsonian Institute.

Factions of Ponca tribe in dispute. 1992. *Lincoln (Nebraska) Journal-Star.* September 26.

Fletcher, A.C., and F. La Flesche. 1911. *The Omaha tribe.* Twenty-Seventh Annual Report of the Bureau of Ethnology. Washington, DC: Smithsonian Institute.

Green, N.K. 1969. *Iron Eye's family: The children of Joseph La Flesche.* Lincoln, NE: Johnson Publishing.

Grobsmith, E. The Ponca tribe of Nebraska: History, socio-economic status and current efforts to obtain restoration of tribal status (Omaha: Northern Ponca Restoration Committee, n.d.), 16–26.

Howard, J.H. 1950. *Peter Le Claire—Northern Ponca. An autobiographical sketch.* Published Monograph. University of Nebraska. Lincoln, NE.

———. 1965. *The Ponca tribe*. Smithsonian Institute Bureau of American Ethnology. Bulletin 195. Washington, DC.

Indian Affairs: Laws and Treaties. June 25, 1817. 7 Stat., 155. Proclamation, December 26, 1877. Compiled and edited by C. J. Kappler. Washington: Government Printing Office. Vol. II. Page 140. 1904.

Indian Affairs: Laws and Treaties. March 12, 1858. 12 Stats., 997. Ratified March 8, 1859. Proclamation, April 11, 1859. Compiled and edited by C. J. Kappler. Washington: Government Printing Office. Vol. II, Pages 875–76. 1904.

*Indian Historian.* (Author Unknown). The prairie Potawatomie: Resistance to allotment. (Fall. 1976).

Jablow, J. 1974. *Ponca Indians*. Ethnohistory of the Ponca with reference To their claim of certain lands. A Report for the Department of Justice, Lands Division, Indian Claims Section. New York: Garland Publishing.

King, J. T. 1969. "A better way": General George Crook and the Ponca Indians. *Nebraska History* 50 (Fall 1969): 239–56.

*Knox County plat book.* 1903. Map of Raymond Township. Des Moines, IA: Anderson Publishing Co.

———. 1920. Map of Raymond Township. Des Moines, IA: Anderson Publishing Co.

Le Claire, P. 1947. *Ponca history*. Letter written on tribal history by Ponca Indian. August, 26. Niobrara, Nebraska.

———. 1965. *In the Ponca tribe* by J. H. Howard. Oral Interview. 1965.

Leroy, F. 1994. Northern Ponca Chairman candidate. Statement in his campaign materials for the 1994 tribal elections.

———. 1998. Chair, Northern Ponca Tribe of Nebraska. Oral history and personal research on Ponca tribal sites.

Mardock, R. W. 1971. *The reformers and the American Indian*. Columbia: University of Missouri Press, 168–91.

———. 1979. Standing Bear and the reformers. In *Indian Leaders: Oklahoma's First Statesmen*, ed. H. G. Jordan and T. M. Holm, 101–13. Oklahoma City: Oklahoma Historical Society.

Meriam, Lewis, et al. 1928. *The problem of Indian administration*. The Institute for Government Research. Baltimore, MD: Johns Hopkins Press.

Ponca Agency. 1864–1870. Letters and other documents. Washington, DC. The National Archives of the United States. Microcopy No. 234. Roll No. 671.

———. 1871–1873. Letters and other documents. Washington, DC. The National Archives of the United States. Microcopy No. 234. Roll No. 672.

———. 1874–1875. Letters and other documents. Washington, DC. The National Archives of the United States. Microcopy No. 234. Roll No. 673.

———. 1876–1877. Letters and other documents. Washington, DC. The National Archives of the United States. Microcopy No. 234. Roll No. 674.

———. 1878–1879. Letters and other documents. Washington, DC. The National Archives of the United States. Microcopy No. 234. Roll No. 676.

Ponca Census. 1860. Census roll of the Poncas tribe taken at the Poncas camp July 6, 1860 by I. Shaw Gregory U.S. Special Agent. Niobrara, NE.

Ponca Elders. 1979. Ben Laravie, Omar and Alec Knudson, and Bill Smith. Stubben's Discount Store. July. Niobrara, NE.

Ponca Tribe of Nebraska Newsletter. Omaha, NE. November 1990.

Ponca tribe's revival restores link to history. *Omaha World-Hearld.* Omaha, NE. November 10, 1990, 34.

Powell, J. W. 1886. Bureau of Ethnology Annual Reports—1882–1886. Washington, DC. Fourth Annual Report. PL. XXXVII, 132–33.

Santee Agency. 1885–1898. Santee and Flandreau Sioux and Ponca Indians. Washington, DC. The National Archives of the United States. Indian Census Rolls. Microcopy No. 595. Roll No. 475.

Smith, B., Sr. Oral Story. Stubben's Discount Store. Niobrara, Nebraska. July 1981.

Tibbles, T. H. 1972. *The Ponca chiefs: An account of the trial of Standing Bear.* Lincoln: University of Nebraska Press.

Wishart, D. J. 1994. An unspeakable sadness—The dispossession of the Nebraska Indians. Lincoln: University of Nebraska Press.

Wood, R. W. 1955. Historical and Archeological Evidence for Arikira visits to the Central Plains. *Plains Anthropologist* 2:(4), 27–39.

Yerington Paiute Tribe Council. 1985. Introduction to Tribal Government. Yerington, Nevada.

## WEBSITES RELATED TO THE OSNI PONCA

http://www.mnisose.org/profiles/ponca.htm
http://www.nebraskastudies.org/0600/stories/0601_0103.html

# 8

# Wounded Knee, 1890: Battle or Massacre: A Treaty Context

*Hugh J. Reilly*

In 1868, in the frontier outpost of Fort Laramie, a treaty was signed between the American government and the Sioux and Arapahoe nations that promised, "From this day forward all war between the parties to this agreement shall forever cease" (Kappler 1971, 968).

The Brule, Oglala, Miniconjou, Yanktonai, Hunkpapa, Blackfeet, Cuthead, Two Kettle, San Arcs, and Santee bands of the Sioux nation and their friends, the Arapaho, met with General William T. Sherman, General William S. Harney, General Alfred H. Terry, and several commissioners appointed by the government. The treaty, which began with great hopes, lasted less than a half-dozen years.

The Sioux initially thought they had won a great victory. The Forts on the Bozeman trail were abandoned, the Sacred *Pa Sapa,* the Black Hills of South Dakota, were to be preserved forever for the Sioux and their descendants. Furthermore, the government promised:

> The Government of the United States desires peace, and its honor is pledged to keep it. The Indians desire peace, and they now pledge their honor to maintain it. If bad men among the Whites, or among other people subject to the authority of the United States, shall commit any wrong upon the person or property of the Indians, The United States will,

upon proof made to the agent and forwarded to the
Commissioner of Indian Affairs at Washington City, proceed
at once to cause the offender to be arrested and punished
according to the laws of the United States, and also
re-imburse the injured person for the loss sustained. (Kappler
1971, 998)

The treaty created a reservation for the Sioux that began on the
east bank of the Missouri River and stretched west, north, and south
to include what is basically the current state of South Dakota west of
the Missouri River. It also pledged to give them permanent and
exclusive hunting grounds in the wilderness beyond the North Platte
and Republican Rivers, taking in parts of what are now the states of
North Dakota, Wyoming, Nebraska and Montana. The caveat was
that these hunting grounds existed only so long as sufficient number
of buffalo roamed there to make a hunt worthwhile. Once the herds
were gone, the tribe would be limited to the reservation.

Still the government promised that ". . . no persons, except
those herein designated and authorized to do so, and except such
officers, agents, and employees of the Government as may be authorized to enter upon Indian reservations in discharge of duties
enjoined by law, shall ever be permitted to pass over, settle upon or
reside in the territory described in this article . . ." (Kappler 1971,
998, 999). In addition, the treaty stipulated that, "no white person or
persons" would be permitted to settle upon or occupy any portion of
the hunting grounds, ceded to the tribe, without the consent of the
Indians (Kappler 1971, 1002).

The Sioux saw the treaty as a return to the old ways. However, it
soon became apparent that the government intended to use its provisions to clear a path for the proposed Union Pacific Railroad. In
fact, buried within the treaty was a line specifically requiring the
Sioux to ". . . withdraw all pretense of opposition to the construction of the railroad now being built along the Platte River and westward to the Pacific Ocean . . ." (Kappler 1971, 1002).

One of the more interesting aspects of the Fort Laramie Treaty of
1868 was a provision that was essentially a "Homestead Act" for
Indians. It allowed individual Indians, who had occupied a section
of land for at least three years and made at least $200 worth of
improvements upon it, to receive ownership rights for 160 acres of
land. In addition, ". . . any Indian or Indians receiving a patent for

land under the foregoing provisions, shall thereby and from thence-forth become and be a citizen of the United States, and be entitled to all the privileges and immunities of such citizens . . ." (Kappler 1971, 1000).

While it is uncertain if any Sioux ever qualified for his or her 160 acres of land, it is certain that none were granted citizenship until more than fifty years later, in 1924, when all Indians were finally granted citizenship in a country where their ancestors had lived for untold generations.

It would have been wise for the Sioux to have not put too much faith in the Fort Laramie Treaty of 1868. Just three years later, in March of 1871, Congress officially ended the practice of making treaties with Indians. Many members of Congress felt the practice was obsolete and that treating the Indians as if they were sovereign nations was ridiculous. "Agreements" and "Special Laws" were now passed to handle the complicated relationship between the govern-ment and more than 100 distinct Indian tribes. They were no longer independent nations and yet neither were they citizens. They were now "wards of the state."

The Fort Laramie Treaty never really lived up to its promise. There were violations of the treaty's provisions almost immediately. In 1874, it was shattered forever by General George A. Custer's inva-sion of the Black Hills. Custer's expedition was said to be merely an exploration, but its real purpose was to confirm the rumors about the existence of gold in the Black Hills. Custer traveled with geologists, mineralogists, and newspaper correspondents to make sure the infor-mation would be credible and widely reported. He got his wish. Within a year, the Sioux's sacred *Pa Sapa* swarmed with more than 25,000 miners and speculators. Custer's violation of the Fort Laramie treaty led inevitably to the great Sioux War of 1876 that culminated in the Battle of the Little Big Horn.

Years of turmoil followed Custer's defeat at the Little Big Horn. In 1876, the Indians gave up the western fifty miles of their reserva-tion, including the *Pa Sapa,* the sacred Black Hills. The agreements of 1882 and 1888 officially dismembered the Great Sioux Reservation. The "agreement" of 1882 forced the Sioux to ". . . relinquish and cede to the United States all of the Great Sioux Reservation—as reserved to them by the treaty of 1868 . . ." (Kappler 1971, 1065). The bands of Sioux were assigned to smaller, separate reservations, including Pine Ridge, Rosebud, Standing Rock, Cheyenne River,

Lower Brule, and Crow Creek. The Great Sioux Reservation was now a fraction of its original size. However, the agreement of 1882 did stipulate that ". . . the provisions of the treaty of 1868, and the agreement of 1876, except as herein modified, shall continue in full force" (Kappler 1971, 1066).

The Agreement of 1888 reinforced the fracturing of the reservation and whittled it down even further. By 1890, the Sioux were desperate, as described by historian Robert M. Utley in his book, *The Lance and the Shield:*

> . . . The reservations had destroyed the very foundations of the Indian way of life. The customs, values and institutions of war and the hunt—overwhelmingly the central concerns of the people in the old days—withered into nostalgic memory. The government warred on spiritual beliefs and practices, on the office of chief, and on the tribe itself, which provided the political setting and the kinship ties that held the people together in meaningful relationship. For the loss, the government offered only unsatisfying substitutes: plows, work oxen, log houses, schools and Christian churches, together with an alien, repugnant ideal of what people should strive to be. . . . (Utley 1993, 281)

The Sioux were ripe for the coming of the latest Indian Messiah, Wovoka, and his message of a return to the old ways. Wovoka was a Paiute, living in Nevada close to Lake Tahoe. On New Year's Day in 1889, there was an eclipse of the sun. The Paiutes called it "the day the sun died." On that same day, Wovoka had a vision that he was taken up to heaven. He was told the old world would be destroyed and replaced by a fresh one. The dead would live again and everyone would be young and happy. The buffalo would return and the white man would disappear. All the Indians had to do was to perform the dance of the souls departed—the ghost dance.

Wovoka's vision was peaceful, but as it radiated out to other Indians it was imbued with the flavor of individual tribes. The Sioux added a strain of militancy. Historian Rex Allen Smith stated, ". . . The Sioux read more hostility to the whites into the prophets words than did the other tribes. When the Sioux thought they heard Wovoka speaking of knocking the soldiers into 'nothingness,' other tribes heard him to say that he would send soldiers against any tribe that 'misbehaved.' And whereas the Sioux believed he had come to earth for the Indians alone and would destroy any Indian who 'tried to be on the white's side,' others understood that he had come for all of God's children and that 'all whites and Indians are brothers . . . they are going to be all one people.' However, all of the tribes that adopted the Ghost Dance religion agreed that their domination by the whites was soon to end and that a beautiful new world was coming in which everyone would live forever . . ." (Smith 1981, 67–68).

It made little difference to settlers living in areas near the Sioux reservations that the Ghost Dance was supposed to be peaceful. They did not understand it. It smacked to them of some pagan ritual, and they felt certain it was merely a precursor for a general Indian uprising.

Adding impetus to the volatile mix of desperate Sioux and nervous settlers was the presence of the famous Sioux medicine man, Sitting Bull. He and his followers had fled to Canada after the battle of the Little Big Horn. In 1881, hungry and homesick, he returned to the United States and was settled, along with his people, on the Standing Rock Reservation. Life on the reservation did not suit him, and he longed for the old ways. Among his own people, he became a symbol of resistance and a hindrance to the plans of men such as James McLaughlin, agent at Standing Rock Reservation.

Elements of the frontier press alternately feared and despised Sitting Bull. In October of 1890, the *Omaha Bee* claimed that he was ". . . again inciting his followers to an uprising" ([*Omaha*] *Bee*, October 28, 1890, 1). Just two months prior, the same paper had mocked Sitting Bull as a coward and claimed he had gathered his family and fled from the battle ". . . westward for safety. Miles he galloped before he dared stop for breath" ([*Omaha*] *Bee*, August 29, 1890, 7).

It is likely that the Ghost Dance would have spread on the Sioux reservations without Sitting Bull's support, and in fact, he was never an overly enthusiastic supporter of the Messiah craze. However, his mere presence lent a potent symbol to the cause of the new religion. For a people who had seen their way of life unalterably changed, requiring adjustment to strange new customs and rhythms, the lure of a return to the old ways promised by the Ghost Dance was hard to resist. There were no reliable figures regarding the number of converts to the new religion across the Sioux reservations, but according to some, it was thought that perhaps one-third of the Sioux were involved with the Ghost Dance at some time (Jensen, Paul, and Carter 1991, 12).

With the spread of the new religion, increasing numbers of Indians professed a belief in a Christian God. In addition, Wovoka told his adherents to farm and send all of their children to school. These were all things that should have been desirable to the white man. In fact, one of the primary duties of an Indian agent was to replace native religious beliefs with Christian dogma. It would seem that the new Indian religion was doing just that. However, Standing Rock Indian agent James McLaughlin, called it an "absurd craze" and described the dance as "demoralizing, indecent and disgusting" (Jensen, Paul, and Carter 1991, 6). He found no reason to change his opinion when he finally witnessed a dance a month after submitting his original assessment.

Historian Elmo Scott Watson states that although the Ghost Dance was called variously an "uprising," an "outbreak," and a "war," it was "none of these—except in the columns of the contemporary press." He quotes Dr. Valentine T. McGillicuddy, former Indian Agent at Pine Ridge, as telling General L. W. Colby, commander of Nebraska's mobilized state troops that no citizen of either Nebraska or Dakota has been killed or molested and that no property had been destroyed off the reservation. Watson adds that when it seemed likely that the Sioux would again "take the warpath, the journalistic practices of a quarter of a century earlier were repeated. Unverified rumors were presented as 'reports from reliable sources' or 'eye-witness accounts;' idle gossip became fact; and once more a large number of the nation's newspapers indulged in a field day of exaggeration, distortion and plain faking" (Watson 1943, 205).

Almost unique among its frontier contemporaries, the (*Omaha*) *World-Herald* tried to maintain an editorial balance when reporting about the Ghost Dance. In a story headlined, "Let Them Alone," it declared that

> An epidemic, fierce as any that marked the middle ages, has seized upon the Indians of the southwest. The Kiowas, Comanches, Apaches, Arapahoes and northeastern Sioux are infected. This mental disease is the belief in an Indian messiah, who is at present, according to his disciples, about four days by rail and four more by horseback, northwest of the Pine Ridge agency. This man was dropped somewhere in Asia two years ago, and reached America by building a bridge across the Pacific. He raises the dead, changes the

living, restores the earth as it was before the curse, resur-
recting the dead buffaloes and all the other dead animals.
His camp consists of millions of people, who move a days
journey a month, but not by locomotion of their own. The
solid earth shifts itself, bearing them along.

The United States takes this matter very stupidly—it
always takes everything connected with the Indian stupidly. Troops have been sent to the agencies most affected
by this belief, and all the ministers are preaching fiercely
against this new Jesus and endeavoring to break up the
"Jesus dance." All this is but a part of the new general
impression which this government and the people in it
have always cherished, that the Indian has no right to any
ideas of his own, or indeed to any nationality of his own.

The Indian is not an idolater. He is distinctly religious.
His ideas concerning the unknown are far from contemptible,
yet they have never been respected and they are not respected
now. . . . ([*Omaha*]*World-Herald*, October 4, 1890, 1)

Some frontier newspapers like the Omaha *Bee* inflamed the situation with headlined stories such as, "Terrorized Dakotans Flee the
Followers of the New Messiah" where they wrote about Indians ". . .
armed in an extraordinary way and loaded down with ammunition."
They argued, ". . . Nothing but the immediate appearance of troops
will prevent an uprising in the judgment of old soldiers" ([*Omaha*]
*Bee,* November 18, 1890, 1).

Many of the settlers "fleeing" the Indians were on land reserved
for the Sioux in the Fort Laramie Treaty of 1868 and the subsequent
agreements of 1882 and 1888. Even the drastically reduced reservations were not free of white settlement. The Fort Laramie treaty was
being used as a way to keep the Sioux under control, but very little
effort was given to keeping the promises made to the tribe.

The two Omaha newspapers, the *Bee* and the *World-Herald,* were
among the first to send reporters to cover the events and took very
different approaches in their coverage. Charles H. Cressey represented the *Bee.* The *World-Herald* was initially represented by
Carl Smith, and later by Thomas Tibbles and Susette La Flesche.
La Flesche was a member of the Omaha tribe, making her one of the
first female war correspondents and certainly the first female, Native
American war correspondent.

The correspondents professed to be providing their readers a factual account of the events, in actuality:

> . . . Smith and Cressey proved to be not only reporters of, but catalysts for the events that followed their arrival. The Omaha *Bee* was a gossipy tabloid, strewn with stories about sex, violence, crime and intrigue. In his first report, wired when he was en route from Cody, Nebraska, Cressey wrote about the Sioux who had been traveling with the Wild West Show. His story hinted of dark and diabolic conversations and of their furtive glances out the windows and gestures toward the familiar landscapes that they had last seen three years previously. He interpreted these actions as a prelude to an Indian plot to attack the train at Valentine, Nebraska. There confederates of the returning Sioux would join those on the train and thus begin the rumored revolution. This report was typical of the ones that Cressey would later file. He depended on imagination, rumor, and hearsay to keep his stories exciting. Whether by assignment or disposition, Cressey's stories about Pine Ridge seethed with impending violence and conflict. His sensational accounts spread to newspapers around the nation and, amazingly, he became a prime source of information about the Pine Ridge troubles. . . . (Jensen, Paul, and Carter 1991, 43)

The conduct of the newspapers, and their reporters, was having a direct effect on military actions, just as it would eight years later during the Spanish-American War. The rhetoric in the newspapers provoked and frightened the populace until they began to flood the government for protection from a crisis that had been primarily manufactured by the media. Besides, it was good for business to have the soldiers in their towns. Somebody had to supply them food and supplies, and the local merchants were happy to oblige.

The *Bee* relished the idea that it was driving public opinion in the ghost dance business. It took credit for a "flood of appeals for aid and arms," citing an exclusive story it had run in its morning paper alleging a plot by "supposed friendly" Indians to murder local soldiers. It wrote, ". . . A panic seems to have seized the settlers living near the Pine Ridge agency. All day long telegrams have come pouring into Governor Thayer's office appealing for aid and arms" ([*Omaha*] *Bee,*

November 24, 1890, 7). The fact that the plot was nonexistent did not seem to matter to the *Bee* or its correspondent.

The *Bee's* correspondent even credited his writing as helping to create an atmosphere of excitement among the Sioux living on the reservation. He stated, "without the trimmings and spirit given it by reflections from the ghost dance and the military, life on Indian reservations must be dull enough to cause the half-animated, long-haired, blanket-swathed musk bags that make up nine-tenths of the inhabitants, swim their teepee in tears and then go blind" ([*Omaha*] *Bee*, December 8, 1890, 3).

Susette La Flesche, also known by her Indian name of Bright Eyes, was asked by the *World-Herald* to try and offer its readers a glimpse of the ghost dance from the Indian perspective. Under the headline of "What Bright Eyes Thinks," she opined:

> . . . Picture to yourself the effect were you to have lived your life thus far with all its dissatisfactions, unsatisfied aspirations and weariness, without having heard of the life of Christ, and someone were to come suddenly before you, someone in whom you had perfect faith and trust, and were to tell you for the first time the story of the Bible in all its simplicity, and of a deliverer who would satisfy all of your needs and aspirations. Would you not feel tempted to believe because of your need? And if you have lived all your lives in the environment which the highest know to the world has brought around you, a civilization based on the idea of the Messiah, can you not realize what that story would seem when told to a human being for the first time, even though the human being were only an Indian who had lived all his life without the blessings of your civilization . . .
>
> . . . I have no doubt that the excitement in the belief of the Messiah's coming added to the excitement of the religious dances. Many knowing of no other way by which they could do homage to the coming deliverer, wrought the Sioux up to such a pitch that a newly arrived agent in his alarm would call for help. ([*Omaha*] *World-Herald*, December 7, 1890, 1)

However, the conciliatory tone in the *World-Herald's* pages was rarely found on the pages of the other newspapers covering the story.

The agitation caused by this sensationalist reporting not only added to the tension, it helped push the Pine Ridge Indian agent into making rash judgments.

> . . . Agent Royer lost his nerve and sent for the troops. The presence of the troops complicated matters. They cannot long maintain a masterly inactivity. They must soon do something or "get out." If they interfere with the religious rites of the Indian they provoke vengeance and bloodshed. War would be probable. If, on the other hand, they withdraw from the Agency, after having excited and provoked Indian resentment, chaos will reign and disorder run riot. Mr. Royer would then be in the predicament which he erroneously thought he was in when he sent for the military.
>
> In short, General (John Rutter) Brooke and his soldiers appear to be in the awkward position of the traditional gentleman who had hold of the bear's tail—it is dangerous to let go and dangerous to hang on. ([*Omaha*] *World-Herald*, November 27, 1890, 2)

Unfortunately for the Sioux, that "something" was about to occur that would set events on a collision path between the Sioux and the soldiers. In December of 1890, the long-standing feud between James McLaughlin, agent at Standing Rock Reservation, and Sitting Bull came to a head. Sitting Bull had retained his influence among his fellow tribesman despite all of McLaughlin's efforts to denigrate him. He had even allowed Sitting Bull to leave on tour with Buffalo Bill Cody's Wild West Show in hopes that his influence would be lessened, but Sitting Bull returned more respected than ever. Now McLaughlin had had enough. He told reporters that there was no reason why Sitting Bull would not be arrested as soon as he came within reach. He had broken his promise to send his children to school and had not come in on ration day as he had been ordered. McLaughlin added that, "Sitting Bull should be captured and confined. His influence is strongly and constantly for evil, and while he does not take part in the ghost dance to the extent of jumping about and yelling, he keeps the frenzy at the highest pitch" ([*Omaha*] *World-Herald*, December 2, 1890, 1). McLaughlin's decision to arrest Sitting Bull was the first step in the tragedy that was to follow.

Shortly before 6:00 A.M. on December 15, 1890, Lieutenant Bull Head and forty-three other Indian policemen, arrived at Sitting

Bull's cabin to arrest him. According to historian Robert M. Utley, Sitting Bull initially agreed to go peacefully, but as he was leaving his cabin, a crowd began to gather. They jostled the policemen and shouted at them to release Sitting Bull, who began to struggle with his captors. Catch-the-Bear, one of Sitting Bull's followers, shot Lieutenant Bull Head in the leg. As he fell, Bull Head fired a shot into Sitting Bull's chest and Red Tomahawk, another policeman, fired a shot into the back of the unarmed chief's skull, killing him instantly. A fierce, brutal skirmish erupted and when it was all over, Sitting Bull, his young son Crow Foot, and six other tribesmen lay dead. In addition, four Indian policemen were dead and three were wounded, two of them mortally (Utley 1993, 293).

The *Bee*'s reaction to the news was somewhat predictable:

> . . . No sentiment should be wasted on the death of Sitting Bull. Whatever the circumstance of his taking off, he deserved his fate as a rebellious and implacable enemy. . . . He was a savage without any sense of gratitude, and he fell ingloriously while in revolt against the authority which had spared his life when justice demanded its sacrifice in atonement for the many crimes he had incited, if not committed. His death removes the most potent disturbing influence among the Sioux, and there is every reason to believe it will bring the existing trouble to a speedy termination. It cannot fail to have a salutary effect on his bloodthirsty followers. ([*Omaha*] *Bee,* December, 17, 1890, 2)

In contrast, the *World-Herald* saw it as a tragic event for which someone must bear responsibility:

> Somebody is responsible for the death of Sitting Bull and the other Indians killed at the same time.
>
> The killing was only part of the unwarranted severity and oppression that the United States is now inflicting on the Indians.
>
> Somebody is responsible. Not those, merely, who did the killing. Nor those merely who ordered the military to the scene of the so-called trouble. Nor those merely who misjudged the danger and called for troops. Nor even those who annually cheat, rob and despoil the miserable red men through Indian rings. Not one of these alone, but all

together, forming as they do, our so-called "system" are responsible for the unhappy death of Sitting Bull.

The killing of Sitting Bull at this time is not an ordinary crime, because it may precipitate more bloodshed out of desperation and revenge.

There seems to be no end to the blunders, crimes and atrocities into which the government is led in the treatment of Indians.

It is time for a change. ([*Omaha*] *World-Herald,* December 17, 1890, 2)

While most historians assign little relationship between the death of Sitting Bull and the Wounded Knee massacre, the majority agrees that Sitting Bull's death caused the Indians to distrust the soldiers and whites even more.

Frightened that the killing of Sitting Bull might be the first action in an all out war, a mixed band of Sioux under the leadership of Minneconjou chief Big Foot fled the Cheyenne River Reservation. Several fugitives fleeing Sitting Bull's camp joined him en route. Big foot was headed for the safety of Pine Ridge hoping that the influential chief Red Cloud could protect his people. However, some feared he was leading his band into the Bad Lands to join the hostile ghost dancers who were already gathered there. Major Samuel Whitside with four troops of the seventh Cavalry was ordered to intercept and capture him.

Historian Elmo Scott Watson relates that the correspondents hanging around Pine Ridge thought that the military would have no trouble rounding up Big Foot, so the majority decided to stay where they were believing that the expected surrender of Kicking Bear, a leader of the ghost dance, would be a bigger story. Only William Fitch Kelley of the *Nebraska State Journal,* Charles W. Allen of the Chadron *Democrat,* and Cressey of the *Bee* accompanied Whitside's troops. Tibbles of the *World-Herald* grabbed a horse and followed two hours later (Watson 1943, 213).

Three days after Christmas of 1890, Whitside and the Seventh Calvary caught up with Big Foot and his band of 120 men and 230 women and children. During the night, Whitside's commander, Colonel James W. Forsyth, assumed command. He told Whitside that the Sioux were to be disarmed and shipped to a military prison in Omaha, Nebraska. The Indians were clothed in rags, and the children were hungry and cold. Big Foot had developed pneumonia during the flight across the Badlands in subzero weather. He was so weak he could barely sit up.

A council was called and Forsyth told the assembled warriors they would be asked to give up their guns. With the recent slaughter at Sitting Bull's camp fresh in their minds, the Sioux were fearful of being unarmed and vulnerable. They decided to give up their broken and useless guns and keep the working guns handy. Forsyth soon surrounded the camp. He had 470 soldiers and a platoon of Indian scouts under his command. Four Hotchkiss artillery pieces ringed the encampment.

According to Brigadier General and military historian S. L. A. Marshall, the army was confident the situation was well in hand. Only a third of the Sioux were warriors and they seemed to be passive. Marshall wrote that the army felt the Sioux were simply too weary and hungry to make any more trouble (Marshall 1972, 252).

The next day, the Indians provided only an assortment of broken and outdated weapons. Forsyth knew there were more guns, so he ordered a search of the camp to gather up all the remaining weapons. Forsyth knew it was a delicate process that could easily lead to a violent reaction. As a precaution, only officers were allowed to enter teepees and search the women.

Despite all of these precautions, the tension rapidly increased with the Sioux warriors angrily objecting to the searches of their women. Historian Rex Alan Smith writes that, as the search continued, Yellow Bird, a Minneconjou medicine man, began to dance and chant and throw handfuls of dirt into the air. He called upon the young men to have brave hearts and told them their "ghost shirts" would protect them from the soldier's bullets. One young man leapt to his feet angrily brandishing his gun saying he had paid good money for it and would not give it up. Some said it was a man named Black Coyote while other witnesses claimed it was a man named *Hosi Yanka*, which means "deaf." Two soldiers came behind the young man and tried to seize his weapon. In the ensuing scuffle, it went off. At that point, several young warriors threw off their blankets and fired a brief and ragged volley into the ranks of the soldiers. Lieutenant James Mann remembered thinking "The pity of it! What can they be thinking of?" Almost simultaneously the soldiers lines erupted with gunfire. Big Foot was one of the first to die (Smith 1981, 184–186).

General Marshall does not believe that a weapon fired by a solitary Sioux warrior was responsible for melee:

> Nothing could be more erroneous than that; it leads to a false interpretation of all that thereafter happened.
>
> Instantly, as though they had been awaiting a signal, the other warriors did the same, volley-firing into the massed soldiers with rifles theretofore carefully concealed under their blankets.
>
> There is no doubt who started that day's fight, though it is often called a massacre. Forsyth may have been clumsy and his soldiers could have been rude and provocative, but deliberate Sioux action, so timed as to indicate that it had been well plotted, initiated the slaughter. Bury My Heart at Wounded Knee may be a lovely phrase. It is still a false and misleading sentiment, dignifying conspiracy and honoring treachery. (Marshall 1972, 255)

Marshall protests that the Sioux had been given no legitimate cause to complain. "To brush off the fact is to bury more hearts at Wounded Knee than rightly belong there." Marshall feels that Wounded Knee has become a convenient symbol for those who prefer to portray the army as villain and Indian as victim (Marshall 1972, 256).

Marshall states that the initial trading of fire cannot have lasted more than a minute. He then underlines his argument for calling the engagement a battle by stating that after the Sioux had run out of ammunition, they attacked the soldiers with clubs and knives they had hidden under their blankets. To Marshall, this proves beyond any doubt that the Indians intent was not simply to defend themselves but to attack (Marshall 1972, 257).

Thomas H. Tibbles, correspondent for the *Omaha World-Herald*, was just a short ride from the camp when the firing began:

> Suddenly I heard a single shot from the direction of the troops—then three or four more—a few more—and immediately a volley. At once came a general rattle of rifle firing. Then the Hotchkiss guns. I saw curls of smoke rise through the still air. I could see the Indians moving on the hills between me and the camp. What did it all mean?
>
> Later I learned that the first volley had come from the troops on the north side of the square, and that its bullets

had whizzed across straight through the thin line of
Cheyenne scouts opposite. These promptly retired pell-mell
eastward to escape the fire of their own forces. . . . A
moment later the Hotchkiss guns, too, opened fire on the
little central band of Indians—106 men, all told and
252 women and children. Every warrior, including Big Foot
himself, who was ill in his tent with pneumonia, was killed
or seriously wounded. Only five men and 51 women and
children escaped and were brought later to Pine Ridge. . . .
(Tibbles 1957, 312)

Tibbles's account seems to be at odds with Marshall's theory of a
planned attack by the Sioux warriors. His description of the initial shot
matches the accepted story of a single shot being fired, either in a scuffle or deliberately. The few scattered shots that followed would seem
to more accurately describe the reactions of a few startled warriors
rather than any cohesive, organized "volley" of shots from the Sioux.

Tibbles returned to the camp only in time to see the end of the
fighting and the initial rounding up of survivors. However, he was
able to interview participants shortly after the event. His firsthand
account claims that the first "volley" came from the soldiers and not
the Indians. Marshall's own assertion that the Sioux firing lasted less
than a minute before they "came on with clubs and knives for the
final death grapple" would seem to indicate that the Sioux were not
able to fire many shots before their ammunition was exhausted.
Marshall prefers to assign a conspiratorial motive to the action of the
Sioux when the more likely, and logical, explanation was they were
desperately trying to protect their women and children with the only
functional weapons they still possessed.

Marshall describes the events after that first exchange of shots as
one of mass confusion. He describes the crews manning the
Hotchkiss guns on the nearby hills responding nervously to the
sound of shots in the valley and to the few stray bullets that kicked
up dirt near them. According to Marshall, due to the distance, they
had no clear idea of what was happening, but responded "naturally"
as all soldiers will do when they feel threatened. They opened fire on
the village below with all four guns, ". . . setting tepees ablaze and
killing indiscriminately the noncombatants and warriors trying to
flee the fight." Marshall goes on to describe the fire as rapid, imper-
sonal and inaccurate and states that several soldiers were killed by
the friendly fire of the Hotchkiss guns. He describes the few Indian

survivors stampeding into the surrounding hills pursued by "frenzied cavalrymen and Indian scouts" who showed them "no mercy."

Marshall writes that this is the "sequence that is most generally condemned" and admits that it is hard to find justification for the soldier's actions. He explains it by stating, "Rarely in such episodes does the heart take over when the brain is less than half functioning. . . . The grisly chase and killing went on for more than three hours and the trail of bodies extended outward from the camp for more than three miles (Marshall 1972, 257, 258).

Marshall bases his opinion that Wounded Knee was a battle and not a massacre on the fact that approximately sixty cavalrymen were killed or wounded. Marshall believes that such a death toll would be impossible if it had not been a well-planned attack rather than a tragic accident. He states that the "mute statistical evidence is sufficient proof that the surprise, like its shock impact, was nigh total, though the figures say that about half the Indians survived. All of this is brushed aside by the bleeding hearts who make of this mournful affair an unmitigated military atrocity, a massacre that need not have been" (Marshall 1972, 258, 259).

Marshall, himself a former member of the Seventh Cavalry, uses the military's total of approximately 170 dead Indians. Contemporary accounts like Tibbles place that figure much higher at around 300. The Smithsonian Institution Bureau of Ethnology's Fourteenth Report also gives the total Indian deaths as about 300, almost twice the figure the military uses. The vast majority of those killed were women and children. Marshall admits that women and children were slaughtered for hours after the initial gunfire exchange and many miles away from the action. This denigrates, somewhat, his position of calling Wounded Knee a battle rather than a massacre, because of the number of soldiers killed and wounded. When the true casualties are given, it is quickly apparent that ten times as many Sioux (300) were killed than soldiers (30). In addition, even Marshall admits that many soldiers were killed by the indiscriminate firing of the Hotchkiss guns and not by the Sioux. It is also probable that other cavalrymen were killed or wounded by their comrades as they fired across the Indian camp and into the ranks of their fellow soldiers encircling the Indian village. In fact, during later Court Martial proceedings, the Army itself criticized Colonel Forsyth for ". . . placing his troops so that when the battle began they fired upon each other" ([*Omaha*] *World-Herald*, January 5,

1891). It seems likely that only a relatively few of the cavalry's casualties were inflicted by the Indians, thus taking away Marshall's principal argument for calling Wounded Knee a battle.

Not surprisingly, the first stories about Wounded Knee in the Omaha *Bee* were headlined "Ghastly Work of Treacherous Reds" and "Capt. [George] Wallace Tomahawked to Death." They claimed the soldiers had "shown themselves to be heroes in deed of daring" (*[Omaha] Bee,* December 30, 1890, 1).

The *Omaha World-Herald* took a different approach in its coverage of the conflict at Wounded Knee. Its first story on the tragedy was headlined, "All Murdered in a Mass" with subheads such as "Big Foot and His Followers Shot Without Regard to Sex" and "Men, Women and Children Said to Have Been Shot Wherever Found" (*[Omaha] World-Herald,* December 30, 1890, 1).

In a story headlined "Horrors of War," the *World Herald*'s correspondent, Bright Eyes, told of wounded Indian mothers with their babies and the agonies endured bravely by the injured:

> . . . There was a woman sitting on the floor with a wounded baby on her lap and four or five children around her, all her grandchildren. Their father and mother were killed. There was a young woman shot through both thighs and her wrist broken.
>
> Mr. Tibbles had to get a pair of pliers to get her rings off. There was a Little boy with his throat apparently shot to pieces.
>
> . . . They were all hungry and when we fed this little boy we found he could swallow. We gave him some gruel and he grabbed with both his little hands a dipper of water. When I saw him yesterday afternoon, he looked worse than the day before, and when they feed him now, the food and water come out the side of his neck. . . . (*[Omaha] World-Herald,* January 2, 1891, 1)

When he heard the reports about Wounded Knee, the Commanding General for the District, General Nelson Miles, removed Colonel Forsyth from command. Miles was said to be incensed at the indiscriminate killing of women and children and also upset at Forsyth endangering his own men by misplacing them on the battlefield. Despite General Mile's best efforts, Forsyth was found to have

Burial of the dead at Wounded Knee, 1890. (*Nebraska State Historical Society*)

acted reasonably and was eventually restored to command (Smith 1981, 202–03). In a possible attempt to justify the events at Wounded Knee, the Army awarded almost twenty Medals of Honor to participants in the engagement. It remains the record for the highest number of Medal of Honor winners for any single engagement in United States history.

The *World-Herald* left no doubt as to how they felt about the tragedy of Wounded Knee:

> Somebody is to blame that over thirty brave soldiers lie dead and forty more are suffering from their wounds, that over 300 Indians, men, women and children, lie dead under a winter sky with coyotes and dogs preying on their unburied bodies, and over 4,000 destitute people are fleeing from their homes in midwinter, fearing the same fate. . . .
>
> Of course the Indian is always to blame. He neither writes nor owns a newspaper. His opinions are never

consulted. He has been starved, robbed, and lied to until he has no right to expect anything else and he should at once be put to death or lamely submit to an unending succession of Royer's [Indian Agent] that will be inflicted upon him whether he wants them or not.

Yet we are a Christian people, for murder, starvation and death is still the portion of the heathen as it was in the days of Pizzarro, Cortez and the noble Pilgrims of New England. ([*Omaha*] *World-Herald,* January, 4, 1891, 2)

In the few weeks following Wounded Knee, there was a mass exodus of Indians into the Badlands. Furious warriors fired upon agency buildings, and it looked like the massive uprising predicted by Cressey was finally going to happen. By January 17, 1891, however, it was all over. The Indians came back to their reservations. A "war" that had begun with panic over the pathetic attempt by the Indians to dance back the old days, and was fueled by wild stories from breathless correspondents, had ended with a whimper.

The Fort Laramie Treaty of 1868 was all but forgotten. Finally, after twenty-two years, there was no war between the whites and the Sioux, but that was the only part of the treaty that was fulfilled. The land promised to the Sioux was splintered and being offered for sale to white men from big eastern cities in newspaper ads featuring a stoic Indian brave looking forlornly in the distance. The promise to deal with the Indians justly had been buried in the blood and snow of Wounded Knee where 300 men, women, and children died because a pathetic attempt to dance back the old days had frightened the leaders of a progressive, new society.

## REFERENCES

Kappler, C. J. 1971. *Indian affairs: Laws and treaties Vol. II.* Compiled & Edited, Washington, Govt. Print Office, 1904-41. New York: AMS Press.

Jensen, R., Eli, Paul, and John E. Carter. 1991. *Eyewitness to Wounded Knee.* Lincoln: University of Nebraska Press.

Marshall, S. L. A. 1972. *Crimsoned prairie: The Indian wars on the Great Plains.* New York: Charles Scribner & Sons.

(*Omaha*) *Bee,* August 29, 1890–December 30, 1890.

(*Omaha*) *World-Herald,* October 4, 1890–January 4, 1891.

Smith, R. A., 1981. *Moon of the popping tree: The tragedy at Wounded Knee and the end of the Indian wars.* Lincoln: University of Nebraska Press.

Tibbles, T. H. 1957. *Buckskin and blanket days: Memoirs of a friend of the Indians*. New York: Doubleday and Company.

Utley, R. M. 1993. *The Lance and the shield: The life and times of Sitting Bull*. New York: Henry Holt and Company Inc.

Watson, E. S. 1943. "The last Indian war, 1890–91: A study of newspaper jingoism." *Journalism Quarterly* 20 (September): 205–19.

# 9

# How the Osages Kept Their Oil

*Teresa Trumbly Lamsam
and Bruce E. Johansen*

Sometime in the early 1900s, after a century of dealing with the U.S. federal government, the Osage tribe began to say "No" to the White Hairs in Washington, DC. They signed over land to the United States some six times only to have to buy back part of it from a former enemy, the Cherokee Nation. At the government's insistence, they gave up hunting for farming—a vocation they would never take to. They were forced to move their permanent villages each time some group of whites pressured the U.S. government for the land.

After being shuffled through several treaty councils, moved from their ancestral homelands, and deposited in 1871 in Indian Territory, nature had a surprise waiting for them. The lands assigned them contained some of the richest oil deposits in the United States. The Osage oil fields were the largest single oil discovery of the day and would soon become the origin of two of this country's largest oil companies, Phillips Petroleum Company and Conoco, now known as Conoco-Phillips. In a matter of decades, the Osages became the wealthiest people per capita in the world, and some would say, the most frequently murdered.

Many, if not most, Native American tribes and nations have experienced colonial-style exploitation of their natural resources, which have been taken from them with little or no compensation or benefit. By and large, the Osages have tenaciously maintained control of their oil and mineral rights throughout a century that has included greedy, murderous attempts to take that oil and the more clever, sustained attempts through U.S. law and business dealings. This chapter will explore how, in historical and legal context, the Osages arranged and maintained this control.

The Osage Reservation occupies all of the roughly 1.5 million acres of Osage County in north-central Oklahoma, adjacent to the Kansas border, a land that varies from woods to open plains and grasslands. The land was purchased in 1871 by the Osages from the Cherokees. The land was part of Osage ancestral land that had been ceded in 1825 in a treaty with the U.S. government.

Osage County, which is roughly the size of Delaware, is the largest county in Oklahoma, and it is the only one created explicitly to correspond to the boundaries of an Indian reservation. The county was created because the Osages feared that Oklahoma statehood might crimp their ability to control their own affairs (Wilson 1985, ix).

Osage leases and royalties from oil and gas generated in the 1990s a high of $25 million in 1990 to a low of $10 million in 1998. During that decade, the average price of oil in 1990 was just under $25 a barrel to just more than $12 a barrel in 1998. The reservation's grasslands also support about 150,000 head of cattle (Tiller 1996, 523).

What emerges from Osage history is an irony; in the case of the Osages, allotment legislation, originally meant to break up collective tribal identity and rights in favor of individual landholding and Anglo-Saxon-style property rights, was used at a key juncture to uphold collective Osage control of oil and other mineral rights. The key was insertion of a clause to that effect into the legislation, passed in 1906, that initiated allotment for the Osages. At every turn, the Osage tribal government has protected its rights to manage oil production for the common good of the nation, even as private interests and internal tribal factions have tried to assail it. Through several decades, the Osages have used legal resources to lobby Congress to use its plenary power vis-à-vis Native nations to maintain its right to manage the nation's natural resources.

The Osage originally migrated from the banks of the Ohio River to the present-day Missouri before contact with Europeans, which occurred in 1673 on the banks of the Osage River. The Osage hunted throughout the northern half of Oklahoma, southeastern Kansas, and much of Arkansas from the 1600s to the 1800s, although their permanent villages were in Missouri. In 1802, the Chouteaus, French traders who had official trading agreements with the U.S. government, convinced a large group of Osages to move to Three Forks in current Oklahoma. Clermont (also known as Claremore) was the ranking Osage chief who led this group.

In 1808, the "Great and little Osage nation of Indians" entered a treaty with the U.S. government signed at Fort Clark on the Missouri, November 10. The Osage ceded most of the state of Missouri and the northern half of Arkansas, all the land north of the Arkansas River. The treaty also established at the signing site a year-round store of goods for barter on moderate terms for Osage furs (Lowrie and Clarke 1832, 4:392). However, U.S. negotiators had forgotten about the necessity of Clermont's signature. He did not sign the 1808 treaty, which was a main reason for the 1818 treaty in which he ceded the land in Arkansas and Oklahoma.

Only a few years after the Fort Clark treaty, the Osage again ceded land as set forth by U.S. President James Madison to the U.S. Senate, January 16, 1810. The treaty with the Osage set a boundary "beginning at Fort Clark, on the Missouri, five miles above the Fire prairie, and running thence a due south course to the River Arkansas and down the same to the Mississippi," relinquishing to the United States all lands to the east of that line, "and north of the southwardly bank of the said River Arkansas, and all lands situated northerly of the river Missouri" (Lowrie and Clarke 1832, 4:763).

A treaty in 1818 contained more land cessations due to the absence of Clermont's signature on the 1808 treaty and increasing pressure by squatters. The 1818 treaty, signed on September 25 by the Osages and a representative for the United States, William Clark, governor of Missouri Territory, ceded the remaining northern section of Arkansas and a section of eastern Oklahoma. The treaty established U.S. rights to "the tract of country . . . beginning at the Arkansas River, where the present Osage boundary line strikes the river, at Frog Bayou, thence, up the Arkansas and Verdigris, to the falls of the Verdigris River, thence, eastwardly, to the said Osage boundary line, at a point twenty leagues north from the Arkansas river, and with that line, to the place of the beginning" (Lowrie and Clarke 1832, 4:167–168). Another treaty was signed in 1822 abrogating the provision of the store mentioned in the treaty of 1808. Payment of $2,329.40 was stipulated. An 1823 treaty with the Osage, Sac, and Fox tribes abolished Indian trading establishments entirely.

With the Osage being squeezed treaty-by-treaty out of their aboriginal land, the U.S. government finally decided in 1825 to designate a permanent strip of land for their villages. The first Osage Reservation occupied a southern strip of land in the present day state of Kansas. In 1825, the Great and Little Osages relinquished claim to all lands in the state of Missouri and Arkansas territory for a twenty-year annuity of $7,000 per annum, plus 600 head of cattle, 1,000 domestic fowls, 600 hogs, ten yoke of oxen, and six carts, plus farming utensils, and the services of a blacksmith. Land was set aside for the Osages beginning due east of White Hair's village and 25 miles west of the western boundary line of the state of Missouri, fronting on a north and south line, as to leave ten miles north, and forty miles south, of said beginning, and extending west to the width of fifty miles.

Another treaty was signed with the Osages at Fort Gibson, "west of Arkansas," in 1839, containing land cessions of all land claimed under treaties of 1808 and 1825, except for explicit exceptions. The Osages were to be paid an annuity of $20,000 a year for twenty years, $12,000 in cash, and $8,000 goods, stock, provisions, or money "as the President may direct." Provisions included a grist mill and saw mill, a grist miller, two blacksmiths, and two assistants, plus 1,000 cows and calves, 2,000 breeding hogs, 1,000 ploughs, 1,000 sets of horse gear, 1,000 axes, and 1,000 hoes.

The Osage lived on the Kansas reservation for sixty years, but a growing number of squatters who occupied the little houses on the prairie pressured to have the Osage removed from prime farmland. In addition, the U.S. government had another problem that could be solved by moving the Osage. The Cherokee tribe was not using a strip of land along the Kansas border called the Cherokee Outlet, which had been set aside as a corridor to the Plains for buffalo hunting (Hogan 1998). The U.S. government sought to effectively block the Cherokees' path to the Plains to counter their support for the Confederate Army during the Civil War.

In 1865, arrangements were made for the Osage to buy the land, which they had ceded in an earlier treaty, and sell the 8 million acres of treaty lands in Kansas, two-fifths of which were sold for $1.25 per acre. The government then advanced $300,000 to the Osages and sold the land for $1.1 million, keeping the funds for the "civilization" of other Native nations, according to the House of Representatives Report No. 1212, 76th Congress, First Session, July 18, 1939. An inquiry by the Court of Claims, presented in the Congressional

Record, March 9, 1877, found that the treaty had been presented to a hastily convened "council" of full bloods who could not read the sixteen-page typewritten document that was presented for their approval. The treaty was rushed through the approval process, aided by interpreters, in three hours (Congressional Record 1877).

After the turn of the century, the Osage, now considerably wiser in the ways of the U.S. government, requested to have the excess $776,742.03 returned to their account, having waived several millions of dollars in accrued interest. The Osages' protested the diverted funds until at least 1909 (Osage Civilization 1909). The Court of Claims agreed, after several years of protracted paper shuffling and considerable waffling over treaty language, in 1928. Eleven years later, the U.S. Senate moved to reimburse the funds (Osage Civilization 1909). The bill passed the Senate three times and the House once before the money was finally, in 1941, ordered to the Osages' account.

Congressional records indicate that the Osage fought several proposals or attempts to abolish their tribal government early in the twentieth century. As early as 1874 and 1875, they also protested to Congress establishment of a territorial government that would have had powers superior to those of the Indian nations in the Territory.

Just a few decades away in a new century, the Osage would discover just how far greed could drive individuals. Land-hungry squatters and disreputable government agents had been only an indication of times to come. Then came oil and the hundreds of white people who were attracted by its scent of wealth.

Oil was discovered under the land in 1896, but the first well drilled in that year was a dry hole. The first successful drilling came just a year later in 1897. Oil was first discovered in Oklahoma (then Indian Territory, before statehood) during 1884. By 1939, more than 500 million barrels had been taken from lands of the Osage Nation (Annual Summary 1939).

Court records show that on March 16, 1896, the Osage Tribe executed an oil and gas lease to Edwin H. Foster for ten years, allowing him to explore anywhere on the 1.5 million acres of the reservation. The lease expired March 16, 1906. This lease was extended ten years to March 1916 during which Foster executed subleases to several corporations. One of these was Barnsdall Oil, which continued to extract oil between March 16, 1916, and June 20, 1916, after its lease had expired.

By 1906, the Osage knew that they wanted to hold the oil rights in common. In an unprecedented use of the national-scale allotment

This photo was taken on a portion of the old Chapman-Barnard Ranch, now owned by the Nature Conservancy and known as the Tallgrass Prairie Preserve, in the north-central part of the reservation. The first producing oil well was completed in 1896. The buffalo were brought back in 1995. (*Joe A. Trumbly*)

legislation, the Osage charted the course of a new history. By that time, smallpox and intermarriage had reduced Osage population to about 2,200 people, about half of whom were of mixed blood. In the mid-1990s, the tribal roll contained about 12,000 people (Tiller 1996, 522). The Osage seemed to have a strong sense that oil, gas, and other mineral resource should remain common property of the tribe from early in the twentieth century. Several congressional reports and resolutions related to allotment of land, many dating to 1906, require that oil and gas remain under common title. For example, House Report Number 3219, 59th Congress, First Session (H.R. 15333, 1906): "The bill as presented by the Indians asked for the reservation of the oil, gas, coal. And other mineral lands to the tribe [be] in common for twenty-five years" (Rice 2001, 8–9).

These oil and mineral rights brought unprecedented wealth to the Osage. In 1880, an Osage received $10.50 per year from the tribe's common fund. In 1900, the amount was $200 per year. In 1920, that yearly amount jumped to $8,090 (per headright, not per household).

By 1923, two years after increasing numbers of Osages were murdered, a headright was bringing in $12,440 per year, equivalent to more than $980,000 per year in 1998 dollars (Hogan 1998, 26).

The average Indian family numbered four persons. Two or three members of the family often owned one or more of the Osage headrights, which numbered 2,229. Thus, for a time, the Osages became the richest people, per capita, in the world (Hogan 1998, 26).

The Congressional Allotment Act of June 28, 1906, provided for the Osages that the mineral rights would revert to the property of the individual owner at the end of the twenty-five years, unless otherwise stipulated by the U.S. Congress. In part, the legislation stated that "having reserved the oil, gas, coal and other minerals covered by the lands for the selection and division of which provision is herein made to the Osage tribe for 25 years from April 8, 1906, and provided for leases by, and payment of royalties to, the Osage Tribe" (Rice 2001, 14). Up to $50,000 a year worth of these royalties were set aside for support of schools on the reservation (Rice 2001, 15).

Even during these twenty-five years, the Osage had to make repeated trips to Washington, DC, to protect and amend the legislation. On July 1, 1912, President Howard Taft approved a recommendation from the secretary of the Interior to fix the royalty rate for oil and gas taken from Osage lands at one-sixth of gross proceeds. In 1915, President Wilson maintained the one-sixth rate for well on any quarter-section producing less than 100 barrels a month. For production greater than that, the royalty was raised to one-fifth. Payments may be taken in cash (from sales) or in oil. A letter from the Secretary of the Interior (July 16, 1917) contained regulations for the leasing of Osage lands for oil and gas mining (Rice 2001, 17). In 1921, House Report No. 1377 (Feb. 26) extended Osage Tribal mineral estate to April 7, 1946, while at the same time allowing Oklahoma to collect a production tax "in lieu of all other State and county taxes" (Rice 2001, 18). The same legislation also declared Osages to be U.S. citizens and allowed collection of an additional 1 percent gross production tax for roads and bridges in Osage County. On April 28, 1922, House Resolution 10401 (66th Congress, First Session) contained an amendment adding a provision "preserving Osage tribal ownership of all oil, gas, coal, or other minerals" (Rice 2001, 17).

In 1925, according to Senate Report 1126, the Secretary of the Interior was explicitly directed to lease Osage oil and gas at market (as opposed to fixed) rates. This intent was stated shortly thereafter in two other Senate bills, both considered during 1928 (Rice 2001, 19). Tribal ownership of the mineral estate was confirmed again in 1938 in House Report 2700, 75th Congress, 3rd Session. In 1950, House Report 2079 (81st Congress, 2nd Session) "authorizes the Osage Tribal Council to determine the royalties that are to be paid, subject to the approval of the Secretary of the Interior, in lieu of that function being in the President of the United States" (Rice 2001, 23). The 95th Congress in the 1978 amendment to the 1906 Act extended the mineral estate in perpetuity. The first paragraph of Section 3 of the Act of June 24, 1978 (52 Stat. 1034.1035), as amended, extended the mineral estate reserved to the Osage Tribe by the Act of June 26, 1906 (24 Stat. 539), was further amended by striking the phrase "until the eighth day of April 1983, and thereafter until otherwise provide by Act of Congress" and substituting, in lieu of thereof, the phrase "in perpetuity" (Rice 2001, 21).

The reservation of oil and other mineral rights to the Osage tribe in the 1906 Allotment Act has been often cited in several court cases since. See, for example, *Utilities Production Corporation v. Carter Oil Co.* and *Carter Oil Co. v. Utilities Production Corporation,* Circuit Court of Appeals, 10th Circuit 72 F. 2d 655 U.S. App. LEXIS 4645 (August 4, 1934), dealing with ownership of "residue gas," casing-head gasoline recovered during the drilling of oil wells (Utilities 1934).

In 1931, twenty-five years after the 1906 act, the Texas Company and the Indian Territory Illuminating Oil Company, holders of mineral leases from the Osage Tribal Council, made a case that they owned the land (and any oil, gas, et al. below its surface), having purchased it from individual Osage allottees. In *Adams et al. v. Osage Tribe of Indians et al.* (No. 642 District Court N.D. Oklahoma 50 F. 2d 918; 1931 U.S. Dist. LEXIS 1436) a federal district judge found that "the contention of the complainants is untenable. A careful consideration of the various acts of Congress involved discloses that the complainants have never by reason of their purchase become vested with the title in and to the oil and gas and other minerals found under the lands involved in this action" (Adams 1931). The court upheld the Osage Nation's right to control mineral rights.

By Act of Congress March 3, 1921 (41 Stat. 1249) the Osage government's right to control mineral rights was extended to April 8, 1946; by act of Congress March 2, 1929, the mineral estate was extended again to April 8, 1958 (Wilson, in The Underground Reservation, p. 185, says 1959). The right of Congress to extend the terms of the 1906 Allotment Act was justified was use of its plenary power in relationships with Indian nations, stemming from *Worcester v. Georgia* (6 Peters 515) and several other federal cases. In a 1978 amendment to the allotment act, the 95th Congress extended the mineral estate "in perpetuity."

The Osages' collective control of oil and gas leasing was extended by Congress over the protest of the Osage County Homeowners' Association, a group of whites who sought to control reservation oil and gas production. In 1957, tribal control vis-à-vis the 1906 provision was extended from 1959 to 1984 (Wilson 1985, 185). The 1906 clause encountered more challenges in other oil-related court cases, including *United States v. Stanolind Crude Oil Purchasing Co.; U.S. v. Gulf Oil Corp.; U.S. v. Sinclair Prairie Oil Co.* (Numbers 1975–1977; United States Court of Appeals for the Tenth Circuit; 113 F. 2d 194; 1940 U.S. App. LEXIS 4817 June 29, 1940). These cases evolved from a dispute over royalty rates owed the Osage by companies producing oil from its leases, specifically the industry custom of deducting 3 percent from the volume of oil pumped to account for impurities, sediment, and shrinkage. The court found that the companies were entitled to the 3 percent deduction. This case, however, shows how aggressively the United States sometimes exercised its responsibility to act as the Osages' legal advocate in oil-related cases (*U.S. v. Stanolind* 1940).

U.S. Justice Department representation of Osage oil interests could become quite aggressive, even (according to subsequent court rulings) overzealous. One example was a court battle with Barnsdall Oil. The company had overstayed its lease by three months but was not taken to court for the proceeds and accumulated interest until fourteen years later. The United States took Barnsdall Oil to court on behalf of the Osages in an attempt to find Barnsdall to be a trespasser. The opinion of the court does not explain the gap of twenty-two years between the infraction and the circuit court's opinion. It does say that the United States instituted the action March 13, 1940, "seeking recovery of the value of the oil received by Barnsdall during the interim period, together with interest thereupon" (*United States v. Barnsdall Oil* 1942). The Interior Department had allowed Barnsdall to operate the extra three-plus months on grounds that closing its wells could decrease their future value to the Osages. The Appeals Court agreed, finding the Justice Department and the Osage tribe at fault for a too-narrow interpretation of the 1906 provisions allowing for Osage tribal control of resources. "We think the acts of the

Secretary of the Interior are well within the discretionary powers reposed in him by Section 12 of the Act of 1906," the appeals court ruled (*United States v. Barnsdall Oil*, 1942).

What cases like this and others that proceeded and followed do not reveal, however, are the motivations and actions of those involved. Nor do these examples reveal the rifts that were created within the tribe and the growing distrust of the federal government. The U.S. government has been a fickle guardian and adviser, at times protecting and upholding Osage interests, but as years of tribal council meeting minutes would disclose, more often they acted as an obstacle to justice and progress for the tribe. In the end, the Osage have kept their oil despite greedy individuals and companies, a disinterested federal government, a contentious state government, and at times, despite themselves.

## REFERENCES

*Adams et al. v. Osage Tribe of Indians et al.* (No. 642 District Court N.D. Oklahoma 50 F. 2d 918; 1931 U.S. Dist. LEXIS 1436).

Annual Summary of Production and Pipeline Runs, Oklahoma and Kansas, for the Year 1939. Petroleum Statistical Guide, p. 11, cited in *United States v. Stanolind* (1940).

Congressional Record, 42d Congress, 2d Session. Ex. Doc. No. 146, n.p. The Adams case was upheld on appeal to the tenth Circuit [59 F. 2d 653; 1932 U.S. App. LEXIS 3435].

Congressional Record. 44th Congress, 2d Session, Ex. Doc. No. 186. Committee on Indian Affairs, March 9, 1877.

Hogan, L.J. 1998. *The Osage Indian murders.* Fredrick, MD: Amlex.

Lowrie, W., and M. St. Clair Clarke. American State Papers. Documents Legislative and Executive of the Congress of the United States. 1789 through 1815. Et seq. Washington: Gales & Seaton, 1832. Vol. 4.

Osage civilization fund. Hearing on Joint Resolution No. 67. Committee on Indian Affairs, House of Representatives. Washington, DC: Government Printing Office, 1909.

Rice, G.W. Osage nation: Initial draft of the analysis of the current situation of the Osage Indian Reservation in Oklahoma. October 28, 2001. Typescript from Rice and Bigler, Attorneys at Law, Cushing, OK.

Tiller, V.E.V. 1996. Osage Reservation. In *Tiller's guide to Indian country: Economic profiles of American Indian reservations.* Albuquerque, NM: BowArrow Publishing Co., 522–524.

*United States v. Barnsdall Oil.* U.S. Court of Appeals for the Tenth Circuit. 127 F. 2d 1019 U.S. App. LEXIS 4792 April 30, 1942.

*United States v. Stanolind Crude Oil Purchasing Co.; United States v. Gulf Oil Corp.; United States v. Sinclair Prairie Oil Co.* (Numbers 1975–1977; United

States Court of Appeals for the Tenth Circuit; 113 F. 2d 194; 1940 U.S. App. LEXIS 4817 June 29, 1940.

*Utilities Production Corporation v. Carter Oil Co.* and *Carter Oil Co. v. Utilities Production Corp.* Circuit Court of Appeals, 10th Circuit 72 F. 2d 655 U.S. App. LEXIS 4645 (August 4, 1934).

Wilson, T. P. 1985. *The underground reservation: Osage oil.* Lincoln: University of Nebraska Press.

# 10

# Kennewick Man: The Facts, the Fantasies, and the Stakes

*Bruce E. Johansen*

Was he European? Norse, perhaps? Was he Asiatic, perhaps Ainu, the indigenous people of Japan? Was he Native American, from the earth of Turtle Island (North America)? Is Kennewick Man, perhaps, a combination of the worldly elements of his own time, a reminder in our time that human origins in the Americas are much more complex (and much more multicultural) than has been commonly supposed?

If "Kennewick Man," a 9,300-year-old, nearly complete skeleton of roughly 350 pieces found in eastern Washington during 1996 could come to life, he might be surprised to find that he has become the object of an exercise in racial heritage fantasies (and related political tensions) in our time. The debate over the origins of Kennewick Man says as much about the racial politics of the very early twenty-first century as it does about the skeleton's actual origins.

Kennewick Man is one anecdote in a long story, one reminder of the increasing complexity of our knowledge about human origins in the Americas. The discovery of Kennewick Man is part of an ongoing rewriting of the story of human origins in the Americas. A number of archaeological discoveries (and speculations) during the past generation have effectively jettisoned the neat and tidy myth that I read in my childhood (the 1950s): that one group of Asiatic people traversed the Bering Strait more or less at one time and populated the continents of the Western Hemisphere in one fell swoop. The racial politics evoked by the discovery of Kennewick Man (and other, similarly ancient remains) has presented us with a number of very diverse opinions, but one thing that nearly all serious observers of human antiquity in the Americas now share is this: Human origins in the Americas are much more diverse, and cover a much greater time span, than the simplistic Bering Strait "theory" allows.

Speculation on human origins in the Americas now reaches to a relatively "safe" 30,000 years (based on finds at Monte Verde, Chile), with speculation (by the noted African archaeologist Louis Leakey) ranging to more than 200,000 years, based on a site at Calico, in San Bernadino County, California. On this time line, Kennewick Man was not one of the first human beings to trod Turtle Island. An overview of the evidence suggests that the Americas were inhabited by many people, from many places, by land and by sea, over a longer period of time than most archaeological professionals have heretofore suspected. In some cases, migration may have reached Asia from the Americas, reiterating a position taken two hundred years ago by Thomas Jefferson. Jefferson, a student of human languages, suspected that Native cultures in America were of great antiquity based on the number and complexity of their languages. Jefferson supposed that the Old World might have been partially populated from the Americas.

Some present-day linguistic analysis supports Jefferson's supposition. Johanna Nichols, a professor of Slavic languages at the University of California (Berkeley) says that from Alaska to the southern tip of South America, Native Americans speak (or have spoken) 143 language stocks that are mutually unintelligible. Nichols says that it takes roughly 6,000 years for a language to split into two mutually unintelligible tongues. Based on this calculation, she estimates that human languages were being spoken in the Americas at least 60,000 years ago.

It's amazing how quickly the discovery of one skeleton can be plugged into contemporary racial agendas—especially some non-Indians' crying need for attachment (mattering not how tenuous) to the land they have come to call America. This has persisted despite acknowledgment by those who first called Kennewick Man a European type that he is really, on second thought, just as much like the ancient Ainu, native peoples of Japan. If they came from Europe at all, peoples such as Kennewick Man may have gone through a lot of changes before arriving in America, making of him a racial mosaic who stumps today's racial classifications.

Despite confusion over his origins among scientists, much of the popular commentary on Kennewick Man has been sifted through racial assumptions. Some of these assumptions have been erroneously attributed to Native Americans, even though most native nations did not define membership racially until the advent of European classifications.

Some present-day Native American peoples do not fit the racial classifications designed by non-Indian scientists that originated in century-old doctrines. Many Haudenosaune (Iroquois) are light-skinned, for example. It takes some imagination to assign a Lakota Sioux and a Maya to a single 12,000-year-old ancestor. Many Native nations adopted people who were not racially similar to them. The texture of the debate changes when it is viewed through this lens. Kennewick Man could have Asian (or even European) facial features and still be defined as a member of a Native American nation, using criteria accepted by many Native American peoples. Very few of the media reports say anything about this aspect of the debate.

At the same time that Kennewick Man has thrown some assumptions of mainstream academia into doubt, the skeleton has become a stalking horse for non-Indian academics who have an interest in limiting Native American nations' legal rights to newly discovered human remains. Kennewick Man has become a focus around which attempts to limit the Native American Graves Protection and Repatriation Act (1990) have taken definitive shape, to allow (for example) inspection of remains found on federally owned land (including Kennewick Man) before they are reburied by Native peoples.

Assertions that Kennewick Man was from Europe have made of him something of a hero to non-Indians who would like to abrogate the treaties and limit Native American sovereignty in our time. Architects of racial fantasies have built an entire racial pedigree for him on scant evidence and used claims that he was "white" to support a theory that he and his kind were the first human immigrants to the Americas. The more extreme variations of these tales assert that Kennewick Man and his kin were slaughtered by the ancestors of present-day Native Americans.

Kennewick Man also has been made over into something of a civic booster by the *Tri-City Herald,* the daily newspaper published nearest to the site of his discovery. The *Herald,* which serves the three neighboring small cities of Kennewick, Richland, and Pasco, maintains an Interpretive Center describing the life and times of Kennewick Man. The local battle for bragging rights to the discovery site of Kennewick Man was joined when civic boosters in the other two small cities proposed (with straight faces) that the skeleton be renamed "Kennewick-Pasco-Richland Man."

## THE FACTS

A human skull that would come to be called "Kennewick Man" was stumbled upon (literally) by two college students, Will Thomas, 21, and Dave Deacy, 20, on July 28, 1996. The two residents of nearby West Richland, home for the summer, were looking for a spot on the banks of the Columbia River from which to watch the annual hydroplane races.

James Chatters of Applied Paleoscience, who routinely conducts skeletal forensics for Benton County Coroner Floyd Johnson, helped police gather what eventually became a skeleton which was complete except for its sternum and a few small bones in the hands and feet. Recent flushing from Columbia River Dams, an attempt to preserve salmon runs for commercial and Indian fishing, had disturbed the sediments and exposed the human remains that became known as Kennewick Man.

The skeleton seemed to Chatters to have belonged to a man who was old by the standards of his time (between 40 and 55 years), about five-foot nine or ten inches, tall for a human being that old, who had led a rough life. He had compound fractures in at least six ribs and damage to his left shoulder, which probably caused his arm to wither. He also had a healed-over skull injury. Kennewick Man, whose dietary staple was fish, probably died of injuries sustained after a stone projectile point pierced his thigh and lodged in his pelvis. The projectile probably caused a fatal infection that may have festered for as many as six months. Kennewick Man also suffered from advanced osteoporosis in one of his elbows and minor arthritis in his knees, according to Chatters.

Kennewick Man had a long, narrow skull, a projecting nose, receding cheekbones, a high chin, and a square mandible. The lower bones of the arms and legs were relatively long compared to the upper bones. These traits are not characteristic of modern American Indians in the area, though many of them are common among Caucasoid peoples, said Chatters.

"The man lacks definitive characteristics of the classic mongoloid stock to which most Native Americans belong," Chatters said shortly after examining Kennewick Man's remains. He continued:

> The skull is dolichocranic . . . rather than brachycranic, the face narrow and prognathous rather than broad and flat. Cheek bones recede slightly, and lack of an inferior zygomatic projection. . . . Many of these characteristics are definitive of modern-day Caucasoid peoples, while others . . . are typical of neither race. Dental characteristics . . . indicate possible relationship to south Asian peoples. (http://www.nmnh.si.edu/arctic/html/kennewick_man.html)

Chatters said that without further study of the skeleton, many of the characteristics by which people usually assign "race" will remain unknown: the form and color of his eyes, color of skin and hair, whether his lips were thin or broad, and whether his hair was straight, wavy, or curly. No one at present knows what language he spoke, nor anything about what type of religion, if any, he practiced. In other words, the game of racial classification which so preoccupies much of the popular discourse about Kennewick Man is being constructed on a very scant evidence base. On such small foundations, however, castles of imagination have been built.

Kennewick man's teeth were well worn, a trait common to prehistoric Indian skulls, and its color indicated great age. The skull contained nearly all its teeth, very unusual for a skeleton that would be dated to more than 9,000 years of age. The teeth also contained remarkably little decay compared to most other remains of similar age.

At first, Chatters had thought that the skeleton might have belonged to the victim of an unreported homicide, or a relatively recent settler in the region, perhaps a century old. The bones seemed to be in too good a condition to guess an age any older than that. Chatters speculated that the man might be an Anglo settler because a homestead was located nearby. After some reflection and much controversy, Chatters backed off his initial quick call that Kennewick Man had European origins. He may have been Caucasoid, but an immigrant to America by way of Asia.

Chatters began to suspect the skeleton might be older than a century or two after he noticed that the projectile point that had lodged in Kennewick Man's pelvis was a leaf-shaped, serrated Cascade projectile point of a type that had been dated, under other circumstances, to ages of 4,500 to 8,500 years. The arrowhead had healed into Kennewick Man's pelvis, causing an infection that probably killed him. Once the question of great antiquity was raised, Johnson ordered radiocarbon and DNA tests to date the skeleton. The remains dated to 9,300 to 9,600 years before the present.

Anthropologist Grover S. Krantz of Washington State University also examined the bones at Chatters's request. The skeleton "cannot be anatomically assigned to any existing tribe in the area, nor even to the western Native American type in general," he wrote to Chatters on September 2 (Slayman 1997, 17). "It shows some traits that are more commonly encountered in material from the eastern United States or even of European origin, while certain other diagnostic traits cannot presently be determined" (Slayman 1997, 17).

The experts sometimes disagreed on some fundamental points, such as Kennewick Man's conjectured diet. One picture of Kennewick Man's eating habits was sketched in the *Tri-City Herald* by Staff Writer Loretto J. Hulse:

> Rich, lean roasts and steaks from the herds of elk and bison that grazed on the lush grasslands of the Basin. Those same grasses also yielded a crop of seeds in the fall that were ground into a crude meal. In the spring, Kennewick Man's small band dug young roots and tubers by the rivers, journeyed to the mountains for juicy huckleberries in the summer and gathered grains in the fall. . . . When he was in his early 40s, Kennewick Man roamed land that supported luxuriant stands of grass and scrubby brush, and some pine trees may have broken the horizon on the higher slopes of the Horse Heavens. (http://www.tri-cityherald.com/BONES/recipes/index.html)

David Rice, of the Army Corps of Engineers office in Seattle, told Hulse that "Most likely, rabbits and deer were their main source of meat. . . . The elk of that time were substantially larger and heavier than any alive today and would have taken some coordinated effort to bring down" (Ibid). Both Hulse and Rice seem to have ignored Chatters's opinion that Kennewick Man's diet was based largely on fish, probably the rich salmon runs that course up and down the Columbia River.

Kennewick Man and his band (which probably numbered twenty-five to thirty people, including children) may have ranged as far north as Spokane, east and west to the Cascades and Blue mountains and south to the Hermiston (Oregon) area. To protect his feet, Kennewick Man likely negotiated the hills and valleys of Eastern Washington and Oregon in sandals made of sagebrush bark. Kennewick Man and his kin may have woven dog hair with the bark fibers to make cloth. The dogs may have been used in hunting and as beasts of burden.

Once Chatters had examined Kennewick Man, the story was picked up quickly by the Seattle *Times* and numerous local papers. Within days of Kennewick Man's discovery, the *New York Times,* and *Washington Post* had picked up the story. Later, *Time* covered the controversy. The *Lehrer News Hour* (on the Public Broadcasting Service) did a segment from the scene, showing Chatters climbing along the banks of the Columbia. *Sixty Minutes* did a segment as well, during which Lesley Stahl wondered in front of millions of viewers whether Native Americans wanted Kennewick Man reburied to extinguish questions about their sovereignty and casino profits. She was sharply criticized by Tim Giago, in his weekly column for *Indian Country Today,* November 2, 1998. Eventually, the story ran around the world. Television crews descended upon Kennewick from as far away as France and Korea, and journalists arrived from Germany and elsewhere. The *New Yorker* profiled the Kennewick area's oldest known resident, as did scribes from nearly every major newspaper in the United States, as well as the Associated Press, and other wire services.

Chatters initially said that he "hoped the skeleton's Caucasoid features would help heal some of the suspicion between whites and Indians by showing how superficial racial differences can be" (Lemonick 1996). He was quoted in the Seattle *Times* (Dietrich 1996) as saying that in a world full of racism, human understanding would be best served by realizing that we are not as different from each other as some may suppose. As the Army Corps of Engineers ordered him to surrender the remains on two hours' notice, Chatters was learning that at least some of his faith in human nature had been misplaced. He quickly sealed the bones into Ziploc bags, and gave them to the government.

As publicity about Kennewick Man spread, the Army Corps of Engineers received more than a dozen claims for the skeleton, including one from the Asatru Folks Assembly and another from

Old Norse, a California-based religious organization. The Asatru Folks Assembly, self-described as an indigenous European religion (said to have been practiced by the Vikings) believes that scientific examination of the bones is justified as "a means by which this long-dead kinsman of ours can tell his saga and renew his glory." Sometimes called Odinists (after the chief deity of Nordic religion), the Asatru Folks Assembly publishes a newsletter, *The Runestone*, which traces Kennewick Man back to what they regard as his ancestral home in Europe. In England, argues a piece in *The Runestone's* Summer, 1997 issue, a 9,000 year-old set of remains was found in the village of Cheddar. The remains of "Cheddar Man" were traced by DNA testing to Adrian Targett, a history teacher in Cheddar. The Asatru Folks Assembly asserts that Kennewick Man should be similarly tested (*Runestone* 1997).

During October 1998, parts of the contested skeleton turned up missing. Doug Owsley, the Smithsonian anthropologist who had inventoried the skeleton on October 28, called the apparent theft "a deliberate act of desecration" and called for "diligent efforts" to recover the missing portions of a missing femur. "Femurs contain invaluable information to assess stature, size, robustness, functional morphology, age and population affiliation," Owsley stated in his report. Chatters retained videotapes that included images of the bones later found to be missing (Lee 1998).

Amidst the adamant statements of some non-Indians that they had found a long-lost "white" brother, Vine Deloria, writing in the Denver *Post*, reminded his readers that, "In September, 1997, the American Anthropological Association sent a report to the Bureau of the Census, saying one could not determine race scientifically. So much for narrow skulls and high cheekbones" (Deloria 1998, G-1). University of Washington Anthropologist Charles Keyes agreed fundamentally with Deloria: "Race does not exist. Racism does exist" (Dietrich 1996).

The complexity of human origins often does not fit racial categories invented after the fact. In the Tarim Basin of western China, for examples, more than a hundred mummies have been unearthed. The mummies are so well preserved that their pale skin and blonde hair are evident. The ancient Ainu of Japan also have light skin and prominent foreheads. The more we learn about the complexity of human origins in the Americas (and elsewhere), the less well-fitting contemporary racial labels seem to become.

Mark Trahant, writing as a columnist at the Seattle *Times,* reminded his readers that science, like all other aspects of culture, is socially defined:

> Of course science, like religion, evolves with each generation's perceptions about its world. American anthropology practically began on the battlefield where dead warriors, and everything they owned, were collected for study under the direction of the Surgeon General. When the freshly dead didn't have enough to offer science, graves were robbed. Anthropology has criminal roots. (Trahant 1998, B-1)

## THE FANTASIES

It would warm my Norwegian-American heart immeasurably to learn that I have a 9,300-year old "brother" on this continent. As strong as my sympathies may be, however, the claim to Kennewick Man lodged by the Asatru Folks Assembly seems, upon examination, to be about as specious as they come. The claim seems to lodge most securely in the shape of Kennewick Man's skull, which one Internet commentator, Colin, "Son of Freedrich," likened to that of Captain Picard of the Starship Enterprise (Freedrich n.d.).

Colin "Son of Freedrich's" quote stems from James Chatters, who told Douglas Preston of the *New Yorker* that discovery of Kennewick Man's remains led him to look for similar racial types in his daily life. One evening he turned on his television set to an episode of *Star Trek,* and thought: "My God! There he is! Kennewick Man!" (Preston 1997, 73). Chatters may have made this statement as a disinterested "scientific" observer. He was not prepared, it appears, for the racial fantasies that would be built in Kennewick Man's name, or his own.

Sometimes, the claim to a "white" ancestor obscures racial agendas of European Americans who assert that the law gives Native Americans what they regard as special privileges, such as treaty rights. This line of reasoning, long popularized in Kennewick Man's home state by Senator Slade Gorton (et al.), resonates through some of the commentary on Kennewick Man. In some of its more racist versions, this type of rhetoric posits that North America was first occupied by Europeans, who were then exterminated by immigrating Proto-Mongoloids from Asia. This conflict is sometimes personalized (with no supporting evidence at all) by the fact that Kennewick Man died with an arrowhead in his pelvis. In this version of the race fantasy, Kennewick Man laid down his life as a racial martyr, the exclamation point in a case claiming that Europeans are the *real* "landlords" of North America. After so many leaps of faith, one more (that the treaties are invalid) is not at all difficult in this version of the race fantasy that has grown up around assumptions that Kennewick Man was "white."

Into this rhetorical stew must be tossed a few remarks on the nature of race, or the socially constructed practice of placing people in classes based on their physical characteristics. One must understand first that this concept, like any other (including the "laws" of science and the doctrines of organized religion) are socially constructed. That is, they are reflections of the mental assumptions held by individual members of certain cultures. The "laws" of science may be taken to be immutable only until someone (such as Albert Einstein) arrives to redesign humankind's conceptions of scientific reality.

The social construction of race, as a system of categorizing people, is a European invention. Before the advent of settlers and slavers from Europe in Turtle Island (North America), skin color, cranial capacity, size and shape of skull, texture of hair, (nor any of many other racial differences) was not usually used by American Indians to define themselves and others. The Haudenosaunee (Iroquois) Confederacy, for example, adopted people of many ethnic origins, European and Native American.

The fact that "race" is hardly a precise concept has not kept the race fantasy around Kennewick Man at bay. Louis Beam, who identified himself as an amateur archaeologist, commented, of the arrowhead found in Kennewick man's pelvis. "Some have jokingly speculated that this was the first incidence of 'cowboys and Indians' with the Indians winning." Beam's racial fantasy grows as he writes: "Shattered will be the myth of the 'Indians' as the first Americans . . ." (Beam n.d.).

According to many of those who claim Kennewick Man to be a long-lost Caucasian brother, seven skeletons with similar features have been discovered in North America since 1938. The first such discovery, at Fork Rock Cave, Oregon, has been radiocarbon dated to about 9,000 years of age. Spirit Cave Man is presently caught in the same sort of crossfire as Kennewick Man; the Northern Pauites have a NAGPRA claim for his remains, which is being contested by several non-Indian scientists. Researchers also contested the return of a skeleton found near Buhl, Idaho, to the Shoshone-Bannock tribe. This set of remains has been radiocarbon dated to roughly 10,600 years ago. Most of the skeletons and associated artifacts were found in the west because the eastern side of the continent is much more humid and acidic, which makes long-term preservation of bones unlikely.

From this evidence base, some of Kennewick Man's Caucasian boosters have hypothesized that there was a large group of similar people who were exterminated by the ancestors of American Indians, who are said to have arrived later, from Asia, usually by way of the Bering Strait "land bridge," or by island-hopping around the Pacific Rim using small boats. Boats suitable to the trip were in use in Japan 20,000 years ago. In our time, the human ability to negotiate long oversea voyages on rafts or small indigenous seagoing boats has been illustrated by personal example.

In this version of American prehistory, some advocates say they have found (or heard of) tools that resemble others found in European sites. These advocates often insist that NAGPRA returns such skeletons to Indian tribes for reburial when they are actually European (or, in some cases, Asian) in origin. One commentator remarks that "There are remarkable similarities to the Old World Solutrean people, who are believed to have come from Eastern and Southern ice-age Europe, and who themselves also hunted large game from twenty-two to eighteen thousand years before the present." The flint tips used to kill game appear strikingly the same, according to this writer (Archive n.d.).

These immigrants are said to have made their way across the European steppes, into Siberia, then to Alaska, then south and eastward along the northwest Pacific coast of North America. Proponents say that these immigrants hunted mammoths, mastodon, giant bison, antelope, and other creatures now extinct. Some of these immigrants have been found with evidence that they wore sagebrush intricately woven sandals. Other items found in the vicinity of their remains include projectile points, scrapers, drills, small baskets (found in pieces), as well as awls for making leather or other tailored clothing for the Kennewick Man and others.

The Clovis people (assuming that they are related to the Kennewick Man) had advanced weaponry for hunting and most likely wore sandals and tailored clothes. Several of the archaeologists and anthropologists who are suing the government for the remains of Kennewick Man have asserted that these technological achievements are completely unrelated to anything developed by Proto-Mongoloids. Proto-Mongoloid clothing is said to have been primitive by comparison, ignoring the historical fact that a number of innovative clothing styles (such as the parka) were invented by Native Americans. One architect of this race fantasy asserts that Native Americans (even in cool climates) wore few or no clothes! (Archive n.d.).

Douglas Owsley, division head of physical anthropology at the National Museum of Natural History (Smithsonian Institution) in Washington DC, has examined all of the seven well-preserved skeletons found in North America and found that they all share some Caucasoid features. The seven skeletons were found at seven different sites and at different periods of time. All are said to have lived during the end of the later glacial era, during which the Clovis people disappeared (Archive n.d.).

Proponents of the Kennewick Man race fantasy build a mountain of speculation on a scant base of physical evidence. In the following, the author invests Native Americans, Proto-Mongoloids, with European attitudes vis-á-vis race as he speculates that present-day Native people may want to bury the remains to escape accusations that they perpetrated an act of genocide against the "whites." All of this very neatly turns recorded history on its head and allows the author to claim that "white" people are oppressed by "Indians."

> The competition for food and land that arose . . . could have ignited a war of some type that lasted several hundred years. As the extinction of big game forced all early Americans to develop new methods of hunting and gathering, the Clovis people began to invade the territories of other peoples or were invaded by them, invasions which prompted violent confrontations. Rising tensions between peoples led to wars. It is quite possible that the larger number of Indians, being different tribes themselves and often at war even with each other, all attacked the Clovis people because they were easily identified as an enemy by their physical and racial differences. *And thus the Red Man exterminated the White Man utterly* [emphasis added]. (Archive n.d.)

Kennewick Man's "white brother" boosters have not faced a definitional problem. Caucasian is a cultural term. While it is usually associated with Europeans, the Caucasoid type used by archaeologists also includes features common to some Southern Asians, as well as the Ainu, the indigenous people of Japan. Any Caucasoids found in North America are far removed in place and time from whatever European origins they may have had. Even people who made their way from southeastern Europe to Asia, then to America, probably mixed with many other peoples along the way. This is probably why the origins of Kennewick Man and the other "white" remains are so hard to classify. He may have been very much a multiracial man.

Taken to extremes, fantasizing about Kennewick Man takes on a fantasy air. In a letter to the editor of the Santa Fe *New Mexican,* Corine Flores asked whether Kennewick Man might have been an ancient visitor from another planet. Mochtezuma thought Cortes was a god. Extraterrestrial origins have been aired to explain the origins of civilization in Egypt. "Statues of Toltec warriors in the tenth century eighteen-foot-tall pillars hold ray guns of advanced design." Associating all of these otherwise random speculations, Flores pops the inevitable question: "Could they have been extraterrestrial from outer space, and could Quezalcoatl have been one of those ancient astronauts?" (Flores 1998, A-9).

Among some white commentators, there is a palatable envy of Native Americans' treaty rights, which stem from original occupancy in the Americas. "From this moment on, kindly refer to my family as 'indigenous,'" lamented Stephen Lyons of Pullman, Washington, in the *Idaho Statesman.* "Or, if you prefer, 'first peoples.' With the discovery of what could be my long-lost European relative—Kennewick Man—it's time to respect my elders." Lyons flippantly suggested that Indian tribes that want to rebury Kennewick Man are motivated by potential loss of their sovereignty and a "change in the tried-and-true story that Native Americans arrived first and then we came and screwed up everything." On that subject, Lyons closes: "I want a large tract of land. I want a culture that doesn't worship mini-vans. I want to play basketball with Sherman Alexie. I want the rest of you to copy my rituals, commercialize my culture, and romanticize my every twitch. Now, how about those casino profits" (Lyons 1998, B-8).

## THE STAKES

The lawsuit filed against the Corps of Engineers regarding Kennewick Man by eight anthropologists represents the first major legal challenge by scientists to the Native American Graves Protection and Repatriation Act (NAGPRA), a 1990 law that provides for the repatriation to tribes of Indian skeletons and ceremonial and mortuary artifacts.

The NAGPRA is, by and large, a reflection of Native views on repatriation; Kennewick Man has been seized by opponents of these practices, such as the eight anthropologists, who would like to use Native remains for scientific study. Against such explorations are arrayed a number of Native American groups, including the Native nations who also have claimed the remains of Kennewick Man. "Native remains are not objects for scientific curiosity. They are relatives. They are grandmothers and grandfathers," said Debra Harry, coordinator of the Indigenous Peoples Coalition Against Biopiracy, in Nixon, Nevada. "When these relatives are put away . . . they're not to be disturbed by anyone . . . and the place that they rest is sacred ground" (Harry 1998).

In the case of human remains inadvertently discovered on federal land, NAGPRA regulations require the government to notify Indian nations "likely to be culturally affiliated with" the remains, tribes "which aboriginally occupied the area," and "any other Indian tribe . . . reasonably known to have a cultural relationship to" the remains in question. Kennewick Man was found within the traditional territory of the Umatilla tribes (as determined by the Indian Claims Commission). The Umatillas' claim to the land on which Kennewick Man was found is supported by a treaty signed with the United States government in 1855. The Corps of Engineers initially determined that the remains might be affiliated with the Yakama and Nez Perce as well. On August 27, the Corps notified these three tribes; Chatters informed the Colvilles himself.

Shortly after Kennewick Man's antiquity was disclosed, the Umatillas issued a statement:

> Our elders have taught us that once a body goes into the ground, it is meant to stay there until the end of time. If this individual is over 9000 years old, it only substantiates our belief that he is Native American. From our oral histories, we know that our people have been part of this land since the beginning of time. We do not believe that our people migrated here from another continent, as the scientists do. . . . Scientists believe that because the individual's head does not match ours, he is not Native American. Our elders have told us that Indian people did not always look

the way we look today. Some scientists believe that if this individual is not studied further, we, as Indians, will be destroying evidence of our history. We already know our history. It is passed on to us from our elders and through our religious practices. (Archive n.d.)

Armand Minthorn, a Umatilla political and religious leader, said:

Scientists have dug up and studied Native Americans for decades. We view this practice as desecration of the body and a violation of our most deeply held religious beliefs. Today thousands of native human remains sit on the shelves of museums and institutions [200,000 as of 1997] waiting for the day when they can return to the earth, and waiting for the day that scientists and others will pay them the respect that they are due. . . . Our tribal policies and procedures, and our own religious beliefs, prohibit scientific testing on human remains. Our beliefs and policies also tell us that this individual must be reburied as soon as possible. Our religion and elders have taught us that we have an inherent responsibility to care for those who are no longer with us. We have a responsibility to respect all human burials, regardless of race. (Minthorn 1996)

To Minthorn, the Umatillas, and others, Kennewick Man's "race" is not an issue. They have a treaty, which is a legal relationship with the United States, not a racial one. The racial origins of the remains does not modify the legality of any treaty.

On September 13, 1996, two weeks after the skeleton's discovery, the Army Corps of Engineers, which had impounded the bones, said it was preparing to give them to a coalition of Columbia Valley Indian tribes (Umatilla, Yakama, Nez Perce, Wanapum, and Colville) for reburial. Once the Corps aired its intention to return the bones to the Native coalition, the scientists' counteroffensive developed rapidly. Plans to rebury Kennewick Man were put on ice by the eight scientists' lawsuit. Shortly thereafter, the Asatru Folk Assembly, a group of Nordic cultists with about 500 members, arrived at the scene of Kennewick Man's discovery, laying ceremonial claim to the remains. They, too, filed suit. U.S. Rep. Richard "Doc" Hastings introduced a bill to amend NAGPRA and allow study of Kennewick

Man. On April 1, 1998, the Army Corps of Engineers gave Kennewick Man to the Department of Interior. Five days later, the Corps of Engineers proposed to bury the site at which Kennewick Man had been found.

Writing to the Corps of Engineers, physical anthropologists Douglas W. Owsley of the Smithsonian Institution and Richard L. Jantz of the University of Tennessee, Knoxville, warned, "If a pattern of returning [such] remains without study develops, the loss to science will be incalculable and we will never have the data required to understand the earliest populations in America" (Slayman 1997, 19). In a letter to the editor in the *New York Times,* William D. Lipe, president of the Society for American Archaeology, asked that the "tribe that has claimed the ancient Washington skeleton . . . reconsider and permit additional studies to be conducted" (Slayman 1997, 19).

On October 4, Rep. Doc Hastings of Washington wrote to Lt. Gen. Joe Ballard, commander of the Army Corps of Engineers, expressing alarm that the corps planned to give up the skeleton before it could be studied. He urged Ballard to "postpone action until the [skeleton's] origins are determined conclusively or until Congress has the opportunity to review this important issue" (Slayman 1997, 19). In the meantime, Rep. Hastings requested that the corps allow scientists access to the bones. A second letter followed a week later, signed by Hastings as well as by Sen. Slade Gorton and Reps. Jack Metcalf and George R. Nethercutt, Jr., all of Washington State.

On October 16, the eight scientists filed their suit against the Corps of Engineers in Federal District Court, Portland, Oregon. They sought access to the skeleton and an indefinite delay of its repatriation. The scientists are Robson Bonnichsen, director of the Center for the Study of the First Americans at Oregon State University; C. Loring Brace, curator of biological anthropology at the University of Michigan's Museum of Anthropology; Dennis J. Stanford, chairman of the Smithsonian's anthropology department; Richard Jantz; Douglas Owsley; and anthropologists George W. Gill of the University of Wyoming, C. Vance Haynes, Jr., of the University of Arizona, and D. Gentry Steele of Texas A&M University.

The scientists' complaint asserts that the Corps of Engineers decided that Kennewick Man's remains are culturally affiliated to the five Native nations without sufficient evidence. NAGPRA regulations stipulate, "Evidence of . . . cultural affiliation . . . must be established using . . . geographical, kinship, biological, archeological, anthropological, linguistic, folklore, oral tradition, historical, or other relevant information or expert opinion." The suit also asserts that the Corps' decision violates the Archaeological Resources Protection Act of 1979, which they maintain, allows them to examine the remains legally (Slayman 1997, 22, 23).

The Archaeological Resources Protection Act (ARPA) requires that any archaeologist who wishes to excavate on federal land must obtain a permit from the agency that manages the land. Chatters said that he applied to the Corps' Walla Walla, Washington, district for a permit, which was granted on July 31, retroactive to July 28. After receiving the permit, he returned to the site several times and excavated more bones from the sand at the river's edge.

The scientists' suit also contends that the Corps' refusal to allow scientists to study the remains violates the Civil Rights Act of 1966. This law guarantees nonwhites the same legal protection as whites, but over the years, it has been read also to offer the same protection to whites as to nonwhites, according to Paula A. Barran, another of the scientists' lawyers. In essence, according to Schneider, they are arguing that their clients are "being denied the right to study [the skeleton] because they're not Native American" (Slayman 1997, 23).

At a hearing in Federal District Court in Portland, Oregon on October 23, U.S. magistrate John Jelderks warned lawyers for both sides to prepare to argue how to define the term *indigenous,* which figures into the NAGPRA's definition of *Native American.* In its notice of intent to repatriate, The Corps indicated only the skeleton's age and its discovery within the Umatillas' aboriginal territory in its notice of intent to repatriate Kennewick Man. "Antiquity says nothing about ancestry," the scientists' lawyers argued. "Forensic anthropology does." They noted that results of the various studies carried out on the bones raise some doubt as to whether the skeleton is related to modern Indian tribes. The NAGPRA defines *Native American* as "of, or relating to, a tribe, people, or culture that is indigenous to the United States." If the skeleton is not related to any modern indigenous group, the lawyers held, it cannot be Native American within the NAGPRA's definition. Furthermore, they contended, "A reliable determination of whether the skeleton is Native American within the meaning of [NAGPRA] cannot be made without . . . further study" (Slayman 1997, 22).

The dividing line between science and politics has become rather difficult to divine, since just about everyone concerned has jumped into the fray over Kennewick Man's remains with a contemporary agenda. For example, Senator Gorton, perennial advocate of anything that separates Native Americans from their land, resources, (or human remains) inserted language into an Appropriations Committee report stating that "It is in the public interest that information providing greater insight into American pre-history should be collected, preserved, and disseminated for the benefit of the country as a whole" (Miller 1997). These are legal code words for severe modifications in the intent of the NAGPRA.

In the meantime, James Chatters, the first scientist to examine Kennewick Man, seemed to be trying to negotiate what he had determined to be a middle ground. He spoke in favor of modifying the NAGPRA to allow scientific examination of human remains before they are reburied by Native peoples. Speaking to a House Committee on Resources hearing on modifications to the NAGPRA, Chatters said that he has a personal stake in seeing that justice is done to Native Americans: his mother-in-law is Haida. Temporizing words aside, Chatters favors a position endorsed by many non-Native scientists: he wants a time limit written into the NAGPRA, a date beyond which claims to remains by present-day Native American political entities would not apply. He also favors abolishing the "geography clause" in the law that gives preference to Native peoples whose reservations are nearest the site where remains are found.

Writing in the *Wall Street Journal,* Mark Lasswell, a contributing editor of *Allure* magazine, cited Native American religious objections to study of Kennewick Man, then ignored them as he ascribed it all to a Clinton administration "attuned, as always, to the nuances of multiculturalism." Because of this, wrote Lasswell, Kennewick Man had been cast into "a strange sort of culture-war hell" (Lasswell 1999, W-11). Lasswell disregarded the fact that many Native American remains reside in many other culturally defined hells: 200,000 Indian skeletons are still being held by museums (Dietrich 1996). Hold a man who might have been "white" under such conditions, and Lasswell loses his intellectual lunch.

Salvation, as one could guess, comes to Lasswell in the form of political pressure to modify the NAGPRA. According to Lasswell, the Clinton Administration directly ordered the $160,000 cover-over of the Kennewick Man site (with 500 tons of rock and fill dirt) by the Corps. He cites a letter describing a "White House inquiry," in the interest of "stabilizing" the riverbank on which Kennewick Man and associated artifacts were discovered in the interest of erosion control. The scientists who had sued the Corps for Kennewick Man's remains compared burying the site to burning the library of Alexandra, ancient Egypt's largest library.

The scientists' lawsuit and legislation pending in Congress will determine, during the next few years, whether Native American tribes and nations will retain human remains found on their aboriginal territories. This course of events also will influence the development of scientific knowledge about human origins in the Americas as it shapes the often-contentious relationships between Native American peoples and the academic specialists who explore the prehistoric past. We will be hearing about Kennewick Man for many years to come.

## CONCLUSION

During August of 2002, after more than a year of deliberation (much of it spent reading several thousand pages of documentation) U.S. District Court Judge John Jelderks found for the scientists, denying the four tribes possession of Kennewick Man's remains under the NAGPRA. "Allowing study is fully consistent with applicable statutes and regulations, which are clearly intended to make archaeological information available to the public through scientific research," Jelderks wrote (Judge 2002, 10).

James C. Chatters, who had first handled the remains, joined the scientists in maintaining that he could support the provisions of the NAGPRA and oppose returning Kennewick Man to the tribes for reburial. "I have conducted repatriations for some of the same tribes who claimed this skeleton," Chatters wrote in the *Wall Street Journal*. "I support the purpose of the law" (Chatters 2002, D-10). Chatters maintained that Kennewick Man's remains were outside the scope of the NAGPRA. "The act," he wrote, "was not intended to turn over all ancient skeletons to some Indian tribe, regardless of relationship. . . . The past is not a possession." (Chatters 2002, D-10) To the tribes that had sought to rebury the remains, Chatters's statement came as something of a simplification, because the point of the NAGPRA is that, when it comprises human remains, the past is indeed a possession.

The question was—and remains—how far back in time the legality of possession reaches.

## REFERENCES

Beam, L. Dead 'Indians' don't lie. n.d. http://www.louisbeam.com/kennewick.htm.

Chatters, J.C. 2001. Affidavit in Federal District Court, Portland, Oregon. May 15, http://www.quilters.com/science/kennewic/court/chatters.htm.

———. 1998. Committee on Resources, United States Congress. Hearing to Amend the Native American Graves Protection and Repatriation Act . . ." June 10. http://www.house.gov/resources/105cong/fullcomm/98june10/agenda980610.htm.

———. 2002. Politics aside, these bones belong to everybody. *Wall Street Journal,* September 5, D-10.

Deloria, V. Jr. 1998. Balancing science, culture: Do scientists have rights to all finds? *(Denver) Post,* November 29, G-1.

Dietrich, B. 1996. Skeleton might be reburied before scientists can study it. *(Seattle) Times,* September 22. http://www.seattletimes.com/.

Flores, C. 1998. [Letter to the editor] *(Santa Fe) New Mexican,* December 19, A-9.

Freedrich, C., Son of. n.d. Patrick Stewart, *Star Trek's* Captain Picard: Spitting image of the Kennewick Man. http://home.earthlink.net/~theedrich/Kennewick.htm.

Harry, D. 1998. Statement on Biopiracy. Associated Press dispatch in *Tri-City Herald,* December 11. http://www.tri-cityherald.com/.

Interpretive Center [of the *Tri-City Herald*]. http://www.tri-cityherald.com/.
    February 14, 1998: Old bones bringing world to Tri-Cities;
    August 31, 1997: Pagan sect blasts corps' handling of Kennewick Man;
    August 28, 1997: Ancient ritual pays tribute to Kennewick Man;
    August 27, 1997: Tribes upset by ritual for Kennewick Man;
    August 23, 1997: Pagans battle corps over old bones;
    August 20, 1997: Pagan group plans ceremony over Kennewick Man Bones;
    July 27, 1997: One year after Kennewick Man surfaced, battle over 9,200-year-old skeleton rages on.

Judge: Scientists can study ancient bones of man Indian tribes claim as ancestor. 2002. Associated Press in *Indian Time* 20(35) (September 5): 10.

Lasswell, M. 1999. The 9,400 year old man; the White House keeps trying to bury him; Scientists are furious. *Wall Street Journal,* January 8. W-11.

Lee, M. 1998. Kennewick Man pieces gone, report says. *Tri-City Herald,* December 11. http://www.tri-cityherald.com/.

Lemonick, M.P. 1996. Bones of contention: Scientists and Native Americans clash over a 9,300-year-old man with Caucasoid features." *Time* 148(18) (October 14, 1996). n.p.

Lyons, S. 1998. [Editorial] Old bones create new views of ancient beliefs. *Idaho Statesman,* December 5, B-8.

Miller, J.J. 1997. Bones of contention: A federal law stands between scientists and America's prehistoric past. *Reason* (October). http://www.reasonmag.com/.

Minthorn, A. 1996. Human remains should be reburied. September. Web page: Confederated Tribes of the Umatilla Indian Reservation. http://www.umatilla.nsn.us/kennman.html.

O'Brien, E. 1997. Sketetal remains discovered in Washington State. *(Philadelphia) Inquirer,* February 3.

Petit, C.W. 1998. Rediscovering America: The New World may be 20,000 years older than experts thought. *U.S. News and World Report,* October 12.

Preston, D. 1997. The lost man. *The New Yorker,* June 16, 70–77.

*Runestone, The.* 1997. Religious group outlines plans for skeleton. http://www.runestone.org/km3.html.

Slayman, A.L. 1997. A battle over bones. *Archaeology* 50(1) (January/February): 16–23.

Trahant, M. 1998. Oral histories are speaking: Will we hear? *(Seattle) Times,* November 12. B-1.

# 11

# The New Terminators: A Guide to the Antitreaty Movement

*Bruce E. Johansen*

A s an increasing number of Native American governments exercise the nuts and bolts of sovereignty—developing infrastructure, managing land use, and levying taxes—more non-Indian landowners within reservation boundaries are crying "taxation without representation." Non-Indians, who own at least half of many reservations, are organizing locally and nationally with renewed vigor around efforts to strip reservation governments of their legal powers.

Antisovereignty efforts are not new. They are as old as the colonization of Turtle Island itself. When John Fleming, Skagit Valley Republican, persuaded Washington State Republicans to adopt a resolution advocating the dissolution of reservation governments in their election year platform during the spring of 2000, the action evoked memories of Andrew Jackson, the Trail of Tears, and 1950s era termination efforts. Fleming then stoked the controversy red hot by advocating that the armed forces be used to evict Native peoples who refuse to surrender their sovereignty without a fight.

Fleming is a prototype of the newest wave of termination advocates—reservation landowners who complain that they are being treated as an oppressed minority. Members of these groups reject the notion of semi sovereign Native nations, as they reject nearly two centuries of legal precedent in the United States, which began with the landmark Supreme Court rulings of Chief Justice John Marshall in the Cherokee cases of the 1830s.

During 1995, for example, the Crows levied a 4 percent tax on businesses that cater to the many tourists who visit the Little Bighorn battlefield where George Armstrong Custer and 209 of his men lost their lives June 25, 1876. Many of these businesses are owned by non-Indians, who immediately branded the levy "taxation without representation," and refused to pay it. As owners of the Custer Battlefield Trading Post and Custer Battlefield Museum refused to pay the Crows' tax, they filed liens for $51,730 on the trading post, which is owned by James Thompson.

As these protests gained momentum, Senator Conrad Burns, Montana Republican, readied a bill that would exempt Montana reservation land owned by non-Indians from Native jurisdiction. Burns' proposal would grant Montana civil jurisdiction over non-Indians living and conducting business on private lands within Montana's reservations. About 40 percent of the Crow reservation is owned by non-Indians (Egan 1998). Nationally, non-Indian land-holdings on specific reservations range from none (the Akwesasne Mohawks, for example, will not allow it) to about 90 percent of the land on the White Earth Reservation in Minnesota.

Montana's Native leaders have categorically rejected Burns's proposal, calling it a blindsided assault on jurisdictional issues on which the tribes have already prevailed in court. All of Montana's seven Native governments lined up against the bill.

Michael T. Pablo, chairman of the Montana-Wyoming Tribal Leaders' Council, pointed out that the Enabling Act for the State of Montana specifically excludes Indian reservations from state jurisdiction. "The Enabling Act language is all-important, yet it was not even mentioned in Burns' bill," Pablo wrote in the Billings *Gazette* (Pablo 1998).

## THE POLITICS OF NAMES

Antisovereignty groups' names often combine patriotic symbols to evoke notions of political fairness and equality. In Upstate New York, for example, the major group opposing Native sovereignty calls itself the Upstate Citizens for Equality (UCE). National groups include the Citizens' Equal Rights Alliance (CERA) and the Interstate Congress for Equal Rights and Responsibilities (ICERR). Other names are similar: Citizens' Rights Organization, Montanans Opposing Discrimination, Concerned Landowners Association, All Citizens Equal, Flathead [Montana] Residents Earning Equality (FREE).

In both the United States and Canada, antisovereignty groups often assume names that focus their energies on non-Native access to fish and game. The Ontario Federation of Anglers and Hunters, which is affiliated with Canada's Conservative Party, has expressed a special interest is ending Native fishing rights under an "equal rights for all" rubric. Howard Hanson, a major figure in Minnesota's Proper Economic Resource Management (PERM) and a board member of CERA, also founded another organization called The Hunting and Angling Club. Another group (in Minnesota) calls itself Sportsmen Protecting Every American's Right (SPEAR).

Protect Americans' Rights and Resources (PARR) was formed during the early 1990s in Wisconsin to battle the Chippewas, who reasserted their rights to spearfish in area lakes. PARR's agenda has since branched out to include everything from blanket opposition to U.S. federal Indian policy to gun control to curbs on smoking. All Citizens Equal goes beyond the usual complaints about Indians'; "special rights," to a broad attack on Native sovereignty. This group specializes in lobbying Congress to affirm absolute rights of private property.

FIRE (Federation for Individual Rights and Equality) operates in several Canadian provinces, calling for the application of Canadian law to Native peoples. This group argues that Native nations' powers should be restricted to those exercised by a municipal government. The Center for the Defense of Free Enterprise, another antitreaty private-property lobby, is headed by Alan Gottlieb, a firearms activist, and Ron Arnold, founder of the "Wise Use" movement. The British Columbia Real Estate Association's position on Native sovereignty is close to that of FIRE: that indigenous nations should be subsumed under Canadian provincial and federal governments. Like many of its allies, the BCREA favors municipal-style governmental models for Native groups.

## MAJOR THEMES IN THE ANTISOVEREIGNTY MOVEMENT

Zoltan Grossman, author of *When Hate Groups Come to Town* (1992), identified three major factors that unite antisovereignty advocates:

1. The call for "equal rights for whites." This concept is based on the assumption that increased political and jurisdictional power of the tribes infringes on the liberties of the individual American taxpayer.

2. Access to natural resources. These resources can be fish or game, land or water, but the case is the same: no citizens should have "special rights" to use the resources. The case is made in anti-treaty pamphlets such as "Are We Giving America Back to the Indians?," "200 Million Custers," and the ironically titled book "Don't Blame the Indians: Native Americans and the Mechanized Destruction of Fish and Wildlife" by Massachusetts writer Ted Williams.

3. Economic dependency. In a rural reflection of the "welfare Cadillac" myths used against urban African-Americans, all reservation Indians are said to wallow in welfare, food stamps, free housing and medical care, affirmative-action programs, and gargantuan federal cash payments, all tax-free, of course. (No one has to pay state sales tax on reservations, but otherwise Indians have had virtually identical tax obligations as non-Indians) (Grossman 1992).

## JOHN FLEMING'S SKAGIT COUNTY CONTEXT

John Fleming, who catapulted the antisovereignty movement into Washington State party politics during 2000, lives within the borders of the Swinomish Reservation in Western Washington, where non-Indians who own almost half the reservation's 6,000 acres have formed the Fidalgo Alliance for an Informed Republic (FAIR), which lobbies against the Swinomish tribal government. "The tribe doesn't own it [the land]," contends Larry Collinge, a spokesman of FAIR. "We own it as citizens and taxpayers of this republic" (Parr n.d.). To this, Swinomish Tribal Attorney Jamie Weber replied: "It was their choice to come live on an Indian reservation. If you own a summer home in Canada, you don't get to vote, but you pay taxes and you follow the laws. It doesn't make the Canadian government not a real government" (Parr n.d.).

Members of FAIR have presented Skagit County commissioners with a petition demanding an end to an agreement between the Swinomish and the county that instructs both to work together on land-use planning for privately owned reservation land. Collinge, who has lived on the Swinomish Reservation for twenty years, gathered about 200 signatures from non-Indian property owners on the petition, which advocates repeal of the "memorandum of understanding," between the Swinomish and Skagit County (Parr 1998). Under the joint arrangement, landowners must apply for permits from both Skagit County and the Swinomish. FAIR believes that county zoning should prevail. The net result: the Swinomish would lose authority over land use on nearly half their reservation to which non-Indians hold title.

During the late fall of 1998, FAIR hosted an informational meeting for a capacity crowd at the Hope Island Fire Hall in LaConner, "to address the Swinomish Tribe's new 3 percent business privilege tax ordinance" (Angry Group 1998). The tax, approved by the Tribal Senate in August, "will be charged to utility providers, who will likely pass down the cost to their customers" (Angry Group 1998). Utilities falling under the tax include water, power, garbage collection, cable, local and long-distance telephone services, wireless communications (cell phones and pagers), septic services, gas, propane, heating oil and sewer. Many of the non-Indian landowners at the meeting complained that they are being doubly taxed: by the Swinomish, and by Skagit County. Once again, the non-Indians who live on the Swinomish Reservation complained of "taxation without representation" (Angry Group 1998).

## REACTION TO THE WASHINGTON REPUBLICAN RESOLUTION

During the weeks between passage of Fleming's resolution and the 2000 National Republican Convention in late July, many Republican political figures in Washington State distanced themselves from the termination plank in their party's platform. One of the most prominent was Senator Slade Gorton, who found himself in the awkward position of handling his state party's platform as one might carry an agitated skunk. "He absolutely disagrees that we should do away with tribal governments," Gorton spokeswoman Cynthia Bergman said. According to an account in the Yakima *Herald-Republic*, Bergman then sketched Gorton's position: "Tribes have the right to govern their own members, but Gorton doesn't think tribes can govern nontribal members living on reservations" (Barenti 2000). This is the core demand of the antisovereignty movement.

Within days of the Washington Republicans' resolution that Fleming initiated, the California Democratic Party and the

Democrats' Native American Caucus passed resolutions denouncing it. The resolutions for both bodies were coauthored by Art Torres, chairman of the California Democratic Party, and Frank LaMere, a vice chair of the Nebraska Democratic Party, who is Winnebago. "It is an outrage. I call upon the Republican National Committee to publicly repudiate the wayward and blatantly racist actions of the Washington Republican party," LaMere said. "It is divisive to even speak of turning our military against our own. That's what they have done in Washington and they need to be ashamed," said LaMere, who lost a brother in the Vietnam War (DeArmond 2000). An editorial in the Billings *Gazette* called Fleming's remarks about calling out the armed forces to put an end to Native governments "shades of Gen. George Armstrong Custer" (Semantics 2000).

Aside from a few Indian supporters of the antisovereignty cause (described below), Native American reaction to antisovereignty proposals has been nearly completely negative. Ron Allen, chairman of the Jamestown S'Klallam Tribe in Washington State, and a Republican, said: "The mentality of this is such an anachronism in our society. This . . . goes back to the old Indian wars" (Montana 2000). "It's pretty sad to see that happen in this date and time," said Susan Masten, president of the National Congress of American Indians (Montana 2000).

"I think what you are seeing nationally are a series of attacks on the centuries-old right of Indian self-government," said Robert Coulter, Potawatomi, and executive director of the Indian Law Resource Center in Helena, Montana (Egan 1998). Senator Ben Nighthorse Campbell, Republican of Colorado, pointed out that tribal self-determination is a Republican idea established by President Nixon during the early 1970s, part of a long history of Republican Party support for the idea (Montana 2000).

Mark Trahant, a Seattle *Times* columnist (who is Nez Perce) wrote July 6, 2000: "Political termination of tribal governments is a policy that's been tried before—and it failed. Only a few decades ago, the Colville Confederated Tribes in this state barely survived termination attempts by the Congress. That tribe is stronger today—economically, politically and culturally—because it convinced its own membership, and then the greater community, that the U.S. ought to continue to honor its word. This position is mainstream Republican. It was, after all, President Nixon who told the Congress that termination had been a mistake" (Trahant 2000).

## MULTICULTURAL FACES IN THE ANTISOVEREIGNTY MOVEMENT

The Citizens Equal Rights Alliance extends an extra warm welcome to Native Americans who share the CERA's loathing of reservation governments and federal policy. The CERA's home pages brim with quotes from the likes of Franklin Delano Roosevelt, Martin Luther King, and the Nez Perce Chief Joseph the Younger, emphasizing its assumed appeal to peoples of all races and cultures, as long as they share its antigovernment ideology.

All Citizens Equal's materials also often include nondiscrimination statements and disclaimers. ACE's bylaws proclaim that it does not tolerate racism in any form. Newsletters and other publications are full of civil rights jargon. On its Web page, ACE says it "is dedicated to the civil rights and equal protection" under the Constitution. It goes on to proclaim, "Persons of Native heritage should not be subject to law based on racial heritage" (Alliance 7:4, 1998). By this, ACE seems to be endorsing the late-nineteenth-century assimilative visions of Helen Hunt Jackson and Richard Henry Pratt.

Exhibit A in CERA's definition of itself as a multicultural organization is Roland Morris, a resident of the Flathead Indian Reservation and a member of the Minnesota Chippewa Tribe, who was elected to the CERA's national governing board during June 1999. In August, Morris also became chairman of All Citizens Equal (ACE), based in Ronan, Montana.

Morris spoke for the CERA and ACE at hearings convened in Seattle during 1998 by Senator Slade Gorton to publicize his legislative efforts (subsequently defeated) to strip Native American governments of their sovereign immunity, a power they share with other governmental bodies. Repeal of sovereign immunity would open reservation governments to a flood of debilitating lawsuits from anti-sovereignty advocates, who have been licking their legal chops at the prospect of suing reservation governments into insolvency.

In his testimony, Morris characterized the CERA and ACE as "grassroots, multi-racial groups dedicated to the promotion of equal rights for all citizens within Indian Country" (Morris 1998). Morris told Senator Gorton's hearing that "Basic human rights other Americans take for granted that allow people to live in dignity with their neighbors are not guaranteed on Indian reservations under the present version of 'sovereignty.'" Second, said Morris, "Tribes are dependent on Federal government help. Through this dependency, many tribal governments have become corrupt with unchecked power and money" (Morris 1998). Morris called Senator Gorton's bill, The American Indian Equal Justice Act, "wonderful news for anyone, either tribal or non-tribal. By providing federal district courts jurisdiction over civil-rights actions brought, under the Indian Civil Rights Act, tribal governments will be held accountable for their actions. This bill will not hurt tribal members, it will only hurt corrupt tribal government" (Morris 1998).

The Montana Human Rights Network has compiled a thirty-year history of antisovereignty organizing in that state, written by Ken Toole and Christine Kaufmann. This report found that "loose affiliation between anti-Indian groups and the religious right is also evident, primarily in the electoral arena [and] State Legislature." Despite their disavowal of racism, antisovereignty organizers "often stumble into the overt white supremacist movement," according to this report (Seldon 2000).

Toole called antisovereignty efforts in Montana inherently racist: "The basis of their disagreement strikes at the core of the concept of sovereignty. And it is here we find the answer to the question of whether the anti-Indian movement is racist. This movement, taken at face value, is a systematic effort to deny legally established rights to a group of people who are identified on the basis of their shared culture, history, religion, and tradition. It is racist by definition" (Are They Racists? 1999).

The Morris family was deeply offended by charges that they were racist. They engaged an attorney and sought an apology from the Montana Human Rights Network. As a partial rebuttal to a charge of racism leveled by the Montana Human Rights Network and its Director, Montana state Senator Ken Toole, Democrat of Helena, against Roland and Lisa Morris, MHRN was required to post it on MHRN's Web site and to notify MHRN members of this posting as part of the settlement reached in September 2001 of a defamation and infliction of emotional distress suit brought by Roland and Lisa Morris against Toole and the MHRN.

According to Jon Metropoulos, of Helena, Montana, attorney for Roland and Lisa Morris [jonmetro@gsjw.com], Toole's report

> Consisted of little more than reading newspaper clippings kept by a tribal activist and speaking with a half-dozen or so individuals, almost all of whom were members of the

Flathead Tribes or employees or former employees of those tribes. None of the people he spoke with represented any view contrary to the one he held. And this was it: Roland, a struggling upholsterer and full blood Indian, and Lisa, a mother to nine Indian children, are "anti-Indian" and "racists," primarily because they oppose the exercise of tribal governmental power over nonmembers, including themselves and their children. But the U.S. Supreme Court agrees with Roland and Lisa that [Indian] tribes rarely, if ever, should have such power. Why? Because of the serious deprivation of civil liberties implicit in allowing a tribal government to control people—non-tribal members— whom it excludes from equal rights of participation in the political process because of their race.

Note the word "conclusion." After years of simmering the work and months of drafting, Toole betrayed no uncertainty. No equivocal "opinions" for him. Not one sentence in the report states or even hints that it is relaying mere opinions of the Montana Human Rights Network and Toole. No, after so much scholarly research, analysis, and deep pondering only hard conclusions, judgments really, will do.

So why does Toole say this is "racist"? The charge of racism against Roland and Lisa Morris by the Montana Human Rights Network and Toole, of course, is absurd. It is defamation arising from willful ignorance or malice. (Morris and Morris 2002)

## MINNESOTA: ZERO-FOR-THREE AND ON A ROLL

Speaking on behalf of non-Indian sports fishermen in Minnesota as the Mille Lacs fishing-and-hunting treaty rights case was being readied for appeal, former Minnesota Vikings football coach Bud Grant wrote to the Minneapolis *Star-Tribune*: "We are behind at halftime, but the appeals process, and hence the game, isn't over" (When Is a Treaty 1997). Two years later, the game was over, with Grant's team having been sent to the showers not only in district court, but by a regional appeals court and the U.S. Supreme Court as well. Like any another coach who has lost three straight, Grant and his colleagues at Proper Economic Resource Management (PERM) were looking for a new game plan. The new game, for PERM and many like-minded antisovereignty advocates, is to end-run the Supreme Court through Congress.

PERM's "game," a campaign called "Save Minnesota," was waged against the fishing, hunting, and gathering rights of several Anisinabe (a.k.a. Chippewa or Ojibway) bands in Minnesota who retained these rights under a treaty signed in 1837. The treaty gave the Mille Lacs bands rights to hunt and fish "during the pleasure of the president" on 13 million acres ceded to the United States. The State of Minnesota's lawyers contended that an order President Zachary Taylor signed thirteen years later took those rights away and ordered the Mille Lacs bands removed from the previously ceded lands.

The Mille Lacs Band of Chippewa sued the state in 1990, challenging Minnesota's authority to impose hunting and fishing regulations on its members. The Mille Lacs bands claimed that the state government was infringing on their treaty-guaranteed rights to fish, hunt, and gather on 13 million acres of east-central Minnesota ceded to the United States by a treaty signed in 1837. The federal government and seven other Chippewa bands in Minnesota and Wisconsin joined the lawsuit.

A federal trial judge ruled in 1994 that the package of rights guaranteed by the Chippewas' 1837 treaty with the United States continues to exist. A district court judge upheld the Mille Lacs' treaty rights in 1997. The Eighth U.S. Circuit Court of Appeals agreed; The appeal court's three-judge panel unanimously ruled in favor of the band and upheld all previous rulings in the dispute. In March 1999, the U.S. Supreme Court ruled 5–4 in *Minnesota v. Mille Lacs Band* (97-1337), that the Native bands retain their rights and that neither an 1850 presidential order nor Minnesota's statehood in 1858 stripped the Mille Lacs bands of the rights guaranteed by the treaty, as the state had contended.

The Minnesota case was similar, in some ways, to earlier treaty-based decisions in Washington State (the "Boldt Decision") and in Wisconsin (the "Voight Decision"). Both of these cases spurred antisovereignty organizing by non-Indian fishing and hunting interests that maintained the treaties gave Native peoples access to fish-and-game resources not shared by the general non-Indian population. In each case, treaties stipulated that while Native peoples gave up large areas of land, they retained rights to harvest food.

"After an examination of the historical record, we conclude that the Chippewa retain the . . . rights guaranteed to them under the

1837 treaty," Justice Sandra Day O'Connor wrote for the U.S. Supreme Court (Mille Lac 1999). O'Connor wrote that Taylor's order requiring the Chippewas' removal from the land was not authorized by federal law and that other provisions in Taylor's order revoking the hunting and fishing rights could not stand separately.

Mark Rotz, PERM's chairman, wrote in the April 1996 issue of PERM's newsletter, "It will take a long time to change Federal Indian Policy . . . the very fact that we have an 'Indian policy' is racist and divisive for our country" (Aamot 1999). PERM's spin doctors worked to downplay an image of them popularized by columnist Nick Coleman of the St. Paul *Pioneer-Press,* who (on February 10, 1997) characterized PERM members as "Bud-Heads, Yahoos, and Bony-headed Walleye Worshippers" (Aamot 1999)

PERM describes itself as being "dedicated to balanced solutions to natural resource-management issues." *Balance,* in this case, is defined this way: "PERM believes that allowing special privileges, for any group, to our public natural resources is unconstitutional. Allowing a nonpublic entity, in which we the public have no voice, management authority and control over publicly owned fish and game is not sound conservation policy" (Welcome Page 1999). At its height, Rotz boasted that PERM, based in Elk River, Minnesota, had gathered 15,000 members under its antitreaty rights banner.

The content of the PERM newsletter reflects PERM members' conviction that they are being ripped off. In PERM's January 1997 newsletter, for example, a cartoon appeared that depicted a Native man driving a truck emblazoned with the company title "Native Son Fish Co." The truck is overflowing with fish. A non-Native man walking toward the vehicle, carrying a string of six small fish, says to the man, "My limit is six—yours is six hundred! How did you work that?" To which the Indian man replies, "You racist!" (Aamot 1999).

After the Supreme Court ruling, Rotz said that PERM members must acknowledge the decision "and respect the rights of our Chippewa neighbors" (Rotz n.d.). He said, however, that PERM members will have a "seat at the table to fight to keep tribal harvest levels to a minimum, as issues of allocation were left unsettled by the District Court. . . [A] battle has been lost, but the war is not over" (Rotz n.d.).

PERM is also a member of the Citizens Equal Rights Alliance, the national antisovereignty coalition. Howard Hanson, an important figure in CERA, hails from Minnesota and is closely allied with antisovereignty activities there. After the Supreme Court ruling in the

Mille Lacs case, Hanson said he was sure that "All PERM supporters were as devastated as I was by the [ruling]." However, said Hanson, "There are still plenty of battles to be fought, especially with regard to our B.I.A. and failed federal Indian policies. PERM is the only organization educating and protecting the citizens of our state from these corrupt and lawless agendas. . . . Let's start by demanding that our elected officials abide by their oaths of office and abide by the Constitution and Bill of Rights. . . . This battle is over, but the war for equal rights and the resources continues" (Hanson 1999). Translation: See you in the halls of Congress, where PERM and its allies will be arguing that "abiding by the Constitution" means doing away with "special rights" guaranteed by treaties.

## ANTISOVEREIGNTY, "WISE USE," AND THE ALLIANCE FOR AMERICA

Tracing the antisovereignty movement through the Internet, one finds many cross-references to alliances with the Wise Use movement, an alliance of groups that focuses on natural resource development and property-rights issues from an antienvironmental perspective. The Web pages of the CERA also cross-reference regularly to Web links with the Alliance for America, self-described as "a national coalition of over 650 local, regional and national groups . . . founded to coordinate and advance the anti-regulatory, anti-environmental agenda of the 'wise use' movement . . . to disseminate 'wise use' information and generate opposition to environmental laws" (Clearinghouse n.d.).

CERA's National Chairman Howard Hanson has been saluted as "prominent in Alliance for America activities" (Alliance 7(1), 1998). The Alliance for America organizes an annual "Fly In For Freedom" rally in Washington, DC, a five-day event during which Wise-Use activists converge on the national capital to network with each other and lobby members of Congress.

A March 1997 report, HONOR (Honor Our Neighbors Origins and Rights), a Wisconsin-based organization that monitors the anti-Indian movement, described links between the CERA and several states' county associations working to do away with tribal sovereignty, treaty rights, and the federal role in Native American life. What's more, the CERA was an active player in the 1994 Republican agenda to whittle away federal power over states. "For CERA's part," writes one commentator, "this would make it easier to eliminate tribal sovereignty, state by state" (Aamot 1997).

A Web site maintained by STAND UP!, in eastern Washington, provides its readers a brief tour of connections between the antisovereignty movements, Wise Use, and other organizations: "The 'Wise Use,' 'Property Rights,' and organized anti-Native movements converge most strongly in Washington State. UPOW, formed in 1989, was formerly known as the Steelhead and Salmon Protective Association and Wildlife Network (S/SPAWN),which the Environmental Working Group called 'an anti-Indian organization disguised as a fishermen's group.' UPOW is a coalition of groups and individuals, some of whom have been actively involved in organized anti-'sovereignty' and anti-tribal activities for years. The group headed the legal and political fight against tribal shell-fishing rights, along with their co-counsel, the Defenders of Property Rights" (Stand Up! 2000).

The STAND-UP! Committee opposes the Yakama Nation's attempt to form an electric utility and the possibility that the Yakamas may assume control of two Columbia River hydroelectric dams. STAND UP also supports the termination resolution of the Washington Republicans and advocates its inclusion in the platforms of all political parties. Elaine Willman, who has helped organize the STAND-UP! Committee, believes that Native nations should have the status of nonprofit organizations, such as the Elks, Eagles, and Boy Scouts, rather than governments (Barenti 2000).

Intensifying pressure from antisovereignty advocates has forced many Native peoples into a familiar defensive posture: organizing to protect land and rights guaranteed by treaties. "Whether he knows it or not, Senator Gorton has done the tribes a favor," said Nisqually leader Billy Frank, Jr., a four-decade veteran of fishing-rights disputes in Washington State. "He brought us together and underscored the need for Congress to get to know us better" (Egan 1998).

## THE ANTISOVEREIGNTY MOVEMENT ON CAPITOL HILL

The antisovereignty movement has been busy on Capitol Hill, doing its best to erode Native American treaty rights on the road to "devolution" of federal power to the states which has been emphasized in the Republican-controlled House and Senate. When the new Congress convened early in 2001, Native American nations braced for the return of an old nemesis: attempts to collect state sales and excise taxes on transactions by reservation businesses. They also may be facing new modifications to existing tax, environmental, and other laws aimed at circumventing the powers of Native governments.

The sales-tax proposals may be replated versions of House Resolution 1814, introduced in 1999, which threatened loss of trust land if state taxes are not paid. Such a proposal, if enacted, would empower the Interior Department to remove from reservation status if a retail business located on that land "consistently and willfully" refuses to pay state taxes. The land would then be subject to all state and local laws, including forfeiture for the unpaid taxes. This issue has assumed a new salience as more Native nations have developed economic infrastructure by (among other things) levying taxes of their own. In this context, state efforts to impose their taxes on reservations may amount to double taxation.

H.R. 1814, was introduced by Representatives Pete Visclosky, Democrat of Tennessee and Ernest Istook, Republican of Oklahoma. Under their proposal, Native American nations that allow collection of state taxes would be provided a priority status in competition for federal-government contracts. "In addition," according to sponsors of the bill, "each tribe will be notified by the Interior Department if they are under investigation for tax liability by the local governments to ensure the tribe will receive due process in meeting tax obligations" (Gray 2000).

Loss of trust status would, according to the National Congress of American Indians, "eliminate tribal authority regarding taxation and make the property subject to all applicable state and local sales taxes" (Legislative Update 1999). The bill proposed that trust status be restored once tax payments are made. According to the National Congress of American Indians, "Not since the Allotment Era of 1877 to 1934 has Congress passed legislation designed to take tribal land out of trust status. After stealing more than 90 million acres of tribal lands . . . less than 8 percent [has] been recovered" (Legislative Update 1999).

Reservation businesses face a stiff test on this issue from the National Governors' Association, as well as from off-reservation business interests. Addressing hearings on the proposal before the House Committee on Resources during October 1999, N.G.A. Executive Director Ray Scheppach asserted that "The failure of retail establishments on Indian trust lands to collect sales taxes and excise taxes on tobacco and gasoline places merchants who comply with the law at unfair price disadvantages. On products like gasoline and tobacco, the tax is a very large percentage of the cost of the good" (Testimony 1999).

The New York Supreme Court during July 2001, let stand a lower-court decision that said the state does not have to collect sales taxes from Indian nations. The Oneida Indian Nation operates nine gasoline stations and convenience stores. Such stores also operate on Seneca reservations in western New York, at Onondaga near Syracuse, and at Akwesasne in the northeast.

The appeal had been brought by gas station and convenience store owners, who asserted that Indian-owned businesses have an unfair advantage because they do not pay sales taxes. At about the same time, the Supreme Court's Appellate Division unanimously rejected arguments by non-Indian retailers who had fought to get the state to tax their reservation-based counterparts. In July 2001, the state's highest court—the Court of Appeals—declined, without comment, to hear the appeal of the New York Association of Convenience Stores. James Calvin, president of the association, said the group's only remaining option was a long shot: an appeal to the U.S. Supreme Court. "That is a very expensive and lengthy proposition, and the likelihood of prevailing is probably rather remote," Calvin said. "It's unlikely we will pursue it," Calvin said (Coin 2001).

Michael Holahan, chief executive officer of the North American Truck Stop Network and member of the NATSO (National Association of Truck Stop Owners), told the same hearing that the problem of tax-free sales on tribal lands is growing, threatening tax-collecting businesses and state governments across the country. "Native American business owners who aren't collecting state taxes from non-tribal members can gain a significant advantage selling two principal products—fuel and cigarettes," he said (Holahan 1999).

Measures that would impose state taxes on Native businesses are only the tip of the proverbial iceberg of antisovereignty efforts in the House and Senate. The American Indian Research and Policy Institute of Minneapolis-St. Paul issued a detailed report, "Contemporary Threats to Tribal Sovereignty From Congress," describing antisovereignty legislation in Congress during the 1990s. The report found that "Much of this legislation is designed to strip tribal authority and to grant states more regulatory power in Indian Country" (Contemporary Threats 2000).

The report found that legislative attempts to curtail Native sovereignty fell into several areas, including proposed amendments to existing laws affecting the Child Welfare Act (1978); proposed amendments to the Indian Gaming Regulatory Act (1988); proposed taxation of Indian gaming; extension of state sales taxes to non-Indians on trust lands, and proposed amendments to regulatory authority of Indian tribes in the name of environmental protection.

The AIRPI noted that "The federal government has historically carried out its trust responsibility to Indians in education, health and welfare via federal social programs. As devolution proceeds and social programs are transferred to states, many Indian programs at the federal level risk being similarly transferred (Contemporary Threats 2000). "The intent of this legislation is to move people off welfare and into the job market. The point is lost in Indian Country where most reservations have little economic base and there are few jobs for Indian people" (Contemporary Threats, 2000). For example, funds for Indian social programs have been defined as discretionary spending, not as an obligation mandated by treaties and the trust obligation.

Also during the 105th Congress, Senator Slade Gorton introduced a provision to the fiscal year 1998 Department of Interior appropriations bill that would have imposed a means test for federal funding. This provision was dropped after pressure from reservation governments. Another of Slade Gorton's proposals would have waived sovereign immunity for Native American nations. This idea also went down to defeat in the Senate. Another of Senator Gorton's proposals would require tribal governments to purchase tort liability insurance and would place jurisdiction over tribal liability suits in federal district courts, bypassing tribal courts (Keeping Watch 1999).

The federal-power devolutionists have other ideas, as well. One of them is H.R. 325 (1997), which would amend the Indian Gaming Regulatory Act (1988) to grant states greater leverage in negotiation of gaming compacts, including a capacity to tax gaming revenues. House of Representatives Resolution 334 (1997), "The Fair Indian Gaming Act," sought to shift the burden of proof from the states to Native nations in gaming-compact negotiations. This bill, another example of devolution at work, would have transferred IGRA oversight from the Department of the Interior to the Office of the Governor or a given state's legislature. This proposal also called for a two-year moratorium on class III gaming. This bill also contained increased record-keeping requirements for Indian gaming establishments. State attorney generals also are directed to investigate Native gaming—an extension of state legal jurisdiction.

In the realm of environmental protection, amendments have been proposed to the Clean Water Act (1977) that would strip Native American governments of their authority to regulate water policies on reservations. Amendments proposed during the 105th Congress to environmental legislation, such as the Endangered Species Act (1973), Superfund (1994), the Clean Water Act (1977), and nuclear-waste storage law, could affect Indian country (Contemporary Threats 2000). The U.S. House of Representatives also has considered H.R. 193 (1997), which prohibits any area from being declared a historic district, site or national monument which is defined as "unimproved" or "unmodified natural landscape." According to one analyst, "This would affect tribal sacred lands. Tribal land is also threatened by H.R. 253 (1997) which gives holders of mineral claims exclusive rights to possession and use of land for mineral activities" (Contemporary Threats 2000).

## "WHITE PRIDE—WORLD WIDE": THE NEO-NAZIS AND TREATY RIGHTS

If you want your racism raw, the Web page to visit is Storm front.org. No quotes from Martin Luther King or Chief Joseph here—just paeans to George Armstrong Custer as oppressed white man and a philosophy that takes pride in no-regrets conquest. The message for Native Americans at Stormfront.org is simple: "We" are the superior race. "We" kicked your ass and took your continent. Tough shit.

Stormfront.org is the place to go for interviews with David Duke, an on-line version of Adolf Hitler's *Mein Kampf,* and the latest in white-pride chic, including a bewildering variety of swastikas and Celtic-cross pendants, T-Shirts, and flags. Don't forget the hot-selling Stars and Bars, the Confederate Battle Flag, which is one of the American neo-Nazis' favorite icons. Visit the graphics library and download your own swastikas, iron crosses, and SS insignia.

Before dismissing all this as someone's sick joke, check the hit-meter on the Stormfront home page, which said (on January 22, 2002) that I was visitor number 5,583,330 since March 27, 1995. This high-tech Web page tells me that I am "visitor number 792 today." It's 9:05 A.M. Central Daylight Time. The page also offers itself in Spanish and German.

This is no joke. This is "White Pride—World-wide: The White Nationalist Resource Page," maintained by Don Black, "a 6-foot-3-inch man with the helmet of gently graying hair" (Abel 1998). Black's personal Internet page shows the Internet White Pride webmaster pecking away at his personal computer in West Palm Beach, Florida, backed by a large Confederate flag.

Stormfront.org's resident sage is "Professor" Revilo P. Oliver, who is described on the Web page as "one of America's greatest patriots." Nearly two hundred of Oliver's commentaries have been reproduced at Stormfront.org. All of them, like the rest of the site, is accessible through Stormfront.org's own internal search engine. In these hundreds of thousands of words, Oliver has a few choice thoughts on Native Americans, although most of his tirades are directed against African Americans (if you're searching, try "niggers"), Jews, Latinos, Asians, homosexuals (see: "queers"), and just about anyone else without a very high quantum of Nordic (search: "Aryan") blood.

Here is Oliver's take on Native American character: "The aborigines could be brave and exhibit an almost heroic superiority to pain and hardship, and that encouraged sentimentalists to forget that they were also cowardly and treacherous, filthy and squalid, innately cruel and savage, and incapable of the discipline that makes civilization possible" (Oliver 1991).

Oliver endorses "the right of a superior people to seize the country of an inferior people and exterminate them."

> A superior race has a moral right, perhaps even a moral imperative, to displace an inferior race in desirable territory. Aryans were obviously greatly superior to Indians and therefore had a natural right to take North America for themselves. I do not say that our race's superiority to the Indians was shown by our greater intelligence and our unique culture, for that would be only a tautology. Our superiority was conclusively demonstrated by the fact that we subjugated the Indians and conquered the country that was ours until we discarded it. (Oliver 1991)

Oliver sneers at suggestions that Native American confederacies, notably the Iroquois, may have shaped democracy: "How far our imbecility has gone may be seen from a recent instance in the state of New York, where the gang of racketeers who call themselves 'educators' are ramming into the minds of their child victims the lie that the American Constitution was imitated from a confederation formed by savages" (Oliver 1991). He is referring to the curriculum guide "Haudenosaunee: Past, Present, Future," which was part of the New York State Department of Education "Curriculum of Inclusion."

In another commentary, Oliver refers to George Armstrong Custer's "efficient defeat of the Cheyenne at Washita in 1868" as "a brilliant victory." "Liberal pests . . . who yelp about Custer's 'massacre' of the savages . . . are beneath contempt," he writes (Oliver 1990).

Black, a former member of the Ku Klux Klan, maintains one of the better-known of several hundred "hate speech" sites on the Internet. The Wiesenthal Center by 1998 was spending 80 percent of its resources tracking on-line hate (Koppel 1998). The German government has tried (and failed) to block Stormfront.org at the border. Much of the site's content is illegal under German law, but protected by the First Amendment to the U.S. Constitution's Bill of Rights.

Black makes the most of his First Amendment rights, riding the airwaves as well as Web links. At one point in 1998, Black appeared on *Nightline* with Ted Koppel. When Black tried to enlist Thomas Jefferson in his cause as a supporter of free expression, Koppel leaned into the camera and replied: "If you'll forgive me, most of us won't have trouble distinguishing between you and Thomas Jefferson" (Koppel 1998).

Black began his career as a white nationalist by handing out White Power literature while a student at Athens High School (near Huntsville, Alabama). In college, as a political science major at the University of Alabama, Black joined the Reserve Officers Training Corps (ROTC) but was expelled for racism. Later, Black graduated to leading local rallies of the Ku Klux Klan (KKK). Black joined the KKK in 1975, the year after David Duke took over the group. Black then moved to Birmingham as the KKK's Alabama organizer. Black's career in the Klan culminated when he became grand wizard, after Duke stepped aside.

Black resigned from the KKK in 1987. "I concluded the Klan could never be a viable political movement again," he said. "It had a reputation for random and senseless violence which it could never overcome. There were several events around [at] that time that reinforced that opinion" (Faulk 1997, 1). Black, who was divorced, moved to West Palm Beach, Florida, the same year and married Duke's former wife.

Black was among fifty-nine individuals and thirty-two organizations profiled in the Anti-Defamation League's report "The Major Vehicles and Voices on America's Far Right Fringe"—"a sort of who's who of such hate groups" (Faulk 1997, 1). The league also has issued another report that focuses on Black and Stormfront.org. "He [Black] was really the first white supremacist on the Internet," said Rick Eaton, senior researcher with the Simon Wiesenthal Center in Los Angeles (Faulk 1997, 1).

## THE DONALD TRUMP CONNECTION

Opponents of Iroquois land claims and casino development also have expressed themselves through the New York state legislature, where attempts to subject tribal-state gaming compacts to county and legislative approval were stalled after intense lobbying on both sides. This proposal arose largely in opposition to federal approval of a casino proposed (with participation by the St. Regis Mohawks) in southern New York's Sullivan County, in the Catskills. The St. Regis Mohawk Tribal Council signed a contract with casino developer Park Place Entertainment, with the intention of building a major gaming resort. The legislative measure arose suddenly, quickly passing the state Senate. It was poised for a positive vote in the Assembly, when a Sullivan County legislator asked the state Democratic leadership to put it on hold.

During the lobbying efforts, an advertising campaign accused the St. Regis Mohawks (at Akwesasne) of drug smuggling, money laundering, trafficking in illegal immigrants, and violence. The advertising was published in several newspapers. The advertising campaign was conducted under the aegis of the New York Institute for Law and Society. The text of the advertising campaign read, in part: "Are these [St. Regis Mohawks] the kind of neighbors we want? The St. Regis Mohawk record of criminal activity is well documented" (Kibbe 2000). Many Akwesasne Mohawks complained that while illegal activity—much of it associated with cross-border smuggling—does take place there, implying that all Akwesasne Mohawks support such activities is something of a racial slur.

According to *Indian Country Today,* the institute's advertising was "clearly informed by the racist attitudes prevailing in the area. The Institute admitted that its extremely objectionable ads were bankrolled by non-Indian casino interests. . . . The transparent setup by casino mogul Donald Trump, who sees a competitive threat to his Atlantic City, N.J., casinos, makes sense. It is in his interest to limit tribal gaming in states surrounding his enterprises" (Trying to Kill 2000). Jim Adams, a reporter for *Indian Country Today,* traced some of the advertising, as well, to an organizer for the short-lived presidential campaign of New York City property magnate Donald Trump.

## STREET THEATER IN UPSTATE NEW YORK

The Upstate Citizens for Equality (UCE) group is comprised largely of property holders who believe that some or all of what they own may become part of several land claims being pursued by the original five nations of the Iroquois Confederacy, the Mohawk, Seneca, Cayuga, Ononodaga, and Oneida. An Internet home page maintained by the UCE leads with a question: "People are facing eviction from their homes for expansion of Indian reservations. Are you next?" (Upstate Citizens n.d.).

The UCE characterizes itself as "a citizen organization that is working to fight Indian land claims in Central New York and change the course of Federal Indian policy . . ." (Seely 1999). The UCE has opened chapters in Oneida, Madison, Seneca, Cayuga, and Niagara Counties, and claims a statewide membership of more than 8,200. The UCE chapter in Madison County, New York, specializes in street theater, especially outside the Oneidas' Turning Stone casino. A UCE "border patrol" marks the boundary of the Oneida Nation with yellow "caution" tape, telling patrons that they leave their rights under the U.S. Constitution at the border. Colorfully-dressed "border guards" stand at attention as lines of picketers mill around them. Protesters rally around mock "Patriot" missiles; signs carry the name of Ray Halbritter, the Oneida Nation representative. The John Birch Society put Halbritter's face on the cover of its *New American* magazine, calling him "High-Rollin', Land-Grabbin' Ray." A sign along Route 46 displayed a rifle and the words: "Ray, come and get your rent." The mock missile making the rounds near Verona bore the inscription, "Heads up, Ray," and "Come get your rent" (Seely 1999). "They created the atmosphere," said Mark Emery, Oneida Nation spokesman, "We're not tying them to it, certainly. But how can you cry crocodile tears over the fact that you wouldn't do this yet condone the same type of language" (Threats Made 1999).

The specific concern of the UCE in Madison County (and the reason its members spend so much time picketing the Turning Stone Casino) is the use, by the Oneidas, of casino profits to buy land that was once part of their traditional estate. Before the casino opened, Oneida landholdings had been reduced to thirty-two acres near Oneida Castle, New York.

The Turning Stone Casino, twenty-five miles east of Syracuse, has produced 1,900 jobs and has become the fifth most popular tourist attraction in New York State. By 1997, the casino and other Oneida businesses were employing 2,400 people, making the Oneida Nation the second largest employer in central New York. Eighty-five percent of the Turning Stone's employees are non-Indian.

While Halbritter pointed to the economic benefits of the Oneidas' growing payroll, local public officials complain that the Oneidas' business ventures pay no sales or excise taxes to cities, counties, or the state. In addition, more than 7,000 acres purchased by the Oneidas with casino profits have been taken off the property-tax rolls.

In September 1997, the Oneidas attempted to assuage these criticisms by paying Oneida County $71,080 and Verona County (in which the casino is located) $55,230 in lieu of property taxes. The payments, called "Oneida Nation Silver Covenant Chain Grants," are named for the covenant chain image that was used in early treaty councils.

Most of the Oneidas' economic development has taken place since 1985, when 90 percent of Oneidas in Central New York lived in poverty. Oneida County Executive Ralph Eannance believes that the Oneidas' business boom has been the single biggest factor in central New York's economic recovery during the late 1990s, following the closure of a major U.S. Air Force base and large layoffs at major defense contractors.

A U.C.E. Web page appeals to class biases as it recruits: "Instead of going to the Turning Stone for entertainment, why not join the U.C.E. picketers? You'll meet a much better class of people at U.C.E. than at the Turning Stone!!" One day on the picket lines, brags the Web page, "Ten cars turned around and left after reading a picket sign that said 'No health inspectors. Enjoy your meal'" (Upstate Citizens n.d.).

For almost three weeks during the summer of 1999, Oneida radio station WMCR canceled its daily call-in show, "Open Line" due to remarks made in poor taste on land-claims issues. The show resumed September 17, "with a vow by management to maintain civility" (Seely 1999). At one point in the radio free-for-all, Susan Galbraith, former DeRuyter [New York] town supervisor who often speaks on behalf of UCE, called the Oneidas' government "parasitic." Later, she recanted that comment, revising her opinion of the Oneidas' government to "shakedown artists and schoolyard bullies" (Seely 1999).

In a quieter moment, Galbraith later told a newspaper reporter: "There has been a lot of damage done to hearts over the past few years. There's a great deal of anger and estrangement among folks who used to be congenial with each other" (Seely 1999). Rather than face protests in Canastota, the Oneidas canceled their annual cultural fair during the summer of 1999. Friendships have soured. Some Oneidas avoid shops or restaurants where they feel unwelcome. "You can tell they don't want us there," clan mother Marilyn John said. "But you get used to it" (Seely 1999).

Rising tensions regarding Haudenosaunee (Iroquois) land claims were accentuated by a threat, delivered to a newspaper anonymously during 1999 to kill an Oneida every three days, beginning on Thanksgiving Day. The threats were made in a one-page typed letter delivered to the Utica *Observer-Dispatch* during the last days of October. Details of the letter were published by the newspaper November 1, detailing the assertions of a group calling itself the United States National Freedom Fighters (USNFF), which threatens to kill Oneidas, bomb their businesses, and attack their non-Indian customers.

The threats probably were related to the Oneidas' long-standing land claim. The Oneidas, with the support of the U.S. Justice Department, are seeking the return of 270,000 acres of ancestral land in Oneida and Madison counties. The U.S. Supreme Court found in 1975 that most of the land was seized in questionable transactions with the state and private individuals in violation of the Non-Intercourse Acts. The court ruled that the Oneidas were entitled to compensation.

The United States National Freedom Fighters claimed thirty-four members in the letter delivered to the newspaper. The letter said that group members were willing to "give and shed blood for what we believe." The letter continued: "We will begin the blood shedding. We will execute one Indian approximately every three days, starting Thanksgiving Day. We will also execute one U.S. citizen (from Upstate N.Y. area) who is noticed by one of the U.S.N.F.F. members as a person who contributes to the Indian nation by supporting the Casino and SavOn Gas Stations. Women will not be spared. Those who contribute to the Indians are traitors, not worthy of sympathy" (Threats Made 1999).

The USNFF letter ended on an ominous note: "Several bombs WILL BE PLANTED sometime after December. THERE WILL BE NO NOTICE. . . . Four VERY courageous people in the USNFF have offered to give their lives for this cause. They will do so by driving two to four trucks carrying explosives into the Oneida Nation's Casino" (Dill 1999).

The UCE, which has kept its protests peaceful, condemned the letter and said it has no connection to the group making the threats. "We view this [the USNFF letter] as absolutely horrendous," Scott Peterman, president of the 8,000-member group, said. "We can see no justification for any of this. We would certainly not have anything to do with a view like this. . . . We agree that it is cowardly and despicable" (Threats Made 1999).

Following publicity attending the threats to Oneidas, security was tightened at the Turning Stone Casino, the Oneida's gas stations, and other businesses. The businesses did not close, however. The Turning Stone and its 285-room luxury hotel draw about 3 million visitors annually. "We think the purpose of the letter is to hurt the businesses," Emery said (Threats Made 1999). The threats were being taken seriously by law enforcement. State police and the FBI are investigating. A copy of the letter was analyzed for fingerprints and DNA evidence. State Police Lt. Robert Patnaude said troopers have never heard of the group making the threats. If the authors are discovered, they could face state misdemeanor charges for aggravated harassment or federal charges because they used the U.S. mail to send the threats.

In December 1998, the Oneidas and the Justice Department announced that they planned to include 20,000 private landowners as defendants in the land-claims lawsuit, a proposal that was dropped after a deluge of non-Indian protests. During the summer of 2001, one of the New York State antitreaty activists' main organizing incentives was demolished when the U.S. Justice Department, which is representing the various Iroquois nations regarding land claims, said it would not sue individual property owners. Some of the activists asserted that they still faced threats. Lawyers for Madison-Oneida Landowners, Inc., said that non-Indian property owners are still facing potentially severe threats to their property.

"We have not had that threat (of eviction) removed," John Benjamin Carroll, chief counsel for the group during a press conference at the offices of Carroll, Carroll, Davidson & Young (Drought 2001). Carroll said that individual property holders can still be held liable in some cases and concessions that may come from the state could have an impact on them. He cited papers filed earlier this month by U.S. Department of Justice trial attorney Charles Jakosa. Those papers ask for a judgment against the state "awarding monetary and possessory relief, including ejectment where appropriate" (Drought 2001).

Carroll said that an eventual resolution also could include the state losing the right to major highways in the area, including the New York State Thruway, as well as routes 31, 13, and 5, as well as state parks. "Obviously, if we cannot get on and off our properties, they have no value," he explained (Drought 2001).

## REFERENCES

Aamot, M. 1997. The anti-treaty movement: The latest, racist rage against Native Americans. *The Circle* [magazine]. Minneapolis, MN, (September, n.p.).

Abel, D. S. 1998. The racist next door: Don Black fills the Internet with hate and calls for a revolution to split the country along racial lines. *New Times*. http://www.stormfront.org/.

*Alliance for America's Trumpet Call* 7 (1), January/February, 1998. http://www.allianceforamerica.org/tcall01.htm.

———. 7 (4) July/August, 1998. http://www.allianceforamerica.org/tcall04.htm#CERA.

Angry group protests Swinomish utility tax. *Native News* On-line, from *Channel Town Press* (LaConner, Washington. December 2, 1998). http://www.mail archive.com/nativenews%40mlists.net/msg00896.html.

Are They Racists? The Anti-Indian Movement in Montana. Montana Human Rights Network News, November 1999. http://www.mhrn.org/news/1199anti.html.

Barenti, M. 2000. GOP politicians break with platform on tribes. *Yakima Herald-Republic*, July 9. http://www.yakima-herald.com/cgi-bin/liveique.acgi$rec=13745?home.

Benedict, J. 2000. *Without reservation: The making of America's most powerful Indian Tribe and Foxwoods, the world's largest casino.* New York: Harper-Collins.

Black, D. Personal Home Page. http://www.stormfront.org/dblack/.

Casinoworld Wire. 2000. Foxwoods tribe produces controversial document to prove ancestry. September 20. http://www.casinowire.com/archive/200009/1976.shtml.

CERF/CERA Welcome Page, Montana Chapter, Ronan, MT. June 26, 2000. www.citizensalliance.org/main/.

Clearinghouse on Environmental Advocacy and Research (CLEAR). Alliance for America, n.d. http://wyl.ewg.org/pub/static/CLEAR/ALLAM.nhtml.

Coin, G. 2001. Sales tax appeal fails. *(Syracuse) Post-Standard,* August 16. http://www.syracuse.com/news/syrnewspapers/index.ssf?/newsstories/20010816_rnsales.html.

Contemporary Threats to Tribal Sovereignty from Congress. American Indian Research and Policy Institute, St. Paul, MN, 2000. http://www.airpi.org/st98cont_congress.html.

DeArmond, M. 2000. Democrats, Indians denounce GOP plan seeking to ban tribal governments. Associated Press. July 8. http://www.sfgate.com/cgi-bin/article.cgi?file=/news/archive/2000/07/08/state2025EDT0165.DTL.

Dill, J.S. 1999. Assault on the Oneida. October. http://www.dickshovel.com/oneida2.html.

Drought, C. 2001. Non-Indian property owners still face threats. *Oneida Daily Dispatch,* August 13. http://www.zwire.com/site/news.cfm?newsid=2212636&BRD=1709&PAG=461&dept_id=68844&rfi=6.

Egan, T. 1998. Backlash growing as Indians make stand for sovereignty. *New York Times,* March 9. http://darkwing.uoregon.edu/~jbloom/race/nativams/backlash.htm#1.

Faulk, K. 1997. White supremacist spreads views on Net. *Birmingham (Alabama) News,* October 19, 1. http://www.stormfront.org/dblack/press101997.htm.

Federal Indian Policy in the News. CERF/CERA Home Page. Ronan, M., July 2000. http://www.citizensalliance.org.

Gransbery, J. 1998. Burns: Jurisdiction obscurity harms Indian reservations. *(Billings) Gazette,* January 7. http://tlc.wtp.net/sovereig1.htm.

Gray, J. 2000. House resolution 1814 targets Indian tribes. *Oklahoma Indian Times,* July. http://www.okit.com.

Grossman, Zoltan. 1992. Indian treaty rights. In *When hate groups come to town: A handbook of effective community responses.* Atlanta, GA: Center for Democratic Renewal. http://conbio.rice.edu/nae/docs/anti_indian.html.

Groups Actively Fighting Native Sovereignty. 1999. http://www.finearts.uvic.ca/~vipirg/SISIS/links/anti.html.

Hanson, H. 1999. The Mille Lacs Treaty case is over, but don't stop fighting for what you believe in. http://www.perm.org/articles/a073.html.

Hauptman, L.M. 2000. [Guest commentary.] Poughkeepsie (New York) *Journal,* June 2.

Holahan, M. 1999. NATSO testifies on tax-free sales on Native lands. U.S. House of Representatives, Committee on Resources. October 12. http://www.natso.com.

Keeping watch—Native people and current legislation. *Native American Voices.* (United Methodist Church) 4 (14), 1999. http://www.umc.org.

Kibbe, D. [Ottaway News Service]. 2000. Casino foe has ties to horse racing. *Press-Republican,* February 20. http://www.pressrepublican.com/Archive/2000/02_2000/022020004.htm.

Koppel, T. 1998. Hate Web sites and the issue of free speech. American Broadcating Company News *Nightline* with Ted Koppel, January 13. http://www.stormfront.org/dblack/nightline011398.htm.

Larsen, K. 2000. L[atter] D[ay] S[aints] author takes on rich Indian tribe: Are Pequots really Pequots? *News about Mormons* [and] *Mormonism.* May 25. http://www.mormonstoday.com/000528/P2Benedict01.shtml.

Legislative Update, National Congress of American Indians "Representative Istook Unleashes Latest Attack." May 17, 1999. http://www.ncai.org.

Mille Lac Chippewa win in Supreme Court; Court upholds Indian hunting, fishing rights. Associated Press, March 24, 1999. http://www.alphacdc.com/treaty/mil-court.html.

Montana, C. 2000. Washington GOP plank to terminate tribes ignites firestorm. *Indian Country Today,* July 12. http://indiancountry.com.

Morris, R., and L. Morris. Personal Communication, April 30, 2002. The complete text of their rebuttal to Toole may be referenced on the Internet at http://www.mhrn.org/.

Morris, R., Sr. Testimony of Mr. Roland Morris, Sr., Board Member Citizens Equal Rights Alliance. Oversight Hearing before the Committee on Indian Affairs, U.S. Senate, Concerning S. 1691, The American Indian Equal Justice Act [ref. Sen. Slade Gorton] Seattle, Washington, April 7, 1998. http://www.senate.gov/~scia/1998hrgs/0407_rm.htm.

New face for ACE—New era for CERA: Anti-Indian groups put Indian in leadership positions. *Montana Human Rights Network News.* February 1998. http://www.mhrn.org/news/298face.html.

Oliver, R.P. 1990. Hero a la mode. Stormfront.org: White Pride Worldwide. November. http://www.stormfront.org/.

———. 1991. Scalping the unwary. Stormfront.org: White Pride Worldwide. July. http://www.stormfront.org/.

Pablo, M.T. 1998. Burns and Gazette editorial ignore treaty rights, tribal sovereignty. *(Billings) Gazette,* January 4.

Parr, M. 1998. Non-tribal reservation residents petition county they want to see an end to county-tribal cooperation. *Skagit Valley Herald,* December 15. http://www.skagitvalleyherald.com.

———. n.d. Sovereignty comes under fire. *Skagit Valley Herald.* www.newswest.com/naissues/skagit/skagit.html.

Rotz, M. n.d. From the chairman: Mille Lacs Treaty case. Proper Economic Resource Management. http://www.perm.org/articles/a069.html.

Scarponi, D. 2000. Another document bolsters the Pequots' claim of authenticity. *New York Times* On-line, September 21. http://www.newstimes.com.

Seely, H., and M. Breidenbach. 1999. C[entral] N[ew] Y[ork] communities split over land claims: Hate mail, name-calling, threats fly as Indians sue. *(Syracuse) Herald-American,* September 26. http://www.syracuse.com/news/stsunday/19990926_apnrace.html.

Seldon, R. 2000. Anti-Indian movement thrives in Montana. *Indian Country Today.* March 17. http://www.walkingant.com.

Semantics of Indian sovereignty: Nation's courts use narrow definition. (Editorial), *(Billings) Gazette,* July 7, 2000. http://www.egroups.com/group/ndn-aim.

Stand Up! The Citizens Stand Up Committee, Toppenish, Washington. May, 2000. http://yakvalnews.com.

Testimony . . . by Ray Scheppach [Executive Director, National Governors' Association] on Collection of Transactional Taxes on Indian Trust Lands. Before the House Committee on Resources, United States House of

Representatives. October 12, 1999. http://www.nga.org/NaturalRes/Testimony19991012Taxes.asp.

Threats made against tribe over land claim lawsuit. 1999. *Gambling Magazine,* http://www.gamblingmagazine.com/articles/21/21-86.htm.

Trahant, M. 2000. Termination has been tried before. *(Seattle) Times,* July 6. www.seattletimes.com.

Trying to kill a good thing: Indian sovereignty is economic stimulant. *Indian Country Today* (editorial), July 12, 2000. http://www.indiancountry.com.

Upstate Citizens for Equality. Seneca and Cayuga Chapter Home Page. Whose land is it, anyway? http://www.ucelandclaim.com/.

Welcome Page. Proper Economic Resource Management, 1999. http://www.perm.org/frames/fwelcome.htm.

When is a treaty not a treaty? 1997. *Crooked Creek Observer,* May 20. http://www.emily.net/~schiller/treaty.html.

# Selected Bibliography

*Adams et al. v. Osage Tribe of Indians et al.* (No. 642 District Court N.D. Oklahoma 50 F. 2d 918; 1931 U.S. Dist. LEXIS 1436). Congressional Record, 42d Congress, 2d Session. Ex. Doc. No. 146, n.p. The Adams case was upheld on appeal to the tenth Circuit. [59 F. 2d 653; 1932 U.S. App. LEXIS 3435]

Adams, James Truslow, and Kenneth T. Jackson, eds. *Atlas of American History.* 2nd rev. ed. New York: Charles Scribner's Sons, 1984.

"Agreement in Principle Reached to Settle Land Claim." Turtle Island Native Network. February 16, 2002. http://www.turtleisland.org.

*American State Papers.* Class II. Vol. 1. 1832. Buffalo, NY: William S. Hein & Co., Inc., 1998.

Anderson, Terry, and R. Patrick Corbett. "Oneidas Rip Offer for Land: Wisconsin Tribe Rejects New York Settlement." *Green Bay Press-Gazette,* February 17, 2001. http://www.greenbaypressgazette.com.

Annual Summary of Production and Pipeline Runs, Oklahoma and Kansas, for the Year 1939. Petroleum Statistical Guide, p. 11, cited in *United States v. Stanolind* (1940).

Aquila, Richard. *The Iroquois Restoration: Iroquois Diplomacy on the Colonial Frontier, 1701–1754.* Detroit: Wayne State University Press, 1983.

*Aroostook Band of Micmac Settlement.* Pub. L. 102–71. Nov. 26, 1991, 105 Stat. 1143. http://www4.law.cornell.edu/uscode/25/1721.notes.html.

Assembly of Governors and Chiefs, Minutes. December 7, 2001; December 1, 2000. December 3, 1999. Maine Indian Tribal-State Commission.

Associated Press. "Atlantic Indian Tribes Balk at Signing New Fisheries Deals with Ottawa." *Boston Globe,* March 9, 2001.

———. "Canadian Negotiator Expects Fewer Tribal Chiefs to Sign Fishing Deals." *Boston Globe,* April 7, 2001.

———. "Judge Rules against Wisconsin Tribe's Claims Against Homeowners." *Boston Globe,* September 5, 2002.

———. "Judge: Scientists Can Study Ancient Bones of Man Indian Tribes Claim as Ancestor." *Indian Time* 20, No. 35 (September 5, 2002):10.

———. "Maine Town Rejects Casino Idea." *Boston Globe,* May 20, 2002.

———. "Mystery of Missing Femurs May Be Solved." *Indian Country Today,* July 4, 2001, A-8.

———. "Oneidas File 20 Lawsuits Seeking Private Land." *Syracuse Post-Standard,* February 21, 2002. http://www.syracuse.com/newsflash/regional/index.ssf?/cgi-free/getstory_ssf.cgi?n0611_BC_NY—Oneida LandClaim&&news&newsflash-newyork-syr.

———. "Three Southwestern Ontario First Nations to Vote On Land-Claim Deal." Syracuse.com, March 26, 2001. http://www.syracuse.com/ newsflash/index.ssf?/cgi-free/getstory_ssf.cgi?n0961_BC_Canada—Land Claim-Vo&&news&newsflash-newyork-syr.

*Atkins v. Penobscot Nation.* 130 F.3d 482 (1st Cir. 1997).

*At Loggerheads—The State of Maine and the Wabanaki: Final Report of the Task Force on Tribal-State Relations.* January 15, 1997. Revised, June 2000. 46 pages.

Aupaumut, Hendrick. "A Narrative of an Embassy to the Western Indians, from the Original Manuscript of Hendrick Aupaumut, 1791 and 1793." *Memoirs of the Historical Society of Pennsylvania* 2.1 (1827):9–131.

Axelrod, Alan. *Chronicle of the Indian Wars from Colonial Times to Wounded Knee.* New York: Prentice Hall, 1993.

Barsh, Russel, and James Henderson. *The Road: Indian Tribes and Political Liberty.* Berkeley: University of California Press, 1980.

Barton, Benjamin Smith. *New Views of the Origin of the Tribes and Nations of America.* 1798. Reprint, Millwood, NY: Kraus Reprint Co., 1976.

Beatty, Charles. *The Journal of a Two Months Tour.* London: William Davenhill and George Pearch, 1768.

Beauchamp, William M. *Aboriginal Place Names of New York.* Bulletin 108: Archaeology 12 of the New York State Museum. Albany, NY: New York State Education Department, 1907.

Bell, Stewart. "Dispute Looms over Salmon Fishing in N[ova] S[cotia]." *The National Post,* October 10, 2000. http://www.nationalpost.com.

Bemis, Samuel Flagg. *Jay's Treaty: A Study in Commerce and Diplomacy.* Rev. ed. New Haven: Yale University Press, 1962.

Bentwell, Mike. Personal communication via Internet from Kahanawake. January 28, 2002.

Berkeley, Edmund, and Dorothy Smith Berkeley. *Dr. John Mitchell: The Man Who Made the Map of North America.* Chapel Hill, NC: University of North Carolina Press, 1974.

Berkes, Fikret. "Fishery Resource Use in a Subarctic Indian Community." *Human Ecology* 5(1977):289–307.

Bilodeau, Mike. "Protest at Nation Sparks More Controversy." *Oneida Daily Dispatch,* January 3, 2002. http://www.zwire.com/site/news.cfm?newsid =2886439&BRD=1709&PAG=461&dept_id=68844&rfi=6.

———. "State: Land Claims Left to Courts." *Oneida Daily Dispatch,* March 29, 2002. http://www.zwire.com/site/news.cfm?newsid=3697175&BRD =1709&PAG=461&dept_id=68844&rfi=6.

———. "Homer to Be Demolished Soon." *Oneida Daily Dispatch,* September 7, 2002. http://www.zwire.com/site/news.cfm?newsid=5279651&BRD =1709&PAG=461&dept_id=68844&rfi=6.

———. "Patterson's Mobile Home Leveled." *Oneida Daily Dispatch,* October 24, 2002. http://www.zwire.com/site/news.cfm?newsid=5803138&BRD =1709&PAG=461&dept_id=68844&rfi=6.

Birenbaum, Joanna, Suzanne Birks, D. Bruce Clarke, Tracey Cutcliffe, David English, Olivier Fuldauer, Nigel G. Gilby, Stuart C. B. Gilby, Coilin Gillespie, Ron S. Maurice, Candice S. Metallic, Martha Montour, Guy Morin, James O'Reilly, Andrew Orkin, Sara Thibodeau, Helene "Sioui" Trudel, Bruce Wildsmith, Kenneth J. Winch, and Eric Zscheile. "Fisheries and Oceans Makes Legal Error at Burnt Church." September 7, 2000. portfolio@newswire.ca.

Blackwell, Tom. "Return of Violence Feared in Burnt Church Native Fishery Dispute." *The National Post* (Canada), August 28, 2001, n.p. http:// www.nationalpost.com/.

*Boudman v. Aroostook Band of Micmac Indians.* 98-174B. 1999. http://216.239.35.100/search?q=cache:bb0G9_9l_TIC:www.med.uscourts .gov/Site/opinions/brody/1999/mab_1-98cv174_boudman_v_aroost-ook_doc14_ jun.pdf+boudman+v+aroostook&hl=en&ie=UTF-8.

Bourrie, Mark. "Supreme Court Scales Back Indigenous Rights." Interpress Service, November 22, 1997. http://www.tips.org/IPS/human.NSF/ 86afef403a5ab0ca802565b0004cc6df/4700159811f7c6338025683c004ea 873?OpenDocument.

Bowersox, Charles A. *A Standard History of Williams County, Ohio.* 2 vols. New York: The Lewis Publishing Company, 1920.

Boyd, Julian P., ed. *Indian Treaties Printed by Benjamin Franklin, 1736–1762.* Philadelphia: Historical Society of Pennsylvania, 1938.

Brinton, Daniel G. *The Lenâpé and Their Legends; with the Complete Text and Symbols of the Walam Olum, A New Translation, and Inquiry into Its Authenticity.* 1885. Reprint, Lewisburg, PA: Wennawoods Publishing, 1999.

Brodeur, Paul. *Restitution: The Land Claims of the Mashpee, Passamaquoddy, and Penobscot Indians of New England.* Boston: Northeastern University Press, 1985.

Brown, Bruce. *Mountain in the Clouds: A Search for the Wild Salmon.* New York: Simon & Schuster, 1982.

Butler, Mann. "Treaty of Fort Stanwix, 1768." In *A History of the Commonwealth of Kentucky.* Louisville, KY: Wilcox, Dickerman and Co., 1834, 379–94.

Campisi, Jack, and Laurence M. Hauptman. *The Oneida Indian Experience: Two Perspectives.* Syracuse, NY: Syracuse University Press, 1988.

Canadian Broadcasting Corporation News. "Court Rules against Native Rights on N[ova] S[cotia] Crown Land." March 8, 2001. http://cbc.ca/cgi-bin/view?/news/2001/03/08/native-logging010308.

Canadian Press. "Court Rules Natives Don't Have Logging Rights." *Toronto Globe and Mail,* March 8, 2001.

———. "Marshall Decision Used in Native Logging Case." September 21, 1999. http://www.lawcanada.com/.

———. "Native Lobster Dispute Heats Up as Officers Seize Traps Off Burnt Church." *National Post,* August 30, 2001. http://www.nationalpost.com/.

———. "Natives Lay Claim to Nova Scotia Forests." *Toronto Globe and Mail,* February 5, 2002, A-6.

———. "Tribe Skips Agreement Ceremony." *Toronto Globe and Mail,* March 11, 2001. http://www.globeandmail.com/.

———. "Widely Opposed 'Historic' Land Deal at Site of 1990 Oka Conflict Is Signed." December 22, 2000.

Canby, William C., Jr. *American Indian Law.* St. Paul: West Publishing, 1981.

Carter, Clarence Edwin, ed. *The Correspondence of General Thomas Gage, 1763–1775.* 2 vols. New Haven, CT: Yale University Press, 1931 and 1933.

———. *The Territorial Papers of the United States.* Washington, DC: Government Printing Office, 1934.

Carter, Diana Louise. "Outside Tribes Dispute Talk of Land Claim Deal." *Ithaca [New York] Journal,* March 19, 2002, n.p.

Carter, Harvey Lewis. *The Life and Times of Little Turtle: First Sagamore of the Wabash.* Chicago: University of Illinois Press, 1987.

"Casino Study." Editorial. *Bangor Daily News,* April 2, 2002, 8. http://www.penobscotnation.org/articles/study040202.htm.

Chatters, James C. "Affidavit in Federal District Court, Portland, Oregon." May 15, 2001.

———. "Committee on Resources, United States Congress. Hearing to Amend the Native American Graves Protection and Repatriation Act . . ." June 10, 1998.

———. "Kennewick Man: Encounters with an Ancestor. Northern Clans." In *Northern Traces: Journeys in the Ancient Circumpolar World.* Washington, DC: Smithsonian Institution, 1997. http://www.nmnh.si.edu/arctic/html/kennewick_man.html.

Chavaree, Mark. Tribal Counsel, Penobscot Nation. "Tribal Sovereignty." *Wabanaki Legal News* (Winter 1998): 10 pp. http://www.ptla.org/wabanaki/sovereign.htm.

———. Telephone Interview. August 27, 2002.

Chen, David W., and Charlie LeDuff. "Bad Blood in Battle over Casinos; Issue Divides Tribes and Families as Expansion Looms." *New York Times,* October 28, 2001, A-29.

*Cherokee Nation v. Georgia.* 30 U.S. 1 (1831). http://odur.let.rug.nl/~usa/D/1801-1825/marshallcases/mar06.htm.

Churchill, Ward. *A Little Matter of Genocide: Holocaust and Denial in the Americas, 1492 to the Present.* San Francisco: City Lights Books, 1997.

Clark, Harrison. *All Cloudless Glory: The Life of George Washington, from Youth to Yorktown.* Washington, DC: Regnery Publishing, Inc., 1995.

Clark, Jerry E. *The Shawnee.* Lexington: The University Press of Kentucky, 1977.

Clinton, De Witt. "A Discourse Delivered before the New-York Historical Society, at Their Anniversary Meeting, 6th December 1811." In *Collections of the New-York Historical Society for the Year 1811.* Vol. 2. New York: I. Riley, 1811–1859.

Cohen, Felix S. *Handbook of Federal Indian Law.* 1942. Reprint, Albuquerque: University of New Mexico Press, 1971.

Coin, Glenn. "Nation Offers Rental House as Option." *Syracuse Post-Standard,* December 19, 2001. http://www.syracuse.com/news/syrnewspapers/index.ssf?/newsstories/20011219_rnnatio.html.

———. 2002. "Ruling Upholds Forced Inspections: Judge Says Oneida Nation's Ordinances Allow for Checks of Homes on Indian Territory." *Syracuse Post-Standard,* February 10. http://www.syracuse.com/news/syrnewspapers/index.ssf?/newsstories/20020210_rnrule.html.

———. "No Settlement, but Governor, Oneidas and Counties to Announce 'a Big Plus.'" *Syracuse Post-Standard,* February 16, 2002, A-1.

———. "Hearing Focuses on Safety of Trailer. Oneida Nation Official Testifies Mobile Home Had Numerous Hazards." *Syracuse Post-Standard,* June 22, 2002, n.p.

———. "Oneida Nation Called Unjust: Peacemakers Liken Oneida Woman's Plight to that of Palestinians, Mayans." *Syracuse Post-Standard,* September 14, 2002. http://www.syracuse.com/news/poststandard/index.ssf?/base/news2/103199253112290.xml.

———. "Lawyer Says Danielle Patterson Doesn't Plan to Appear at her Assault Trial." *Syracuse Post-Standard,* September 24, 2002, n.p. http://syracuse.com/news/poststandard/index.ssf?/base/news-2/ 1032856565100493.xml.

———. "Tribal Jail Deal Violates State Law; Housing of Oneida Nation Prisoners in Lewis County Forbidden, Officials Say. *Syracuse Post-Standard,* September 26, 2002, n.p.

———. "Nation Jails Woman in Trailer Dispute; Danielle Patterson Is Ordered Held through Weekend. Her Trial Is Set to Begin Monday." *Syracuse Post-Standard,* October 19, 2002. http://www.syracuse.com/news/poststandard/index.ssf?/base/news-2/103501301360180.xml.

———. "Deal Lets Nation Tear Down Trailer; Danielle Patterson Admits One Count in Tribal Court. Sentencing Is Wednesday." *Syracuse Post-Standard,* October 22, 2002.

———. "Turning Stone's One-year Profit: $70 Million." *Syracuse Post-Standard,* December 19, 2002, n.p.

———. "Tribe to Ask to Inspect Five Homes." *Syracuse Post-Standard,* May 9, 2003, n.p.

———. "Nation Opponents' Letter Criticized." *Syracuse Post-Standard,* May 13, 2003, n.p.

Commager, Henry Steele, ed. *Documents of American History.* 9th ed. Englewood Cliffs, NJ: Prentice-Hall, 1973.

*Congressional Record.* 44th Congress, 2d Session, Ex. Doc. No. 186. Committee on Indian Affairs, March 9, 1877.

———. "Proceeding and Debates of the Forty-Ninth Congress, Second Session." Government Printing Office: Washington, DC. Vol. XVIII. 1887.

Connelley, William E. "Notes on the Early Indian Occupancy of the Great Plains." *Collections.* Vol. 14. Kansas State Historical Society (1915–1918). 1918.

Cook, Ray Wahnitiio. "When 'Scholars' Pour Vinegar on Indian Wounds." *Indian Time,* February 21, 2002, 4.

Coon-Come, Matthew. "Remarks of the National Chief Matthew Coon-Come: Peoples Summit of the Americas Environment Forum." April 18, 2001. http://www.afn.ca/Press%20Realeses%20%20speeches/april_18.htm.

Corbett, R. Patrick. "Casino, Vernon Downs: The Gambling Connection. Harness Track Hopes to Cash in on Turning Stone's Success." *Utica Observer-Dispatch,* October 27, 2002. http://uticaod.com/archive/2002/10/27/news/8195.html.

*County of Oneida, New York, et al. v. Oneida Indian Nation of New York State, et al.* 470 U.S. 226 (1985).

Cox, Kevin. "N.B. Natives Lose Court Fight over Fishing." *Toronto Globe and Mail,* July 10, 2002, A-5.

Cronon, William. *Changes in the Land: Indians: Colonists, and the Ecology of New England.* New York: Hill & Wang, 1983.

Cusick, David. "Sketches of Ancient History of the Six Nations." 1825. In William M. Beauchamp, *The Iroquois Trail or Foot-prints of the Six Nations, in Customs, Traditions, and History.* Fayetteville, NY: H. C. Beauchamp, 1892.

Dana, Barry. *Chief's Report.* n.d. http://www.penobscotnation.org/notes/chiefreport.htm.

"Dead 'Indians' Don't Lie." n.d. http://www.louisbeam.com/kennewick.htm.

Deloria, Vine, Jr. *Behind the Trail of Broken Treaties: An Indian Declaration of Independence.* 1974. Reprint, Austin: University of Texas Press, 1985.

———. "Balancing Science, Culture: Do Scientists Have Rights to All Finds?" *Denver Post,* November 29, 1998, p. G-1.

Deloria, Vine, Jr., and Raymond J. DeMallie. *Documents of American Indian Diplomacy: Treaties, Agreements, and Conventions, 1775–1979.* 2 vols. Norman, OK: University of Oklahoma Press, 1999.

———. *Documents of American Indian Diplomacy.* 2 vols. Norman: University of Oklahoma Press, 1999.

Dennis, Matthew. *Cultivating a Landscape of Peace.* Ithaca, NY: Cornell University Press, 1993.

Dewan, Shaila K. "After 5 Days, Oneida Deal Is Unraveling." *New York Times,* February 22, 2002, sec. 2, p. 1.

Diamond, Billy. *Highlights of the Negotiations Leading to the James Bay and Northern Quebec Agreement.* Val d'Or: Grand Council of the Crees of Quebec, 1977.

———. "Villages of the Damned: The James Bay Agreement Leaves a Trail of Broken Promises." *Arctic Circle,* (November/December 1990):24–34.

Dietrich, Bill. "Skeleton Might be Reburied before Scientists Can Study It." *Seattle Times,* September 22, 1996. http://www.seattletimes.com.

Dodge, Jacob Richards. *Red Men of the Ohio Valley: An Aboriginal History of the Period Commencing* A.D. 1650, and ending at the Treaty of Greenville [*sic*], A.D. 1795. Springfield, OH: Ruralist Publishing Company, 1859.

Dorchester, Lord. Archives of Ontario. August 15, 1791, Speech to the Confederated Indian Nations. F47, A-1, Letterbook 17.

Dorsey, J. O. "Omaha Sociology." In *Third Annual Report of the Bureau of American Ethnology.* Smithsonian Institute Bureau of Ethnology. Washington, DC, 1884.

———. "Migrations of the Siouan Tribes." *American Naturalist* XX, no. 3. (1886). Philadelphia.

———. "A Study of Siouan Cults." In *Eleventh Annual Report Bureau of American Ethnology.* 1889–90. Smithsonian Institute. Washington, DC. 1894.

Duncan, Barbara R. *Living Stories of the Cherokee.* Chapel Hill, NC: University of North Carolina Press, 1998.

Eckert, Alan. *That Dark and Bloody River: Chronicles of the Ohio River Valley.* New York: Bantam Books, 1995.

Edel, Wilbur. *Kekionga! The Worst Defeat in the History of the U.S. Army.* Westport, CT: Praeger Publishers, 1997.

E-mail (personal communication) from Victoria Halsey, Oneida 32 Acres, NY. June 19, 2003.

Ernst, Robert. *Rufus King: American Federalist.* Chapel Hill, NC: University of North Carolina Press, 1968.

"Europa: The History of the White Race, Chapter 6: To The Ends of the Earth: Lost White Migrations." 1999. http://www.stormfront.org/whitehistory/hwr6.htm.

"Factions of Ponca Tribe in Dispute." *Lincoln Journal-Star.* Lincoln, NE. September 26, 1992.

"First Nations Advised Not To Sign New Fishing Agreements with Ottawa." Canadian Broadcasting Corporation News On-line. April 2, 2001. http://cbc.ca/cgi-bin/view?/news/2001/04/02/native010402.

Fitzpatrick, John C., ed. *The Diaries of George Washington, 1748–1799.* 4 vols. New York: Houghton Mifflin, 1925.

———. *The Writings of George Washington from the Original Manuscript Sources, 1745–1799.* 39 vols. Washington, DC: Government Printing Office, 1938.

Fleck, John. "Bones of Contention." *Albuquerque Journal,* April 18, 1999, p. 6.

Fletcher, A. C. and F. La Flesche. *The Omaha Tribe.* Twenty-Seventh Annual Report of the Bureau of Ethnology. Smithsonian Institute. Washington, D.C. 1911.

Flores, Corine. [Letter to the editor] Santa Fe *New Mexican,* December 19, 1998, p. A-9.

Freedrich, Colin, Son of. "Patrick Stewart, Star Trek's Captain Picard: Spitting Image of the Kennewick Man." n.d. http://home.earthlink.net/~theedrich/Kennewick.htm.

Gagnon, Dawn. "HoltraChem Woes Similar to Sister Plant." *Bangor Daily News,* July 15, 2002, 1.

Galbreath, Charles B. *History of Ohio.* 5 vols. New York: The American Historical Society, Inc., 1925. Vol. 1.

Girard, M., and C. Dumont. "Mercury Exposure of James Bay Cree to Methylmercury during Pregnancy for the Years 1983–1991." *Water, Air and Soil Pollution* 80(1995):13–19.

Girard, M., F. Noêl, and C. Dumont. "Varying Mercury Exposure with Varying Food Source in a James Bay Cree Community." *Arctic Medical Research* 55(1996):69–74.

Graettinger, Diana. "Education Next Step in Casino Bid" *Bangor Daily News,* June 18, 2002, 1. *Great Northern Paper v. Penobscot Nation.* 2001 ME 68. May 1, 2001. http://www.courts.state.me.us/opinions/documents/01me68gr.htm.

Gransbery, Jim. "Burns: Jurisdiction Obscurity Harms Indian Reservations." *Billings Gazette,* January 7, 1998. http://tlc.wtp.net/sovereig1.htm.

Gray, Barbara. (Kanatiiosh) "Vine Deloria Spoke: I Listened, Will You?" *Indian Time* (Akwesasne) 19, no. 48 (December 7, 2001):14.

Gray, Barbara A. "The Eagle's Cry: A Warning for Native American Indians Concerning Political Trials." A paper presented at the School of Justice Studies, Arizona State University, Tempe, 2002.

Green, Michael D. "The Expansion of European Colonization to the Mississippi Valley, 1780–1880." In *The Cambridge History of the Native Peoples of the Americas,* edited by Bruce G. Trigger and Wilcomb E. Washburn, 461–538. Cambridge, England: Cambridge University Press, 1996.

Green, Norma Kidd. *Iron Eye's Family: The Children of Joseph La Flesche.* Lincoln, NE, Johnson Publishing, 1969.

Gregoire, Marie-Lauren. "Kanesatake Land Governance Recognized by Federal Government." The Six Nations and *New Credit* (Ontario) *News,* n.d. http://www.tekanews.com.

Griffin, James B. *The Fort Ancient Aspect.* University of Michigan Anthropological Papers. No. 28. Ann Arbor, MI: Museum of Anthropology, 1943.

———. ed. *Archaeology of Eastern United States.* Chicago: University of Chicago Press, 1952.

Grinde, Donald A., Jr., and Bruce E. Johansen. *Ecocide of Native America: Environmental Destruction of Indian Lands and Peoples.* Santa Fe, NM: Clear Light, 1994.

Grobsmith, Elizabeth. The Ponca Tribe of Nebraska: History, Socio-Economic Status and Current Efforts to Obtains Restoration of Tribal Status. Omaha: Northern Ponca Restoration Committee, n.d.:16–26.

Groening, Tom. "Thirty-Three Mile Trek Protests State's Control." *Bangor Daily News,* May 24, 2002, 1. http://www.penobscotnation.org/articles/trek052402.htm.

Hale, Horatio. *The Iroquois Book of Rites.* 1883. Reprint, Toronto: University of Toronto Press, 1963.

Harry, Debra. Statement on Biopiracy. Associated Press dispatch in *Tri-City Herald,* December 11, 1998.

Hauptman, Laurence M., and L. Gordon McLester III, eds. *The Oneida Indian Journey: From New York to Wisconsin, 1784–1860.* Madison: University of Wisconsin Press, 1999.

Haywood, John. *The Natural and Aboriginal History of Tennessee, Up to the First Settlements Therein by the White People, in the Year 1768.* Nashville: George Wilson, 1823.

Heckewelder, John. *History, Manners, and Customs of the Indian Nations Who Once Inhabited Pennsylvania and the Neighboring States.* 1820. 1876. Reprint, New York: Arno Press, 1971.

———. *Narrative of the Mission of the United Brethren among the Delaware and Mohegan Indians from Its Commencement, in the Year 1740, to the Close of the Year 1808.* 1818. 1820. Reprint, New York: Arno Press, 1971.

Heinzl, Toni. "Growing Prison Religion Stirs Concern," *Omaha World-Herald,* February 28, 1999, pp. A-1, A-2.

Henderson, Diedtra. "Scientists Examining Kennewick Man Hit a Snag: Glue on Bones." *Seattle Times,* February 28, 1999. http://www.seattletimes.com/news/local/html98/kenn_19990228.html.

Higgins, A.J. "Chief Dana Makes Case for Casino 'The Bottom Line in Life Is Improved,' He Says." *Bangor Daily News,* June 6, 2002, 1. http://www.bangornews.com.

Hogan, Lawrence J. *The Osage Indian Murders.* Frederick, MD: Amlex, 1998.

Horsman, Reginald. "American Indian Policy in the Old Northwest, 1783–1812." *William and Mary Quarterly* 18, no. 1 (January 1961):35–53.

Hosen, Frederick E., comp. *Rifle, Blanket, and Kettle: Selected Indian Treaties and Laws.* Jefferson, NC: McFarland, 1985.

Howard, James. H. *Peter Le Claire—Northern Ponca. An Autobiographical Sketch.* Published Monograph. University of Nebraska. Lincoln, NE. 1950.

———. *The Ponca Tribe.* Smithsonian Institute Bureau of American Ethnology. Bulletin 195. Washington, DC, 1965.

Indian Affairs: Laws and Treaties. June 25, 1817. 7 Stat., 155. Proclamation, December 26, 1877. Compiled and edited by Kappler, Charles J. Washington: Government Printing Office. Vol. II. Page 140. 1904.

Indian Affairs: Laws and Treaties. March 12, 1858. 12 Stats., 997. Ratified Mar. 8, 1859. Proclamation, April 11, 1859. Compiled and edited by Kappler, Charles J. Washington: Government Printing Office. Vol. II, Pages 875–76. 1904.

*Indian Historian.* "The Prairie Potawatomie: Resistance to Allotment." Fall. 1976.

Interpretive Center [of the *Tri-City Herald*]. http://www.tri-cityherald.com. February 14, 1998: "Old Bones Bringing World to Tri-Cities"; August 31, 1997: "Pagan Sect Blasts Corps' Handling of Kennewick Man"; August 28, 1997: "Ancient Ritual Pays Tribute to Kennewick Man";

August 27, 1997: "Tribes Upset by Ritual for Kennewick Man";

August 23, 1997: "Pagans Battle Corps over Old Bones";

August 20, 1997: "Pagan Group Plans Ceremony over Kennewick Man Bones";

July 27, 1997: "One Year After Kennewick Man Surfaced, Battle over 9,200-year-old Skeleton Rages On."

Israel, F.I., ed. *Major Peace Treaties of Modern History, 1648–1967*. 4 vols. New York: Chelsea House Publications, 1967.

Jablow, Joseph. *Ponca Indians*. "Ethnohistory of the Ponca with reference to Their Claim of Certain Lands." A Report for the Department of Justice, Lands Division, Indian Claims Section. New York: Garland Publishing, 1974.

Jacobs, Wilbur. *Diplomacy and Indian Gifts: Anglo-French Rivalry among the Ohio and Northwest Frontiers, 1748–1763*. Stanford, CA: Stanford University Press, 1950.

Jemison, G. Peter, and Anna M. Schein, eds. *Treaty of Canandaigua 1794: 200 Years of Treaty Relations between the Iroquois Confederacy and the United States*. Santa Fe, NM: Clear Light Publishers, 2000.

Jensen, Richard, Eli Paul, and John E. Carter, *Eyewitness to Wounded Knee*. Lincoln: University of Nebraska Press, 1991.

Johansen, Bruce, and Roberto Maestas. *Wasi'chu: The Continuing Indian Wars*. New York: Monthly Review Press, 1979.

Johansen, Bruce E. *Life and Death in Mohawk Country*. Golden, Colorado: North American Press/Fulcrum, 1993.

———. "Oneida: Historical Sketch," In *The Encyclopedia of the Haudenosaunee (Iroquois Confederacy)*, edited by Johansen and Barbara Alice Mann, 224–229. Westport, CT: Greenwood Press, 2000.

Johansen, Bruce E., and Donald A. Grinde, Jr. *The Encyclopedia of Native American Biography*. New York: Henry Holt, 1997.

Johansen, Bruce Elliott, and Barbara Alice Mann. *Encyclopedia of the Haudenosaunee (Iroquois Confederacy)*. Westport, CT: Greenwood Press, 2000.

Johnson, Elias, Chief. *Legends, Traditions and Laws, of the Iroquois, or Six Nations*. 1881. Reprint, New York: AMS Press, 1978.

Johnson, Tim. "The Dealer's Edge: Gaming in the Path of Native America." *Native Americas* 12, nos. 1 & 2 (Spring/Summer 1995):16–25.

Kappler, Charles J., ed. and comp. *Indian Treaties, 1778–1883*. 1904. Reprint, New York: Interland Publishing, Inc., 1972.

———. comp. and ed. *Indian Affairs: Laws & Treaties*. Vol. II. Washington, DC: Government Printing Office, 1904–1941/New York, A.M.S. Press, 1971.

Kates, William. "Oneidas' Enterprises Bolster Struggling Central New York." Associated Press in *Omaha World-Herald,* November 5, 1997, pp. 22, 25.

King, Charles, ed. 1894–1900. *The Life and Correspondence of Rufus King*. 6 vols. New York: G.P. Putnam's Sons, 1894–1900.

King, James T. "'A Better Way': General George Crook and the Ponca Indians," *Nebraska History*, 50 (Fall 1969, 239–256).

*Knox County Plat Book*. Map of Raymond Township. Anderson Publishing Co. Des Moines, Iowa. 1903.

———. Map of Raymond Township. Anderson Publishing Co. Des Moines, Iowa. 1920.

Knox, Henry. "The CAUSES of the existing HOSTILITIES between the UNITED STATES, and certain Tribes of INDIANS North-West of the OHIO." *Territorial Papers of the United States*. Edited by Clarence Edwin Carter. 28 vols. Washington, DC: Government Printing Office, 1934; 2:359–366.

Kriss, Erik. "Halbritter Protest Held in Albany; Supporters of Oneida Nation Woman Rally at the Governor's Mansion." *Syracuse Post-Standard*, September 21, 2002, n.p.

Kutler, Stanley I., ed. *Dictionary of American History*. 10 vols. New York: Charles Scribner's Sons, 2003. Vol. 6.

Lafitau, Joseph François. *Customs of the American Indians Compared with the Customs of Primitive Times*. Edited and translated by William N. Fenton and Elizabeth L. Moore. 2 vols. 1724. Reprint, Toronto: The Champlain Society, 1974.

Laghi, Brian. "Policy for Land Claims Abject Failure." *Toronto Globe and Mail*, January 2, 2001, n.p.

Lambie, Chris. "N[ova] S[cotia] Natives Get Combat Training for Lobster Wars; 'Tired of Being the Victim.'" *National Post*, December 22, 2000. http://www.nationalpost.com.

LaRusic, Ignalius. *Negotiating a Way of Life: Initial Cree Experiences with the Administrative Structure Arising from the James Bay Agreement*. Ottawa: Canada, Department of Indian and Northern Affairs, Policy Research and Evaluation Group, 1979.

Lasswell, Mark. "The 9,400 Year Old Man; the White House Keeps Trying to Bury Him; Scientists Are Furious." *Wall Street Journal*, January 8, 1999, p. W-11.

Lawlor, Allison. "Strict Enforcement Planned at Burnt Church." *Toronto Globe and Mail*, August 28, 2001.

Lawton, Valerie and Kelly Toughill. "Chiefs Call Temporary Truce in Fish War." *Toronto Star*, October 7, 1999, n.p.

Le Claire, Peter. *Ponca History*. "Letter Written on Tribal History by Ponca Indian." August, 26. Niobrara, Nebraska. 1947.

———. In *The Ponca Tribe*. by J. H. Howard. Oral Interview. 1965.

Lee, Mike. "Kennewick Man Pieces Gone, Report Says." *Tri-City Herald*, December 11, 1998. http://www.tri-cityherald.com.

———. "Experts bringing Kennewick Man to Life." *Tri-City Herald*, February 28, 1999. http://www.tri-cityherald.com.

Leidy, Edgar Earl. "The Extinction of the Indian Title in Ohio beyond the Greenville Treaty Line." Ph.D. Diss. Ohio State University, 1929.

Lemonick, Michael P. "Bones of Contention: Scientists and Native Americans Clash over a 9,300-Year-Old Man with Caucasoid Features." *Time* 148:18 (October 14, 1996). http://marauder.millersv.edu/~tctirado/papers/time-4.html.

Leroy, Fred. Northern Ponca Chairman candidate. Statement in his campaign materials for the 1994 tribal elections. 1994.

———. Chair, Northern Ponca Tribe of Nebraska. Oral history and personal research on Ponca tribal sites. 1998.

Libby, Dorothy. "An Anthropological Report on the Piankashaw Indians." *Piankashaw and Kaskaskia Indians.* Edited by David Agee Horr. New York: Garland Publishing, 1974, 27–341.

Lola, Wenona. "What Are the Real Issues About Casino?" *Bangor Daily News,* April 4, 2002. http://www.penobscotnation.org/articles/wenona_lola.htm.

Lowrie, Walter, and Matthew St. Clair, Clarke, eds. *American State Papers. 1832. Class II. Indian Affairs. Documents, Legislative and Executive, of the Congress of the United States, From the First Session of the First to the Third Session of the Thirteenth Congress, Inclusive: Commencing March 3, 1789, and Ending March 3, 1815.* Washington, DC: Gales and Seaton, 1789–1815.

———. *American State Papers. Documents Legislative and Executive of the Congress of the United States. 1789 through 1815.* Et seq. Vol. 4. Washington: Gales & Seaton, 1832.

Lyons, Stephen. "Old Bones Create New Views of Ancient Beliefs." *Idaho Statesman,* December 5, 1998, p. B-8.

"Maine Tribal Leaders Give Historic Speeches to State Legislature: Excerpts from State of the Tribes Addresses. March 11, 2002." *Indian Country Today,* April 10, 2002, A-5.

Makin, Kirk. "Natives Fail in Bid to Regain Land." *Toronto Globe and Mail,* December 22, 2000.

———. "Court Recognizes Metis as a Distinct People." *Toronto Globe and Mail,* February 24, 2001. http://www.globeandmail.com.

Manley, Henry S. "Red Jacket's Last Campaign, and an Extended Bibliographical and Biographical Note." *New York History* 31, no. 2 (1950):149–68.

Mann, Barbara Alice. *Iroquoian Women: The Gantowisas.* New York: Peter Lang Publishing, 2000.

———. ed. *Native American Speakers of the Eastern Woodlands: Selected Speeches and Critical Analyses.* Westport, CT: Greenwood Press, 2001.

Mann, Barbara Alice, and Jerry L. Fields. "A Sign in the Sky: Dating the League of the Haudenosaunee." *American Indian Culture and Research Journal* 21, no. 2 (1997):105–63.

Mardock, Robert Winston. *The Reformers and the American Indian.* Columbia, University of Missouri Press, 1971, 168–91.

———. "Standing Bear and the Reformers." In *Indian Leaders: Oklahoma's First Statesmen.* Edited by H. Glenn Jordan and Thomas M. Holm. Oklahoma City, Oklahoma Historical Society, 1979, 101–13.

Marshall, Audrey. "Commentary: Charter Protects Rights of Aboriginal People." *The Eastern Door* [Kahnawake Mohawk Territory], September 15, 2000, 3.

Marshall, S. L. A. *Crimsoned Prairie: The Indian Wars on the Great Plains.* New York: Charles Scribner & Sons, 1972.

Mason, W. Dale. *Indian Gaming: Tribal Sovereignty and American Politics.* Norman: University of Oklahoma Press, 2000.

Mathews, John Joseph. *The Osages: Children of the Middle Waters.* Norman: University of Oklahoma Press, 1961.

May, James. "Fate of Kennewick Man in Hands of Judge; Ruling Expected in Several Weeks." *Indian Country Today,* July 4, 2001, A-8.

McAndrew, Mike. "Iroquois Nations Install Leader." *Syracuse Post-Standard,* April 15, 2001, n.p.

McCutcheon, Sean. *Electric Rivers: The Story of the James Bay Project.* Montreal: Black Rose Books, 1991.

McElwain, Thomas. "'Then I Thought I Must Kill Too': Logan's Lament: A 'Mingo' Perspective." In *Native American Speakers of the Eastern Woodlands: Selected Speeches and Critical Analyses.* Edited by Barbara Alice Mann. Westport, CT: Greenwood Press, 2001, 107–21.

[McKee, Alexander]. "Minutes of Debates in Council on the Banks of the Ottawa River, (Commonly Called the Miami of the Lake), November, 1791." Philadelphia: William Young, Bookseller, 1792.

McKinley, James C. "Wisconsin Oneidas Vow to Persist in Their Lawsuit, Jeopardizing Pataki's Settlement." *New York Times,* February 18, 2002 http://www.nytimes.com/2002/02/18/nyregion/18ONEI.html ?todaysheadlines.

———. "Judge Rejects Many Defenses by New York State in Oneida Lawsuit." *New York Times,* April 3, 2002. http://www.nytimes.com/2002/04/03/ nyregion/03CLAI.html.

McKinley, James C., Jr. "Pataki Works Out Deal with Indians for Upstate Land." *New York Times,* February 17, 2002, 1.

McNutt, Debi, and Zoltran Grossman. Midwest Treaty Network, Madison, Wisconsin. Personal communication, September 5, 2000.

Meissner, Dirk. "Treaty Nears for Vancouver Island's Largest Aboriginal Group." *Vancouver Sun,* March 4, 2001. http://www.vancouversun.com.

Meriam, Lewis, et al. *The Problem of Indian Administration.* The Institute For Government Research. Baltimore, MD: John Hopkins Press, 1928.

"Micmac Dispute May Go to Top Court." *Toronto Globe and Mail,* March 21, 1997, n.p.

Miller, Bruce J. "The Press, the Boldt Decision, and Indian-White Relations." *American Indian Culture & Research Journal* 17:2(1993):75–98.

———. "Bones of Contention: A Federal Law Stands between Scientists and America's Prehistoric Past," *Reason* (October, 1997). http://www .reasonmag.com/.

Minthorn, Armand. "Human Remains Should Be Reburied." September 1996. Web page: Confederated Tribes of the Umatilla Indian Reservation. http://www.umatilla.nsn.us/kennman.html.

MITSC (Maine Indian Tribal-State Commission). "Maine Indian Land Claims Case." February 14, 1995. 22 pages. http://www.wabanaki.com/ land%20Claims%20Settlement.htm.

Mofina, Rick. "Treaty Ruling Causing 'Chaos'; Federal Cabinet May Suspend Top Court Ruling on Native Fishing." *Ottawa Citizen,* September 28, 1999, A-3.

Morris, Richard B., and Jeffrey B. Morris. *Encyclopedia of American History.* 7th ed. New York: HarperCollins Publishers, 1996.

Murphy, Grace. "Tribes' March to Protest Court Order." *Portland Press Herald,* May 21, 2002. http://www.penobscotnation.org/articles/march052002.htm.

Murphy, John A., ed. *The Greenville Peace Treaty: The Actual Speeches of the Council.* 1882. Columbus, OH: Brockston Publishing Company, 1997.

Murphy, Tom. "Nation's Home Condemnation Disputed; Contractor Says Residence Needs Some Repairs but None that Require Tearing It Down." *Syracuse Post-Standard,* November 24, 2001. http://www.syracuse.com/newsstories/20011124_rmevict.html (Murphy 2001b).

Murphy, Tom, and Glenn Coin. "Tension Mounts in Home Dispute; Oneida Claims Nation Police Assaulted Her; Nation Says She Attacked Police." *Syracuse Post-Standard,* November 20, 2001. http://www.syracuse.com/news/syrnewspapers/index.ssf?/newsstories/20011120_cfoneida.html (Murphy, 2001a).

New York State. "Special Committee to Investigate the Indian Problem of the State of New York." In *Report of Special Committee to Investigate the Indian Problem of the State of New York.* Albany, New York: Troy Press, 1889.

O'Brien, Ellen. "Skeletal Remains Discovered in Washington State . . ." *Philadelphia Inquirer,* February 3, 1997.

O'Callaghan, E. B., and Fernow, Berthold, eds. *Documents Relative to the Colonial History of the State of New York.* 15 vols. Albany: Weed, Parsons and Company, 1856–1883.

Office of Strategic Research. Ohio Department of Development. "Population of Ohio and Ohio's Top Ten Cities, 1800 to 1990." Posted November, 1995. Accessed December 11, 2001.

*Omaha Bee,* August 29, 1890–December 30, 1890.

*Omaha World-Herald,* October 4, 1890–January 4, 1891.

"Oneida Families File Federal Suit to Prevent Eviction from Reservation Homes." Press Release. 11/14/02.

*Oneida Indians Nation of New York, et al. v. County of Oneida, New York, et al.* 94 S. Ct. 772 (1974).

"Oneida Iroquois Urgently Need Legal Observers," December 2, 2001. http://mytwobeadsworth.com/OneidaPet3.html.

"Oneida Nation Clanmother Assaulted by Oneida Nation Police." In Personal Communication, Barbara Gray (Kanatiyosh). November 17, 2001, from Oneida Indian Territory, Oneida, New York.

"Oneida Protest: Letter From Danielle Patterson." January 2, 2002.

Oneidas for Democracy chat page, August 31, 2002. oneidasfordemocracy@ yahoogroups.com.

Orkin, Andrew, and Stephen Hazell. *Second International Water Tribunal, Spring 1992, Case Document [on] The James Bay Hydroelectric Project.* Ottawa: Canadian Arctic Resources Committee and Rawson Academy of Aquatic Sciences, 1991.

"Osage Civilization Fund." Hearing on Joint Resolution No. 67. Committee on Indian Affairs, House of Representatives. Washington, DC: Government Printing Office, 1909.

Pablo, Michael T. "Burns and Gazette Editorial Ignore Treaty Rights, Tribal Sovereignty." *Billings Gazette,* January 4, 1998.

Parker, Arthur C. *The Constitution of the Five Nations, or the Iroquois Book of the Great Law.* New York State Museum Bulletin, No. 184. Albany: The University of the State of New York, 1916.

———. *An Analytical History of the Seneca Indians.* Researches and Transactions of the New York State Archaeological Association, Lewis H. Morgan Chapter. 1926. Reprint. New York: Kraus Reprint Company, 1970.

Parr, Marina. "Sovereignty Comes Under Fire." *Skagit Valley Herald.* No date. www.newswest.com/naissues/skagit/skagit.html.

*Passamaquoddy Tribe v. Maine.* 1st Cir. Appeals. No. 95-1922. February 9, 1996. http://www.law.emory.edu/1circuit/feb96/95-1922.01a.html.

Patterson, Danielle. Personal communication, June 22, 2002. oneidasfordemocracy@yahoogroups.com.

———. Personal Communication. August 22, 2002. oneidasfordemocracy@ yahoogroups.com.

———. Personal Communication, September 1, 2002. oneidasfordemocracy@ yahoogroups.com.

Patterson, Danielle Schenandoah. Statement Given at Oneida Indian Territory, Oneida, New York 13421. January 2, 2002. www.oneidasfordemocracy.org.

" 'Peace Camp' Grows around Condemned Trailer in Oneida Nation Homelands, N.Y." Knight-Ridder Business News. August 30, 2002. via oneidasfordemocracy@yahoogroups.com.

*Penobscot Nation v. Cynthia Fellencer* 98-1326 (1st Cir 1999). http:// www.law.emory.edu/1circuit/jan99/98-1326.01a.html.

Peters, Richard. *The Public Statutes at Large of the United States of America.* 8 vols. Boston: Little, Brown, and Company, 1853.

Peters, Richard. "Fallen Timbers Battlefield Archaeological Project at Heidelberg College. Accessed December 12, 2001. http://www.heidelberg.edu/ offices/ chma/fallen-timbers/.

Petit, Charles W. "Rediscovering America: The New World May be 20,000 Years Older Than Experts Thought." *U.S. News and World Report,* October 12, 1998.

Pevar, Stephen L. *The Rights of Indians and Tribes: the Basic ACLU Guide to Indian and Tribal Rights.* 2nd ed. Carbondale: Southern Illinois UP, 1992.

Phillips, William. Chief, Aroostook Micmacs. Telephone interview. August 27, 2002.

Ponca Agency. "Letters and Other Documents." Washington, DC: The National Archives of the United States. Microcopy No. 234. Roll No. 671. 1864–1870.

———. "Letters and Other Documents." Washington, DC: The National Archives of the United States. Microcopy No. 234. Roll No. 672. 1871–1873.

———. "Letters and Other Documents." Washington, DC: The National Archives of the United States. Microcopy No. 234. Roll No. 673. 1874–1875.

———. "Letters and Other Documents." Washington, DC: The National Archives of the United States. Microcopy No. 234. Roll No. 674. 1876–1877.

———. "Letters and Other Documents." Washington, DC: The National Archives of the United States. Microcopy No. 234. Roll No. 676. 1878–1879.

Ponca Census. Census Roll of the Poncas Tribe taken at the Poncas Camp, July 6, 1860 by I. Shaw Gregory, U.S. Special Agent. Niobrara, NE. 1860.

Ponca Elders. Ben Laravie, Omar and Alec Knudson, and Bill Smith. Stubben's Discount Store. July. Niobrara, NE. 1979.

Ponca Tribe of Nebraska Newsletter. Omaha, NE. November, 1990.

Ponca Tribe's Revival Restores Link to History. *Omaha World-Herald.* Omaha, NE. November 10, 1990. p. 34.

Powell, J. W. Bureau of Ethnology Annual Reports—1882–1886. Washington, D.C. Fourth Annual Report. PL. XXXVII. Pages 132–33. 1886.

Pratt, G. Michael. "The Battle of Fallen Timbers: An Eyewitness Perspective." *Northwest Ohio Quarterly* 67, no. 1 (Winter 1997):4–34.

Preston, Douglas. "The Lost Man." *The New Yorker,* June 16, 1997, pp. 70–77.

Prittie, Jennifer. "Court Orders Ontario to Recognize Metis and Their Right to Hunt; Province Has Year to Work Out Deal; Harris May Appeal." *The National Post,* February 24, 2001. http//:www.nationalpost.com.

Prucha, Francis Paul. *American Indian Treaties: The History of a Political Anomaly.* Berkeley: University of California Press, 1994.

Quakers at Peace Camp. Personal Communication, August 31, 2002. oneidasfordemocracy@yahoogroups.com.

Rafert, Stewart. *The Miami Indians of Indiana: A Persistent People, 1654–1994.* Indianapolis: Indiana Historical Society, 1996.

Ranco, Darren John. *Environmental Risk and Politics in Eastern Maine: The Penobscot Indian Nation and the Environmental Protection Agency.* Diss. Harvard University, 2001.

*Rhode Island v. Narragansett Indian Tribe.* 19 F.3d 685 (1st Cir. 1994).

Rice, G. William. "Osage Nation: Initial Draft of the Analysis of the Current Situation of the Osage Indian Reservation in Oklahoma." October 28, 2001. Typescript from Rice and Bigler, Attorneys at Law, Cushing, OK.

Richards, Cara E. *The Oneida People.* Phoenix: Indian Tribal Series, 1974.

Royster, Charles. *The Fabulous History of the Dismal Swamp Company: A Story of George Washington's Times.* New York: Knopf, 1999.

*Runestone, The.* "Religious Group Outlines Plans for Skeleton." No date. http://www.runestone.org/km3.html.

St. Clair, Arthur. *A Narrative of the Campaign against the Indians, under the Command of Major General St. Clair.* 1812. Reprint, New York: Arno Press & The *New York Times,* 1971.

Santee Agency. "Santee and Flandreau Sioux and Ponca Indians." Washington, DC. The National Archives of the United States. Indian Census Rolls. Microcopy No. 595. Roll No. 475. 1885–1898.

Sargent, Winthrop. "Winthrop Sargent's Diary While with General Arthur St. Clair's Expedition against the Indians." *Ohio Archaeological and Historical Quarterly* 33(July 1924):237–82.

"Saskatchewan Indian Band Ponders $38 Million." Canadian Broadcasting Company News, March 6, 2001. http://cbc.ca/cgi-bin/view?/news/2001/03/06/sask_landclaim010306.

Savery, William. *A Journal of the Life, Travels, and Religious Labors of William Savery.* Edited by Jonathan Evans. Philadelphia: Friends' Bookstore, 1873.

Schenandoah, Diane. "Oneida Struggle Not a 'Family Dispute.'" Oneidas for Democracy, December, 2001. www.oneidasfordemocracy.org.

———. "A Plea from Onyota'a:ka Oneida Indian Territory." September 13, 2002. Via Oneidas for Democracy. www.oneidasfordemocracy.org.

———. Personal communication, June 11, 2003, via e-mail.

Schmitz, Cristin. "'Ill-defined Rights' Disputes Better Solved through Negotiation, Judge Bastarache Argues." *Ottawa Citizen,* January 14, 2001. http://www.ottawacitizen.com/national/010115/5100458.html.

Schweinitz, Edmund de. *The Life and Times of David Zeisberger, the Western Pioneer and Apostle of the Indians.* Philadelphia: J. B. Lippincott & Co., 1870, 36–37.

Scully, Diana. Telephone Interview. August 13, 2002.

Seager, Robert II, and Hay, Melba Porter, eds. *The Papers of Henry Clay.* 11 vols. Louisville, Kentucky: University of Kentucky Press, 1959–1992.

Sence, Bruce. "Exclusive Jurisdiction Argument Could Put Canada to The Test; Court's Failure to Provide Clear Rulings Threatens Treaty and Aboriginal Rights." *The First Perspective: News of Indigenous Peoples in Canada.* June, 2001. http://www.firstperspective.ca/commentary.html.

Shanahan, Mark. "Cash Cow or Sin City?" *Portland Press Herald,* March 17, 2002. http://www.penobscotnation.org/articles/cashcow031602.htm.

Sherer, Michael. "Dem Bonz." *Salmon River Gazette,* 1997. http://salmonriver.com/issues/dembonzrevised.html.

Slayman, Andrew L. "A Battle Over Bones." *Archaeology* 50, no. 1 (January/February 1997): pp. 16–23.

Smith, Bill, Sr. Oral Story. Stubben's Discount Store. Niobrara, NE. July. 1981.

Smith, Dean Howard. *Modern Tribal Development: Paths to Self-sufficiency and Cultural Integrity in Indian Country.* Walnut Creek, CA: AltaMira Press, 2000.

Smith, Dwight L. *Wayne's Peace with the Indians of the Old Northwest, 1795.* Fort Wayne, IN: The Public Library of Fort Wayne and Allen County, 1950.

Smith, Rex Allen. *Moon of Popping Trees: The Tragedy at Wounded Knee and the End of the Indian Wars.* Lincoln: University of Nebraska Press, 1981.

Smith, William Henry, ed. *The St. Clair Papers.* 2 vols. Cincinnati: Robert Clark & Co., 1882.

Sohappy, David. "This has been a Long Road . . ." *Native Nations* (June/July, 1991):7–8.

Sosin, Jack M., ed. *The Opening of the West.* Columbia, SC: University of South Carolina Press, 1969.

Southworth, Natalie. "A Native Band Has Turned to Ottawa in Bid to Reclaim Land it Says Was Never Surrendered to the British." *Toronto Globe and Mail,* January 15, 2001. http://www.globeandmail.ca.

Sparks, Jared, ed. *The Writings of George Washington.* 12 vols. Boston: Little, Brown, and Company, 1855.

Speck, Frank G. *Penobscot Man.* Philadelphia: University of Pennsylvania Press, 1940.

Stevens, Sue. Statement. "Behind the Scenes of the Maine Indian Land Claims Settlement." N.d. http://www.geocities.com/CapitolHill/9118/history5.html.

Stout, David B. "The Piankashaw and Kaskaskia and the Treaty of Greene Ville." *Piankashaw and Kaskaskia Indians.* New York: Garland Publishing, Inc., 1974, 343–75.

Sullivan, James, Alexander C. Flick, Almon W. Lauber, Milton W. Hamilton, and Albert B. Corey, eds. *The Papers of Sir William Johnson.*14 vols. Albany, New York: University of the State of New York, 1921–1965.

Sword, Wiley. *President Washington's Indian War: The Struggle for the Old Northwest, 1790–1795.* Norman: University of Oklahoma Press, 1985.

Tanner, Helen Hornbeck. "The Greenville Treaty, 1795." In *Indians of Ohio and Indiana Prior to 1795.* 2 vols. New York: Garland Publishing, Inc., 1974. 1:51–463.

Taylor, Alan. *William Cooper's Town.* New York: Knopf, 1995.

Thwaites, Reuben Gold, ed. and trans. *Les Relations de Jésuites, or The Jesuit Relations: Travels and Explorations of the Jesuit Missionaries in New France, 1610–1791.* 73 vols. New York: Pageant Book Company, 1959.

Tibbles, Thomas Henry. *Buckskin and Blanket Days: Memoirs of a Friend of the Indians.* New York: Doubleday and Company, 1957.

———. *The Ponca Chiefs: An Account of the Trial of Standing Bear.* Lincoln: University of Nebraska Press, 1972.

Tiller, Veronica E. Velarde. *Tiller's Guide to Indian Country: Economic Profiles of American Indian Reservations.* Albuquerque, NM: BowArrow Publishing Co., 1996. Cf. Pp. 522–524, "Osage Reservation."

Toughill, Kelly. "Mi'kmaq Own Entire Province, N[ova] S[cotia] Court Told." *Toronto Star,* December 9, 2000, n.p.

Trahant, Mark. "Oral Histories are Speaking: Will We Hear?" *Seattle Times,* November 12, 1998, p. B-1.

Trelease, Allen W. *Indian Affairs in Colonial New York: The Seventeenth Century.* Ithaca, NY: Cornell University Press, 1960.

Trowbridge, C[harles] C[hristopher]. *Shawnese Traditions.* Edited by Vernon Kinietz and Erminie W. Voegelin. Ann Arbor, MI: University of Michigan Press, 1939.

United States. Eleventh Census. 1995. Donaldson, Thomas, Carrington, Henry B., and Jackson, Timothy W. Reprint of 1892 ed. *The Six Nations of New York: The 1892 United States Extra Census Bulletin.* Ithaca, NY: Cornell University Press, 1995.

*United States v. Barnsdall Oil.* U.S. Court of Appeals for the Tenth Circuit. 127 F. 2d 1019 U.S. App. LEXIS 4792, April 30, 1942.

*United States v. Stanolind Crude Oil Purchasing Co.; U.S. v. Gulf Oil Corp.; U.S. v. Sinclair Prairie Oil Co.* (Numbers 1975–1977; United States Court of Appeals for the Tenth Circuit; 113 F. 2d 194; 1940 U.S. App. LEXIS 4817 June 29, 1940.

"U.S. Citizen Asks United Nations for Asylum from U.S. Government." Press Release. Oneidas for Democracy, May 22, 2003.

*Utilities Production Corporation v. Carter Oil Co.* and *Carter Oil Co. v. Utilities Production Corp.* Circuit Court of Appeals, 10th Circuit 72 F. 2d 655 U.S. App. LEXIS 4645 (August 4, 1934).

Utley, Robert M. *The Lance and the Shield: The Life and Times of Sitting Bull.* New York: Henry Holt and Company Inc., 1993.

Van Every, Dale. *Ark of Empire: The American Frontier, 1784–1803.* New York: William Morrow and Company, 1963.

Venables, Robert W. "Iroquois Environments and 'We the People of the United States.'" *American Indian Environments.* Edited by Vecsey, Christopher, and Venables, Robert W. Syracuse, NY: Syracuse University Press, 1980, 81–127.

Wallace, Paul A. W., ed. *Thirty Thousand Miles with John Heckewelder.* Pittsburgh: University of Pittsburgh Press, 1958.

Walsh, William Patrick. "The Defeat of Major General Arthur St. Clair, November 4, 1791: A Study of the Nation's Response, 1791–1793." Ph.D. Diss. Chicago: Loyola University of Chicago, 1977.

Washburn, Wilcomb E., ed. *The American Indian and the United States: A Documentary History.* 4 vols. 1973. Reprint, Westport, CT: Greenwood Press, 1979.

*Washington v. Washington State Commercial Passenger Fishing Association* 443 U.S. 658, 686 (1979).

Waters, Frank. *Brave Are My People: Indian Heroes Not Forgotten.* Santa Fe: Clear Light Publishers, 1993.

Watson, Elmo Scott. "The Last Indian War, 1890–91: A Study of Newspaper Jingoism." *Journalism Quarterly* 20 (September 1943):205–19.

Welcome Page. Proper Economic Resource Management, 1999. http://www .perm.org/frames/fwelcome.htm.

Wilkinson, Charles F. *American Indians, Time, and the Law: Native Societies in a Modern Constitutional Democracy.* New Haven, CT: Yale University Press, 1987.

Wilson, Frazer Ells. *The Treaty of Greenville.* Piqua, OH: The Correspondent Press, 1894.

———. *The Peace of Mad Anthony: An Account of the Subjugation of the North-Western Indian Tribes and the Treaty of GreeneVille [sic].* Greenville, OH: Chas. R. Kemble, 1909.

————. *Around the Council Fire: Proceeding at Fort Greene Ville in 1795 Culminating the Signing of the Treaty of Greene Ville.* Greenville, OH: Frazer E. Wilson, 1945.

Wilson, Terry P. *The Underground Reservation: Osage Oil.* Lincoln: University of Nebraska Press, 1985.

Wishart, David J. *An Unspeakable Sadness: The Dispossession of the Nebraska Indians.* Lincoln, NE: University of Nebraska Press, 1994.

Wood, Raymond W. *Historical and Archeological Evidence for Arikira Visits to the Central Plains.* Plains Anthropologist, no. 4, 1955.

Yerington Paiute Tribe. *Introduction to Tribal Government.* Yerington, Nevada. 1985.

Young, Susan. "Maine Indian Tribes Gain Nationwide Support." *Bangor Daily News,* November 17, 2000, 1.

————. "Tribes Reject Water Compact." *Bangor Daily News,* May 11, 2002, 1. http://www.penobscotnation.org/articles/051102rejection.htm.

Young, Susan, and Diana Graettinger. "Gambling on the Future of Casinos May Help Tribal Economies, but Face Legal, Philosophical Battles." *Bangor Daily News,* May 4, 2002, 1. http://www.bangornews.com.

Zemel, Kara Dawne. "Burnt Church Human Rights Observer Arrested." *The Eastern Door* (Kahnawake reservation), October 20, 2000, 10.

# Index

# About the Editor
# and Contributors

**Vine Deloria, Jr.** (Standing Rock Sioux), is author of more than twenty books that have provoked debate across many fields, is widely known as an important founder of Native American Studies as a scholarly discipline.

**Granville Ganter** is an assistant professor of English at St. John's University in Queens, New York. His research focuses on antebellum oratorical culture, and he is currently working on a collected edition of the speeches of Sagoyewatha (Red Jacket), a Seneca orator of the early nineteenth century.

**Bruce E. Johansen,** Frederick W. Kayser research professor of Communication and Native American Studies at the University of Nebraska at Omaha, has written and edited several books in Native American Studies, as well as other works dealing with various environmental issues, most recently *Indigenous Peoples and Environmental Issues: An Encyclopedia* (Greenwood Press, 2003).

**Teresa Trumbly Lamsam** is an assistant professor in the Communication Department at the University of Nebraska at Omaha where she teaches print journalism. Lamsam is a member of the Osage Nation and grew up on the reservation. Her journalism career included a few years as the editor of the *Osage Nation News,* a monthly tribal newspaper.

**Barbara Alice Mann** is a lecturer at the University of Toledo, specializing in Native American Studies and English. Seneca-descended (Bear Clan), Mann is a widely published author. Her most recent books include *Native Americans, Archaeologists, and the Mounds* (2003), *Native American Speakers of the Eastern Woodlands* (2001), and *Iroquoian Women: The Gantowisas* (2000).

**John C. Mohawk,** who is Seneca, is an associate professor in the American Studies Department at the State University of New York at Buffalo and author of *Utopian Legacies: A History of Conquest and Oppression in the Western World* (2000).

**Hugh J. Reilly** is an assistant professor in the Communication Department at the University of Nebraska at Omaha. Reilly is the coauthor of three books and has written dozens of articles for regional and national publications. He has just completed work on a photo-history of Omaha which has been published by Historical Publishing.

**Jerry Stubben** (Ponca) is a descendent Osni Ponca and member of the Osni Ponca Heduska Society. He grew up in Niobrara, Nebraska, and presently is an Adjunct Associate Professor and Extension State Communities Specialist at Iowa State University. His research involves tribal government and politics, the development and implementation of tribally based research and programs, and tribally specific and spiritually based substance abuse prevention and treatment modalities.

At Cornell University since 1988, **Robert W. Venables** is a member of the Department of Landscape Architecture. He teaches American Indian studies and courses dealing with comparative cultural landscapes. He has been, and continues to be, an expert witness for the Haudenosaunee in both Canada and the United States in various legal cases. He has also edited *The Six Nations of New York: The 1892 United States Census Bulletin* (1995). With Christopher Vescey, Venables coedited *American Indian Environments: Ecological Issues in Native American History* (1980).